IMPLEMENTING STRATEGIC PROCESSES

Implementing Strategic Processes:

Change, Learning and Co-operation

Edited by Peter Lorange, Bala Chakravarthy, Johan Roos and Andrew Van de Ven

Copyright © Basil Blackwell Ltd, 1993

First published 1993

Blackwell Publishers
108 Cowley Road
Oxford OX4 1JF
UK

238 Main Street
Suite 501
Cambridge, MA 02142
USA

British Library Cataloguing in Publication Data
A CIP catalogue record for this book is available from the British Library.

Library of Congress Cataloging-in-Publication Data

Implementing strategic processes: Change, learning and Co-operation edited by Peter Lorange ... [et al.].
    p.   cm.
  Includes index.
  1. Strategic planning. 2. Management.   I. Lorange, Peter.
HD30.28.I48 1993
658.4'012 — dc20   92–20359
                                                       CIP

ISBN 0-631-185658

Typeset in 10 on 12 pt Plantin
by Central Typographers, Hong Kong
Printed in Great Britain by T.J. Press Ltd, Padstow, Cornwall.
This book is printed on acid-free paper

Contents

Figures

Tables

Editors

Peter Lorange

Born in Oslo, and a citizen of Norway, Peter Lorange is President of the Norwegian School of Management in Oslo and President-elect of IMD in Lausanne, Switzerland. He is also a Visiting Professor of Multinational Management at the Wharton School, University of Pennsylvania. He received his undergraduate education from the Norwegian School of Economics and Business, was awarded an MA in Operations Management from Yale University, and his DBA degree from Harvard University.

Dr. Lorange is a Strategic Management Consultant to major corporations worldwide.

He was elected President of the Norwegian School of Management in 1989, and is on a leave of absence from the Wharton School. Before going to Wharton in 1980, he taught at the Sloan School, MIT, at IMEDE Management Development Institute, Lausanne, Switzerland, and has also been a visiting professor at the Stockholm School of Economics in Sweden.

Dr. Lorange has written extensively on the subject of corporate planning, strategic management, strategic alliances and control, including writing, cowriting, or editing the following volumes: *Cooperative Strategies in International Business*; *Corporate Planning: An Executive Viewpoint*; *Implementation of Strategic Planning*; *Managing the Strategic Process: A Framework for Multibusiness Firms*; and *Strategic Alliances: Formation, Implementation and Evolution*.

Balaji S. Chakravarthy

Balaji Chakravarthy is Professor of Strategic Management at INSEAD, in Fontainebleau, France, while on leave from the University of Minnesota. He has also taught at the Wharton School and at Tulane University.

He has a B.Tech in Mechanical Engineering from IIT, Madras, India, an MBA in Business Administration from IIM, Ahmedabad, India, and a DBA in Business Policy and Planning from Harvard University.

Prior to his academic experience, he worked for six years with the Tata Engineering and Locomotive Company Ltd (TELCO), a leading automobile manufacturer in India.

Professor Chakravarthy's work has appeared in top academic journals, including the *Strategic Management Journal, Academy of Management Review* and *European Journal of Operations Research*. His most recent book, *Managing the Strategic Process: A Framework for Multibusiness Firms*, co-written with Peter Lorange, was published by Prentice-Hall in 1991.

He is an active consultant to major multinational corporations in North America, Europe and Asia.

Johan Roos

A Swedish citizen, Johan Roos is an Assistant Professor in Strategy at the Norwegian School of Management in Oslo, Norway, where he teaches strategic management.

He holds a doctorate in International Business from the Stockholm School of Economics, a MSc in Agriculture from the Swedish University of Agricultural Sciences, and was previously a Research Associate at the Wharton School, University of Pennsylvania.

His work has been published in journals such as *Management Science, Long-Range Planning, European Management Journal, Management International Review, Journal of Organizational Change Management*, and *Journal of Business Strategy*. His book, *Strategic Alliances: Formation, Implementation and Evolution* (with Peter Lorange) was published by Basil Blackwell in 1992.

Johan Roos does research within international management with special focus on co-operative strategies and the competence-based perspective of the firm. He is an active consultant within his fields of expertise.

Currently, he is heading the Council on Cooperative Strategies, a knowledge-sharing group for Scandinavian executives.

Andrew H. Van de Ven

Andrew Van de Ven is 3M Professor of Human Systems Management in the Curtis L. Carlson School of Management and Director of the Minnesota Innovation Research Program in the Strategic Management Research Center of the University of Minnesota.

He received his Ph.D from the University of Wisconsin at Madison in 1972, and taught at Kent State University (1972–5) and the Wharton School of the University of Pennsylvania (1975–81) before his present appointment.

Currently, he and his colleagues are undertaking a major longitudinal research programme on the management of innovation. It involves 13 research teams tracking technological, product, process and administrative innovations as they develop over time.

Preliminary findings from this research have been published in A.H. Van de Ven, H.L. Angle and M.S. Poole (eds), *Research on the Management of Innovation: The Minnesota Studies*, New York: Ballinger/Harper & Row, 1989.

In addition to innovation, Dr Van de Ven's books and journal articles over the years have focused on the Nominal Group Technique, the Program Planning Model and the Organization Assessment Framework.

Contributors

Baden-Fuller, Charles W.F.
Professor of Strategic Management
University of Bath
Claverton Down
Bath BA2 7AY
UK

Bonora, Elda A.
Research Assistant
Linköping University
Sweden

Brandes, Ove
Professor of Industrial Marketing
Linköping Institute of Technology
S-581 83 Linköping
Sweden

Brege, Staffan
Associate Professor of Industrial Marketing
Linköping Institute of Technology
S-581 83 Linköping
Sweden

Camillus, John C.
Donald R. Beall Professor of Strategic Management
Joseph M. Katz Graduate School of Business
University of Pittsburgh
Pittsburgh, PA 15260
USA

Carroll, Charles
Professor
Department of Business Administration
University of Illinois at Urbana-Champaign
350 Commerce Building (West)
1206 South Sixth Street
Champaign
Illinois 61820-6271
USA

Datta, Deepak K.
Associate Professor
School of Business
University of Kansas
Lawrence, KS 6045
USA

Durand, Thomas
Professor, Stratégie d'Enterprise
Directeur, Strategy and Technology Research Unit
Ecole Centrale Paris
France, 92295 Châtenay Malabry

Frayne, Colette A.
Associate Professor of Management and Human Resources
School of Business Administration
California Polytechnic State University
San Luis Obispo
California 93407
USA

Geringer, J. Michael
Associate Professor of Strategy and International Business
School of Business Administration
California Polytechnic State University
San Luis Obispo
California 93407
USA

Govindarajan, Vijay
Professor of Strategy and Control
The Amos Tuck School of Business Administration
Dartmouth College
Hanover, NH 03755-1798
USA

Gupta, Anil K.
Professor, Strategy and Organization
College of Business and Management
The University of Maryland at College Park
College Park, MD 20742
USA

Hedlund, Gunnar
Professor
Institute of International Business
Stockholm School of Economics
P.O. Box 6501
S-11383 Stockholm
Sweden

Krogh, Georg von
Associate Professor
The Norwegian School of Management
P.O. Box 580
N-1301 Sandvika
Norway

Levenhagen, Michael
Assistant Professor
Western Business School
University of Western Ontario
London
Ontario
Canada N6A 3K7

McKern, Bruce
Visiting Professor of International Business
Director, Stanford Executive Program
Stanford University
Graduate School of Business
Stanford, CA 94305-5015
USA

Narayanan, V.K.
Professor and Associate Dean
School of Business
University of Kansas
Lawrence, KS 66045
USA

Nonaka, Ikujiro
Professor
Institute of Business Research
Hitotsubashi University
Tokyo
Japan

Paton, Douglas
Lecturer
Curtin University

Pettigrew, Andrew
Professor of Organizational Behaviour
Director, Centre for Corporate Strategy and Change
Warwick Business School
University of Warwick
Coventry CV4 7AL
UK

Porac, Joseph F.
University of Illinois at Urbana-Champaign
350 Commerce (West)
1206 South Sixth Street
Champaign, Ill. 61820-6271
USA

Rajagopalan, Nandini
Assistant Professor
Department of Management and Organization
School of Business Administration
University of Southern California
Los Angeles, CA 90089-1421
USA

Rasheed, Abdul M.A.
Assistant Professor
Department of Management
College of Business Administration
University of Texas at Arlington
Arlington, TX 76019
USA

Revang, Øivind
Associate Professor
Norwegian School of Management
P.O. Box 580
N-1301 Sandvika
Norway

Snow, Charles C.
Professor of Business Administration
Smeal College of Business Administration
The Pennsylvania State University
411 Beam Business Administration Building
University Park, PA 16802
USA

Stopford, John M.
Professor of International Business
London Business School
Sussex Place
Regent's Park
London NW1 4SA
UK

Thomas, Howard
Dean, College of Commerce and Business Administration
and James F. Towey, Professor of Strategic Management
University of Illinois at Urbana-Champaign
350 Commerce (West)
1206 South Sixth Street
Champaign, Illinois 61820-6271
USA

Thomas, James B.
Assistant Professor of Management
The Smeal College of Business Administration
Pennsylvania State University
411 Beam Business Administration Building
University Park, PA 16802, USA

Vicari Salvatore
Professor
SDA Bocconi
Via F. Bocconi 8
20136 Milano
Italy

Whipp, Richard
Professor of Human Resources Management
Cardiff Business School
University of Wales
UK

Wilson, Fiona
Lecturer
University of St Andrews
UK

Zimmerman, Brenda J.
Assistant Professor
York University
Faculty of Administrative Studies
4700 Keele Street
North York, Ontario
M3J 1P3
Canada

Introduction

The present volume is the result of an international research conference on the strategy process which was held at the Norwegian School of Management in June 1991. The conference drew more than fifty-five researchers representing seven countries. Of over fifty papers given at the conference, we present here seventeen that were selected by the editors as providing an overview of some of the latest thinking on managing the strategy process. This book should, therefore, serve as an important resource to the thoughtful practitioner as well as become an invaluable guide to researchers interested in the strategy process.

In the context of an increasingly global, multicultural economy with rapid technological, political and socio-economic changes, organizations are being challenged to rethink their strategies. To achieve this, they must redesign their organizations and become more proactive in their strategies. The attendant challenges for the design of the strategy process are many, including: (1) increasing the organization's change capabilities; (2) enhancing organizational learning; (3) strengthening the capacity for co-operation in networks, (4) reinforcing strategic systems design capabilities; and (5) preparing the organization for more self-examination.

The first challenge, increasing the organization's change capabilities, has to do with creating a flexible organization, one that can cope with the multitude of changes that face a global firm today. Often this means dismantling traditional hierarchical structures, developing closer relationships with customers, and having the ability to internalize emerging technological innovations. The strategy process must encourage speedy decision making close to where expertise resides within the firm.

The second important challenge, organizational learning, also stems from the rapid changes that are taking place today in a firm's business environment. The amount of knowledge being created is growing exponentially due to the technological, political and social transformations that are occurring at an accelerating pace. As a case in point, the changes in Eastern Europe call for entirely new business knowledge. The events from 1990–2 alone altered the world economic order in a manner that no firm could have anticipated. Rapid change is also stimulated by fast-expanding global communication. Many firms have invested heavily in developing global information and communication systems, further facilitating both individual and organizational learning. In this context, the strategy process must help organizations to update their knowledge base continuously and protect their knowledge from attrition due to possible departure of organizational members.

A third challenge for the strategy process has to do with networks of co-operative strategies. Firms are no longer self-contained citadels. The borders of the firm are blurring, with many firms becoming a network of alliances often with different purposes. Today's firm is part of a larger network which consists of other firms, customers, suppliers, the public sector, etc. The reasons for this are twofold.

First, it is simply too expensive, risky and/or impractical to have all the necessary resources in-house to cope with an increasingly global economy, even for large multinationals. Second, open-systems networks, based on strategic alliances in various forms, will simply become the norm. Alliances may be a faster way to achieve market penetration, for instance, than going it alone. The networked firm can leverage the capabilities of others with a more established market presence. The strategy process must be designed to help the firm cope with its network partners.

The fourth challenge, re-enforcing strategic systems design capabilities, arises because of the need to develop strategies at an increasingly faster pace. Given the rapidly-changing environmental conditions where the strategic resource dimensions – physical, financial, technological, organizational and human – themselves are inherently unstable, the traditional strategic planning process is no longer adequate. It tends to be bureaucratic, analytically detached, and extrapolative. Similarly, the control process must be more proactive – signals of change, however weak, must be spotted early. It is also critical to design a more flexible and interactive strategy process than that existing in most organizations today. Managing the knowledge workers of tomorrow calls for more lateral communication along with flexible planning and control systems.

The fifth challenge for the design of the strategy process is preparing the organization for more self-examination. The designers of a firm's strategy process must be willing to examine new paradigms, to learn from new experiences that might result in recognized practices, and to incorporate new theoretical and/or empirical insights.

Leading-edge ideas on how the above five challenges can be successfully met by a global firm are presented in the papers selected for this book. All of the papers have been referred and revised several times. The process has been long and painstaking, but has led to what we believe is a rich and high-calibre collection of papers. We deeply appreciate the co-operation and patience of the authors, with whom we have truly enjoyed working. We also wish to thank Peggy Simcic Brønn for her capable management of the strategy process inherent to the production of a major work of this type. In addition, we would like to recognize Knut Haanes and Sven Barlinn for their parts in making the Oslo Conference such a success.

Peter Lorange
Bala Chakravarthy
Johan Roos
Andrew Van de Ven

I

Strategic Change Capabilities

We begin the book with four papers dealing with the change capabilities of an organization. The authors explore this subject through a variety of perspectives: instilling and sustaining a positive orientation to change; entrepreneurship; lessons on change management from a high technology programme; and the management of strategic turnaround and an assessment of the importance of top management involvement.

Pettigrew and Whipp assert that the key to a firm's change capabilities will be the need to sense, or anticipate, when changes are needed and act before actually facing a crisis. The ability to mobilize for constant change as a firm learns to adapt to the political, economic and industrial changes of the 1990s and beyond will be critical to the competitive success of an organization. How a company succeeds in adapting to changes depends on its environmental assessment, management of human resources, coherence, ability to lead change, and ability to link strategic and operational change. Irrespective of the strategy adopted, the key to a firm's success is its capability to carry through the changes implied by the strategy, even transforming the strategy in the process, if necessary.

Entrepreneurship is another key factor for success in today's world. Stopford and Baden-Fuller suggest that entrepreneurship should aim at building deliberate *and* emergent strategies with clear directions from top management but with incremental planning over time. Innovative companies should have, among others, the following characteristics: an entrepreneurial spirit throughout the company, co-operation between specialists/managers across functions and divisions, and a positive attitude towards change in the company. Organizations that do not possess these characteristics are likely to fail, while other, more dynamic, organizations increase their chances of success. The firms must also be prepared to accept that the process of building entrepreneurship takes time; some firms feel they never will finish the process.

Although perhaps not so frequently studied, large-scale, high-technology projects, like those undertaken by NASA and studied by Narayanan, offer a challenging arena for the study of organizational change capabilities. These projects generally necessitate the co-ordination of separate scientific and engineering disciplines, and they have a high visibility accompanied by a high degree of uncertainty regarding their outcome. Therefore, there are many similarities in their management processes to those of large diversified organizations: strong central co-ordination in the early phases, a negotiating organization with strong ties to headquarters, and a top management ready to continually negotiate conflicts across divisions.

Brandes and Brege offer an example from the formative years of an organization, the point where a firm is contemplating a turnaround. Turnarounds are often the result of a major crisis within a firm. Active top management involvement, while necessary, is not a sufficient condition for handling a successful turnaround. Other elements of importance are the initial situation, the dialogue between different management levels, motivation and consensus in the organization, helped perhaps by some positive opportunities in the environment.

1

Managing the Twin Processes of Competition and Change

THE ROLE OF INTANGIBLE ASSETS

Andrew Pettigrew and Richard Whipp

Introduction

How do firms compete with one another over long periods of time? What factors explain the relative performance of firms in the same and different sectors over time? What contributions do skill and knowledge in managing strategic change processes make in determining the relative performance of firms? These are the critical questions to be posed in this chapter. Drawing on our recent research on competition and managing strategic change (Pettigrew and Whipp 1991) we point to a range of organizational and managerial capabilities now known to be essential to competitive performance in times of great upheaval.

We characterize such capabilities as intangible assets (Budworth 1989). Intangible assets include knowledge about markets and technologies and of how to exploit them, as well as brands and reputation for quality of products, services and human resources. However, the most fundamental intangible assets, and those most linkable to competitive performance, are organizational capabilities to learn and change.

In simple terms, the ability of an enterprise to compete rests on two qualities. First is the capacity of the firm to comprehend the competitive forces in play and how they change over time. Second is the linked ability of a business to mobilize and manage the resources necessary for the chosen competitive response through time. Yet irrespective of the strategy adopted, the key intangible asset is the capability to carry through the changes implied by the strategy and if necessary transform the strategy through use. This is the significant message from our research linking managing change to competitive success, and the central mobilizing idea of this chapter.

This chapter has four main sections. The first contains a brief assessment of the dominant understanding of competition and strategic change; it goes on to propose an integrated approach based on a multi-level view of competition, linked to a processual orientation to strategic change. The second, third and fourth sections offer a summary of the findings of a major research project on competition and strategic change which has used such an orientation (for a fuller account see Pettigrew and Whipp 1991). The second section presents the research design. The third section gives an empirical comparison from two book publishing companies involved in the project, showing their differing capacities to manage strategic change and the outcome for performance. The fourth section is then able to identify a pattern among the companies studied in managing change for competitive success in the four mature industry and service sectors of automobiles, book publishing, merchant banking, and life assurance. Linking the development and use of intangible organizational assets to the relative success of firms marks a distinctive contribution to the literature on strategy and competition.

The main conclusion to be drawn from examining the firms in the four sectors is twofold. First, a common pattern emerges from the key features of managing strategic and operational change among the firms; and second, there is an observable difference in the way the higher-performing firms manage change from their counterparts over time. That pattern is best represented by a model composed of five interrelated factors, the five central factors are:

1 Environmental assessment
2 Leading change
3 Linking strategic and operational change
4 Human resources as assets and liabilities
5 Coherence

Each of the five factors is built upon a combination of conditioning features and secondary mechanisms. The conditioning features and secondary mechanisms gain their power from being developed in combined form. Their potency is built up through repeated application and across differing circumstances. This building process is measured in years rather than months. In terms of competitive success, the management of strategic change is the result of an uncertain, emergent, and iterative process. There are no grand blueprints for long-term success or quick fixes for immediate salvation. The process of change relies on the development and use of less immediately visible organizational capabilities, what we call intangible assets. Managing such an uncertain process places heavy demands on the ability of firms to learn and adapt over time in relation to all five factors in our model.

The following sections are devoted to presenting new evidence about the links between a firm's ability to manage strategic change and its relative competitive performance; it is to these issues we now turn.

Competition and Strategic Change

The study of competition has attracted the interest of scholars from several schools of thought in the fields of economics and management. Each of the above traditions has made its contribution to the understanding of competitive performance. The strength of the industrial organization (IO) approach has been in teasing out the links between the firm and industry levels of analysis. Returns to the firm are determined by the structure of the industry of which it is a part. The key features of that structure include not only the number and relative size of firms but also the existence of barriers to entry. Firm conduct and performance are said to follow directly from these structural characteristics.

Yet in spite of the strength of the contribution of IO to the understanding of competition it is by no means complete or without its limitations. There are three important deficiencies. Above all, each of the IO schools confine themselves to the firm/industry levels of analysis. The contribution of the national economy and its attendant social formations is never tackled directly (for a recent move in this direction, based on the clustering of successful firms in certain industries, see Porter 1989). Second, even where the IO instruments are handled with great sensitivity the underlying assumption is still one of rational 'homo economicus'. Third, the dynamic of the process of competition (especially within the firm) always remains richly implicit but never explored in their work (for the attempts of game theory to capture dynamic relationships see Schotter 1981). Consequently their appreciation of time and their concept of competition as a process has remained stunted (cf. Barney 1986).

The new competition writers (e.g. Abernathy, Clark and Kantrow, 1983) place the main blame for the deterioration in the competitive strength of US business at the doors of the executive suite. They highlight the importance of specific technological bases of competition, the potential role of management and some of the key temporal frameworks for analysing competition in industry. The approach, however, has a number of gaps. In common with IO specialists the important contribution of the political and social environment is not covered. Given their backgrounds the authors concentrate on manufacturing and engineering industry at the expense of the service sector. There is also a danger in the way their work gives such prominence to technology. It is noticeable, too, how in spite of identifying the key role of management in effecting technological and related changes, the new competition writers do not pursue the issues. Consequently they say little on how such processes of change are to be managed within the firm or what less-tangible assets might be necessary.

The institutional economists have appeared from within the mainstream of traditional economics. Nonetheless they differ from the neo-classical understanding of economic relations in a number of fundamental ways. They have produced an attractive conception of competition. Institutionalists do not assume that such agents are rational in the sense of maximizing their resources within a framework of known alternatives; instead economic relations are in large measure the result of experience and learning over time. Economic explanation should therefore be a dynamic exercise. Economic activity is not co-ordinated simply through price-mediated transactions. It is informed by a range of social institutions (Schotter 1981:11) which are themselves a worthy topic of inquiry (for a detailed account see Hodgson 1988).

There is a noticeable gap, however, in the way they have applied their analytical tools. The process of strategic management is hardly covered. Yet, as will become clear, the process of managing strategic change is particularly suited to such an inspection. In what follows we suggest how some of the concerns of the institutionalists can be fruitfully met in the study of strategic change.

The UK economic retardation literature and the excellence and turnaround writers each add their contributory influences on competition. Thus Wiener (1981) highlights the role of UK cultural conservatism and Pavitt (1980) the relative inability of UK firms to convert product inventions into marketable innovations. Instead of developing corporate management skills, British industrialists remained wedded to family control. Bankers lacked direct involvement in industry and did not use their positions to facilitate changes in industrial structures (Elbaum and Lazonick 1986). The excellence and turnaround literature has specified some generic recipes based on the experience of apparently successful companies (Peters and Waterman 1982). The drawbacks of the excellence and turnaround school for the study of competition are readily apparent. The concern with managerial remedies has necessarily led to an over-emphasis on the firm at the expense of the competitive environment. The problem of competition is immanent within their accounts. Seldom are the firm's competitors dealt with directly or the concept of competition addressed. The urge to prescribe sometimes seems to have overcome the need to show how the data was collected. There is, of course, the danger of reductionism since the impression is often left that successful management can be encapsulated in neat 'laundry lists'.

If the preceding pages offer a rudimentary SWOT (Strengths, Weaknesses, Opportunities, Threats) analysis on the main schools of thought on competition, then what sort of analytical framework might utilize identifiable strengths, make good apparent weaknesses and exploit opportunities? A possible answer is provided in the next section.

Competition and strategic change: an integrated approach

The distinctive characteristics of the Warwick study of competition are manifold. The primary feature is that it sees competition and strategic change as intimately linked. It regards strategic change and competition as joint and inseparable processes. In particular the research contends that these processes occur at multiple levels across time. In other words these processes move forward within their firm, sector and national contexts. The study's framework is also unusual to the extent that it pays due regard to the way such processes are structured by a trinity of forces. These include not only the objective decisions of managers using information derived from their competitive environment; they also embrace the subjective learning and political dimensions which operate both within and outside the firm.

These features can best be understood by first examining an outline of the framework and then considering its more unusual attributes in close-up. The central aim of the study was to link the competitive performance of British firms to their ability to adapt to major changes in their environment. This motivation stems from the way existing literature appears to have minimized the role of management in the debates over competition. Little analytical weight in the prevailing accounts of competition has been attributed to the capacity of management to adjust to external change. Most policy discussion of competition in the UK has concentrated on policies at the expense of processes. Comparatively little is said of how such policies should be carried out or in what way the changes which they require might be managed. Too often these processes are assumed to follow policies automatically. In practice the situation is far less straightforward.

The overriding intention of the Warwick framework is to capture strategic change and competition as holistically as possible (figures 1.1 and 1.2 set out the main constituents of that framework). This implies major judgements about the nature of these twin processes which have been described at length elsewhere (Pettigrew, Whipp and Rosenfeld 1989). Here it is important to explain the central features.

The purpose of figure 1.1 is to communicate the three essential dimensions necessary to an understanding of strategic change. In short, strategic change should be regarded as a continuous process which occurs in given contexts (Pettigrew 1985). The point to appreciate is the richness of these contexts and their simultaneous shaping of strategic change. The hallmark of the processual dimension is that strategy does not move

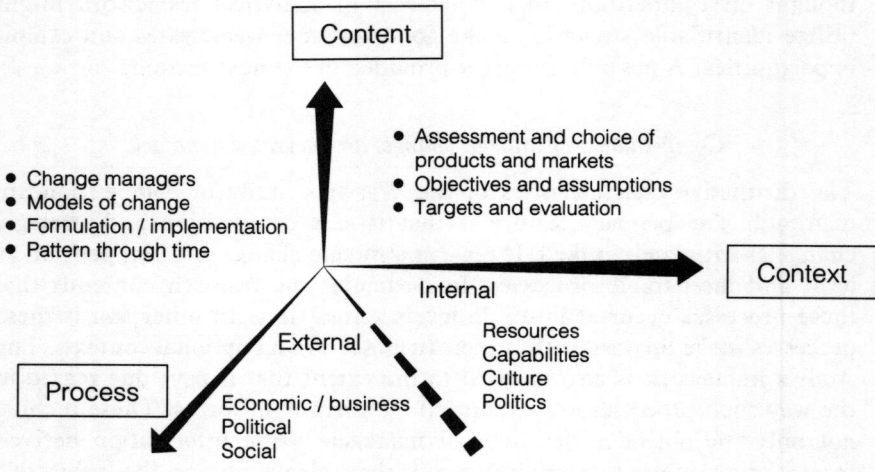

Figure 1.1   Understanding strategic change: three essential dimensions

forward in a direct, linear way, nor through easily identifiable sequential phases. Quite the reverse, the pattern is much more appropriately seen as continuous, iterative and uncertain.

Competition, similarly, is best appreciated in a multidimensional way (Whipp, Rosenfeld and Pettigrew 1989a). Two dimensions stand out: the levels at which competition operates and the element of time as indicated in figure 1.2. Along the vertical axis are the three major levels with their associated characteristics and measures. The competitive performance of a firm hinges therefore on the recognition that businesses compete not merely against one another but *at the same time* within sectoral and national/international structures and relationships.

A number of differences will already be apparent between the framework and those presented in the previous sections, including the composite dimensions of strategic change and competition. One of the most critical contrasts is with the way traditional economics concentrates on the singular competitive traits of a firm. Even the new competition writers emphasize one key base of competition related to technology. We argue that the competitive performance of an enterprise is the result of a collection of abilities and modes of action. One must appreciate, therefore, the bases on which a firm competes and above all their process of creation. Rarely is there a single base. Most firms develop many tiers of advantages which explain their over-all competitive strength. These may combine both price and non-price characteristics, involving assumptions about quality, production efficiency and distribution networks.

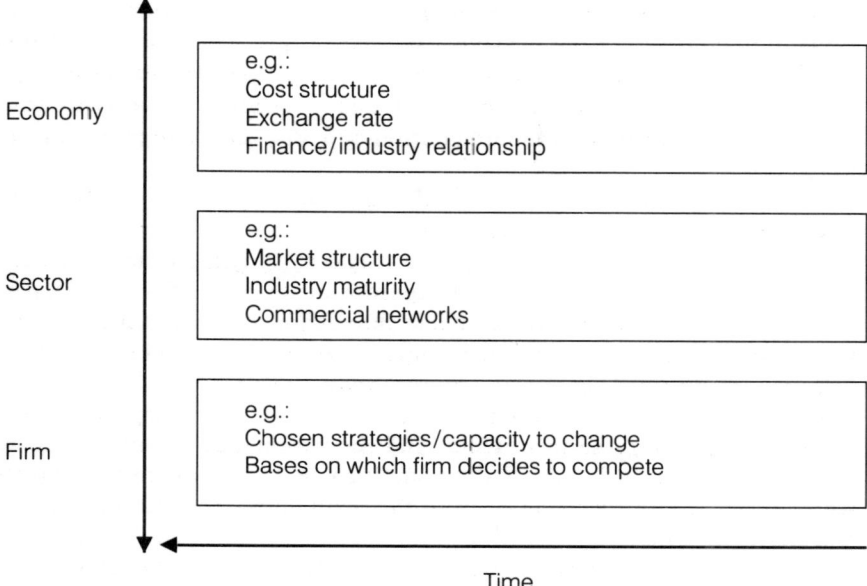

Figure 1.2 Competition: three levels across time

As the horizontal axis suggests, the sectoral and national conditions in which a firm operates, and hence the bases on which it competes, are quintessentially unstable. They are never static. It is to these changes that management has to respond continuously and which provide part of the major external impulsions for strategic change. Yet there is a critical differential. The ability to perceive those changes and to take necessary action diverges considerably between and within firms. It is those divergences of choice and execution which interest us (Whipp, Rosenfeld and Pettigrew 1987).

This multi-level and dynamic view of competition is greatly strengthened by uniting it with a contextually and processually sensitive understanding of strategic change. Put simply, the ability of an enterprise to compete within the prevailing settings relies on two qualities:

1 The capacity of the firm to identify and understand the competitive forces in play and how they change over time, linked to:
2 The competence of a business to mobilize and manage the resources necessary for the chosen competitive response through time.

None of the schools of thought in the previous section address this core point. Yet irrespective of the strategy adopted, the capacity to carry out the changes it implies is critical. The need for management to assess the environment, make choices and mount the necessary alterations is vital to explaining contrasting performances between firms. Three aspects of this analytical approach deserve highlighting: (1) the distinctive view of strategy used; (2) the levels of analysis employed; and (3) seeing the ability to manage the compound process of competition and strategic change as an asset in its own right.

As Figure 1.1 indicates, the intended content of a strategy is continuously and reciprocally influenced by the inner and outer context of the firm. Seldom is there an easily-isolated logic to strategic change. Instead that process may derive its motive force from an amalgam of economic, personal and political imperatives. Their interaction through time requires that those responsible for managing that process make continual assessments, repeated choices and multiple adjustments.

An essential part of our framework is its multi-level concept of competition encompassing the firm, sector and the national economy (see figure 1.2). It is the appreciation of the combined relevance of these domains which sets the framework apart from the main approaches to competition and strategic change.

The competitive behaviour of a firm cannot therefore be understood solely by reference to the industry structure model. The role of the national economy and a wider conception of the social and economic relations of the sector are vital. Such a perspective has two considerable benefits in the exploration of competition and strategic change. First, it is through these grids of relations that managers make sense of their environment. Second, it would appear that the more successful companies are able to understand and manage both these economic and social relations at each appropriate level of their operation. More than that, they then go on to develop the bases on which their firms compete (for an example see figure 1.4). The result is not the construction of a single comparative advantage but the creation of 'layers of advantage' linked to each level (cf. Hamel and Prahalad 1989:69).

Understanding competitiveness as an outcome and a process

Competitiveness performance may be analysed as an outcome state, where the progress of firms is assessed on the basis of indicators such as profits, market share or various financial ratios. This is a valid, indeed the conventional approach used in most business analysis, but we believe it is insufficient to capture the realities of competitive behaviour. The Warwick approach recognizes the need to pay attention not only to discrete outcome indicators but to examine these in the light of (1) the bases of competition on which a firm competes, and (2) the various capacities which it can

1   Performance as an outcome state
    for example:
    Profits
    Market share
    Turnover
    Various financial ratios

---

2   Bases of competition which are multiple at any time,
    and change over time
    for example:
    Price
    Quality
    Production capacity and efficiency
    Distribution networks

---

3   Creating and maintaining various layers of capacity over time
    for example:
    Apposite knowledge
    Capacity for continuous learning
    Capacity for continuous change

Figure 1.3   Competitiveness as a process: three interlinked areas of analysis

develop to underpin those bases. Our approach to understanding and competitiveness as a process is summarized in figure 1.3.

Thus outcome indicators are but a start in understanding performance. A time-series analysis of the process of competition will explore how firms appreciate the changing bases of competition in their industry, make choices to meet any new bases which they or their competitors create, and then develop the appropriate capacities to enable those bases to be effectively used in practice to the new standards appropriate for that era of competition.

One implication of this approach is overwhelming. Competition and strategic change must be seen together as a compound process. Analysis of competitive forces and strategic management should not be presented as separate activities. The consistent picture which emerges from our research is that in practice management deals with both at the same time. Even when apparently implementing only part of a given strategy, management still has to assess and respond to the perpetual changes in the environment. The processes involved are continuous and analysis should at least attempt to match that fact of life. A helpful way of capturing this compound nature of strategic change and competition is to regard it as a hologram rather than see it through a single lens (cf. Van de Ven 1986). The visual complexity of the hologram seems an apt representation of the way the key dimensions of strategic change and competition combine.

Indeed it is the capacity of a firm to accommodate and manage this compound process which appears as *the* decisive strategic asset. Nor is this finding the figment of an over-heated academic imagination. The weight of evidence from this project can be added to the conclusions of a number of others. A consistent line runs through: Winter's (1987) view of the structures of managerial knowledge and competence underlying competitive advantage; Rumelt's (1988) highlighting of the need for firms to develop 'co-specialized assets'; and similarly Teece's (1987) discovery of the role of 'complementarity' between a plurality of such assets (for a full account see Whipp, Pettigrew and Sparrow 1989). The management of this compound process of competition and strategic change is not only a vital asset in its own right. In practice this asset of handling the demands of simultaneity and continuity must be done in such a way that it cannot be copied or easily appropriated by competitors.

Research Design

The Warwick study of competitiveness and strategic change began at the end of 1985 and finished in January 1989. The study examined the process of managing strategic and operational change in four mature industry and service sectors of the UK economy: automobiles, publishing, merchant banking and life assurance. All the sectors had reached stages in their life cycles where established products, markets and relationships were undergoing marked alterations. A major attraction of the chosen industries is their range and the way they extend from manufacturing to service (for a more detailed account see Pettigrew, Whipp and Rosenfeld 1989).

A pair of firms was chosen for study in each of the four sectors, making a total of eight. Each pair was made up of a higher and lower performer in the same broad product market. An important advantage of the use of high and low performers is the avoidance of the general bias in the business literature towards successful organizations. The list of firms involved is as follows:

- *Automobiles*
  Jaguar
  Peugeot Talbot
- *Book publishing*
  Longman
  Associated Book Publishers (ABP)

- *Merchant banking*
  Kleinwort Benson
  Hill Samuel
- *Life assurance*
  Prudential
  A. N. Other

The object was to discover: (1) why firms operating in the same industry, country and product markets should record such different performances; and (2) what has been the contribution of the way they manage strategic change?

Longitudinal data were collected covering the firms' activities in detail over the past two decades, guided by a detailed question pro forma (see Appendix in Pettigrew, Whipp and Rosenfeld, 1989: 132–6). The sources of data were threefold: (1) semi-structured tape-recorded interviews conducted extensively in each firm and related organizations (e.g. government and industry bodies, competitors); (2) primary documentary evidence from within the firm, such as board and departmental records and internal reports; and (3) secondary published material, ranging from official government documents to book publications. In excess of 350 recorded interviews, conducted at all levels of the firms and sectors involved over a three-year period, indicate the scale and intensity of the research.

Deciding on the higher and lower performers to be studied rested on a combined approach to performance. In other words, reliance on a single indicator, such as profitability or market share, was rejected. Such single indicators can be misleading. Market share can be bought by price cutting in the short term, while profitability in one year can be inflated by the use of exceptional balance sheet items. The recent problems over the confused state of balance sheet conventions (Waters 1989) make the use of a broader approach vital. The same is also true of the flawed condition of many sets of aggregate statistics in the UK (Yamazaki 1989:18). In this study, therefore, a group of appropriate general and specific measures have been employed in each sector. Equal emphasis is given to the performance of companies in the sense of creating the relevant bases, which will enable them to compete in their sector.

Great emphasis has thus been placed on indicators which relate to the sectors concerned. Turnover is therefore included in book publishing since it discriminates immediately between the top six large, international houses, the medium-sized independents and the other 20,000 registered, yet often tiny, inactive publishers in the UK. Longman and Associated Book Publishers (ABP) were chosen for study on the basis of their performance within the top six who account for 70 per cent of sales. Equally the comparisons have been spread over time, usually the past two decades, in order that eccentric one- or two-year windfalls do not mislead the identification of performance. ABP's indifferent market and profitability record prior to its improvement in 1981–5 compares unfavourably with Longman's sustained performance on all fronts from the 1960s.

Similarly, careful attention was paid to the perceived performance of firms by others in each industry. In the book publishing example, therefore, those who work in the industry were able to qualify or underwrite the objective measures of performance. In ABP's case, in spite of its position within the top six, it soon became clear that the rest of the trade interpreted its sales figures critically. Competitors showed that ABP's ranking was reliant almost entirely on its dominance with Butterworths of the single area of legal publishing.

The keynote has been the piecing together of a composite picture of performance in order to understand how firms compete. The next section examines, in outline, one pair of firms taken from UK book publishing – a sector where there has been little published research. The comparison will explain their contrasting perfomance by reference to their capacities to manage change and competition, and in the light of the analytical approach summarised in figures 1.1, 1.2 and 1.3.

Longman and ABP

The experience of the two book publishers, ABP and Longman, presents an intriguing comparison. Although both have been well-known as leading UK publishing houses, closer inspection reveals contrasting competitive strengths.

The book market has rightly been likened to a honeycomb. It is remarkably difficult to compare the activities of book publishers. Each publisher categorizes its products differently. Meaningful statistics covering book publishing have been slow to emerge. The number of unquoted companies and those which are part of larger groups (and therefore do not disclose the results of their book publishing activities) make it difficult to compare company results. With these caveats in mind one can create a competitive profile for ABP and Longman which combines a range of measures.

In terms of total book market share, ABP occupied a middle place in the top ten publishers with around 5 per cent until 1985, whereas Longman led with twice as much. If one breaks that figure down into specialist market share positions then ABP's narrow base is revealed. Longman can rightly claim to be at least among the leaders in each of the specialist product areas in which it competes and in fact the dominant force in almost all (viz. schools, medical, reference, scientific and technical). ABP, in spite of its reliance on legal publishing, only comes second to Butterworths in the law and professional market at 25 per cent and 30 per cent respectively. ABP's academic and scientific divisions combined are still only one of ten main publishers in the area. In medical publishing ABP is not among the top five publishers who dominate the market. Similarly in children's books, ABP's general division is not among the six main houses who between them account for over 50 per cent of the market. Unlike Longman, ABP is a leading publisher in only two specialist areas but is not the market leader in any.

While market share is a good indicator of competitive strength it is not conclusive and must be combined with other indicators. The turnover figures for the main UK publishers confirm ABP as one of the largest but, as in market share, some way behind the leaders. In 1985, before acquisitions totally distorted the picture, Longman recorded a turnover of £122 million, Collins £120 million and ABP £76 million. In other words the figures reflect the expansion of Longman in the 1970s and 1980s, and ABP's more modest recovery and growth of the 1980s.

However, if profitability is then assessed together with market share and turnover the general picture is confirmed. Longman's profitability is hit by its international exposure from 1982 (Longman exported 60 per cent of its production compared to an industry average of 20–43 per cent). Yet in spite of enduring the collapse of its Nigerian market in the early 1980s, Longman achieved a higher profit margin (between 12 per cent and 17 per cent) from a consistently broader sales base than anyone else. ABP by comparison is respectable in profit margin. However, it remains very flat, at around 9 to 10 per cent (much the same as in the 1970s when Longman reached 15 to 25 per cent) yet on a much smaller, safer sales coverage and product range. An outline of the main actions taken by ABP and Longman across the past three decades reinforces Longman's superior position.

Sweet & Maxwell, a highly successful law publisher, acquired ABP in 1964. ABP contained the Methuen, Chapman & Hall, and Eyre & Spottiswoode imprints. In spite of an attempt to create three publishing divisions down to 1973 (law, trade and academic) fragmentation resulted. Linking ABP's inherited interests in Canada and Australia proved difficult: the process in Australia was only completed in 1970.

The period between 1973 and 1980 was dominated by fire-fighting rather than solving the problem of the group's dependence on its successful legal publishing. The aim of expanding and strengthening the trade and academic divisions was not achieved. The 1973–4 recession hit specialist publishing hard. Attempts to respond to the economic recovery from 1976 took the form of entry to the mass paperback market and the establishment of a US operation, based in New York. The second oil crisis brought both to an abrupt halt.

The 1980s for ABP, weve dominated by three main episodes. First was the separation of the UK and overseas operations, together with an internal restructuring, including financial controls. Together with the upturn in demand for consumer goods in the mid-1980s, these actions led to a clear improvement in short-term performance. The second episode of the 1980s began in 1985 when ABP acquired Routledge & Kegan Paul, Croom Helm Ltd and Pitkin Pictorial. Yet neither of these sets of actions had solved ABP's long-term problem: developing other successful publishing to match its legal division's strength.

As the search for increased international market domination by an emerging group of major world publishers intensified in 1985–7, interest in ABP grew. It was the historically high premium prices which bidding companies were paying for publishers in 1986–7 which proved decisive. The Eyre Trust, the major shareholder and previous defence against takeover, simply could not ignore the unprecedented financial opportunity. By 17 June 1987 a bid by International Thomson had been accepted.

The house of Longman had developed a strong reputation in commercial publishing across two centuries. Longman developed a leading profile in not only the trade and general areas but also in education, reference and journal publishing. The company's expansion after the Second World War was based largely on the exploitation of the rapid growth in state educational provision in the UK and then abroad. Longman therefore was a truly international company of long-standing by the 1970s and 1980s. There were companies from Hong Kong to the Caribbean and Latin America, from west, east and southern Africa and across the Arab world to Malaysia, Singapore, Australia and New Zealand. It was easier for Longman to adapt to the marked changes in world markets in the 1980s than some of those houses, such as ABP, who had only limited previous exposure to international publishing.

Unlike ABP, Longman did not choose to rely on its family shareholding. In 1968 Longman became part of S. Pearson and Son Ltd, the engineering, publishing and energy group. Mark Longman explained his decision to join Pearson in terms of finding an acceptable home for Longman rather than being swallowed by a hostile publishing house.

The move into the US market gathered pace in the 1970s as Longman went from being just an import operation to publishing first British and then American authors in the United States. Longman's persistence is explained by the need to find substitutes for threatened Third World markets. The long-term benefits of remaining in the US were to be fully realized in the 1980s. Conversely Longman used international supply sources well. As print material costs rose by 29 per cent from 1970–4, 40 per cent of Longman's UK printing and binding needs were transferred to the Far East by 1978.

The world recession of 1979–81 formed a painful break-point for most publishers. Longman's discomfort was increased by the collapse of the Nigerian market in 1982. Some $7 million worth of sales per annum were lost as the fall in the price of Nigerian oil precipitated an economic crisis and the abrupt termination of import purchases. Yet the breadth of Longman's strength has meant that it has been able to combine growth (a doubling of its business) and internationalism (expanding into Europe and the Far East) across the 1980s. Longman has gone on to deepen its competitive base.

The essential aim of the following pages is therefore to uncover why Longman was able to develop new publishing areas, deepen its international spread of operations and re-create itself over the long-term, when ABP could not. In other words, to discover the way the two companies were able to meet the bases of competition in the book publishing industry (see figure 1.4). The critical differences between the two companies emerge in the way they: assessed their environment; led change; linked strategic and operational change; managed their human resources; and the extent to which they were able to achieve coherence across the process of change as a totality.

Environmental assessment

The experience of Longman and ABP reveals how the way a company assesses its environment is constrained by its internal character. In certain respects both organizations made similar diagnoses of the industry in the 1970s and the relevant markets. Yet they diverged widely in the way they: challenged their cherished strategic formulae; adjusted their structures to open up their businesses to new features of the environment; ensured the shifts in the environment were understood within the companies; and developed specific techniques to ensure a more sophisticated understanding was sustained. As a result, their ability to comprehend and meet the competitive bases of the 1980s could not have been more different. Nowhere has the relevance of the way the internal character of an organization can condition its environmental assessment capability been better illustrated. In both cases there were key people available in senior positions in the 1970s who saw the international opportunities. The difference was in the way they were able to develop their assessments.

In Longman the evolution of its relationship with its overseas operations and its corporate structure facilitated its new market position. Longman's aim was to be both international and multinational. In other words the company sought to export products from the UK but also to publish and produce in a wide range of overseas locations. The UK company became but one unit (albeit large) amongst the collection of international

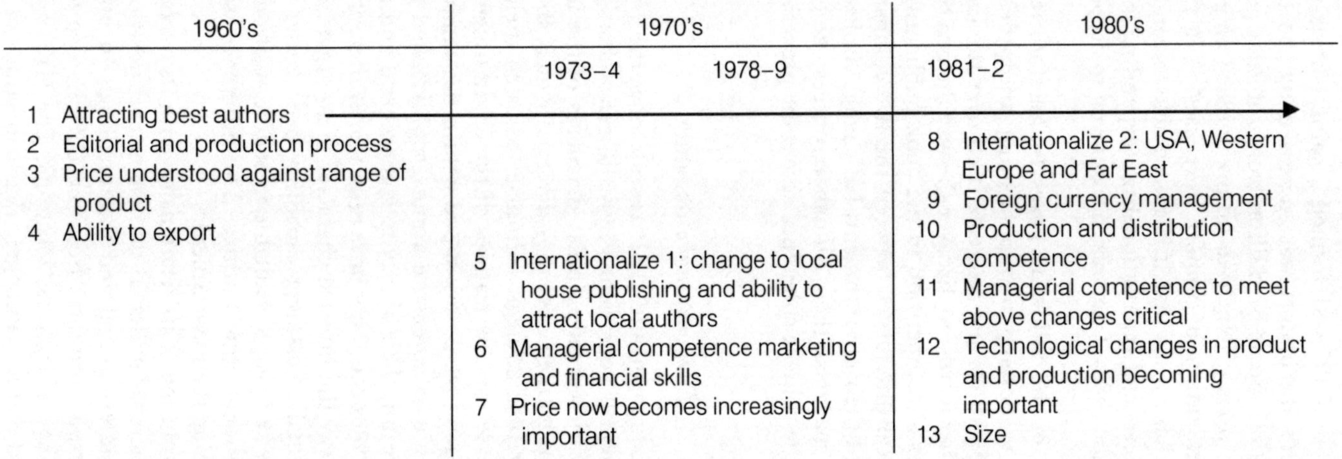

Figure 1.4 Bases of competition in book publishing

1960's	1970's		1980's	
	1973–4	1978–9	1981–2	

1960's
1 Attracting best authors
2 Editorial and production process
3 Price understood against range of product
4 Ability to export

1970's
5 Internationalize 1: change to local house publishing and ability to attract local authors
6 Managerial competence marketing and financial skills
7 Price now becomes increasingly important

1980's
8 Internationalize 2: USA, Western Europe and Far East
9 Foreign currency management
10 Production and distribution competence
11 Managerial competence to meet above changes critical
12 Technological changes in product and production becoming important
13 Size

subsidiaries. The strength of local publishing overseas, from which the UK company derives clear benefits is impressive, especially in market knowledge. Longman Hong Kong therefore has its own integrated sales and production operation. People from Longman UK's English language teaching division can use such local knowledge in selling their own specialist books in the Far East.

Longman has been able to devote time and resources to creating a set of secondary mechanisms which have extended and deepened its understanding of its environment. This is especially true in the way it has felt confident enough to challenge accepted editorial views of the market by recruiting marketing staff from outside the industry. At the same time it has effected a shift from being purely editorially-led to being market-led: the equivalent of Jaguar's move away from its view of a world dominated by engineers.

In ABP there were many readily-apparent strengths. The senior management of ABP were distinguished – some had negotiated the changes to the world book agreement with the USA for the UK Publishers' Association. The excellence of ABP's commissioning editors, especially in the law and academic lists, was widely recognized. In spite of their efforts it was the core problems of the composition of ABP which proved decisive. The companys ability to develop a fuller understanding of its environment suffered as a result.

The nagging unresolved problem of the structure of ABP went back to its creation in 1964 and created problems for the way in which the company engaged with its environment. Three difficulties arose. The first was fragmentation. It proved immensely difficult to reorder the group around three new divisions of law, academic and trade (general) publishing. It was therefore impossible to prevent duplication and overlap of lists in the same markets. The identity of ABP in the wider trade remained unclear. Second, the linking of the inherited overseas interests of the group was far from straightforward. It took two years of personal intervention by John Burk, the original chief executive up to 1970, to merge the law and other publishing areas in Australia. Such activity took senior management away from the market fragmentation within the divisions.

The third problem was one of imbalance arising from the success of the Legal division. The Sweet & Maxwell imprint and its major rival Butterworth accounted for the vast majority of the standard legal texts and continuation works in British law. The direct cost of this legal publishing was much lower than other types and the result was very high gross profit levels of around 70 per cent. The problem was that although the legal imprint contributed the majority of ABP's profits, there was little opportunity for them to be copied by the other divisions since their market position was so unique.

These three main internal problems meant that ABPs environmental assessment capability was conditioned in a number of negative ways that Longman's was not. This meant that ABP was hit severely by the economic dislocation of the 1970s. The rapid onset of inflation and contraction in 1974 led to the cutting back of the academic and scientific divisions by 40 per cent.

ABP, like many other British companies, ended up fire-fighting in the second half of the 1970s. It was almost at the mercy of its environment. Unlike Longman many of the secondary mechanisms, which could have been used for environmental assessment, simply did not get a chance to develop. The early attempts at developing full divisional three-year plans were abandoned and even the group did not have a fully worked-out five-year plan until 1981. There was no corresponding introduction of marketing expertise from other industries to challenge the native book trade sales approach. This defensive posture also meant that ABP was less able to use environmental pressures or crises as means of dramatically demonstrating the need for a new course of action. Longman's planning capacity meant that it both anticipated the effect of the collapse of the Nigerian market in 1982 and used it as a lesson for other divisions.

Leading change

The book publishers ABP and Longman are especially clear examples of the contribution of different styles of leading change to their companies' performance. Useful insights can be derived both from the similarity of their intentions and the contrasts in the means they employed to achieve them.

The aim at ABP, as at Longman, was to secure the benefits of separate divisions devoted to particular types of publishing; in ABP's case law, academic and trade. Yet as management found in the Rootes Group and in other industries the problems of running such structures for the first time were immense.

The difficulties with the divisional system arose from the way it was conceived and managed by ABP's senior executives in the context of the norms of publishing and the model provided by the rest of British industry. It was entirely logical therefore for the leadership of John Burk, and then Peter Allsop from 1972, to concentrate on the most prized asset of any publisher: its editorial strength. Combined with their lack of experience, however, in the trade and specialist areas of ABP, this produced a highly devolved style of leadership. This in turn was reinforced by the problems which arose in the integration of previously distinct businesses in both Canada and Australia, and commanded so much of the group executives' attention. Since it occurred at the beginning of the group's existence, the pattern was set. The result was the separation of senior management – to deal mainly with overseas problems. The divisions became the responsibility of management committees.

The type of leadership which emerged was closest to the leadership-by-exception mould. Apart from the emphasis on the autonomy of the divisions and lists up to 1974, action was directed towards the divisions only where problems arose. Such a style of leadership was consistent with the values and experience of the senior management. It was also made possible by the enduring profitability of Sweet & Maxwell's legal publishing and the satisfaction of the major shareholder, the Crossthwaite-Eyre family trust.

The reliance on a devolved style of leadership meant that the problems of the 1970s were especially hard to face. The reliance on editorial entrepreneurship at the expense of rationalization was sorely exposed by the fourfold rise in oil prices in 1973–4. Understanding the nature of ABP's leadership stance from 1964, the circumstances in which it was formed and the way wider economic upheavals then prevented its development, is highly illuminating. This perspective throws light on why, by the 1980s, ABP had devoted insufficient attention to building the competitive bases which the market now demanded; notably in the areas of marketing and new technology. This is not to argue that there was no change in leadership approach. Unfortunately for ABP the response was too late. Above all the new leaders remained within the devolved mode. They did not move to a more transformational style as was the case at Longman.

The contribution of the leadership at Longman could not have been more different. The core of that difference was in the way the company's strategic changes over the past twenty years were matched by a commensurate alteration in its leadership. Longman had to endure the same economic and market challenges as ABP. In some cases, such as the Nigerian market collapse of 1983, these external shocks were even more acute. However, the sequence of actions taken by Longman's leadership was unlike ABP's. This can be demonstrated by considering the distinctive scope of those actions which Longman sustained over almost two decades.

The starting point has to be the way certain strategic decisions were taken early but then their implications were catered for by a web of interconnecting, smaller, supportive actions built up over the long-term. The best illustration comes from the way, in the 1960s, that Longman refused to rely on milking its major asset – overseas operations in Commonwealth and related markets. The company was already moving to local publishing and joint publishing companies in Europe by the 1970s. In the words of the head of the overseas division they heeded their extensive international networks and were determined not to be caught in the 'unchanging world' created by the activities of the 'colonial entrepreneurs in the markets of the

old commonwealth'. So when the internationalization of English accelerated in the 1970s and 1980s, leading to a boom in demand for English
language teaching outside the commonwealth for example, Longman was
well-placed to respond.

Given these broad early moves Longman had the advantage of having set
in motion a process. At the same time that Longman built up strategic
goals, its leaders were almost equally concerned with fashioning the
internal character of the company. Staff might thereby adapt to the implication of such goals more readily. Longman did not try to retain family
control and shareholdings as at ABP but sought out a position within the
loosely federated Pearson & Son Ltd in 1968. Nor did Longman attempt to
establish a new divisional structure in one go. Unlike ABP, Longman had
already become a group of companies in 1966 in order to reflect its spread
of overseas publishing units. Longman then embarked on what is best described as a progressive divisionalization. The aim was to replace the three
existing departments of overseas, home and general publishing, sales and
production.

Moreover the development of the strategic goals and the preparation of
the internal character of the company were not left to operate alone. They
were augmented by generation of an appropriate capacity for change within
Longman. This entailed parallel shifts effected in the Longman culture.
These centred on a refinement of the attitude towards quality, a reworking
of the notion of professionalism and a movement in the balance of editorial
versus marketing priorities. Without it many of the advances in the production process and list development in the 1980s would have been
still-born.

The pivotal reason for the adoption of these conditioning features in
Longman has been the profound change in the style of leadership. Unlike
ABP, the senior management of Longman represents a shift over time:
from a liberal version of transactional leadership in the early 1970s to a
flowering of transformational leadership in the 1980s. It has been through
the personal development of the chief executive, Tim Rix, that the pitfalls
of ABP have been avoided.

It is worthwhile dwelling on the main aspects of the mechanism which
have been used. From 1976 Rix assembled around him a critical mass of the
'finance committee' and divisional directors who made up the UK board.
His extensive international publishing experience gave him the advantage
of an early insight into the trends and growth possibilities inherent in the
USA, Europe and the Far East. His accomplishments of having achieved
growth overseas, allied to his personality, meant that he was able to transfer
many of his techniques, piloted and proven in the 1960s and earlys 1970s.
He was more able, therefore, to aim for the higher-order goals outlined
above than was ABP. What is commonly referred to as 'Tim's vision' did

not appear in response to the fashion for mission statements but was forged into a robust form over ten years. Such a vision, then, provided the basis for collective action at first board and then divisional level. Robert Duncan, head of the medical division was in:

> no doubt that there was a two-way movement between Tim Rix and myself .... It appeared to me that there was a lot we could do outside our traditional markets, a lot of opportunities open to us, particularly in America. His feeling was that we should do something to get us out of the dependence on Africa and therefore he encouraged it. It was undoubtedly me and Tim, a joint version.

The board has therefore been relatively stable in the 1980s, augmented by key appointments in computer and production services. The finance committee (Rix and his deputy plus the finance director) has therefore grown from its early control and monitoring duties to performing an educative role for the heads and then top teams of each division. Much of the basic communication of the flow of changes is now a mature combination of Rix's regular personal appearance in the divisions, a professional communication apparatus across the company and the home-grown efforts of the divisions. Sector four's 1988 divisional conference on 'planning for development' is a case in point.

Linking strategic and operational change

The singular aspect of the two book publishers is the differing amount of attention devoted to the educative requirements of the translation process. The result is seen in the contrasting strategic awareness displayed at the operational level in the two companies.

Longman's ability to translate strategic initiatives into operational form is shown with clarity in the development of its US market. In the late 1960s it was evident to Longman (with 70 per cent of its business outside the UK) that it was in danger of becoming too reliant on its Commonwealth and related markets. Longman decided therefore to expand its publishing in the developed world and particularly North America. Longman acted early and opened a small import house in New York in 1973. The base was then used to sell UK-published books in the USA while gradually building up Longman's own commissioning from New York. A senior executive was appointed in 1975 to co-ordinate an advance on three fronts: medical, college and English language teaching (ELT). The point to note is that there was no attempt to achieve major change in one jump. Instead smaller, less risky, more manageable steps were tried. The success is shown by the contribution of US sales to Longman in the 1980s: they stood at 2.7 per cent in 1975, 28.5 per cent in 1985 and 35 per cent in 1990.

In the medical field, the Churchill Livingstone imprint was used to sell UK texts to the US. Subsequently, books by American medical and scientific authors were published; the added benefit was that they could in turn be sold in the UK. In college publishing in the 1970s the idea was, according to a commissioning editor, to: 'build on the base of exporting from the UK appropriate books to be sold in America and then gradually publish college books locally for the American market.' Here progress was slower. The mistake was in trying to publish across too wide a band of subjects. Yet this knowledge was used in the subsequent ELT and other initiatives. In spite of the inviting scale of this English-speaking market, for example, Longman learnt that it could not hope to cover the market as a whole (as did native US publishers like Prentice Hall). Instead Longman was able to exploit its strengths within further specialist niches.

In common with Jaguar, Prudential and to an extent Kleinwort Benson, Longman was able not only to deploy a spread of devices which facilitated operational change but to refine them almost continuously. Within the sectoral form, for example, further innovations have been encouraged appropriate to their markets. These include the creation of highly autonomous 'publishing cells' in the scientific area, located not in the Harlow centre but adjacent to their sources and markets. Alongside these new ventures, however, there has been a constant re-tuning of company-wide communications. The need was keenly felt when, after such expansion and innovations, a questionnaire in 1983 to middle managers showed how 'little they knew about the sectors' strategic goals'. The result has been an increasing elaboration of the communications apparatus to include briefing groups, sectoral conferences and company-wide financial commentaries given to all staff.

It is instructive to compare the way ABP attempted to enter the US market with Longman's approach. As the need for expansion into new product areas grew in the 1970s, ABP was forced to attempt a hurried and large-scale venture in 1978. The company found itself competing head-on with established trade publishers in the USA, a product and market of which it had 'hardly any experience'. As with Clerical Medical in the life assurance sector, the enforced and compressed nature of the attempt at change prevented the creation of supportive secondary mechanisms. The problems of almost constant fire-fighting in the 1970s precluded the prior development of such devices.

APB therefore found itself from 1980 weak in such operational areas as stock control, information routines, service and distribution. While Longman was mounting a series of adjustments to its structure to release managerial responsibility, improve market alignment and try out innovative publishing units (e.g. the cell idea), ABP was still struggling to clarify its internal form. The paradox therefore resulted of a company with world-class editorial standards yet undeveloped marketing departments. The skills of monitoring, feedback and adjustment had little chance to grow, given the limitations.

ABP's senior management also found that the preoccupations of the 1970s had left them without the ability to use feedback and adjustment processes as found at Longman. David Croom, a newcomer to ABP, with the key responsibility of the academic division from 1980, makes the point well. He is clear how the new growth objectives for the mid-1980s were given to the imprints. Yet in his words no dialogue, no testing or interrogation followed to develop the objectives at the operational level. The growth targets were not 'drawn out in human terms'. The budget forecasts of each division were not tested for their operational implications and means of implementation – unlike at Kleinworts, for example, or most particularly via the finance committee at Longman's.

Managing human resources

Any company develops its own distinctive knowledge base over time. That base contains both technical and social knowledge. The ability to produce books, for example, in ABP came to rely on a mixture of technical information on the specialist markets it served, the production process and the skills necessary to put such knowledge into practice. There were also the implicit notions of the standards by which such activities were practised. Furthermore, there were the values which informed such action and helped, for instance, to account for the status granted to legal publishing. What becomes critical is the extent to which the knowledge base of a firm matches changing competitive conditions. Altering such a composite base is not simple.

The experience of Longman is useful in two main respects. First the company is an excellent example of the way HRM can be used to develop an appropriate knowledge base. Second, Longman reveals one of the more difficult issues confronting the successful company: how to shed outmoded features of that knowledge base.

At the core of Longman's growth from the 1970s was the creation of an understanding of its own competitive base. It is clear from the above that the company evolved a strong definition of its business purpose involving considerable innovation. Although developed more unevenly, by the mid-1980s Longman's strategic position was underpinned by a growing HRM approach. It had teased out the human resource requirements which such objectives imply as part of its attempt to increase the depth of its business planning. In that sense Longman demonstrated the need for HR change as a result of its own maturing strategic thinking across the 1970s and early 1980s.

In one sense Longman was forced to consider its workforce management. Longman during the 1970s became much more centralized and professional in its personnel and IR approach. In many ways this was forced by the growth of the ASTMS union in the publishing divisions (recognition was given in 1975) and the flow of national employment legislation. The keynote in the company was the centralization of negotiation and information, together with the attempt to develop a new salary structure based on job evaluation. There had been relatively few major disputes after the 1973 strike by SOGAT union members in the distribution area. The problem became the rigidity of work practices, the post-entry closed shop and management which came to restrict the efficiency of the section. Since 1983 most of the existing structure and practices have been changed. The weak supervisory system has been overhauled, new values have been instituted in the bonus scheme and a totally new procedure agreement was negotiated with SOGAT across 1987 which led to Longman leaving the Publishers' Association's national negotiations.

Yet Longman has gone further than only reforming its industrial relations arrangements. From 1982, and with the appointment of the director of personnel to the board of the UK company, a new phase of policy was initiated. The general aim has to make clear, throughout the company, the need for linking personnel policies much more to the strategic objectives of the business. The intention was to diffuse the commitment to HRM beyond the senior management. A series of secondary actions followed.

Devolving the HRM approach to the line was seen as imperative to decentralize some of the responsibility for training and development to line management. The view of the director of personnel was clear: in spite of the training activity which already existed, Longman's divisional method of business planning did not cover the detailed human resource needs and implications of given policies. The result was to begin a process (in 1987) of developing HR plans for each division. The potential benefits are considerable given the hesitancy of other major publishers to move to such orientations.

The HRM approach has not been allowed to become a programme or end in itself. Rather its relevance has been shown to the contribution it can make to Longman's commercial objectives. Nowhere has this been better demonstrated than Longman's need to alter its knowledge base. The senior management and personnel staff have been working consistently since 1982 to alter editorial techniques, values and standards of professionalism. The aim has been to align those more closely with the requirements of diversification. Without such a shift Longman's strategic moves to the USA and the Far East would not be possible.

One of the major needs derived from the business objectives of the company was the creation of a more commercial consciousness among all staff but most especially on the publishing side. One publisher sums up the change neatly when she draws the distinction between: 'being interested in the product for its own sake and being interested in the product as a means to developing the business.' If one takes these two types of approach as extremes then the publishers at Longman have exhibited a behaviour across the range. In general, though, the collection of commercial pressures which Longman faced in the 1980s meant that there was a swing very much towards the entrepreneurial, business developer. The shift was clearly necessary in order to mirror the decision to be market- rather than product-led.

At ABP the extent of the fire-fighting required in the 1970s and then the slump in the company's fortunes in 1980 meant that little time was left for consideration of human resource planning. As with Longman, most attention was given to the increasing requirements of employment legislation and bargaining at the Andover distribution centre with SOGAT and ASTMS members. The small size of the personnel function meant that there was only one training officer and most of her time was devoted to handling the terms and conditions of the freelance copy-editors and proof-readers used by the imprints. An internal review in 1986 noted tersely how the company's 'record in training had not been impressive'.

Unlike Longman, ABP was unable to alter its knowledge base. Indeed this became one of the most powerful impediments to the company's attempt to move away from its legal publishing emphasis. The restricted approach of its personnel department was not able to act as the catalyst for change as in Longmans.

The new managing director of ABP UK in 1980 noted how the principal strength of the business lay in the professionalism of its staff. There was an undoubted commitment, especially on the editorial side to their subject, their lists and their authors. The culture of ABP was founded on the quality and integrity of its publishing. The law lists through to the University Paperback series of Methuen or the Arden Shakespeare editions were united by this common denominator. The quality of the titles was widely accepted in the trade.

This adherence to editorial integrity, however, was often maintained at the expense of commercial requirements. The root of the problem is best summed up by a divisional director. He noted how: 'Most of us came into publishing because we liked the idea of books or the subject behind the books. Most of us did not come into publishing because we were business people to make money.' Therein lay the cause of much of the relatively weak commercial base of ABP. David Croom realized the strength of the feeling behind the approach very quickly after the merger with Croom Helm in 1985. He noted how ABP editors, when considering a potential book, asked: 'Is it worthy of my list?' Croom Helm editors asked: 'Is it worthy of my ratios?'

Similarly, by allowing the adherence to quality among editorial staff to become so dominant, this obscured the need to develop the business. In other words, ABP's editors did not make the vital progression from quality for its own sake to producing quality which the market required. The flatness of ABP's results can in part be explained by the way quality squeezed out the desire to grow.

ABP's ability to learn from its experience was limited. This was evident in the failure to generate learning mechanisms across the divisions. At a lower level it is clear that certain improvements were made in the operation of the divisions and their learning effects were retained. The reporting forms and budget systems not only gained acceptance through their immediate relevance (e.g. in revealing cash flow deficiencies) but by their very nature they became positively self-reinforcing. Elsewhere the mechanisms for learning from past successes or mistakes were essentially ad hoc. In 1979 the striking need was identified for 'post-mortem' forms to be completed for each book. This way there was less chance of failed projects being left unrecorded or taken for granted. Yet without any major alteration in the editorial-led culture of the divisions and the devotion to quality, the new practice was not extensively used. The clearest indication of just how little formal or organized reflection took place within each division was shown in the surprised reaction to David Croom's suggestion in January 1987 for a three day seminar for the Methuen and Tavistock academic imprints. Longman had been holding annual sector conferences throughout the 1980s.

Coherence

The issue of coherence in managing change and competition is the most abstract and wide-ranging of the five central factors. In many ways the requirements for coherence arise from the implications of the other four. In practice the essence of such coherence can be baldy stated: it is the ability to hold the organization together while simultaneously reshaping it.

No previous work deals with the problem directly. Those that have examined the issues of integration or co-ordination are found wanting. Their reliance on the notion of 'fit' (especially in the excellence literature) is unhelpful; it is too static and dwells on a fixed structural metaphor. Recent studies of networks and inter-firm linkages are more promising. The need, however, is to appreciate such relations within a dynamic perspective. The problem for management is how these links can be used within the process of managing change and competition.

As the evidence from Longman shows, employing structures as part of an ongoing process is but one of the puzzles that the process generates. In fact achieving coherence in managing change requires the resolution of a whole series of conundrums. Creating a collective capacity to assess a firm's environment, lead change, link strategic and operational change and manage human resources throws up a host of dualities and dilemmas. These have to be resolved while change takes place. The four central factors outlined above cannot be left to function by themselves.

We have suggested a twin set of actions which appear to be relevant in dealing with such apparent contradictions. As in all the other central factors the crucial need is in ensuring that the primary conditioning features are reinforced through time by a complementary set of mechanisms.

The conditioning features relate to the formation of strategy. A given strategy should therefore bear the hallmarks of consistency, consonance, advantage, and feasibility. Yet as the Longman example shows, how such characteristics are built up is decisive. Thus it was clear that Longman began with certain commercial insights in the 1970s (such as the need to switch to new markets). The company then took infinite pains to develop those over almost a decade. This involved: beginning with a relatively imprecise vision of what such a decision implied; using that imprecison to win over staff gradually; and maximizing the learning-by-doing which followed. The result by 1980 was a robust, well-accepted strategic orientation and flexible business planning method: both have stood the test of the 1980s.

Yet in order for these qualities of a strategy to survive there has to be a range of complementary management action which sustains them. There has to be a coherence of purpose and belief among the senior management team, even though individual styles and methods may differ. HRM initiatives must produce apposite knowledge bases which match the strategic conditioning features. Similarly there must be inter-organizational coherence across the range of customers, suppliers, distributors and collaborators upon which the firm relies. In the case of Longman, this required parallel action in the areas of: breaking with suppliers and distributors (in the face of industry norms) who failed to meet Longman's requirements; educating authors so that they met specific market demands; using contract sub-editors to meet fluctuations in the publishing process; and forging new links with computer hardware manufacturers, software houses and freelance designers in order to develop products which exploit new technology.

Given the scope of the actions necessary in the preceding four factors, then the ability to manage a series of interrelated and emergent changes is vital. This particular conundrum can be addressed by consciously working on the analytical, educational and political problems of the change process.

As Longman vividly shows it was no good Tim Rix becoming ever more sophisticated at strategic analysis. His personal learning had to become generalized and taken on further within both the board and the business sectors. Nor was the company afraid to use outsiders. While this generated in time certain shared assumptions within Longman, almost equal attention was, in due course, given to the contradictions and mistakes which arose. They were acted upon and the new knowledge built in to the cycle of strategic thinking and action. The need for major alterations in markets, products or technology was not met by analysis alone, nor even by major programmes of radical change.

What stands out is the use of modest islands of progress – such as the financial planning techniques or the publishing cells idea. These first tried out possible responses to a problem, were non-threatening, did not raise expectations unduly, and were consequently more amenable to diffusion. Although obvious after the event, realizing and communicating such successes (but not to the point of delusion) was invaluable in sustaining the momentum of a complicated set of changes. The political implications of such actions are far-reaching. Fixed, elaborate hierarchies act as a brake. The exploitation of often impermanent, less formal internal and external networks seem far better suited to managing the necessary changes.

A brief comparison with ABP is instructive. Figure 1.5 summarizes the way Longman has maintained coherence in its management of strategic change and competition. Figure 1.5 also supplies an outline of the difficult-

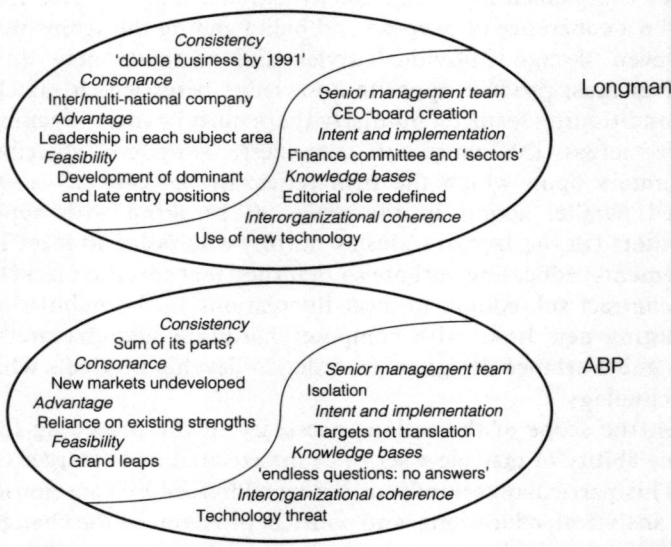

Figure 1.5   Coherence in the management of strategic change: Longman and ABP

ies faced by ABP in this respect. It shows how ABP did not benefit from a strong set of conditioning features. As the previous chapters have shown, ABP's analysis of its competitive advantage relied heavily on its existing market strengths (mainly legal and academic). Thereby the clear identification of the need and means of adapting to the changes in the book publishing markets was slow to emerge. Its strategic thinking and actions were not fully consonant with its environment. The result was that, unlike Longman's long-term learning approach, ABP was forced to attempt grand leaps of much higher risk, to try and break into new markets – as in the case of its Magnum paperback and US projects of the late 1970s.

Similarly, ABP's capacity to achieve coherence in managing the strategic changes it chose had a number of weaknesses in comparison to Longman. Set beside Rix and the development of the Longman board, ABP's senior management appear isolated. The assumption that the divisions within ABP knew best how to translate their business targets into practice put ABP at a disadvantage. This became especially clear in the light of Longman's extensive range of supportive action and its persistence in refining such secondary mechanisms.

Managing Change and Competitive Performance:
Main Research Findings

The Warwick research set out to determine if the way a firm managed strategic change made a demonstrable difference to its competitive performance. The general answer to this core problem was a resounding yes. We were able to demonstrate the widely-assumed but seldom-investigated relationship between strategic change and competition.

Here it is only possible to give a brief synopsis of the main findings of the study, and in particular to describe the pattern which emerges from examining competition among the firms in the four sectors of automobiles, book publishing, merchant banking, and life assurance (see Pettigrew and Whipp 1991). That pattern is represented in the five interrelated aspects of managing strategic and operational change shown in figure 1.6. The higher and lower performing firms contrasted sharply in the way they: assessed their environment; led change; linked strategic and operational change; managed their human resources; and the degree to which they achieved coherence in the management of the change process. We used these five factors in the working example from Longman and ABP in the previous section. Here these factors are examined in their own right.

The key to understanding the model in figure 1.6 is its interconnectedness. No single factor among the five provides the means, by itself, to

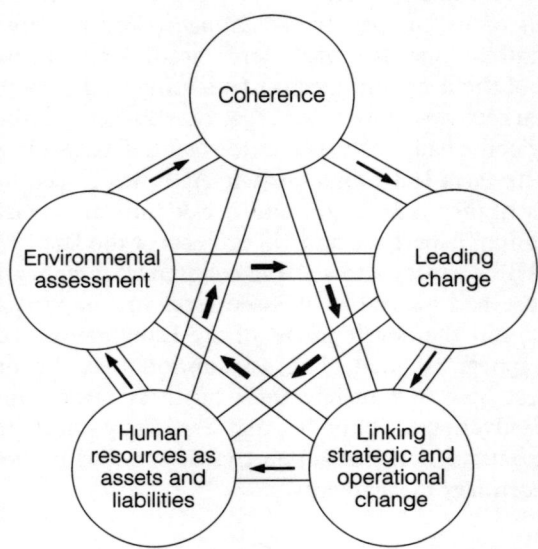

Figure 1.6   Managing change for competitive success: the five central factors

manage change for competitive success. The model attempts to capture the vital flow of energy in the change process and point to the ways by which that energy can be channelled productively or conversely blocked. Jaguar is a good example. The company built totally new ways of leading change, linking the strategic and operational and managing its human resources in the early 1980s. The blockage to its energy level in managing change came in its misassessment of the environment and the capability to maintain coherence.

Each factor contains two main components: (1) the primary conditioning features which logically have to exist before (2) the secondary actions and mechanisms can have any meaningful effect (see figure 1.7).

A further general pattern is that the lower performers seem unable to combine the conditioning features with the subsidiary mechanisms over time. The higher performers were able to derive the benefits which accrue from developing both aspects of each factor. In other words, the lower performers may meet some of the necessary conditions to manage change but they do not satisfy sufficient conditions to manage change for competitive success.

It is worthwhile extracting what the study has revealed of the ways the higher performers used the five factors in practice.

Environmental Assessment

The starting point in the process of competition derives from the understanding a firm develops of its environment. In general terms the research shows that it is insufficient for companies to regard the creation of kowledge and judgements of their external competitive world as simply a technical exercise. Rather the need is for organizations to become open learning systems. In other words, the assessment of the competitive environment does not remain the preserve of a single function nor the sole responsibility of one senior manager. Nor does it occur via isolated acts. Instead strategy creation is seen as emerging from the way a company, at various levels, acquires, interprets and processes information about its environment.

As figure 1.7 shows, there are four conditioning features which help to explain the degree of openness of an organization to its environment and its receptiveness to the changes in its environment. These include: (1) the extent to which there are key actors within the firm who are prepared to champion assessment techniques which increase the openness of the organization; (2) the structural and cultural characteristics of the company; (3) the extent to which environmental pressures are recognized and their associated dramas develop; and (4) the degree to which assessment occurs as a multi-function activity which is not pursued as an end in itself but which is linked to the central operation of the business.

However, even if this set of primary conditioning features existed within an enterprise then that would be no guarantee of the survival of its environmental assessment capacity. In order for it to endure a set of secondary actions are required in order to stabilize and impel the assessment capacity forward. Incorporation of those responsible for planning and marketing is critical, as is the availability of purposive networks which link the firm with key stakeholders and interest groups. The use of specialist task forces or teams, beside their technical relevance, can often reinforce the importance attributed to the assessment process, especially if they are drawn from across functions.

Leading change

Our central finding in relation to leading change is that there are no simple universal rules. In fact the reverse is true: leadership is acutely context sensitive. This is manifested in a number of ways. The very choice of leader clearly relates to those who make the choice and the circumstances in which they do so. The immediate problems which the incoming leader faces are largely supplied by the situation which the leader inherits. The

	Environmental assessment	Leading change	Linking strategic and operational change	Human resources as assets and liabilities	Coherence
Primary conditioning features	1 Availability of key people 2 Internal character of organization 3 Environmental pressures and associated dramas 4 Environmental assessment as a multifunctional activity	1 Building a receptive context for change legitimation 2 Creating capability for change 3 Constructing the content and direction of the change	1 Justifying the need for change 2 Building capacity for appropriate action 3 Supplying necessary visions, values and business direction	1 Raising HRM consciousness 2 Use of highly situational additive features to create positive force for HRM change 3 Demonstrating the need for business and people change	1 Consistency 2 Consonance 3 Advantage 4 Feasibility
Secondary mechanisms	5 Role of planning, marketing 6 Construction of purposive networks with main stakeholders 7 Use of specialist task forces	4 Operationalizing the change agenda 5 Creating the critical mass for change within senior management 6 Communicating need for change and detailed requirements of the change agenda 7 Achieving and reinforcing success 8 Balancing continuity and change 9 Sustaining coherence	4 Breaking emergent strategy into actionable pieces 5 Appointment of change managers, relevant structures and exacting targets 6 Re-thinking communications 7 Using the reward system 8 Setting up local negotiation climate for targets 9 Modifying original visions in light of local context 10 Monitoring and adjustment	4 *Ad hoc*, cumulative, supportive activities at various levels 5 Linking HRM action to business need with HRM as a means not an end 6 Mobilizing external influences 7 Devolution to line 8 Construction of HRM actions and institutions which reinforce one another	5 Leadership 6 Senior management team integrity 7 Uniting intent and implementation 8 Developing opposite knowledge bases 9 Interorganizational coherence 10 Managing a series of interrelated changes over time

Figure 1.7 Managing change for competitive success: the five central factors

zones of manoeuvre open to the new leader in deciding what to change and how to go about it are bounded by the context within and outside the firm.

The critical leadership tasks in managing change appear to be much more fragmentary and incremental than the popular images of business heroism allow. Leading change involves action by people at every level of the business. Nowhere among the five central factors is the set of primary conditioning features so important. Moving directly to bold actions can be costly. Instead, the prior need is to build a climate for change while at the same time raising energy levels and setting out the new directions to be followed *before* precise action is taken.

The primary conditioning set here includes: (1) the building of a climate within the firm which will be receptive to change, which involves justifying why the change should take place. (2) Similarly, there is little point attempting change without first building the capability to mount that change. (3) Equally, establishing a change agenda which not only sets the direction of the business but also establishes the necessary visions and values is by no means simple. It is a process in itself which may take a series of attempts before completion.

Once these conditioning features have been attended to then a more direct set of mechanisms can be put to use (see figure 1.7). These extend from the breaking down of broad strategic intentions into manageable pieces (in, for example, policy initiatives or projects) to the articulation of successful outcomes in order to build confidence.

Linking strategic and operational change

The importance attributed to linking strategic and operational change is because the process has both an intentional and emergent character. The need is, therefore, to appreciate how intentions are implemented – and hence transformed – over time. Indeed the additive effect of otherwise separate decisions and acts of implementation may be so powerful that they over-whelm the original intentions and even help create an entirely new context for future strategic decision making. Strategies are often therefore the post hoc labelling of such series of 'successful' operational acts.

Unsurprisingly the conditioning features involved are similar to those in leading change. They centre on the capability for action and the necessary visions and values which underwrite the chosen business direction.

Great attention is required though to the secondary mechanisms if the operational aspects are not to undermine the general strategic intentions. Not only must those intentions be broken down to actionable pieces, those components must become the responsibility of change managers, operating within appropriate structures at various levels within the organization. Clear and exacting target-setting has in turn to be supported by re-thought communication mechanisms and adjusted reward systems. The modification of overall visions in the light of local conditions is a major requirement, as is the construction of human resource capabilities which can support such a raft of related changes.

Human resources as assets and liabilities

Human resource management relates to the total set of knowledge, skills and attitudes that firms need to compete. It involves concern for, and action in, the management of people including selection, training and development, employee relations and compensation. Such actions may be bound together by the creation of an HRM philosophy.

The differential ability of the eight firms to recognize and carry out a version of human resource management is very evident. Yet on reflection the disparity is less surprising when one considers the time it takes to develop such a capacity and its fragility. An HRM approach cannot be constructed overnight. What is involved is a much longer-term learning process which requires the creation of successive positive spirals of development.

The route to such learning is first through a group of conditioning features. This involves: (1) the raising of a general consciousness of the benefits of HRM in relation to the business needs of the firm by those prepared to champion the cause; (2) there appears to be a highly situational collection of features which can create a positive force for HRM change; (3) there usually have to be enforced alterations in both business and people aspects of the organization which help to produce a receptive context for HRM change.

Thereafter, the mechanisms for confirming and stabilizing such HRM initiatives are less programmatic than ad hoc. When added together, such practical actions can be highly conducive to the survival of the initiatives. These acts embrace the mobilizing of external influences which confirm the link between business needs and the means HRM can supply, through to the creation of linked institutions and structures which reinforce the existence and credibility of policies.

Coherence in the management of change

The last factor in managing change for competitive success is at once the most abstract and wide-ranging of the five central factors. In many ways the requirements for coherence arise from the implications of the other four. As in all the other central factors the crucial need is in ensuring that the primary conditioning features are reinforced by a complementary set of mechanisms.

The conditioning features relate to the formation of strategy. We agree with Rumelt (1988) that a given strategy should present consistent goals, be an adaptive response to its environment, provide for the maintenance of competitive advantage and neither over-tax available resources nor create unsolvable problems.

Yet in order for these qualities of a strategy to survive there has to be a range of complementary management action which sustains them. As figure 1.7 indicates, there has to be a coherence of purpose and belief among the senior management team, even though individual styles and methods may differ. HRM initiatives must produce apposite knowledge bases which match the strategic conditioning features. Similarly there must be inter-organizational coherence across the range of customers, suppliers, distributors and collaborators upon which the firm relies. Given the scope of the actions necessary in the preceding four factors, the ability to manage a series of interrelated and emergent changes is vital.

These conclusions do not claim universal application. Nonetheless, the strength of their insights is confirmed by using two searching tests. That the pattern of managing change and competition represented in our model holds good across four sectors ranging from manufacturing to service and including the hybrid, book publishing, surely commands attention. That claim is reinforced by applying a second check. The model does not only differentiate between high and low performers. It has also been used to explain why certain firms improved or lost their competitive position over time.

Confirmation of the strength of the factors and their components comes from having studied the companies over the long term. Changes in competitive performance emerge by changes being made in each of the central factors. Peugeot Talbot therefore has registered a marked improvement in its record since 1985. This has been closely linked to a series of adjustments made in each of the five factors. In terms of coherence the company now has achieved consistency, consonance and a degree of advantage through reducing its strategic aims. At the same time a new managing director has devoted far more attention to the full range of requirements for leading change outlined in the fourth section of this paper. In the area of human resources Peugeot Talbot found the effort expended there led to sharp productivity gains in spite of the company's relative lack of capital resources for new technology.

The project raises important methodological issues for the study of competition. If the joint process of competition and strategic change is a continuous one which occurs in given contexts, then it should be studied accordingly. This means that the iterative and uncertain nature of the process should be fully recognized. Looking for clearly defined episodes of competitive assessment, strategic decision making and operational implementation is misguided. The need is to explore the cumulative and un-predictable effects of the interplay between managerial decisions and changing contexts.

It is imperative, therefore, that full attention is given not only to the impact of management's analytical techniques (which are never entirely objective) but also to the vital acts of learning and adaptation which have to occur. The range of linked political actions involved should also be in-cluded. By their very nature such compound processes can only be fully understood as they emerge over time. One of the clearest methodological outcomes is that the process of competition demands longitudinal techniques of study which may need to cover decades rather than years (for a fuller account see; Pettigrew and Whipp 1989; Pettigrew 1990; Whipp and Clark 1986: 7–50).

Conclusion

In this chapter we have used new empirical evidence on the relative per-formance of firms over long periods to demonstrate the link between com-petitive success and managing change. The fundamental test for large firms facing up to the business and economic upheavals of the 1990s rests on their ability to create, maintain, and use what we have described as an interconnected set of intangible assets. Empirically we have studied these intangible assets through our five factors of environmental assessment, leading change, managing the link between strategic and operational change, human resources as assets and liabilities, and the management of coherence. In our view the capacity to manage the process of strategic change is deeply embodied in people, and one of the most important intan-gible assets of all.

These conclusions do not claim universal application. None the less, the strength of their insights is confirmed by using two searching tests. That the pattern of managing change and competition represented in our model holds good across four sectors ranging from manufacturing to service and including the hybrid, book publishing, surely commands attention. That claim is reinforced by applying a second check. The model does not differentiate between absolute high and low performers. It has also been used to explain why certain firms improved or lost their competitive pos-ition at different points over time.

Understanding the joint process of competition and strategic change via a contextual and longitudinal approach requires the quality and quantity of data which the project has mobilized. This strength is also a limitation. In spite of embracing the focal firms and the industries concerned the sample size is still restricted. That size is determined by the needs of intensive processual research. However, our findings now provide sturdy patterns which can be tested elsewhere. It is also the case that the original intention of using matching pairs was not totally fulfilled in that the pairs did not form perfect couples. The significance of that outcome should not be lost; in real life commercial competitors are not obligingly matched.

Our findings about the interlinked character of the process of strategic change and competition require emphasis. The evidence from the industries studied does not support any view of that relationship as straightforward. On the contrary, the problem turns out to be multi-faceted and not susceptible to monocausal explanation. In broad terms, the need is to first appreciate competition and strategic change as a joint process. Second, to see that process through a multi-level contextual perspective. This then allows the construction of a more holistic model which can account for the way firms differ in their competitive performance.

In addressing the linked questions of how firms compete and how they handle processes of change, notions of 'fit' do not capture what we have observed. A reliance on contingent thinking and metaphors of 'fit', with their connotations of constancy and rigidity, does not capture the fluidity, unpredictability, and simultaneity of processes of change and competition. The pattern in our data is not of firms seeking to lock the character of an organization and its strategic direction together in some timeless fashion. On the contrary, a more searching requirement is evident–the ability to hold a firm's strategic thinking together, while at the same time carrying out the reshaping and adjustments which new or emergent strategies demand. The ability to maintain such coherence is only demonstrated over time; it is tested by the multitude of alterations which occur, and by ever-present demands for learning and unlearning as actions taken reap their anticipated and unanticipated consequences. In these processes the ability to manage a series of interrelated and emergent changes is vital.

Thus our data points to the uneven capacity of management to acquire and filter information from a competitive environment which is constantly changing its rules and assumptions. It is the impermanence of given strategic positions and fragility of bases of competition which make the process so unpredictable. It is this unpredictable quality which leads the more successful firms to develop learning processes at all levels of the organization. Such learning is seldom through orderly progressions, but occurs through a process of untidy iterations and learning spirals.

This study also indicates the critical role of energy in understanding and managing change processes. The five factor model (see figure 1.6) points to the centrality of energy in the change process. However, there are three aspects of management action which can assist the flow of energy set up by the use of the five factors.

1 In contrast to much current thinking, this research does not conclude that energy generation comes only from new leaders brought in from outside. To be sure, these entrants can have galvanizing effects in the sense of their expectations and assumptions which confront established views. Tension thereby creates energy. Yet these productive tensions can equally be generated from within by management prepared to question company orthodoxies, to use real and constructed crises, or to benefit from deviants and thereby exploit the resulting energy.

2 Sustaining the flow of energy within a change process, especially after crises have been successfully survived, is one of the most recurrent difficulties for management. The evidence from this study points to the need to avoid undue reliance on a single source of leadership. Instead, the creation of leaders at different levels in the organization is more helpful to the maintenance of energy in managing the process of change. The role of these leaders is to problem-sense from their vantage point, to ask fundamental questions, and to uncover data which disturbs and confronts in-house assumptions. Equally relevant therefore is the necessary reworking of HRM policies in order to recognize such responsibilities – this may require new methods of performance review, reward and recognition and the use of internal labour markets to encourage such behaviour.

3 The issue of preventing regression in the change process is important as it is often overlooked. Demonstrating intermediate successes or islands of progress can play a productive role by showing what can be achieved. Attention to the lines of succession also count heavily since it is their breakdown which leads to the leakage of energy. Yet beyond these actions we have identified a way of thinking which is of considerable relevance to stopping the slide into inertia. Managers should be encouraged to see change not only in terms of episodes or events but as an ongoing, continuous process. The keynote of this mode of thought is the ability to not only cope with the dualities and contradictions of the strategic change process but to exploit them. Thus the 'transformations in use' of original strategic intentions should not be seen as failure. The dilemmas and contradictions inherent in the translation process are seldom amenable to being planned out of existence. Instead the flow of questions they give rise to should be captured and their implications confronted as a means of preventing the slump back into conventional thought patterns – once a given challenge is considered to have passed.

Moreover, this study calls into question any easy unitary notion of managing change and competition. Quite the reverse, the research reveals the operation of a range of highly interconnected, subprocesses which are commonly overlooked or assumed. This calls into question therefore the ability of those responsible to not only problem-sense but also to: raise the energy for change; justify the need for change and legitimize chosen courses of action; negotiate the pathways of change for the organization; stabilize successful programmes; set in motion processes which will lead to the generation of relevant knowledge; and resolve the many contradictions which arise between these subprocesses.

Kanter has argued (1989) that the prime characteristics of successful companies in the future will be their degree of all-round innovation. This will embrace: the restructuring to create synergies between different parts of the business; opening boundaries in the furtherance of strategic alliances; and the generation of new ventures from within. Companies may be turned inside-out (Whipp, Rosenfeld and Pettigrew 1989b). She concludes that more than ever before this future company will represent a triumph 'of process over structure'. If that is the case then the extension of the change capacities identified in this chapter may well be the key to the reconstruction of the firm in this 'age of surprises' at the end of the twentieth century.

References

Abernathy, A. J., Clark, K. and Kantrow, A. 1983: *Industrial Renaissance. Producing a competitive future for America*. New York: Basic Books.

Barney, J. B. 1986: Types of competition and the theory of strategy: towards an integrative framework. *Academy of Management Review*, 11, 4, 791–800.

Budworth, D. 1989: Intangible assets of companies. Mimeo, Science Policy Support Group, London, May.

Elbaum, B. and Lazonick, W. 1986: *The Decline of the British Economy*. Oxford: Clarendon Press.

Hamel, G. and Prahalad, C.K. 1989: Strategic intent. *Harvard Business Review*, May–June, 63–76.

Hodgson, G. 1988: *Economics and Institutions*. Cambridge: Polity Press.

Kanter, R. M. 1989: *When Giants Learn to Dance*. New York: Simon & Schuster.

Pavitt K. (ed.) 1980: *Technical Change and Britain's Economic Performance*. London: Macmillan.

Peters, T. J. and Waterman, R. H. 1982: *In Search of Excellence: lessons from America's best run companies*. New York: Harper & Row.

Pettigrew, A. M. 1985: The *Awakening Giant: Continuity and Change in ICI*. Oxford: Basil Blackwell.

Pettigrew. A. M. 1990: Longitudinal field research on change: theory and practice. *Organisation Science*, 1, 3, 267–92.

Pettigrew, A. M. and Whipp, R. 1989: The management of strategic and operational change. End of award Report to the Economic and Social Research Council, F20250006, Jan.

Pettigrew, A. M. and Whipp, R. 1991: *Managing Change for Competitive Success*. Oxford: Basil Blackwell.

Pettigrew, A. M., Whipp, R. and Rosenfeld, R. 1989: Competitiveness and the management of strategic change processes: a research agenda, in, Francis, A. and Tharakan, M. (eds) *The Competitiveness of European Industry: Country Policies and Company Strategies*, London: Routledge, 110–136.

Porter, M. 1989: *The Competitive Advantage of Nations and their Firms*. New York: Free Press.

Rumelt, R. 1988: The evaluation of business strategy. In J.B. Quinn, H. Mintzberg and R. M. James (eds), *The Strategy Process: concepts, contexts and cases*, Engelwood Cliffs, NJ: Prentice Hall, 50–56.

Schotter, A. 1981: *The Economic Theory of Social Institutions*. Cambridge: Cambridge University Press.

Teece, D. J. (ed.) 1987: *The Competitive Challenge: strategies for industrial innovation and renewal*. Cambridge, Mass.: Ballinger.

Van de Ven, A. 1986: Central problems in the management of innovation. *Management Science*, 22, 5, May, 590–607.

Waters, R. 1989: Identity crisis threatens balance sheet values. *Financial Times*, 27.4.89, 35.

Weiner, M. 1981: *English Culture and the Decline of the Industrial Spirit, 1850–1890*. Cambridge: Cambridge University Press.

Whipp, R. and Clark, C. 1986: *Innovation and the Auto Industry: Product, Process and Work Organisation*. London: Frances Pinter.

Whipp, R., Rosenfeld, R. and Pettigrew, A. M. 1987: Understanding strategic change processes: some preliminary British findings. In Pettigrew, A. (ed.), *The Management of Strategic Change*, Oxford: Basil Blackwell, 14–55.

Whipp, R., Rosenfeld, R. and Pettigrew, A. M. 1989a: Culture and competitiveness: evidence from mature UK industries. *Journal of Management Studies*, 26, 6, November, 561–86.

Whipp, R., Rosenfeld, R. and Pettigrew, A. M. 1989b: Managing strategic change in a mature business. *Long Range Planning*, 22, No 6, 92–99.

Whipp, R., Pettigrew, A. M. and Sparrow, P. 1989: New technology, competition and the firm: a framework for research, *International Journal of Vehicle Design*, 10, 4. 453–69.

Winter. S. 1987: Knowledge and competence as strategic assets, in Teece, D. (ed.) *The Competitive Challenge: strategies for innovation and renewal*. Cambridge, Mass: Ballinger, 159–184.

Yamazaki, T. 1989: Corporate investment. *Financial Times*, 29.11.89, 18.

2

Organizational Strategies for Building Corporate Entrepreneurship[1]

John M. Stopford and Charles W. F. Baden-Fuller

The quickening pace of cross-border competition, spurred both by moves towards global competition and by deregulation, has caused firms immense difficulties of adjustment. The record of business failures shows that managing the needed redefinitions of strategy is a task that challenges and can defeat all but the strongest enterprises. Confronted by innovative, often Japanese, competitors, many Western firms have found themselves trapped in outdated assumptions and procedures, ill-suited to the new conditions. To respond effectively, they have had to find new ways of both thinking and acting to manage a process of organizational renewal, in which learning is of critical importance. Conventional, 'planned' approaches to corporate management have frequently proved inadequate to deal with the volatile competitive environments found in many 'mature' international industries. Success in building and maintaining competitiveness seems dependent in part on the ability of the enterprise as a whole to be entrepreneurial.

The seminal ideas of Schumpeter (1934), who considered an entrepreneur to be one who carries out new combinations, can be applied to firms. For large, complex organizations the essential ingredients are changes in the pattern of resource deployment and the creation of new resources that transform the enterprise into something significantly different from what it was. We concur with Stevenson and Jarillo (1990) that the critical need is for the entrepreneurial instincts of individual managers to be shared with colleagues: long-term competitive battles are not won by gifted individuals alone. Thus, conventional notions of strategy need to be combined with those that some have labelled 'corporate entrepreneurship' (Burgelman, 1983a).

We define corporate entrepreneurship in terms of five key variables that have been commanding growing attention. The first of these is the use of teams, both laterally and horizontally, both to identify and to solve problems (Kanter, 1983, 1989; Senge, 1990). The second is the ability of firms to calculate strategic direction, not in terms of a fit between perceived market needs and today's resources, but in terms of the beliefs managers hold as to their abilities to create new resources and capabilities in the future (Hamel and Prahalad, 1989, 1990; Hay and Williamson, 1991). Third is the ability of the firm to conduct experiments and adapt rapidly to unforseen events (Nielsen, Peters and Hisrich, 1985; MacMillan and Day 1987). Fourth, and closely related to the third is the ability of teams to learn new skills (De Geus, 1988, 1990; Tichy and Charan, 1989). Fifth is the ability to resolve dilemmas consistently over time (Hampden-Turner, 1990).

Elsewhere, we have examined the symbiotic connection between corporate entrepreneurship and organizational renewal (Stopford and Baden-Fuller, 1991). In particular, we have shown that the more a firm makes progress in building all five attributes of corporate entrepreneurship, the more it improves its chances of success in implementing innovations in strategy. In this paper, we address the related topic of how firms go about building corporate entrepreneurship. Who starts the process? What are the triggers for starting? How can the inevitable resistance to change be overcome? Can the momentum for continuous change be maintained even after success has become evident?

The analysis that follows necessarily includes both issues of the strategic process and of strategic thinking. Mintzberg (1987, 1990), Quinn (1980) and others have asserted that strategy is often incremental and emergent, rather than deliberate. But is the same true for building the capabilities associated with corporate entrepreneurship?

There are two schools of thought. One emphasises the part played by the top team in general and the particular role of the chief executive in guiding the development of the organization. Even if they do not set a detailed strategic plan, they are responsible for setting the overall direction for desired progress. They exercise leadership by building the organizational climate and style of operating. The other school argues that an organization cannot be driven successfully from the top. Though the top may appear to lead, others may not follow. Moreover, the organization may have a mind of its own. When talking about strategy, Weick (1979, p. 188) struck a chord when he asserted: 'the only thing that can be selected and preserved is something that is already there ... Organizations formulate strategy *after* they implement it, not before'.

We take the position that building entrepreneurship can be both deliberate and emergent. Deliberate in the sense that a clear direction had been established by the chief executive, often in the form of a challenge: emergent in the sense that the details of the actions were seldom planned far in advance, that the words 'corporate entrepreneurship' were never used and that the concepts evolved rather than came into existence fully formed. In successful firms, these evolutions are incremental, but designed to maintain consistency of direction. Far from finding that policies for building entrepreneurship can only be discerned after the event from patterns in the actions taken, we observed that the primary directions were communicated well in advance, sometimes in writing, sometimes only verbally. The clarity of the understanding of the mission was a crucial ingredient in the process that followed.

Without some knowledge of purpose, middle managers are likely to limit their support for new initiatives. Many firms have fallen into the trap of assuming that managers were aware of and committed to the overall strategy and the more detailed policy changes. The consequences of assuming rather than explicitly building a climate for innovation was well expressed by Roger Smith, chairman of General Motors, when he said:

> 'I sure wish I'd done a better job of communicating with GM people ... then they would have known why I was tearing the whole place up ... I never got this across. There we were, charging up the hill right on schedule and I looked behind me and saw that many people were still at the bottom, trying to decide whether to come along'.[2]

One alternative is to set out from the beginning to build an internal climate of understanding that motivates everyone to help find effective responses to new competitive challenges. This takes time. There are no shortcuts: else, like General Motors, firms build castles without foundation. Besides, care taken at the start helps break down resistance to change and provides light to those labouring in the bowels of the ship.

A highly simplified form of such purposeful action is taken in stages in figure 2.1. First is the recognition that the status quo is inadequate to deal with a changed marketplace. Typically it is the chief executive who takes the lead. Even if he is not alone in recognizing the need for change, he alone has the power to initiate actions that will ultimately engender 'holistic', rather than partial, change. Then comes work to 'unfreeze' the organization from past modes of behaviour, focused initially on building a top team capable of sharing and understanding the new 'mission'. To alleviate or even remove the obstacles such team-building typically encounters, changes in many of the performance and control measures are needed. Finally, a series of actions can be undertaken to foster a progressive deepening of strategic understanding until it infuses the entire organization.

The listing in figure 2.1 of activities at each stage is not comprehensive, but serves to highlight some of the issues that are amplified below. It also serves to indicate why we consider our analysis to shed light on a central proposition: 'Building corporate entrepreneurship requires purposeful

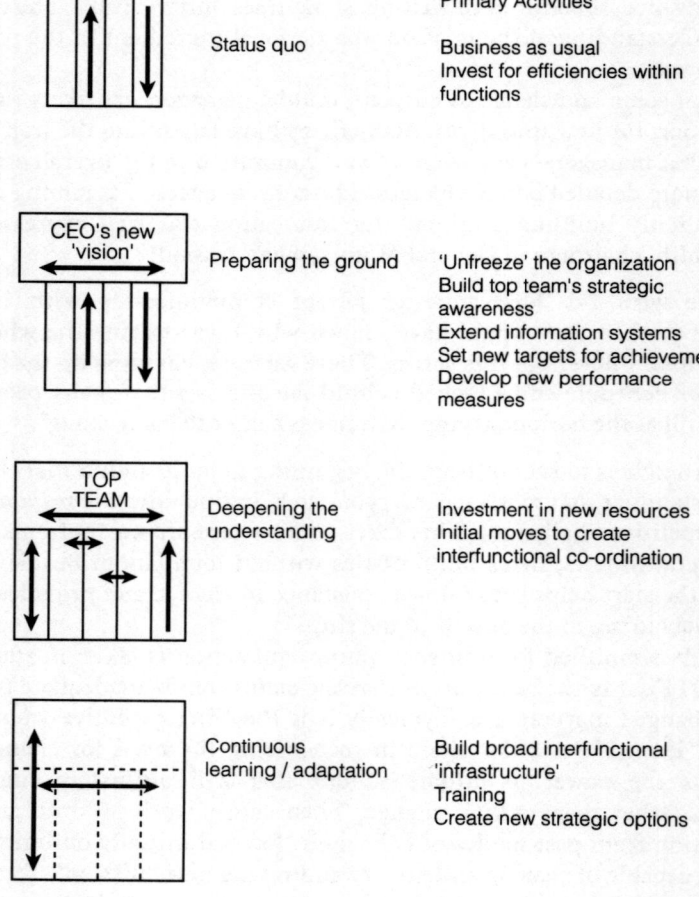

Status quo	Primary Activities	
	Business as usual	
	Invest for efficiencies within functions	
Preparing the ground	'Unfreeze' the organization	
	Build top team's strategic awareness	
	Extend information systems	
	Set new targets for achievement	
	Develop new performance measures	
Deepening the understanding	Investment in new resources	
	Initial moves to create interfunctional co-ordination	
Continuous learning / adaptation	Build broad interfunctional 'infrastructure'	
	Training	
	Create new strategic options	

Note: The arrows indicate the emphasis of the flows of information

Figure 2.1 Building corporate entrepreneurship in stages

organisational strategies that start from the top before being carried forward in all parts of the enterprise.'

Unlike strategy, which is often emergent, we believe that the process of building corporate entrepreneurship is unlikely to occur without central direction and sanction. In this, the continuing role of the chief executive seems to be vital. But no leader can work effectively without the support of others. Thus the purpose of the organizational strategy is to enlist the support and participation of people at all levels and in all functions.

In this paper, we amplify and illustrate our proposition from evidence collected during a prolonged study of the nature of change in mature organizations. Some of this evidence was reported earlier in Stopford and Baden-Fuller (1990a, 1991). There, we reported on the performance of a sample of successful firms in four mature industries. Here, we focus on the five firms listed in table 2.1. All had experienced either severe financial difficulty, or were threatened by new competition, or both. All five faced intense international competition and all succeeded in making decade-long transformations of their organizations. In addition, we draw on partial evidence from other, less successful firms in the same industries, plus data from firms in other industries to test the generality of our conclusions.

Innovation in Strategy

The firms we investigated were all in the so-called mature industries: those older industries where overall growth of demand was slow and the rates of change in product design and technology slower than in the sunrise industries. Many observers consider that managing maturity requires a funda-

Table 2.1   Research sample

Names	Parent	Sector	Approx. sales (£ million, 1988)
Hotpoint	GEC	Appliances	275
Edwards High Vacuum	BOC Group	Pumps	100
Weir Pumps	Weir Group	Pumps	100
Richardson Sheffield	McPherson	Cutlery	15
Wolsey Knitwear	Courtaulds	Knitwear	10

mental strategic choice between stable 'recipes', typically labelled as low-cost, or some form of differentiation (see, for example, Porter, 1980, 1990, ch. 2; Harrigan, 1988). These choices, even if they were ever true, seem no longer valid for the industries we studied. The veneer of stability seen at the level of the industry masks continuous processes of change in the economics of both supply and demand for the firm (Baden-Fuller, Dell'Osso and Stopford, 1991). These changes in turn lead to fundamental shifts in strategic choice, in particular the creation of new strategic options such as 'variety-at-low-cost'.

In each of our industries, there has been growing demand for *variety* of output. Further, the supply technologies adopted by leading players have reduced the minimum scale needed for low-cost output and altered the choices of location of supply and the levels of service provided to customers. We studied these phenomena and the responses of leading firms in white goods (Baden Fuller and Stopford, 1988a and b), cutlery (Grant 1990) and knitwear (Stopford and Baden-Fuller, 1990b). Similar findings have been shown in other industries, such as European automobiles (Bianchi and Volpano, 1990), and in ceramic tiles and similar industries (the work of Utili and others, reported by Porter, 1990, ch. 5).

The knitwear industry provides one of the most visible settings for the forces that have prompted behaviour of the type we explore in this paper. The growing demand for increased variety of knitwear is self-evident on the streets. Knitwear is also an industry where the adoption of computer-controlled knitting machines has now made providing variety-at-low-cost technically possible. The consequence has been an erosion of the boundaries that previously separated players in the various segments of the market. Benetton's innovations have allowed it to provide variety for the mass market (Lorenzoni, 1988) and thus invade the High Street segment previously dominated by firms supplying the multiple retailers on contract; internationally branded producers have been winning contracts from the retailers; and across Europe contract producers have, after considerable hesitation, now invaded the fashion segments previously served exclusively by the branded houses. For many in the industry, responding to these competitive shifts has been delayed because managers have found it difficult to change their mental models of what defines the defensible boundaries of their traditional segments (Porac, Thomas and Baden-Fuller, 1989).

In all these industries, the state of competition has changed from that of a contest among players all following roughly equivalent strategic 'recipes' to a situation where the contest is now among the 'recipes' themselves. Competition has changed not only the cost and differentiation options but also the geographic boundaries to each segment. In white goods, for example, the contest is among three supply 'recipes' – national, export-based and global – with the balance of advantage shifting over time. In the 1960s, export strategies dominated: in the 1980s, it was the national strategy based on a smaller territory, a highly surprising shift given the failing tariff and non-tariff barriers within Europe. In the 1990s the mass-market battle is being fought among increasingly global producers.

It is the *simultaneity* of demand and supply shifts that has allowed clever competitors to spot opportunities to create new combinations of resource allocation, precisely the conditions that foster corporate entrepreneurship. But simultaneity also breeds ambiguity and dilemma. For the innovators, there is no certainty that the new combinations will prove to be of lasting competitive power. How to judge the appropriateness of future strategy cannot be answered solely by logic based on past evidence. Such dilemmas cannot be resolved by restricting change to only one part of the firm: more far-reaching change is typically needed to create new, entrepreneurially inspired, combinations.

Characteristics of Corporate Entrepreneurship

Before describing a general model of the stages through which successful firms have created conditions of corporate entrepreneurship, we need to amplify what we mean by the five critical attributes involved.

Teamworking

Managers add value by working across organization boundaries (Kanter, 1989). This is as true today as it was seventy years ago when mass production processes were pioneered (Hounshell, 1984, especially chapter 6). Measuring what constitutes teamwork is not, however, straightforward. Though all in our sample claimed to value teamwork, some limited the idea to behaviour in meetings of functional heads. Agreement on a common course of action was their measure. An alternative measure, and the one we have used, is based on the actions that follow such meetings. When conflicts occur, is there one dominant function that always wins the argument? Is there a single measure of performance that overrides all others? Is there 'real' collaboration that permits accommodation among the functions or other units to unforeseen events? Teamwork, as measured by active collaboration at the operational level, dominated the behaviour of the successful firms we examined, but was largely absent from the failures.

An example from the furniture business indicates what can go wrong when managers meet, but fail to resolve important issues or to share information. G-Plan needed to adapt its core product range for its export business from the UK. The managing director stated that 'other Europeans don't like our softly sprung seats' but held the view that the investment cost for adaptation was too high, for 'we would have to totally re-engineer the design'. By contrast, the chief designer believed that 'we could make firmer seats. It's no problem to fit different springs' (Bower, 1990). Though a new range was eventually designed by 1990, it had not been produced. Management blamed local high interest rates as an external reason for inaction. An alternative explanation is that the failure to build a team meant the firm could not grasp the opportunity when it arose.

Teamwork is more than collaboration and lateral networks among managers: it also requires close co-operation between upper and lower levels of the hierarchy, as the experience of one white goods producer illustrates. It initiated a major quality-improvement programme, only to find later that defects were still pervasive in the output. Why? One production manager answered that 'we were improving the quality on the assembly line, but pressure from sales meant that we had to encourage staff to send out goods that were *almost* right'. In other words, a sensible policy of great strategic importance was defeated, because middle-level functional managers were unable to share a sense of mission and priority.

The importance of creating teams capable of providing linkage across organizational boundaries was underscored by Ohmae (1982, p. 226) when he claimed: 'the separation of muscle from brain may well be a root cause of the vicious cycle of the decline in productivity and loss of international competitiveness in which US industry seems to be caught'.

Aspirations

The second characteristic involves the level of aspiration set for the future development of the enterprise. An entrepreneurial organization does not constrain its strategic horizon, nor its perception of the available opportunities, to the limits defined by its current resources. Stevenson and Jarillo (1990) stated this idea as a proposition. Hamel and Prahalad (1989, 1990) provide some evidence that many Western firms are weakened by seeing only those opportunities immediately available, whereas the Japanese pursue and achieve much more ambitious goals.

Our evidence makes us more cautious. Though it is clear from interviews and documents that all our successful firms pursued ambitious strategic challenges, it is also clear that many failing firms were equally ambitious in their thinking. The difference lies in the subsequent actions taken. For example, one failure seems, in large part, to have been caused by the adoption of wildly optimistic targets to take on the world leader ten times its size. Like rabbits caught in the headlights, the managers were so paralysed by the enormity of what lay ahead, they did nothing to implement the plans to which they had agreed. High ambition may be necessary, but it is not a sufficient condition for corporate entrepreneurship.

Adaptive behaviour

Teamwork and high ambition are related to the third characteristic of corporate entrepreneurship: the adaptive behaviour of the entire system. The turbulent competitive conditions for all the firms we examined (and most others) pose a challenge for the convention of planning before action. The uncertainties of the market are such that only the most general of directions for change can be predetermined. The notion of detailed forecasting as the base for planning has to be questioned. As the managing director of one highly successful subsidiary put it:

> 'I have difficulty forecasting the next six weeks; forecasting the next year is almost impossible and the idea of long-range projection is absurd. It is true that my masters (at headquarters) require projections, so I give them what they want, but I also tell (the Chairman) they are meaningless'.

In this, and the other successful firms we researched, strategic planning took the form of attempting to define alternative possibilities so as to shorten the reaction time as events occurred: not exercises in forecasting. They had removed the traditional distinction between strategy formulation and implementation. The managing director of Edwards went so far as to assert, 'we never plan here'. His planning director, present at the meeting, did not disagree, for both knew the firm did not rely on formal annual plans, but used ideas and projections of currently *perceived* possibility as the basis for altering plans as frequently as the market conditions seemed to demand.

In other words, there is a false dichotomy implied by the separation of planning and action: both need to be interwoven. Besides, 'the real purpose of effective planning is not to make plans but to change the mental models decision makers carry in their heads' (De Geus, 1988).

Resolving dilemmas

A key feature of successful firms can be expressed in terms of their superior ability to manage and resolve strategy dilemmas. Resolving dilemmas requires an ability to match seeming opposites in the search for needed new combinations. For some of our firms at least, this ability can be shown to be created by consciously building an infrastructure of trust and shared understanding at all levels of the enterprise.

Resolving dilemmas is about making the 'impossible' happen. In the early stages of renewal, it was often the chief executive who made the connections of possibility; later on it was anyone in the top team. When one of our successful firms needed urgently to shorten production lead times to match the performance of newly emergent Japanese competitors, the engineers were adamant that progress was impossible in the UK plants. Top management believed them to be wrong and hired consultants, experienced in new production line layouts and methods, to carry sufficient conviction to start some experiments for one product. As the production director said afterwards: 'We had to make them *believe* in the new opportunities. They then had to create the appropriate data to *prove* the concept.' Afterwards, what had earlier seemed impossible became so obvious that many more people could become involved in the process. Initial successes made the engineers so enthused they rapidly began to discover for themselves possibilities for further improvement to exceed the Japanese performance.

Learning

The general themes of learning have been well discussed by Argyris and Schon (1978), De Geus (1990), Senge (1990) and others. All agree that learning organizations enable managers to review options and to conjure with new possibilities without becoming frozen into fixed patterns of thought. The critical learning is not that of doing familiar tasks more efficiently. 'Managers are usually well equipped to handle *maintenance* learning, but it is the leader's responsibility to ensure *innovative* learning' (Bennis and Nanus, 1985, p. 194). It is also the leader's job to legitimize the sharing of experience and opinion without individuals running the risks normally associated with attacking the 'sacred cows' of yesterday's beliefs.

Taken together, these five characteristics of corporate entrepreneurship may be regarded as the end state for the process of renewal, not the starting point. They are difficult to establish in older firms, long comfortable with conventional canons of managerial behaviour. The obstacles to change in both thought and action are pervasive and have to be overcome by deliberate and sustained processes of organizational investment.

Methodology

Before proceeding with the analysis, some explanation of the research methodology is needed. We had, for example, to confront the issue of how to determine whether or not past events occurred in a 'linear' sequence. To help us disentangle the various strands, we constructed event-histories. In line with Pettigrew (1985), Eisenhardt and Bourgeios (1988) and others, we built these histories on the basis of extensive interviews inside each firm as well as with competitors and other outsiders. We used both oral and written evidence to illuminate and shed light on theory. For many of our firms, oral evidence was the richer and more informative. The work was carried out between 1985 and 1990. In all organizations there were multiple visits; written up cases were circulated for comments, correction and additional discussion.

There is also the question of whether the five firms were distinctive in their renewal and their establishment of the characteristics of corporate entrepreneurship. Their success is shown by the fact that all but one achieved real sales growth over five years during the mid-1980s, growing profitability that eventually exceeded 25 per cent return on capital, well above the industry averages. Though we identified a few other examples of equally far-reaching transformation, limited research funds precluded our investigating them.

The scope of the transformations we observed were distinct from that usually associated with 'turnaround' management, aimed at correcting failure in a single function. Such limited 'turnarounds' have been well documented by Slatter (1984), Grinyer et al. (1988), Lewis (1990). The five firms we studied all changed the scope and relative importance of every function. By contrast, less successful firms changed only one or a few of the functions: such as finance (for financial restructuring), or production (for efficiency).

A Model of Organizational Building

At the outset, none of the five firms exhibited any of the characteristics of corporate entrepreneurship. They all had to build them over time and, more or less, followed the steps outlined earlier in figure 2.1. Any attempt to record what firms did has to deal with the problem of gauging when and how the process actually started. Most experienced numerous false starts and partial actions that together appear to have helped to build a climate conducive to effecting lasting change. The difficulty is that many parallel activities were going on at the same time. Thus, the 'boundaries' between the stages are blurred.

Sensing the need for change

In the special case of renewal in firms that had to escape from the strait-jacket of past stasis, the starting point appeared to be the recognition that the organization needed root-and-branch alteration, not tinkering with some of its parts. Typically, there were individuals at many levels who realized that changes were needed, but we found that the energizing process was primarily the responsibility of the chief executive. In all cases a man, he had to sense the need for a new direction before much of substance could be started. In some cases, progress had to wait until a new boss arrived: in others, the incumbent sensed that the market signals were changing.

We use the term 'sensed' advisedly, for there is much evidence that these men had no hard data on which to base their beliefs. Instead they had to be confident that there were sufficiently promising signs of 'life' somewhere in the organization to make the gamble of pursuing a new direction worthwhile. For example, when Lord Weinstock, the Chairman of GEC appointed Schreiber in 1974 to run the white goods subsidiary, Hotpoint, he reputedly gave Schreiber the brief of closing the operation as cheaply as possible. Yet Schreiber found that amidst the chaos and the losses, there remained valuable capabilities. He set about rebuilding the firm to the point where his successor could show Hotpoint as Europe's most profitable player in the mid-1980s.

Hotpoint was like the others. All had some individuals or small groups that were behaving entrepreneurially, but their efforts were not directed to corporate ends. Typical symptoms of 'life' were the existence of some form of 'skunkworks' (Burgelman, 1983b) infecting part of the organization. In Edwards, there were experiments within the factories with new information systems. All were experimenting with new, flexible production processes, but none fully understood the wider ramifications for other functions. We were told many times that only after such experimentation had become linked across functions could the effort be harnessed to effect the overall strategy. More generally, the data suggests that the locus of the perceived 'life' biased the choices of *where* to start the building.

By stressing the role of sensing in this early stage, we are supporting the observations of many others. Hurst, Rush and White (1989) provide a good summary of much of the literature that bears on the point that intuition and personal feelings have an important bearing on strategic choices. Moreover, the organization that is setting out to facilitate innovative learning should be careful not to suppress the role of intuition (Simon, 1987).

As we indicated earlier, there was never adequate information available to prove or disprove any proposition for change. Information systems tend to support the current strategy and to exclude data deemed irrelevant to the chosen 'recipe'.[3] Just as has been said of control systems, 'what gets measured gets done', so with strategy. What is seen and known informs the choice of strategy; what is unknown is ignored. The cure for strategic glaucoma does not lie in the realm of logic, but in belief in possibility.

A   *Understanding of the problem or opportunity*

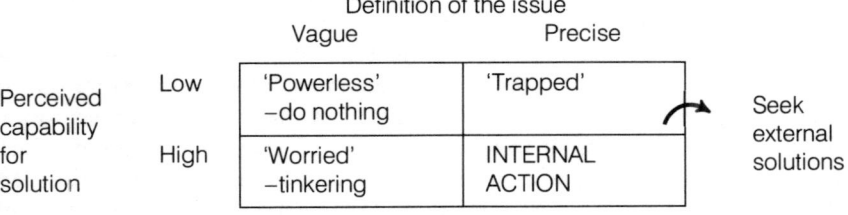

Definition of the issue

		Vague	Precise	
Perceived capability for solution	Low	'Powerless' –do nothing	'Trapped'	Seek external solutions
	High	'Worried' –tinkering	INTERNAL ACTION	

B   *Perceived nature of required internal action*

Scope

		Simple	Complex
Urgency	Low	Marginal change within some functions –efficiency	Turmoil or 'skunkworks'
	High	Major change within functions	RENEWAL

Figure 2.2   Two connected states of thought and action

The intuition that, with hindsight, we can consider as the starting point did not come as a blinding flash of inspiration. In all the cases we reviewed, there were many strands of previous thought, partial action and exploration of other possibilities. Figure 2.2 lays out two sets of general conditions about the state of perception and understanding that needed to be explored before renewal could begin in earnest.

Figure 2.2 highlights several attributes of the problem that are notoriously hard to capture in a research programme. The issue of understanding begs the question of *whose* understanding. So too with perception. Schreiber might have understood the opportunity available when he took over Hotpoint, but it is doubtful whether his managers did. In Edwards, the incoming chief executive found that many of the key ideas and perceptions of opportunity were already recognized and understood by his senior managers. For him, the problem was that the lack of a common focus had dissipated resources by allowing compromises among the functions. He observed later, 'what I could not do was to continue to fiddle around in the middle' (Stopford, 1989).

Referring to section A of figure 2.2, we found that all the firms had been at some stage in one of the three states: 'powerless and unable to do anything', 'trapped but perceive clear issues', 'worried and concerned to do something but unable to define precise actions'. Indeed some of the firms had been in more than one state before they arrived at the point where they were prepared to take internal action. One of the pump companies, for example, had for several years a board agenda so all-encompassing that for every action proposed by one functional head there was a counterproposal from another. Though all were clearly worried about the firm's declining fortunes, collectively they could not agree on priorities, felt powerless, and drifted on the tide of industry fortunes. It took the shock of looming bankruptcy to jerk them into risking internal action, rather than go to the wall. One white goods firm, Thorn, had been highly self-confident about its abilities, but had taken such a narrow view of its served market that it had not seen the changes occurring elsewhere in its industry and had failed to do more than tinker with what was regarded as a winning (and for a time, highly profitable) strategy. When the threats became obvious, the self-confidence evaporated. The division was subsequently sold to Electrolux and most of top management departed.

Closely related to issues of understanding are those of the perceptions of the scope and urgency of the actions required – section B of figure 2.2. In all the cases we studied, action in at least one other box was taken before the firm arrived at the point of departure for renewal. All had taken actions to improve efficiencies within some or all of the functions, though no attempt had been made to link the functions together: a key feature of renewal.

We regard actions in both parts of figure 2.2 as forms of behaviour that exhaust all the 'obvious' actions to improve before the nettle of attempting more deep-seated change is grasped. In some cases, this early behaviour was conventional 'turnaround' management. The difference was that the chief executives were not content to stop when the financial results began to improve; they realized that the base for improvement was fragile. Renewal had to wait until such actions had demonstrably failed to provide a lasting solution to the underlying problems.

In this early stage, there were few signs of any deliberate building of organizational strategies that would promote corporate entrepreneurship. Rather, the period of sensing had the effect of clearing up the existing confusion and setting a clear direction for later progress. It took considerable time to overcome the well-known problem that strategic awareness of issues declines sharply as one descends the hierarchy (Hambrick, 1981).

'Unfreezing' the organization

Undertaking a process of renewal and sustaining action consistently and coherently over long periods of time requires the initial individual entrepreneurial instincts of top managers to be shared among others. This is the point of transition from *individual* entrepreneurship to *corporate* entrepreneurship. It requires all managers at all levels of the hierarchy to be willing to reappraise their own roles and also to be equipped to understand the nature of the problem for the firm as a whole, not just in its parts.

Building teams is a common first step for turning a growing awareness of the need for change into action. Typically, we found such initial efforts to be restricted to the top management group. The weapons were information, questioning, symbolic action and simplification of the strategic task. They succeeded when they harnessed enthusiasm to the point where they could overcome the persistent problem that managers want to tell others what to do. This is especially so in large organizations with long traditions of powerful specialist functions such as engineering. Managers become comfortable in a world where there are specific plans and actions. They can find it acutely uncomfortable to ask themselves or their juniors to think through what the goals ought to be in the first place.[4] A learning organization, reliant on teamwork, must also be a listening organization.

Our evidence shows that the process is complex, for it one thing to generate common understanding; it is quite another to shift behaviour. 'Unfreezing' the organization to the point where new actions are possible requires change in the old internal 'rules of the game' (Crozier and Friedburg, 1980). Sometimes symbolic actions are needed to show the new possibilities or the new requirements. Schreiber abolished the marketing department overnight, in part to remove a layer of 'expert' management that had failed to appreciate the full measure of the competitive challenge. At Edwards, teamwork was promoted by a series of actions running from the abolition of separate dining rooms for management and staff to personnel policies that made it legitimate for managers to move sideways and so gain experience first-hand of other functions and territories. At Richardson, managers are expected to load the delivery vehicles late in the day if there is an urgent order to fill.

Equally important in this stage of the process is the setting of new targets for the achievement of the enterprise as a whole. In some firms the targets were set in terms of market share objectives, first for existing markets, later for new ones. In others, they were in terms of developing supply-side capabilities such as cost levels, quality standards or even time to fill orders. Setting the precise levels for these targets often involved many people: they were not drawn out of thin air. In this respect, target setting became part and parcel of what some call the co-option of middle management energies by processes of social contracting (Starr and MacMillan, 1990) or building management coalitions (Burgelman, 1983b). They were needed because middle managers 'are the only men in the organisation who are in a position to judge whether issues are being considered in the proper context' (Bower, 1970). Yet middle managers need help in judging the appropriateness of the perceived context and in escaping from the straitjacket of past rigidities and limitations to the scope of their thinking. Thus, the process required much educational work by top managers.

Such education was greatly accelerated by reducing the complexities of the strategic scope. All our successful firms eliminated tasks that had come to be seen as peripheral to the central task. Even though it was profitable for Hotpoint, the export network was eliminated. Schreiber's successor thought its existence was being used by some as an excuse for not undertaking the fundamental restructuring of manufacturing, sales and service for the home market. At the knitwear firm, Wolsey, the greatest benefit of cutting some product lines was 'to try to get our business so we (the whole team) can actually manage it'.

A recent study highlighted the two reasons for involving middle managers more fully in strategy (Wooldridge and Floyd, 1990). One was to seek greater consensus in a form that would result in superior implementation actions. The other was to improve the decision making process to gain superior strategies. All our successful firms were specific that the prime motivation for all members of the top team was the creation of both types of benefit *simultaneously*.

Overcoming resistance

Managers used to clear, vertical lines of functional demarcation often feel threatened by the development of teamwork (Kanter, 1989). They do not take naturally to thinking and working across boundaries; to bargaining and selling ideas like politicians; or to exercising greater autonomy in their personal portfolios of activity. Kanter concluded from her case evidence that the promise of freedom has a dark side: loss of control and feelings of insecurity. To compensate for that loss we found many conscious attempts to provide measures of individual success and to symbolise the difference between corporate and individual success.

How, in practice, was resistance overcome? In addition to the informal methods discussed above, our sample produced a battery of more formal weapons, including:

- Removing people, functions and even sales agents that were either resistant to the new order or lacking adequate skills:
- Changing the formal structure to signal a changing balance of importance among the activities.
- Flattening the structure by removing intervening layers of functionaries whose presence could mask mediocrity and impede communications
- Changing the information systems to change perceptions of what was important

- Changing the control systems to provide new measures of performance that directly supported the strategy

We could not tell how radical each of these changes had to be to signal the start of more far-reaching, 'holistic' change and thus have little to add to the extensive literature on these subjects, except the last two. The information system is the intelligence base linking the firm to the market and providing a basis for testing with evidence the entrepreneur's initial hunches. It also provides the information on which performance is measured and rewarded.

The systems installed had to deal with the needs of gaining both internal and external information. At Edwards, the information director stated that 'information has enabled us to keep abreast of change; it has helped us to get beyond the obvious to get to total costs'. Starting from relatively simple factory-based computer systems, the overall information system has progressively been extended to link with other functions and across borders. Initially, the system helped deal with serious problems of ignorance about factory costs. An additional system introduced in 1983 allowed the pricing policies more adequately to reflect the dynamics of factory costs. Later additions reflected the growing ambition of the firm to become a world player and not just an exporter from the UK. At each stage of development, senior managers had to be retrained to harness the power of the system. By 1988, all had a networked computer on their desks and the capability to use it comprehensively. 'Information is our life blood' was an attitude shared by all managers and many others. At Weir, much the same sorts of development occurred as the scope of their systems for costing and pricing bids were extended during the 1980s.

To meet demands for more complex data, information systems have to be tied to procedures that encourage many people to contribute the data in the first place. All our successful firms had to change their systems for measuring and rewarding performance before much happened on this account. For example, at Edwards, the UK salesmen were taken off the commission basis which rewarded volume and put on salary. Though all were paid on a fixed salary, promotion went to those who sold those parts of the range most needed to support the emerging strategic priorities. The sales manager had, therefore, to negotiate closely with manufacturing and others to ensure that the correct instructions were sent into the field. This one change had the unintended benefit of greatly increasing the quality and quantity of valuable information fed back to headquarters about customers' needs: the salesmen could use their greater knowledge of the purpose of the firm. Similar changes in other firms also had the benefit of helping the centre register and act on data that had been available but ignored.

In all our successful firms, the experience gained as performance measures were altered added another spur to linking the functions together. Just as Aaker (1989) found in Californian firms, stronger interfunctional linkage in turn helped to build the multiple sources of advantage needed in these and similar industries.

Deepening the understanding

Figure 2.3 shows the three basic stages of the organizational building that renewal entailed. The first stage of simplification, building the intelligence base and changing the performance measures is focused at senior levels, where the urgencies for team-building are initially greatest. The next stage was repeating the process at lower levels.

The behaviour we observed matches the more general sense of 'holistic' change being advocated by others. Among the more populist writers, Tjosvold (1986) and Cope (1989) both argue that without flexible arrangements at middle and lower levels of the organization, there will be few sources of continuing vitality in the system. This theme was developed in greater detail by Harmon and Peterson (1990) in their examination of what makes for greater productivity within factories. In most cases in the West, they argue, the need is not for new factories or for greater levels of automation, but for specific attention to be paid to the potential for improving existing systems by altering the behaviour of both managers and the workforce.

The recovery of Lucas' Welsh brake factory shows how great such potential can be (Bowen, 1990). There, the need was to match and possibly exceed the levels achieved by their German affiliate. At the shop-floor level, managers and workers alike attribute much of the success to the combination of the familiar list of such factors as training, 'cell' production rather than Taylorist specializations, fewer supervisory levels, competitor benchmarking, quality targets, improved industrial labour relations and so on. Lucas had first to overcome resistance from middle managers fearful that the new patterns of work would diminish their status. Lucas also met resistance on the shop-floor as the messages were pushed further down. Skilled workers disliked the idea that they had to retrain to stay on top pay scales. They were, however, persuaded to adapt, largely by the actions of the union convenors, once they had themselves become converted to the new approach. As one said, 'I told my toolmakers that they were in danger of going the same way as the skilled blacksmith.[5]

Further evidence of the need to build both vertical and lateral networks from top to bottom in the firm is provided by the MIT studies of the world automobile industry. Womack *et al.* (1990) provide convincing evidence for their 'integration' hypothesis, namely high manufacturing performance

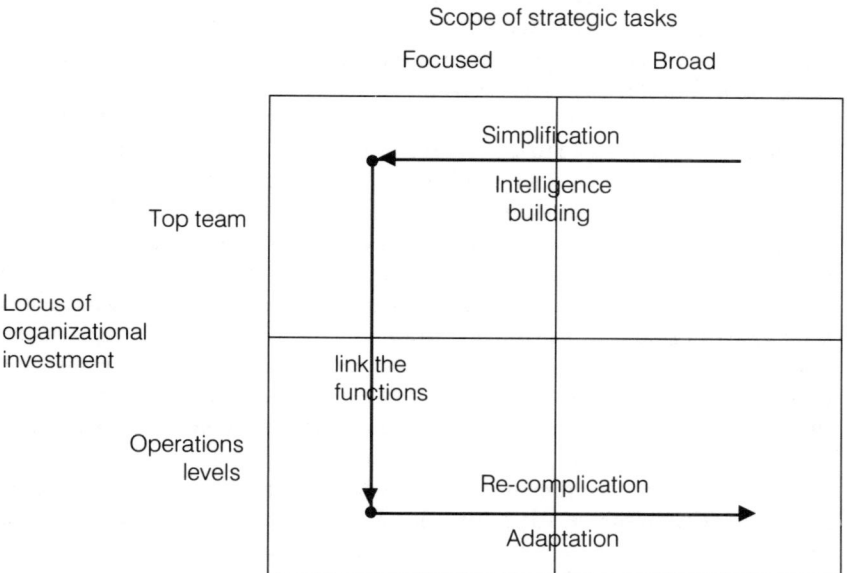

Figure 2.3   Organizational investments

results from the integration of technology and management policies that govern production practices, work organization, and human resource management. They show that achievement of 'world class' status by Japanese firms is much more closely correlated with such integrative practices than it is with other factors such as product mix and complexity and the scale of operations at the plant level.

In our successful firms, the levels of training were generally well above the industry averages; the commitment to constant two-way communication vertically and horizontally was evident at all levels; and the development of new ways of doing familiar tasks had become a way of life. No specific measures were developed to test the later two variables, but the sense of excitement about belonging to a 'winning team' was conveyed to us by almost everyone.

Resolving dilemmas

The first two stages of the rejuvenation process require the firm to become entrepreneurial in its strategic thinking. Earlier on, we emphasized that traditional industries are changing, and that marginal shifts in the environment – in demand, costs and competitors – pose both tactical and strategic challenges for the firms. While the chief executive can provide the vision, the details of the actual strategy need to be built by those lower down the organization. In all the successful organizations, we observed the mould being broken by individuals responding to the challenges by doing new things and doing them in novel ways.

One interpretation of such behaviour is to consider the challenges as dilemmas. Hampden-Turner (1990) noted that managers in static organizations perceive dilemmas as constraints to actions, whereas in dynamic firms they see dilemmas as problems to be overcome. For the latter group, the challenge is not to choose between what are normally regarded as opposites, but to seek ways of combining the best of both worlds. For them, it is not a question of costs or quality, but both. So too for dilemmas that extend to every aspect of the organization.

For the appliance firms, the ability to resolve dilemmas was measured in great detail and related to financial performance. The measures revealed that resolving multiple dilemmas created new sources of advantage that others could not readily match. The results are so striking that caution has to be exercised in the interpretation. As Hampden-Turner said 'For anyone used to teasing weak relationships out of masses of social science data such results are suspiciously strong. Where, we might ask, is the flaw in this methodology? How did we cheat? The answer is obvious: all our work is an attempt to measure multiple dimensions of a single phenomenon, not multiple phenomena' (1990, p. 62). If corporate entrepreneurship is about making new combinations in allocating resources, then these results, even if suspiciously strong, indicate that an ability to manage dilemmas is an essential feature of sustained success in a turbulent market.

How this mental approach to challenge translates into action and superior performance can be illustrated by one of the dilemmas faced by all UK appliance makers in the early 1980s: the rising power of the retailers. Most firms had oscillated between extremes of either succumbing to retailer domination by conceding discounts and by not supplying the smaller outlets, or else openly defying the retailers who subsequently refused to stock or properly display the goods. As a Thorn executive put it: 'The changing face of distribution is that greater and greater power is falling into fewer hands, so that a whim on their part about sourcing has a dramatic impact on our lines.'

Hotpoint's solution to this problem was to promise the smaller retailers stable margins, extensive sales materials and service support, supplemented by generous co-operative advertising and guaranteed twice-a-week delivery. Retail chains that refused to guarantee prices found their support levels cut. Some chains thought they could do without Hotpoint's product range, but found they were wrong. Hotpoint's distribution and product range were so effective for the small stores that they shifted demand away from many major chains. The chains eventually gave way.

Initially, Hotpoint's strategy was regarded as unusually risky: it was not a brand leader. Managers at Thorn noted that this imaginative policy was an attempt to squeeze rivals out of the shops, but like Hoover and the major importers, could not work out how it could be made to work. They were therefore slow to respond, thus giving Hotpoint more time to enhance its strengths. Creda did not see the need to respond at all, and had to rely on other segments not threatened by Hotpoint. Yet, with hindsight, one can regard Hotpoint's strategy as less risky than it seemed to outsiders at the time. They had already established the internal infrastructure needed to make the strategy possible in the marketplace.

Many firms recognize dilemmas, but fail to resolve them by choosing one side or the other, not the combination. Though some firms that had omitted the initial steps of renewal made some progress, the absence of an infrastructure for innovation made their speed of progress slower. Our findings are not just confined to the small sample of domestic appliance firms in the UK: we found evidence in continental appliance firms too. The evidence extends to firms in insurance and computers, and to large oil companies (Hampden-Turner, 1990).

As with the wider processes of renewal, organizations tackled the dilemmas, starting from the simpler ones. For example, when they first purchased new computer-controlled knitting machines, many Scottish knitters initially sought to reduce costs for a given level of variety, later increased variety while keeping costs constant and eventually tackled the issue of adding greater levels of customer service. Because they shuttled among these options, it is impossible to say which really came first: the learning was apparently in loops (Argyris and Schon, 1978). Similarly, the production manager of Creda described the development of flexible manufacturing as 'creating islands of excellence in a sea of chaos' and then extending those islands. The essential feature of progress was the realization that the major prizes were to be won by linking all parts of the firm.

Maintaining the Momentum

Having successfully mastered the earlier stages of building for renewal, firms are then faced with the task of maintaining the vitality and momentum for change and avoiding the trap of refreezing the systems too early. Few managers or workers instinctively prefer to live in an environment of constant upheaval. Once profits and growth reappear, there is a natural temptation to 'hard-wire' the new procedures into managers' mental circuits.

One of the pump companies found this to be a severe problem several years down the road. As the chief executive put it,

I found that success brings repetition; repetition brings efficiencies, but it also brings boredom and employment 'drift'. Managers slowly relax and begin to argue the case for more people to cope with increased volumes. The problem was that such increases were eroding the gains in efficiency, especially in the areas of indirect labour.

He now sees his primary role as that of creating a climate of frank communications among his senior managers where team discussion makes it clear that building overhead is not the way to go. He also relies on his ability to set stringent targets for continuous cost and quality improvement. His cost targets have meant job cuts at a time of rapid growth.

Initially there was much resistance, but I set one man the task of finding out what could be done. His evidence was so overwhelming that it helped reduce opposition. Now everyone says the cuts were necessary and obvious. Even the workforce now agrees, though I have still to convince the unions.

These statements were repeated to us in many forms by the other firms. They all pointed to the continuing criticality of the role of the chief executive in fostering a climate of open communications that could quickly harness the benefits of better information and deepen the nature of the teamworking. In addition, the evidence we have gathered underscores the necessity of setting ever more challenging targets as a prime means of maintaining the early levels of enthusiasm and commitment.

Sometimes these targets were set in response to competitors' moves, as the earlier example from Edwards' engineers illustrated: sometimes by raising the level of internal ambition. One firm became worried about their export margins, because they foresaw that UK inflation rates would not be adequately reflected in sterling adjustments once Britain joined the exchange rate mechanism. They therefore adopted a target for containing cost increases to well below then-existing national levels. With inflation dropping sharply during 1991, this firm now has an additional export margin they had not anticipated. 'We would not now be able to resist claims for higher wages if people did not fully understand why we need this "windfall" gain to generate yet further options for future growth.'

Even more challenging for our firms has been the constant shift in market forces. Their 'simplified' strategic scope has been challenged as market forces have eroded the defensibility of their niches. Since our original research, we have observed the firms to adopt one of three possible responses.[6] First, they could stay small and focused, confronting the challenge of maintaining vitality, but risk invasion. Wolsey has taken this route, but largely for reasons of corporate policy in allocating expansion possibilities to other subsidiaries. Wolsey has, however, had difficulty in maintaining the momentum in the face of a depressed market and intensified competition. Second, they could slow down the pace of investment and risk the re-freezing trap. None of the firms has taken this course. Third, they could further extend their ambitions and exploit their new-found advantages on a wider international canvas. Four of the five have done so and added back much of the complexity they shed earlier.

Playing in a larger arena has required these four to go round the cycle of renewal all over again. For Weir, the challenge has been to transfer their new systems to recent acquisitions at home and abroad and to do so while maintaining vitality at home despite having to transfer some key personnel to the new units. In turn, the original core of the firm has been enhanced by the greater scale of activity and available investment, and the careers of their managers have been enriched by challenges of greater scale and new opportunity. The success of the pumps subsidiary has provided lessons and learning that are now beginning to transform the group as a whole. Hotpoint extended its UK strategy by buying Creda, a local rival, but then appeared to accept the logic of the need for a wider European position. Rather than go it alone, Hotpoint was merged into a European joint venture with GE.

Both Edwards and Richardson extended internationally and raised their ambitions to be among the global leaders. At Edwards, the values of teamwork developed within the UK have been transferred abroad, though as their managers admit not without difficulty. They have developed a complex international matrix organization in which a greatly augmented information system plays a central role. Indeed, Edwards has set a new target for the system: it must 'dynamically link the factory with the customer' and cut manufacturing lead times to a quarter of previous performance. Customer confidence in delivery is so essential, especially at a time when Edwards is facing the emergence of sixteen new Japanese competitors, that Edwards' management regards that target as a minimum. With a continuing stream of new products, processes and services being offered, they exhibit all the symptoms of continued vitality. For them, success has not bred complacency; on the contrary, their managers are more than ever aware of strengthening Japanese competitors, who are, as ever, striving to change the 'rules' of competition. Though Richardson's business is simpler, the story is similar. The strategic horizon was greatly enlarged when they were bought by an Australian firm. The understanding of the international challenge has deepened, now that their 15 per cent share of the world market has attracted a host of imitators. For both, there seems little doubt that such external threat serves the useful purpose of concentrating attention on the need for never-ending innovation and enhanced entrepreneurship.

Conclusions

We started with the proposition that corporate entrepreneurship can be built by deliberate organizational strategies. The evidence suggests that the sense of deliberateness grows slowly over time. Signs of deliberate policy began to emerge in the unfreezing stage of development, but limited to the top team. By the time the changes were well established (deepening the understanding) they were pervasive throughout the organization.

The need for such building is evident in turbulent competitive environments. We have endeavoured to show that static organizations do not possess the characteristics of corporate entrepreneurship and are likely to fail. Dynamic organizations, by contrast, can increase their chances of prosperity. But the process is arduous and takes a long time. After five or even ten years our firms felt they had yet to finish the process; some felt they never would. They all recognized that the steps to energize the process depended critically on the continuing involvement of the chief executive, for the judgments needed at each step required an enterprise-wide view. But that is not to suggest exclusive reliance on one individual. Rather, the role of top management becomes that of orchestrating the works of a growing network of teams and a harnessing of enthusiasm for pursuing rising ambitions.

It seems clear that success helps the process along and that there are feedback loops between successful action and further building the characteristics of corporate entrepreneurship. This indeed is one of the levers used by top management; but only one. Our firms did not use success as an excuse to cruise, but as a signal to increase efforts to change again to reach for more ambitious goals.

This behaviour makes an important point. Managers did not follow the sequence of 'analyse-plan-act' and make change a one-off affair. Instead, progress was by many steps, and followed the logic of 'act-analyse-learn-disseminate-act again'. This is, in effect, a learning process for the firm. We observed not only feedback loops but also a great emphasis on knowledge in its widest sense; our organizations wanted to learn how to succeed. They did not grasp at panaceas, but invested in knowledge and sustained or increased that investment over time. Indeed two of our firms stated that their investment in knowledge and skills cost as much as that on physical plant and equipment.

Given our limited sample, our conclusions must be tentative. Moreover, our data is imperfect: the executives did not keep diaries of actions taken over long periods. We had to rely on memory and (always incomplete) internal documentation, supplemented by only limited real-time tracking of events. More seriously, we did not study any firm which exhibited signs of entrepreneurship and failed. Even so, we believe than our findings provide more than a tool box for analysing the past: they also provide clues about what firms should do in the future, *provided* they are willing to take the risk of experimentation. Sustainable growth comes as much from deliberate organizational building as it does from making wise choices of market positioning.

Notes

1 Partial funding for the research reported here was generously provided by the Economic and Social Research Council and the Centre for Business Strategy, London Business School.

2 Cited in *Strategic Direction*, May 1990, p. 9.

3 We gathered much anecdotal evidence about the nature of the data filtered out by the systems in place. For instance, we found that many of the British and French firms did not know the prices and capacities of their competitors in other European countries, even though there was extensive cross-border trade.

4 This problem has been tackled head-on in Exxon Chemicals. Though progress for has been rated as 'painfully slow', one corporate VP stated recently 'we are making progress and believe we're steadily improving performance. What we have done ... is to drop plan reviews at the company level and replace them with strategy discussions. After all, if the top of the organization isn't thinking in strategic terms, who is? ... When objectives and strategies are clear and understood, planning is no problem and the reviews of plans at lower levels assume a different and more positive character' [cited in *Strategic Direction*, June 1990 p. 8.].

5 Much of the UK programme was led from the top by the manufacturing director. By contrast, in Germany, 'we did it all before him'. There, the sense of constant change as a necessity of life has been deeply engrained for years. 'Everybody is aware that stop means down' says a member of the Works Council. The culture in Wales is as yet shallow and may wither away without constant fostering. The international comparison is important, because it shows the need in research of this type to guard against generalizing from one only unit.

6 At the time of writing, we are engaged in re-visiting all the firms to check and measure progress on further building on all the dimensions of corporate entrepreneurship.

References

Aaker, D. A. 1989: Managing assets and skills; the key to sustainable competitive advantage, *California Management Review*, Vol. 31, No. 2, Winter.

Argyris, C. and Schon, D. A. 1978: *Organizational Learning: A Theory of Action Perspective*, Reading, MA: Addison-Wesley.

Baden-Fuller, C. and Stopford, J. M. 1988a: Restructuring mature industries: the challenge for Europe, in Urabe, K., Child, J. and Kagono, T. (eds), *Innovation and Management: International Comparisons*, Berlin: Walter de Gruyter.

Baden-Fuller, C. and Stopford, J. M. 1988b: Global or national? *L'Industria*, IX, 2, 195–229.

Baden-Fuller, C., Dell'Osso, F. and Stopford, J. M 1991: Competition Dynamics Behind the Mask of Maturity, in Tamburini, G. and Faulhaber, G. R (eds), *European Economic Integration: the Role of Technology*, Kluwer Academic Publishers.

Bianchi, P. and Volpano, G. 1990: Flexibility as the response to excess capacity: the case of the automobile industry, in Baden-Fuller, C. (ed.), *Managing Excess Capacity*, Oxford: Blackwell.

Bennis, W. and Nanus, B. 1985: *Leaders: The Strategies for Taking Charge*, New York: Harper & Row.

Bowen, D. 1990: How Lucas learned to live with the rest of the world, *The Independent on Sunday*, 8 July.

Bower, J. L. 1970: *Managing the Resource Allocation Process*. Boston: Harvard Business School Press.

Bower, T. 1990: Not with a roar but a whimper, *The Times*, February 5.

Burgelman, R. A. 1983a: Corporate entrepreneurship and strategic management, *Management Science*, Vol. 29, No. 12, pp. 1349–64.

Burgelman, R. A. 1983b: A process model of internal corporate venturing in the diversified major firm, *Administrative Science Quarterly*, Vol. 28, No, 2, pp. 223–44.

Cope, R. G. 1989: *High Involvement Strategic Planning: When People and their Ideas Matter*, The Planning Forum/Blackwell.

Crozier, M. and Friedburg, E. 1980: *Actors and Systems*, Chicago: Chicago University Press. (Translation of the original French version by Editions du Soleil, 1977.)

De Geus, A. 1988: Planning as learning, *Harvard Business Review*, March–April.

De Geus, A. 1990: Strategy as learning, Stockton Lecture, London Business School, May.

Eisenhardt, K. M. and Bourgeois, L. J. 1988: Politics of strategic decision making: towards a mid-range theory. *Academy of Management Journal*, Vol. 31 pp. 737–70.

Grant, R. 1990: Exit and Rationalization in the British Cutlery Industry, 1974–1985, in Baden-Fuller (ed.), *Managing Excess Capacity*, Oxford: Blackwell.

Grinyer, P. H., Mayes, D. G. and McKiernan P. 1988: *Sharpbenders: The Secrets of Unleashing Corporate Potential*, Oxford: Blackwell.

Hambrick, D. C. 1981: Strategic awareness within top management teams, *Strategic Management Journal*, Vol. 2, No. 3, pp. 263–79.

Hamel, G. and Prahalad, C. K. 1989: Strategic intent, *Harvard Business Review*, May–June.

Hamel, G. and Prahalad, C. K. 1990: The core competence of the corporation, *Harvard Business Review*, May–June, No. 3, pp. 79–91.

Hampden-Turner, C. and Baden-Fuller, C. W. F. 1988: Strategic Choice and the Management of Dilemma, Centre for Business Strategy working paper no. 51, London Business School.

Hampden-Turner, C. 1990: *Charting the Corporate Mind*, Oxford: Blackwell, and New York: The Free Press.

Harmon, R. L. and Peterson, L. D. 1990: *Reinventing the Factory*, New York: The Free Press.

Harrigan, K. R. 1988: *Managing Mature Businesses*, Lexington, MA: Lexington Books.

Hay, M. and Williamson, P. 1991: Strategic staircases: Planning the capabilities required for success, *Long Range Planning*, Vol. 24, No. 4, pp. 36–43.

Hounshell, D. A. 1984: *From the American System to Mass Production, 1800–1932*, Baltimore, MD: John Hopkins University Press.

Hurst, D. K., Rush, J. C. and White, R. E. 1989: Top management teams and organizational renewal, *Strategic Management Journal*, Vol. 10, pp. 87–105.

Kanter, R. M. 1983: *The Change Masters: Innovation and Entrepreneurship in the American Corporation*, New York: Simon & Schuster.

Kanter, R. M. 1989: *When Giants Learn to Dance*, New York: Simon & Schuster.

Lewis, W. W. 1990: Strategic restructuring: A critical requirement in the search for corporate potential, in Rock, M. and Rock, H. (eds), *Corporate Restructuring*, New York: McGraw-Hill, pp. 43–55.

Lorenzoni, G. 1988, Benetton, London Business School, case series no. 4.

MacMillan, I. C. and Day, D. L. 1987: Corporate ventures into industrial markets: Dynamics of aggressive entry, *Journal of Business Venturing*, Vol. 2, No. 1, Winter, pp. 29–39.

Mintzberg, H. 1987: Opening up the definition of strategy, in Quinn, J. M., Mintzberg, H. and James, R. M. (eds), *The Strategy Process*, Englewood Cliffs, N. J.: Prentice Hall.

Mintzberg, H. 1990: The design school: reconsidering the basic premises of strategic management, *Strategic Management Journal*, Vol. 11, pp. 171–95.

Nielsen, R. P., Peters, M. P. and Hisrich, R. D. 1985: Intrapreneurship strategy for internal markets – corporate, non-profit and government institution cases, *Strategic Management Journal*, Vol. 6, No. 2, pp. 181–9.

Ohmae, K. 1982: *The Mind of the Strategist*, New York: McGraw-Hill.

Pettigrew, A. M. 1985: *The Awakening Giant: Continuity and Change in ICI*, Oxford: Blackwell.

Porac, J. F., Thomas, H. and Baden-Fuller, C. 1989: Competitive Groups as Cognitive Communities: the Case of Scottish Knitwear Manufacturers, *Journal of Management Studies*, Vol. 26, No. 4, July, pp. 397–416.

Porter, M. E. 1980: *Competitive Strategy*. New York: The Free Press.

Porter, M. E. 1990: *The Competitive Advantage of Nations*, London: Macmillan.

Quinn, J. B. 1980: *Strategies for Change: Logical Incrementalism*, Homewood, IL: Richard D. Irwin.

Schumpeter, J. A. 1934: *The Theory of Economic Development*, Cambridge, MA: Harvard University Press.

Senge, P. M. 1990: *The Fifth Discipline: The Art & Practice of the Learning Organization*, New York: Doubleday Currency.

Simon, H. 1987: Making executive decisions: the role of intuition and emotion, *Executive*, February.

Slatter, S. 1984: *Corporate Recovery*, London: Penguin.

Starr, J. A. and MacMillan, I. A. 1990: Resource cooptation via social contracting: resource acquisition strategies for new ventures, *Strategic Management Journal*, Vol. 11, Special Issue, pp. 79–92.

Stevenson, H. H. and Jarillo, J. C. 1990: A paradigm of entrepreneurship: entrepreneurial management, *Strategic Management Journal*, Vol. 11, Special Issue, pp. 117–27.

Stopford, J. M. 1989: Edwards High Vacuum International, London Business School case study.

Stopford, J. M. and Baden-Fuller, C. 1990a: Corporate rejuvenation, *Journal of Management Studies*, Vol. 27, No. 4, July, pp. 399–415.

Stopford, J. M. and Baden-Fuller, C. 1990b: Flexible Strategies – the Key to Success in Knitwear, *Long Range Planning*, Vol. 23, No. 6, December, pp. 56–62.

Stopford, J. M. and Baden-Fuller, C. 1991: Creating corporate entrepreneurship, Centre for Business Strategy, London Business School, working paper, no. 105.

Tichy, N. and Charan, R. 1989: Speed, simplicity, self-confidence: an interview with Jack Welch, *Harvard Business Review*, September–October.

Tjosvold, D. 1986: *Working together to Get Things Done: Managing for Organizational Productivity*, Lexington Books.

Weick, K. E. 1979: *The Social Psychology of Organizing*, Reading, MA: Addison-Wesley.

Womack, J. P. Jones, D. T. and Ross, D. 1990: *The Machine that Changed the World*, New York: Rawson Associates.

Wooldridge, B. and Floyd, S. W. 1990: The strategy process, middle management involvement, and organisational performance, *Strategic Management Journal*, Vol. 11, No. 3, pp. 231–41.

3

Implementing High Technology Programmes

THE CASE OF THE SPACE STATION[1]

V. K. Narayanan

High technology programmes as the term is employed in this paper have several features. First, they require the co-ordination of a large number of separate scientific and engineering skills to solve programmes' technical challenges. Second, during the start-up phase, many decisions have to be made with relatively little understanding of their consequences. Third, start-up phase decisions have long-term effects that will become apparent only ten or twenty years later. Finally, these programmes tend to be visible, and involve large commitments of resources – people, time, and money.

Strategic process studies of high technology programmes, although rare, have primarily been nomothetic (Sayles and Chandler, 1971; Burgleman and Sayles, 1986). Complementary idiographic works, such as the ones available in other settings (e.g., Allison, 1971; Bower, 1972; Pettigrew, 1973; Crozier and Friedberg, 1980, and Quinn, 1980) are non-existent. This has precluded us from understanding the influence of history, context and prominent actors on the evolution of these programmes.

In this paper, I report the results of a field study conducted within National Aeronautics and Space Administration NASA, documenting the evolving management processes of the space station programme during its formative years (1982–6). The space station programme exhibited all the characteristics of high technology programmes: it necessitated the co-ordination of over one hundred separate scientific and engineering disciplines; in 1982 the broad features of the programme were being designed although the launch date was estimated to be some ten years later; the decision makers were quite unsure about the key consequences such as the ultimate beneficiaries or the eventual costs of the programme; it was a highly visible programme, promoted as the 'the next logical step' for NASA and endorsed by President Reagan in 1984.

The paper is organized into four major sections. In the first section, I introduce the major theoretical assumptions underpinning this study, and summarize the study methodology. In the second section, I sketch NASA's historical, environmental and organizational context to highlight the framework within which NASA's decision makers were operating, and to anchor the discussion of the programme management processes. In the third section, I delineate the four major management stages in the programme evolution, and summarize the key management processes within each. Finally, I discuss the data, in light of the extant theory and scholarship in the strategy process field.

Initial Considerations

Theoretical assumptions

Few field researchers of strategic process start with tightly articulated hypotheses. However, most approach the organizational phenomena of their interest with some theoretical prejudices; this researcher is no exception. Although the theoretical positions underpinning this study have been elaborated before (Narayanan and Fahey, 1990, 1982; Dutton, Fahey and Narayanan, 1983; Fahey and Narayanan, 1989), the salient assumptions are summarized to locate the present work in the larger body of literature.

Three sets of assumptions have informed this work:

1 Organizations are viewed as political arenas where srategies emerge from an interplay of information (which is limited), actors' political interests (which are often in conflict) and their cognitive maps (which are moulded by their experiences and organizational roles).
2 The individual actors, especially the upper echelons in organizations, are assumed to operate with an incomplete grasp of situations, but manage to focus organizational attention on some missions to the exclusion of others. They encounter resistance, but manage to forge coalitions powerful enough to carry their strategies to implementation.
3 Flowing from the above, we assume a dialectical relation between organizational contexts and social action. Contexts shape action which in turn mould contexts. This implies that explanations of organizational strategies, intended or realized (Mintzberg and Waters, 1982) invariably take us to the processes from which they emerge.

Taken together, these assumptions bear a close resemblance to the positions of Allison, Bower, Crozier, Pettigrew and Quinn. Technological and environmental uncertainty, exercise of power, strategic action and opportunistic actors, timing, resources and history – variables so often overlooked in the traditional renditions of effective management – are presumed to have explanatory significance in this theoretical position.

These theoretical assumptions permeate the methodological choices in this study, a point to which I now turn.

Methodological details

The 'research design' adopted for the study was the product of two circumstances. First, the entry into NASA was accidental, and resulted from a response to a competitive call for proposals from the History Division of NASA to research and write a 'management history' of the space station programme. Since writing the history of major programmes is a standard NASA practice, this ensured more or less willing co-operation of the organization.[2] Second, since the investigator's familiarity with the internal workings of NASA was low, it was difficult to pose hypotheses in the beginning. Reminiscent of Schein's suggestion (1985) in his diatribe on the extant writings about corporate cultures, we did not know what questions to ask in the early stages of investigation.

These two circumstances led us to adopt an *evolutionary* approach to research design: we decided to start with an initial strategy which would be modified as we gained knowledge of the organization. This initial strategy was to search through all the congressional testimonies presented by NASA officers, and to interview selected individuals at the headquarters to help us develop a general outline of the start-up phase of the programme as well as to get referrals for other interviews. Our initial interviews helped us in three ways: first, we gained four individuals, three then retired, who played central roles in the programme, and had very different views – just by chance but who would serve as our 'tutors' in our research project. Second, it became quite clear that in a public agency like NASA, internal documents, not merely congressional testimonies, are so carefully crafted that knowledgeable insiders would have to provide a 'reading', i.e., interpret the text for us to understand its meaning. Our 'tutors' and some others whom we picked up on the way served this function. Third, these initial interviews helped us to frame the questions in our later interviews.

Out of this initial phase emerged our basic research strategy; it had three major elements:

1 We would bootstrap between interviews and internal documents, each serving to validate the other.
2 Our interviewee selection process would be two-pronged: we would sound off interviewees for names, but would, in addition, make independent choices based on the NASA organization chart, concentrating on

the chain of command in the space station programme organization. In a complex organization such as NASA that had many power centres, had we relied solely on 'knowledgeable' insiders (however high up in the hierarchy they may be) for references as advised in recent literature (Huber and Power, 1985) we would simply have reproduced the reality of one or two major coalitions.

3 The research would proceed from (a) developing a more or less comprehensive chronology of events and decisions; through (b) developing an interpretation in textual form; (c) to validating and where necessary modifying the text with the help of insiders, This text is available as an internal NASA monograph (Lewin and Narayanan, 1990).

The data for the study thus came from interviews, internal documents, video tapes and congressional testimonies. We interviewed the top management (Administrator Beggs, deputy administrator and five associate administrators) and over ten others at headquarters, four field centre directors and their deputies, and nearly fifty others from Space Station Task Force, programme and project management at the field centres. Each interview lasted from twenty minutes to three hours; cumulatively the interviews generated nearly 3000 pages of hand-written notes and where taped, transcribed pages. The internal documents consisted of memos, other letters ('written for your eyes only'), private notes where available, and presentation slides. These documents filled six filing cabinets. In only one case was the author's request for a private file denied; the file belonged to a retired individual in one field centre.

Analysis

We provide a diachronic and synchronic analysis of the data. By diachronic we mean tracing the events over time, breaking them down into meaningful units. In this, we focus on 'critical milestones': an event is deemed critical if it is perceived to be unique to the programme by some within NASA. This criterion rules out normal organizational practices and standard operating procedures within NASA. For synchronic analysis, we break down the start-up phase into four major stages and document the driving forces, management problems and solutions in each stage.

NASA: The Decision-Making Context

NASA's space station initiative in the 1980s was its fourth major attempt to realize one of its long-standing goals. The concept of a manned space station within NASA can be traced back to Von Braun days, even before the agency was formed. Indeed, in the first half of 1959, NASA's Research

Steering Committee on Manned Space Flight had placed a space station ahead of a lunar expedition on its list of priorities. However, although NASA had tried several times over the years to win presidential approval for this programme, it had failed each time. With Kennedy's decision to go to the moon, the chances of developing a space station in the 1960s vanished. In the 1970s, Nixon, Ford, and Carter also rejected funding requests for the space station. By the late 1970s it was clear that any substantial money for a space station would have to wait until the agency demonstrated success with the shuttle, but the shuttle was then experiencing technical difficulties as well as schedule and cost overruns.

Technologically, NASA did not perceive the space station project to be as complex or challenging as some of its previous ventures like the Apollo and the space shuttle. The agency could draw upon its previous experiences with manned projects (Apollo and the space shuttle), many unmanned space projects like skylab, and most importantly, the seventeen technological feasibility studies conducted over the years for its previous attempts to win presidential approval for the space station. The agency's challenge was not the scarcity of alternatives, but the sheer number of contending options; it had to select one from the many feasible alternative space station concepts that had evolved over the years.

The environmental and organizational context of NASA presented greater challenges. Environmentally, NASA faced a period of tight funding, different from the benign days of the Apollo project. Unlike Kennedy, later presidents were not fond of NASA; they could see few political advantages in promoting science. In fact during the 1970s NASA's budget in real inflation-adjusted terms had dwindled. During the 1970s, NASA also faced a period of increasing congressional scrutiny over its activities. The agency's headquarters, 'the Washington Office', had to respond to this 'micro' management. Finally, few influential scientists supported the concept of a manned space station; they viewed this project as an engineering adventure with no scientific value.

NASA's organization structure had evolved over the years in response to its operations, environment and programmes. Operationally, NASA's main tasks were to win approval and funding for programmes, developing the concepts or conducting experiments, and managing and overseeing the industrial contractors who built most of the hardware. In any programme, most of the funds went to the hardware development phase; hence contractor management was a crucial part of the operations. The organizational boundaries of NASA – where NASA ended and contractors began were fuzzy; the movement of employees between these organizations made it fuzzier. From a management perspective, organizational strategies for any programme should take into account the extended network comprised of NASA and its contractors.

NASA's status as a government agency influenced its internal organization in many ways. First, the increasing congressional oversight over the years resulted in a clear separation of functions between the headquarters and the field centres: 'the Washington Office' won the approval of programmes, the field centres implemented them. Over the years, the field centres were granted increasing operating autonomy. Second, this trend was magnified by the regional constituencies that had developed around the field centres. The congressmen from various regions advocated the cause of their respective field centres, since funding meant greater regional employment and other benefits. Although the field centres were officially barred from lobbying, their contractors were not. Thus, the field centres wielded a great deal of power, sometimes to the chagrin of the headquarters.

The agency's field centres had earned distinct reputations for their excellence. Thus, Johnson Space Center (JSC) and Marshall Space Flight Center (MSFC) were engineering centres, primarily responsible for the manned programmes, highly visible to the public eye. Although less visible, Langley, Ames and Lewis were reputed to be technology development centres; Goddard catered to the scientific constituency (space scientists, astronomers). Each centre jealously guarded its reputation. NASA's culture promoted competition among the centres: the rivalry between the engineering centres JSC and MSFC was particularly intense. The decreasing funding exacerbated these competitive forces.

NASA undertook both single centre and multicentre programmes. Most unmanned programmes were confined to a single field centre. The field centre with their long history of matrix organization, could manage these programmes without great difficulty. Manned programmes typically involved multiple centres. Further, over the years, NASA had to undertake multicentre programmes, partly in response to reduced funding. These programmes necessitated co-ordination among field centres, which was difficult partly because of intercentre competition.

The management process during the start up-phase of the space station programme had to take into account the above technological, environmental and organizational contingencies.

Stages of Decision Making

For analytical purposes, the start-up phase of the space station programme was broken down into broad stages. Two rules were employed to isolate the stages. First, each stage represented a clearly identifiable set of decisions that consumed organizational attention. Second, the clustering of the decisions into a stage was not so fine as to deprive the text of meaning. Based on these rules four stages were identified: (1) missions and boundary conditions; (2) organizational strategy; (3) implementing the organization; and (4) re-evaluation and redesign of the organizational strategy. A simplified chronology of the critical events and decisions in each stage is presented in figure 3.1. As can be seen from the table, the four stages overlapped, a contingency that generated its own management challenges.

Missions and boundary conditions

The successful space station initiative began when Beggs, in his confirmation hearings in 1980, asserted that the program is 'the next logical step' for NASA. The central problem was however winning the presidential approval, and building a constituency so that programme funding would be ensured in the years to come. Winning the presidential approval meant that NASA had to persuade President Reagan that the space station was a worthwhile idea. It also meant dealing with several agencies who would be interested in details of the programme – in NASA's terms the mission of the programme – and refuting the opposition of other agencies who would rather have the dollars allocated to them. The space station had then no defined constituency, and this was problematic for future funding.

Four major strategies were adopted at this stage:

1 Space station would be kept at a low profile in the period 1980–2. Issues of timing played a role: Beggs wanted to create a favourable impression about NASA before he would embark on the initiative. He would wait till he could foster a public perception that (1) priority was given to making the shuttle operational, and (2) space science and applications programmes were revitalized. It also gave NASA time to work out the broad details of the programme.

2 Two task forces would provide a starting point for focusing the missions of the programme. One, an internal task force (SSTSC) would examine the technological feasibility of the project; this meant consolidating the available information within NASA and suggesting solutions to any problems. The second, an external one (the Fletcher Committee), would start the process of building political support; this committee was asked to comment on two major options: an incremental approach with low budget and a more ambitious one. Although SSTSC continued till later, the Fletcher Committee was dissolved once its task was accomplished. Its recommendation was later rejected, but the process had been initiated.

3 When Administrator Beggs judged the timing to be appropriate, it was decided to mount a major visible effort to build the constituency. Organizationally, an internal task force (SSTF) was created at the headquarters, headed by a Beggs appointee, but staffed by people from various field centres (as was NASA practice). Thus the field centre operations

Dates

STAGES

| MISSION & BOUNDARY CONDITIONS |

| Early management decisions | Evolution of missions & boundary conditions: space station task force | Gearing for implementation |

1980
1 Key personnel

5/82
1 Formation of Task Force

9/82
PPWG

4/83
CDG ($8 billion)

1/1984
Reagan: →

State of the Union message

4/84
Dissolution of SSTF

← 2 SSTSC/Fletcher Committees
2 SSSC

← 3 Core Task Force members
3 MRWG/SSWG

| ORGANIZATIONAL STRATEGY |

| Early positions | Broad alternatives: Organizational forms | System engineering and integration | Co-opting institutional elements |

1982
Culbertson's position 1 Apollo model vs. lead center
2 Program phasing

9/82

2/83

2/83

Test bed competition Wallops & Langley meetings

5/83

2/84

Decision to Enlarge Participation

LEAD CENTER DECISION

WORK PACKAGE DECISIONS

4/84

6/84

| FIELD CENTRES |

| Early attempts | Refining alternatives | Co-opting Institutional Elements | Field centre negotiations |

82
1 Hook's attempts

83
1 Cramer group

3/84
1 Centre director's meeting

4/84
1 Negotiations between Marshall & Johnson

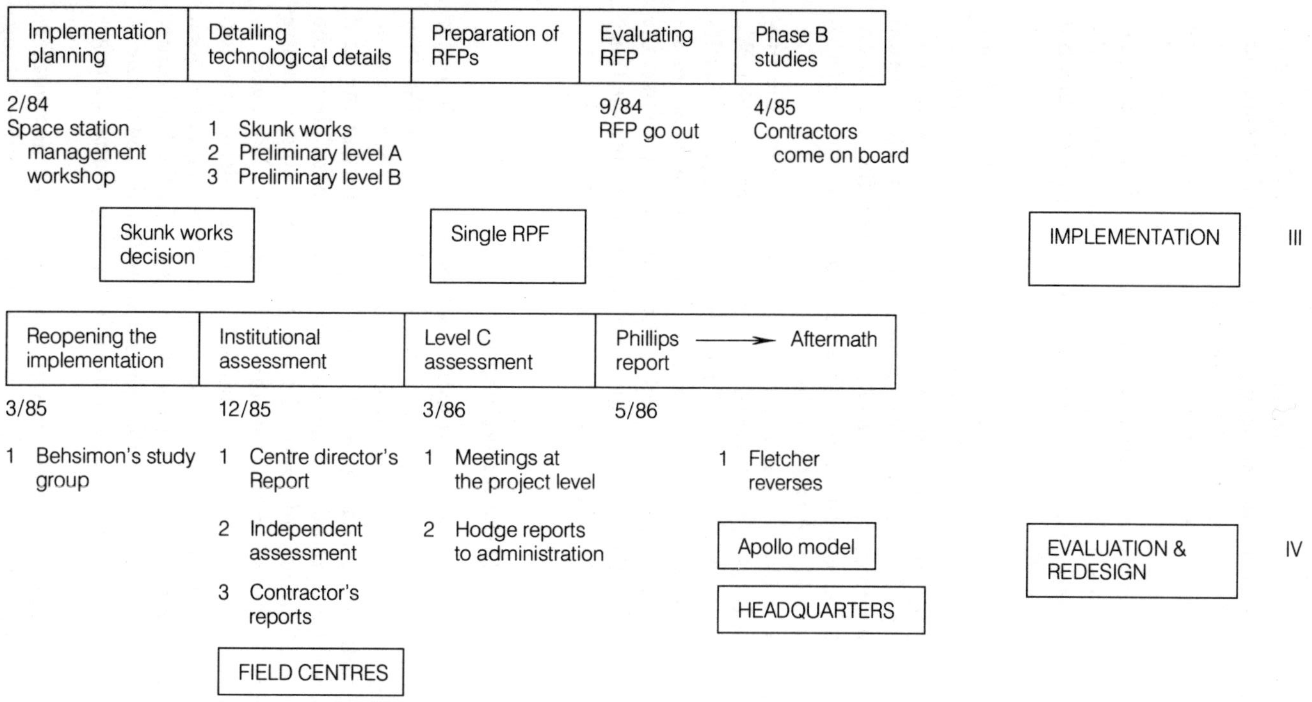

Implementation planning	Detailing technological details	Preparation of RFPs	Evaluating RFP	Phase B studies
2/84 Space station management workshop	1 Skunk works 2 Preliminary level A 3 Preliminary level B		9/84 RFP go out	4/85 Contractors come on board

Skunk works decision

Single RPF

IMPLEMENTATION   III

Reopening the implementation	Institutional assessment	Level C assessment	Phillips report ⟶ Aftermath	
3/85	12/85	3/86	5/86	
1 Behsimon's study group	1 Centre director's Report 2 Independent assessment 3 Contractor's reports	1 Meetings at the project level 2 Hodge reports to administration	1 Fletcher reverses	

FIELD CENTRES

Apollo model

HEADQUARTERS

EVALUATION & REDESIGN   IV

Figure 3.1 Stages of the space station program

were not disrupted, and the strong central co-ordination prevented the intercentre competition from dominating the working of the task force. The task force would work out the details while the broad missions and 'boundary conditions' were deliberated by Beggs.

4 In order to thwart the agencies which played a monitoring role over NASA, and who would question NASA's space station priority, Beggs decided to rule out any other alternative. In public, he held on to the position that NASA had a single alternative for the 1980s and that was the space station. One could quarrel over the details of the programme, but not over the concept itself.

This detailing of missions and constituency building (selling the programme) had to be parallel, since in 1982 there was urgency to get the programme approved. Each President had a term of four years, and it would have been difficult to get his approval during the second term. The political climate was always unpredictable; and had Reagan not won the re-election, the entire effort would have been wasted, since the administrator of NASA was a political appointee. NASA was working against time.

This stage came to a close when President Reagan accorded the programme his public approval in the State of the Union message in 1984. We should note, however, NASA's efforts at managing the budgetary battles were far from over. Presidential approval meant only that the scene of action, the actual budget negotiations, moved to the Congress. Of course, the later negotiations would only focus on what kind of a programme the space station should be, not whether there should be this programme at all.

Organizational strategy

Under the three-tier organization structure NASA used for all major programmes, the top tier was responsible for the direction of the programme (including responding to the Congress), and rested at Washington. The third tier, contractor management, was the responsibility of the field centres. The second tier, programme management, was responsible for the management co-ordination of activities and in all single centre programmes, this tier also rested at the field centres. However, in multicentre programmes like the space station, NASA could draw upon two alternative models for the location of the second tier. In the Apollo model, the programme management was located at Washington. In the lead centre model, then in use for the space shuttle – the major manned programme of the 1970s, one field centre (JSC) was responsible for programme management.

As early as 1982, when the Space Station Task Force had just formed, Beggs had decided that the space station would be a major undertaking, rejecting the Fletcher Committee recommendations; this meant a multicentre programme, since no centre could undertake such a major programme. Even at that time, some of the central players at the headquarters believed that the space station should follow the lead centre organization and that the lead centre should be located at Houston (JSC). However, these opinions were not then made public for the fear of jeopardizing the prospects of programme approval. Programme management brought with it dollars and prestige. In the competitive climate of NASA, premature designation of lead centre would have antagonized the losers and the constituencies supporting them. Others, mostly the Apollo veterans, also at Washington, held very different views regarding the appropriate organizational form.

Although gaining the presidential approval for the programme was then the most important task, NASA began to craft the space station's organization strategy. The details were left to one of the working groups in SSTF, the Program Planning Work Group (PPWG). Just as missions were being crafted, so was the organization strategy. The PPWG refined the organizational alternatives, although its premises were shaped by higher-ups, particularly Beggs. Two of PPWG recommendations were not controversial.

> First it recommended that, unlike the previous programmes, the space station should have an extended definition period, i.e., sufficient time should be expended to define the project to control costs. This was the direct outgrowth of the Hearth Committee, constituted earlier under prodding from Congress to investigate the cost overruns in many NASA programmes.
>
> Second, the programme should incorporate advanced technology development, as recommended by the SSTSC. This also ensured that the technology centres would have a role to play, and would get some funding from the programme.

In two controversial areas, PPWG did not make recommendations, but provided the details. The first was the Apollo versus lead centre controversy for locating the programme management. The second was the distribution of work and hence dollars among the participating field centres.

Lead centre

As the prospects of winning the approval brightened, NASA decided to extend participation in the organization structure decision to field centres. They conducted two major meetings where the issue was debated among the field centre directors. The centre directors unanimously endorsed the lead centre concept, and even suggested an organizational structure. They would rather co-operate with the lead centre than put up with the intrusion from headquarters into their autonomy. Beggs endorsed the decision, and later designated JSC at Houston to be the lead centre.[3]

Many at headquarters, who disagreed with the lead centre concept, interpreted Beggs' decision as an 'experiment' to be evaluated later.

Workpackages

NASA's term for responsibilities allocated to the field centres, workpackages were not so easily decided. In 1982 the lead centre proponents at Washington thought that there would only be three centres involved: JSC, MSFC and GSFC. However, as an outgrowth of its 'strategic planning' under the leadership of its newly appointed centre director, Lewis won a workpackage for itself. This enhanced the complexity of the workpackage decision. The space station project had to be broken down into four meaningful components; technological interdependence and uncertainty about the design, however, made this an extremely difficult task. The space shuttle, from which the lead centre concept was borrowed, had clean interfaces: it could be broken into two relatively separate parts. The space station did not have such clean interfaces.

The workpackage decisions evolved just as the technological concept of the space station was being debated. Unlike the lead centre decision, this decision process did not converge easily. The respective field centres understood only too well during the hardware development phase (which consumed the most dollars), that resources each centre could amass later depended on workpackage decisions made at this stage. Even after many rounds of negotiations contending field centres could not reach agreement. Finally, the headquarters intervened and handed down a decision. Further, to encourage some competition among the centres, the headquarters built some redundancy into the workpackages among the field centres.

Just like the lead centre decision, the workpackage decision was believed to be an experimental one, valid only for the extended definition period.

Implementing the organization

The programme implementation was 'kicked off' at the lead centre with a Space Station Management Workshop where personnel drawn from participating field centres were brought, together to plan the implementation. The major decision made by workshop was that to hold a 'skunk works' at Houston to determine the configuration and to send out the request for extended definition phase proposals (RFP) to the contractors. At the headquarters, the SSTF folded into the first tier (Level A), and continued working with Congress over the actual dollars that would be allocated to the programme. This was the kind of work the headquarters was typically adept at performing.

The skunk works, a standard operating procedure within NASA, inherited the work of CDG, a working group within SSTF charged with defining the configuration. The works operated in parallel with the workpackage negotiation, and each influenced the other.

Although the skunk works produced the RFPS, fissures had begun to appear in the lead centre organization. Although the centre directors had promised co-operation during the lead centre decision, they were not willing to part with their personnel, even for the skunk works. Further, as soon as the workpackage decisions were handed down from the headquarters, the skunk works personnel began to return to their respective field centres. Fissures also began to appear between the headquarters and the programme management. Since the programme manager reported to the JSC centre director, not to the associate administrator in Washington, some at headquarters believed that he neglected the edicts from Washington.

As soon as the industrial contractors came on board, the extended definition period commenced in earnest. By now the programme activity shifted to the lead centre. The technological interdependence among the workpackages made the programme co-ordination difficult. The cumbersome lead centre organization made it worse. The intercentre rivalry was further fuelled by the ties that developed between the contractors and their respective field centres. The contractors, sensing their economic stakes, supported 'their' field centres with data, reasons, and all the symbolic weapons of bargaining and negotiations. The cost estimates of the space station began to soar. The programme manager, someone who had limited project experience, became the focal point of blame for the decision delays.

During this period, there was management turnover which exacerbated the turbulence within the programme. First, deputy administrator Hans Mark, an advocate of the lead centre organization, left to become the chancellor of the University of Texas Austin. Second, Gerry Griffin, the lead center director, resigned to become the president of the Chamber of Commerce at Houston. Third, Neil Hutchinson, the programme manager left for the industry. Finally, and perhaps most devastating, administrator Beggs was indicted, went on leave and later resigned. This also meant that Culbertson, then associate (administrator for the Space Station programme, was taken out of his current job to help the acting administrator.

Re-evaluation and redesign

Even as the extended definition period was in progress, headquarters initiated a review of the workpackage decision. As the space station details were becoming clearer, it was possible to sort out the overlaps and redundancies in the initial workpackage decisions. An independent working group under a headquarters person began to develop workpackage alternatives. This group provided the associate administrator with requisite analyses in his consultations with field centre directors who had to agree to changes in the workpackages.

Most of the centre directors had by now come around to the view that the lead centre was not working properly. The one exception was JSC, the lead centre. JSC continued to advocate the lead centre option, further their workpackage option – based on cost considerations – would have considerably diminished the role of other field centres and indeed other contractors. This was not favoured by Washington, where many attributed the shuttle cost overruns to JSC's long-standing relationship with Rockwell – shuttle's prime contractor. It was getting to be a Washington-Johnson story.

The management turnover left the space station in the hands of the acting associate administrator, and decisions would have to wait till management was clear. Several attempts were made to negotiate the workpackages among the field centres. These negotiations moved from headquarters to the field centres, then to the third tier, and then back to the headquarters. The agreements were hard to come by especially between MSFC and JSC. In NASA, these negotiations came to be known as the 'workpackage wars'.

Meanwhile NASA experienced its worst crisis since Apollo days, the Challenger disaster. The resulting scrutiny, especially the Rogers Commission Report, discredited the lead centre organization then employed in the shuttle. This provided new fuel for the Washington faction that had viewed the lead centre as unworkable. An independent study under Sam Phillips, a retired Apollo veteran, confirmed that the lead centre was not workable, that programme management should be brought to Washington. In the very meeting when Phillips made his recommendations, the newly appointed Administrator, James Fletcher, who had been responsible for the lead centre organizational form in the shuttle programme decided to scrap the lead centre organization in the space station programme and to bring the programme management to Reston, Virginia. A new era in the space station programme began.

Discussion

We organize our discussion into three sections: (1) contextual features; (2) the management challenges created by the context; and (3) ways by which the top management coped with them.

The initial phase of the space station program displayed nine *major features*:

1 The uncertainty of gaining the presidential approval and the need for urgent start-up immediately afterwards contributed to a condition where

the mission development and organizational strategy stages considerably overlapped. These stages occurred in *parallel* unlike the sequential descriptions that dominate most strategy content literature (e.g. Chandler, 1962).

2 Early decisions haunted later decisions; for example, the test bed competition conducted to allocate experimental test beds to various field centres somewhat drove the workpackage decisions. In NASA, the field centres anticipated this later occurrence early on in their efforts to influence headquarters. This occurrence was *not* a failure in planning, but an outgrowth of the context (time pressure and level of decision-making information) in which the decision makers were operating.

3 Since there was no 'one right technological solution' to the problem of the space station, competition among field centres took on an added dimension. It was difficult to separate the arguments for resource acquisition from those made on 'scientific' and 'technological' grounds.

4 In a public agency like NASA, when internal decisions are influenced by and transparent to external constituencies like Congress, field centres could invoke their external constituencies in dealing with the headquarters, especially in the formative years of the programme which determine major resource allocations in the future.

5 The mission statements for the programme were ambiguous and contained priorities among details.

6 The organizational alternatives debated were not tailor-made for the programme nor derived from theoretical concepts (e.g., structure follows mission). The ambiguous nature of the mission statements made it difficult to do so. More importantly, the decision makers reasoned by analogy, *debating alternatives that were already familiar to them.* Calls for outside help in developing these alternatives-were ruled out in the beginning.

7 As the programme moved to the operational phase, external constituencies continued to influence the decisions, sometimes in a way disliked by NASA. For example, even as the concept of the manned space station began to be designed, Congress insisted on developing the 'man-tended option', as an alternative to NASA's preferred alternative.

8 Partly as a result, the headquarters had to continue its efforts to maintain the external constituencies for the space station well into the execution phase. Since headquarters could not pay great attention to the technology evolution of the programme, it had to rely on field centres for execution.

9 Unique to the space station, the major earlier decisions could be reversed mainly because the preceding Challenger disaster destroyed the legitimacy of the programme organization concept – a concept borrowed from the shuttle.

These contextual features created some obvious *management challenges*:

1 It became necessary to co-ordinate parallel processes, to maintain some minimal consistency among decisions.
2 Top decision makers often inherited the consequences of their predecessor's decisions – often made in ignorance – without the benefit of being able to shift responsibility.
3 Since technology concepts reflected self-interests, processes had to be developed to prevent any single field centre's interests dominating the (concept) development process.
4 From headquarters' vantage point, the field centres with their own constituencies often became influential stakeholders, and sometimes refused to remain the subordinates that their formal organization structure demanded.
5 The sheer time pressure precluded the luxury of careful collaborative decision-making.
6 External constituencies had to be placated in a persuasive fashion, and NASA's public positions, sometimes at odds with the constituencies', often made this difficult.
7 Mechanisms had to be found by which field centres conformed to headquarters' direction during execution, without headquarters being able to spend time on monitoring.
8 The top management had to live with the fact that decisions, once made, are difficult to reverse, even if they are implementation-related.

What were the approaches to these problems by the top level NASA decision, makers? We could identify several *operating rules* employed by decision makers:

1 The parallel processes were often coupled by employing *centralized (headquarters-driven) task forces*, broken down into working groups. Where decisions were non-controversial (e.g. scheduling), the working group was left to recommend solutions. In controversial decisions, the major factors in the decision (alternatives studied, participation, guidelines) could be somewhat controlled by the administrator or his immediate subordinates.
2 The past recommendations, when politically non-explosive, were often *incorporated into the present* as in the Hearth Committee recommendations.
3 The adverse consequences of past decisions required *creation of heroes and villains*. The labels were provided in retrospect. Heroes succeeded in convincing Congress and the press of the institutional legitimacy of NASA; villains were recalled from visible positions, retired or reassigned.

4 The *technology concept had to be shaped by the headquarters*, at least modifying some of the concepts developed by a field centre.

5 The mission statements were made *ambiguous*, to provide flexibility in the future, but this in turn necessitated redefining and negotiating later on whenever clarity was required.

6 The decision makers picked up *organization structure alternatives that NASA was familiar with*, rather than inventing new ones. This tactic reduced search time. The choice, in reality, obscured many major operational differences between the 'idealized' alternative and implemented alternative. Thus space station lead centre deviated considerably from that employed in the shuttle, although in the early phases of decision making, the shuttle provided the organizing principle.

7 The top decision makers dealt with both external constituencies and field centres *as nodes in a constituency network* in assessing the impact of a decision. The dichotomy between external and internal had to be suspended.

8 The top level decision makers controlled the *timing and content of announcements and decisions*.

9 Once the activity moved to the field centres the mechanisms of implementation became *the previously decided-upon missions (symbolic), relationships among people (interpersonal), and budgets*. The selection of individuals to key posts became an important issue. Consistency with missions became a decision rule.

10 The headquarters had to create an *atmosphere of legitimacy* for reversing previous decisions. They could accomplish this only marginally through 'rational' mechanisms. They could, however, do this with ease under two conditions: (a) if a major disaster provided a natural opportunity to paint the previous decision as a mistake; or (b) if a senior official, in charge of implementation, made a visible 'mistake'.

Empirically, this study portrays the top management as continually shaping organizational missions and monitoring implementation through its negotiations with the internal and external constituencies. The top management had a clear goal, undertake a major space station programme, although it was not committed to the programme details. This clarity of goal ensured that it was 'muddling through', but with a purpose. The NASA administrator's negotiating strategy with respect to external elements was to take a public position that there was only a single feasible programme alternative – so that the programme could not be shot down in favour of another, but to be inclusive in terms of constituencies (external and internal) so that there was enough support for it. This meant that the mission statement was broad and ambiguous, with no deliberate attempt at priorities. The ambiguous nature of the mission statement, however, created the need for continual negotiations even after programme approval, since there was a lot of manoeuvring room for various constituencies to argue their case (e.g., Lewis).

For a public agency like NASA, negotiating with the external constituencies like Congress is an ongoing and time-consuming activity; hence in major multicentre programmes, the headquarters frees itself during implementation from programme, management and technical details, leaving them to field centres. However, since field centres are often competing among themselves for funds, this sets the stage for a new round of negotiations between headquarters and the field centres. For assistance in this process, the top management creates a 'negotiating organization', a set of carefully chosen individuals at different hierarchic levels. Unlike the dominant coalition of Cyert and March (1963), in NASA this resembles an extended network with a hierarchic structure. The members of this network are committed to maintain the headquarters' premises, act as a conduit for information to the headquarters, and in turn negotiate with the local (field centre) interests, thwarting them access to headquarters for every minute problem. In this negotiated organization, feasibility and time frames drove the process. Consistency – usually applauded in management strategy and organization design literature – was not practical, and, for individuals, sometimes suicidal. The successful individual understood others' self-interests, kept himself flexible, and took advantage of opportunities whenever they arose. In decisions related to implementation, the sheer pressure of time predisposed him to opt from familiar organizational models and operating routines rather than fashioning new ones.

Experience of the space station illustrates the social construction of technology in public agencies, i.e. the technological details emerge not merely from their intrinsic merits, but from political processes. Rationality, which implies some clarity of objectives against which decision alternatives can be ranked, becomes problematic since the goals themselves are in question. In the case of the space station, major segments of scientific community, especially astronomers, continued to deride the manned space station programme since the enterprise siphoned off resources from projects interesting to them. Others continued to cheer the programme on. Different constituencies advocated competing criteria; whoever was dominant managed to skew technological details in their favour.

Although I portrayed a public agency, the lessons may be germane to large diversified organizations undertaking high technology programmes which cut across divisional boundaries. The NASA experience suggests that strong central co-ordination is important in the early phases of such ventures; a negotiating organization, comprised of individuals committed to the premises of the headquarters is crucial to implementation; and that the headquarters must be ready to continually negotiate conflicts across divisions (see also Contractor and Narayanan, in press).

Notes

1 This paper is based on the work done for NASA under contract number NASW-4248. I gratefully acknowledge the financial assistance provided by NASA, the wealth of information and knowledge shared by many NASA personnel during my interviews with them, and especially Dr Sylvia Fries, then Director of History Division, for her patronage. I also thank Professor Thomas Lewin, who was my colleague during the project. The opinions expressed in this paper are completely mine and do not reflect the position of NASA.
2 To date, only one individual refused to participate in our interviews.
3 A figure illustrating the Space Station programme in NASA: the lead centre model is available from the author.

References

Allison, Graham. 1971: *The Essence of Decision*. Boston: Little Brown.
Bower, J. C. 1972: *Managing the Resource Allocation Process*. New York: Irwin.
Burgelman, Robert A. and Sayles, L. R. 1986: *Inside Corporate Innovation*. New York: The Free Press.
Chandler, Alfred, D. 1962: *Strategy and Structure*. Cambridge, MA. MIT Press.
Contractor, F. and Narayanan, V. K. Technology Planning in Multinational Corporations: A Framework for Planning. *R&D Management* (in press).
Crozier, Michel, and Friedberg, E. 1980: Actors and Systems. Chicago: The University of Chicago Press.
Cyert, R. M. and March, J. M. 1963: *A Behavioral Theory of the Firm*. New Jersey: Prentice-Hall.
Dutton, J., Fahey, L., and Narayanan, V. K. 1983: Toward Understanding Strategic Issue Diagnosis. *Strategic Management Journal*, Vol. 4 (4), pp. 307–23.
Fahey, L. and Narayanan, V. K. 1989: Linking changes in revaled causal maps and environment: an empirical study. *Journal of Management Studies*, Vol. 26, No. 4, July, pp. 361–78.
Huber, G. P. and Power, D. J. 1985: Retrospective Reports of Strategic-level Managers. *Strategic Management Journal*, Vol. 6, No. 2, pp. 171–180.
Lewin, T. and Narayanan. V. K. 1990: *A Management History of the Space Station Program* (1982–86). Washington, D. C.: NASA.
Mintzberg, H. and Waters, J. 1982: Tracking Strategy in the Entrepreneurial Firm. *Academy of Management Journal*, Vol. 25, pp. 465–499.
Narayanan, V. K., and Fahey, L. 1990: Evolution of Revealed Causal Maps during Decline: A Case Study of Admiral. In Huff (ed.) *Mapping Strategic Thought*. John Wiley & Sons Ltd, London, pp. 107–131.
Narayanan, V. K. and Fahey, L. 1982: The micro-politics of strategy formulation, *Academy of Management Review*, Vol. 7, No. 1.
Pettigrew, A. M. 1973: *The Politics of Organizational Decision Making*. London: Tavistock.

Pettigrew, A. M. 1990: Longitudinal Field Research on Change: Theory and Practice, *Organization Science*, Vol. 1 (3), pp. 267–92.

Quinn, J. B. 1980: *Strategies for Change*. Homewood, IL: Irwin.

Sayles, L. R., and Chandler, M. 1971: *Managing Large Systems*. New York: Harper & Row.

Schein, E. H. 1985: *Organizational Culture and Leadership*. San Francisco: Jossey-Bass.

4

Strategic Turnaround and Top Management Involvement

THE CASE OF ASEA AND ABB[1]

Ove Brandes and Staffan Brege

Introduction

In the mass media, especially in the business press, myths are cultivated about the powerful actions of the chief executive officer (CEO) during a turnaround process; he/she is proclaimed a hero/heroine after successfully bringing the company out of a serious crisis, a so-called turnaround. In the same manner, the CEO bears the sole responsibility if the firm fails. Swedish examples of company heros are Jan Carlzon, Scandinavian Airlines Systems (SAS) and Percy Barnevik, ASEA and ASEA Brown Boveri (ABB). This trend in the mass media is international.

In the academic world the predominant perspective is different. According to this view, the possibilities for the CEO and top managers to independently choose and implement the strategy are very restricted. Top management is caught between a deterministic environment and an organization characterized by bureaucracy and inertia (Aldrich, 1979; Pfeffer and Salancik, 1978; Cyert and March, 1963; Lawrence and Lorsch, 1967).

Other researchers however, maintain that possibilities exist for management's strategic choice, e.g. Chandler (1962), Child (1972) and more recently, in an article dealing with turnarounds, Greiner and Bhambri (1989). Top management's influence is greatest during periods of revolution, i.e. when the firm dramatically changes its strategic orientation (Tushman and Romanelli, 1985).

Strategic turnarounds

The concept of 'turnaround' has many definitions, using various criteria. We suggest a broad definition here: 'A turnaround is a process that takes a company from a situation of poor performance to a situation of good, sustained performance.'

Hofer (1980; 1988) differentiates between strategic and operating turnarounds. The strategic turnaround process leads, according to Hofer, to a changed strategic position and/or competitive advantage. The operating turnaround processes concentrate upon short-term improvements in profitability through increases in revenue, reduction in costs or asset reductions.

Improved results can derive from either improved effectiveness or improved efficiency. According to Hofer's definition, operating turnarounds imply short-term improvements of efficiency (while the long term effects remain unclear). Furthermore, Hofer assumes that strategic turnarounds lead to improved effectiveness through a repositioning or changed competitive advantage.

Even if there are some definitional problems, we choose to support the concepts of operating and strategic turnaround, but with a somewhat different and broader significance. The operating turnaround emphasizes short-term efficiency within the frame of the established 'strategic orientation' including strategic, structural, resource, and cultural elements (cf. Miller and Mintzberg's, 1984, discussion of configurations).[2] The strategic turnaround aims at a long-term increase of both effectivenes and efficiency through a drastic change of strategic orientation.[3]

Purpose of the paper

The empirical base of our paper is a 'double' strategic turnaround in ASEA (1980–8) and ABB (1988–91). Our purpose is to generate theoretical and managerial understanding of the phenomena. The main questions are:

- How can a strategic turnaround process be described?
- What is the involvement of the CEO and top management team (TMT)?
- Which are the key success factors?

Our presentation of the ASEA and ABB cases is divided into five phases. Each phase can be separated from next by observed changes in the process and we can thereby focus on different aspects of the turnaround process. We summarize by formulation of a set of hypotheses and theoretical discussion.

The Strategic Turnaround in ASEA and ABB

In 1980, ASEA was among the ten largest companies in heavy electrical industry, i.e. generators, turbines, transformers, electrical motors, (railway) engines etc. The firm's technical level was world class, but in a market characterized by excess capacity and a weakened demand, the corporation's growth and profitability had declined. (By 1990 ABB was three times larger than its closest competitor within its core business and showed good profitability, considering the rapid growth and the extensive internal structuring.)

In the late 1970s, ASEA found itself on a downhill course with declining profits and stagnating growth. ASEA considered itself one of the major 'all round' suppliers in the world within heavy electrical equipment, but its position was threatened. Internationalization was still unsatisfactory and did not meet the company's internal goals, although approximately 50 per cent of turnover was exported. The large dependency upon the domestic market, in terms of sales, profits, production and R&D, was a significant problem with the poor demand and high relative costs in Sweden. Excess capacity strained the profits within certain areas, which represented a large portion of ABB sales and heavy losses in steel production were incurred. However, the picture was not completely dark, ASEA had numerous product areas which were both growing and profitable.

ASEA had high functional competence. The production unit was a leader with its modern Manufacturing Planning and Control Systems. A very high level of technical and, to a certain extent, also marketing competence existed within ASEA. The problems were weak integration and co-operation between the different functional departments as well as between headquarters and the international parts of the organization. In general the organization was centralized, authoritarian and bureaucratic.

ASEA had advanced accounting and cost calculation systems, but only a few people were able to interpret the information generated by these systems. Furthermore, the systems were not used for any planning purposes. The long-range planning that existed was primarily a centralized investment plan.

The corporate culture was technocratic. It emphasized technical development, contracting and production at the expense of market orientation. Common values based on the importance of technology kept the organization together. When candidates were sought to fill managerial positions, evaluations were based on technological competence, this created many 'legendary managers and engineers'. Another important ingredient in the corporate culture was employment security. ASEA had not discharged personnel since the 1930s and had maintained this policy during the difficult years of the late 1970s.

Phase 1: Barnevik accepts the position of CEO

The ASEA Board of Directors' choice of Percy Barnevik as the new CEO was both surprising and unconventional. The Board chose a person that represented a very different way of thinking, both strategically and organizationally. However, the developments of the late 1970s, indicated the need for radical changes. A new CEO with strength and skill was needed to change the large and inert organization.

At this time, Barnevik was one of the vice presidents of Sandvik, a multinational company with its base in steel and powder metallurgy, but virtually unknown within the Swedish business community. His experience included a managing position with Sandvik's US subsidiary and experience of working in an international matrix organization. Barnevik was characterized by a strong analytical ability, an exceptional capacity for work and a restless and insistant attitude towards his fellow managers.

Barnevik accepted the offer, but only after having first obtained the Board of Directors' promise of total support for the extensive and radical changes he deemed necessary. He prepared intensively prior to assuming the CEO position.

Phase 2: Structuring one's way out of the Crisis, 1980–1982

Barnevik's appointment as CEO of ASEA's corporation caused a great deal of surprise and scepticism internally, and generated a high level of expectations regarding potential changes. How could an externally-recruited graduate economist manage this extremely technology-oriented and complex corporation? Yet, a larger number of top and middle managers as well as representatives of the trade unions realized that radical change was necessary.

Barnevik took over on 1 June 1980. Directly after the summer holidays, the plans for the first reorganization were presented and implemented. The central plant engineering sector was split up and built into the new product divisions. For the first time production and contracting had been brought together with the marketing function in units with one division manager for each product area.

Several members of the TMT considered Barnevik's initial ideas too short-term profit-oriented and expressed scepticism. They felt that the company's core competence[4] was at risk by scattering and disintegrating its plant engineering and functional competence. Nevertheless, managers were loyal towards both the company and its CEO, in accordance with the ASEA culture. Furthermore, there was at least one person in the TMT who was in complete agreement with Barnevik's visions, namely the vice president of marketing, Mr Arne Bennborn. He had earlier presented his plans for a reorganization but had been turned down. Barnevik showed his talent in political and communicative skills by persuading the trade unions to support the many severe decisions regarding the reorganization and reductions.

Concurrently, Barnevik focused upon the corporation's excess production capacity in Sweden. The first step was to either painfully shut down or substantially reduce the steel operations. This was motivated by the need for short-term profits and the new priorities of ASEA's product portfolio. This decisive action was in direct contrast to ASEA's traditional strategy, e.g. a large degree of backward integration. From now on each business would be judged according to its own merits and its importance within ASEA's new portfolio strategy. Furthermore, another established ASEA principle was altered: guaranteed employment regardless of the economic situation.

This principle had led to a series of unprofitable contracts and marginally-priced business deals with the purpose of maintaining production volume and, thereby, employment. One of Barnevik's immediate short-term actions was to stop marginally-priced business deals, review the pricing system and renegotiate a number of unprofitable contracts. These decisive and successful actions strengthened Barnevik's position within the company and attracted media attention which further strengthened his position internally.

In parallel with these short-term actions, Barnevik presented his long-term strategic visions regarding ASEA's future towards the 1990s. The necessary market orientation of the entire corporation was to be achieved by means of reorganizations. Yet this was not enough. The increasing costs of maintaining a leading R&D position required growth in both volumes and profitability. This had to be achieved through stronger positions in selected international markets under fierce international competition.

The vision was that, in order for ASEA to remain within the 'power equipment industry's highest division' it would be necessary to change from an export-oriented corporation to a multinational corporation with strong international positions in both marketing and production. This demanded an acquisition strategy, especially if ASEA was to compete in industrialized countries with large and government-protected markets. Organic growth was considered insufficient. Barnevik had, in light of his experience from the US market, visions of strengthening ASEA's position in North America through acquisitions.

Barnevik showed his conceptual ability and began early to preach a number of strategic principles: 'spearhead' products, choice of international niches and dominance within these niches. Priority businesses were, from the very beginning, given resources for expansion. The slogan 'to be an insider, not an invader', was created within the company at this early stage and eventually came to be the foundation of ASEA's attitude towards foreign markets. Barnevik took every opportunity to spread his message of the new ASEA'.

For the first time there were profit centres with practically total responsibility for their performance. Divisional managers were chosen among the earlier sector managers but were given new responsibilities based on an evaluation of their capacity and competence. An important ingredient in the divisionalization of the corporation was to provide increased resources for financial control and strategic planning. A central group of younger academics acted as internal consultants to the division management. The motto was 'give those responsible the planning tools'. The TMT demanded immediate action, time-consuming investigations and reports were abandoned. Formal strategic planning became an important means of communication between the TMT and division managers and was an important instrument that facilitated the strategic initiative to be delegated to the divisional level.

The international matrix, a second reorganization, was introduced in 1981. The geographical subsidiaries abroad were tied closer to the divisions of the parent company and other product subsidiaries within the ASEA group's eight business areas. Barnevik had, since the beginning, strived to make the organization 'transparent', i.e., make it possible to follow profit results from the point of purchase to the final delivery. The division and product subsidiary managers were given the responsibility for the very important task of allocating production in the international network of manufacturing units. In the new matrix organization, overlapping responsibility and high demands were set for co-ordination between the managers of the divisions and the managers of the national subsidiaries. The TMT had the assignment for co-ordinating activities within the matrix through its 'parent company responsibility' (PCR) function, i.e. through its work (and responsibility for profits) in the various internal boards. With the organizational changes, considerable resources were invested towards developing a new accounting system.

Many professionals, both internally and externally, criticized the matrix. The TMT felt that this organizational design was necessary, considering among other things the complex interdependences and demands for co-ordination that the plant engineering operations required. 'The matrix was there whether one acknowledged it or not'. The pressure placed upon managers was great. The division managers had to adapt from mainly functionally-based specialists to general managers with profit responsibility. The international subsidiary managers had to better co-ordinate

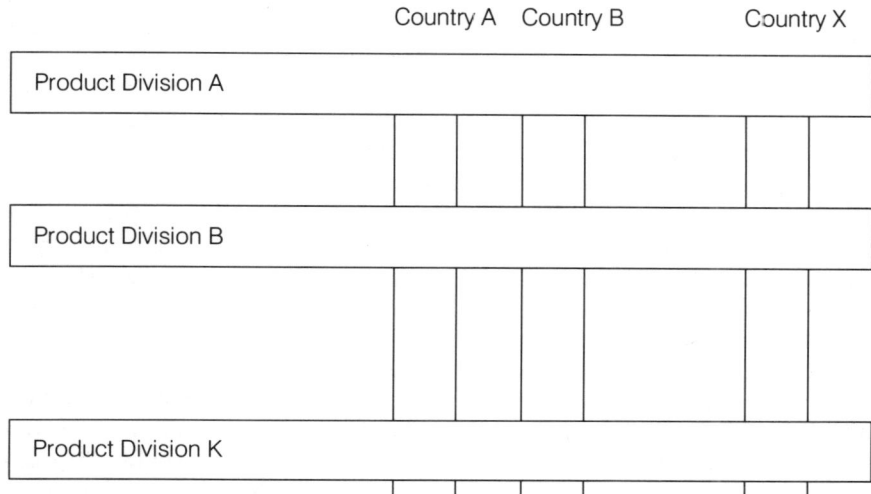

Figure 4.1   ASEA's international matrix

their resources with the division managers. There was high turnover among managers initially. A group of young engineers, 'Percy's Boys', grew to be general managers of important units. Capability and competence rather than seniority became the guiding light for promotion to managerial positions. The matrix even permitted the TMT the possibility to play a partially operative role. It was of critical importance that they did not just abdicate, but rather interfered to keep the organization together.

On the whole, the first years, 1980 and 1981, were a period of upheaval and revolutionary changes. In closing the accounts for 1980, a continued weak profitability was published a result that Barnevik had only limited responsibility for and consciously held low in order to lay the groundwork for a future upswing (it came in 1981). The Board received letters from its personnel and from those external to the company demanding the Board should dismiss Barnevik. The divisionalized organization and profit orientation could only, according to them, lead to short-term solutions as well as a separation and disintegration of ASEA's strongest technological competence. However, the Board stood its ground and continued to give Barnevik their support.

Hypothesis 1

The likelihood for initiating a strategic turnaround increases if: (a) the Board experiences a serious performance gap and realizes that strategic change can only be realized through a change in the CEO; (b) the Board recruits an outsider CEO with experience for solving problems of a similar nature; and (c) the Board gives the new CEO 'carte blanche' for extensive changes and a clear statement of their demand for results.

Studies pertaining to strategic change show that these processes are often induced as a result of a financial crisis combined with a change in CEO and TMT (Starbuck *et al.*, 1978; Bibeault, 1982; Ross and Kami, 1973; Tushman and Romanelli, 1985; Tushman *et al.*, 1986; Hofer, 1988; Greiner and Bhambri, 1989; Brandes and Brege, 1990). The Board's most important task is to select a CEO and together with the CEO, guide the firm through periods of crisis and transition (Zald, 1969; Mintzberg, 1983). One question that has been studied with organization and agency theory perspectives is to what extent the newly appointed CEO should be recruited internally or externally (Zajac, 1990). Zajac ascertains that there is less risk involved for the Board if the CEO is recruited internally since the 'information asymmetry'[5] problem' is then of minor importance. Zajac supports this hypothesis with the finding that internally-recruited CEOs generally lead more profitable corporations.

According to our studies (Brandes and Brege, 1990), the initial position of the firm (in need of a turnaround), at the time of the new CEO's appointment is of great importance for the potential improvement during the next few years. This was not discussed in Zajac's study and one additional explanation for his finding is that the likelihood of appointing an externally recruited CEO increases if the Board realizes a serious performance gap. Internal recruitment of a new CEO, e.g. in the case of retirement, is more likely when performance is satisfactory. Vancil (1987) states, based upon an extensive study of 227 Fortune 1000-corporations, that the trend towards an increase of externally-recruited CEOs is exceptional – from 9 per cent at the end of the 1960s to 27 per cent during the first half of the 1980s. Increased turbulence in the external environment could be a central explanation.

Empirical results also suggest that externally-recruited CEOs implement 'frame-breaking changes' more often than internally-recruited CEOs. According to Tushman, Newman and Romanelli (1986), 'frame-breaking changes' (in 80 per cent of in total 40 cases) were related to a change in CEO and in addition to this, externally-recruited CEOs initiated these changes three times more often. In those cases (six cases) where the incumbent CEO implemented the changes, a significant part of the TMT had been replaced.

Organization theorists favouring an externally-recruited CEO states that he/she is not influenced by the firm's culture, does not have to defend previous actions and is not initially bounded by the political network (Starbuck *et al.*, 1978). This seems critical in those cases where the 'frame-breaking' activities are required.

In ASEA, more so than in ABB, the Board's mandate and support for the new CEO was of great importance to his ability to act forcefully and initiate the extensive changes needed. ASEA experienced a lack of management expertise in the TMT, and, for this reason, decided to recruit an outsider CEO who they believed would have the capability to handle the uncertainty of the actual situation (Pfeffer and Salancik, 1978). Thus, the Board was willing to support a person whose ideas, for the most part, challenged the Board's and management's earlier course of action and some of their fundamental values.

Hypothesis 2a

The likelihood of a quick initiation and a successful implementation of a strategic turnaround increases if: (a) the CEO shows strong visionary, communicative, and political skills – stressing the seriousness of the prevailing situation but simultaneously painting a picture of his optimistic vision for the future; (b) the initiative that the CEO takes in the change process also shows his capability to solve the firm's acute profitability problems; (c) senior managers have thoroughly-prepared plans, some of which the new CEO can incorporate into his programme of change – the 'Bennborn effect'; and (d) the reorganization and appointment of managerial positions make it possible to communicate the strategic vision to the division level and begin a strategic dialogue between the CEO/TMT and SBU (Strategic Business Unit) managers (i.e. division and subsidiary managers).

When an externally recruited-CEO takes over, his earlier career is typically unknown within the organization. His position of power is essentially composed of the legitimate power designated by the Board of Directors. Hambrick (1981) ascertains that the position of power held by the new outsider CEO is both uncertain and questioned. Furthermore, power bases, e.g. the CEO's position as an expert and referent (French and Raven, 1959), must be established. Above all, strong dedication and political skill are needed in order to accomplish the changes at hand (Mintzberg, 1983). To be accepted internally demands expertise in handling important uncertainties related to the environment (Pfeffer and Salancik, 1978; Pearce and Robinson, 1987).

The CEO's choices for action are limited because of the 'contract' he has with the Board. The CEO's dilemma is that short-term improvements in profits, which are perhaps best achieved via an operating turnaround, must be measured against the long-term demands for a strategic turnaround, which often require considerably more resources and time.

Miller and Friesen (1980) illuminate the discussion pertaining to organization inertia and opposition towards change by introducing the concept 'momentum'. According to Miller and Friesen, inertia is not static but rather something connected to movement. Embedded in this direction of movement is a force that typically causes one to go too far. ASEA's central plant engineering operations exemplifies this type of momentum: the continued and excessive drive towards centralization and bureaucratization. There are, however, comparable risks with decentralization as well. Thus strategic change, according to this perspective, deals with radical changes in direction.

This implies that extreme forces are needed to achieve radical changes. It often takes a financial crisis to create awareness and to legitimate difficult decisions related to change – traditional methods of action are considered to have been tried and failed (Tushman and Romanelli, 1985). In the ASEA case, there was widespread understanding among top and middle managers that powerful action was necessary. It was, however, difficult for many to see just what efforts were needed. Many waited for a change in CEO as the starting point for 'putting new life into the company'.

Therefore, the initial position was favourable for Barnevik in this respect, but there was still widespread scepticism towards him as a person and his programme. Barnevik showed great political skill in getting his programme accepted by showing the seriousness in the prevailing situation while giving more positive long-term visions. Greiner and Bhambri (1989) state that: 'What also seems important is to appoint a CEO who stresses a 'positive future' under negative conditions (p. 74).

Greiner and Bhambri also point out that a change in the CEO creates a power vacuum, and strategic change is favoured if the old top management does not organize any opposition towards the new CEO and his initial actions. In ASEA there was, as stated earlier, a great deal of scepticism towards Barnevik's measures among a majority of top managers. These managers were, however, traditionally loyal towards the company and its CEO. Loyalty, a feeling of responsibility, a passion for engineering competence, and hard work were fundamental elements of ASEA's corporate culture. As results began to be realized, several of the managers changed their opinion, while others never accepted the logic of the new strategy and therefore left the company.

One explanation for the low level of visible opposition towards Barnevik's turnaround was that he quickly took command of the change process by means of a thorough reorganization. These actions came like lightning and took many by surprise. Barnevik's fundamental attitude has always been to maintain a fast pace in the change process (without being politically insensitive). Drawn-out changes create unrest, insecurity and, in the worst case, an inability to act among personnel, thus a fast pace keeps these elements to a minimum. Barnevik, quite early, stated: 'It is more important to act quickly than to end up exactly right'. In addition to his legitimate base of power, the Board's trust, Barnevik began to be respected within the organization for his short-term problem solutions which significantly improved operational performance (expert and reference power), and long-term vision. He deviated from established traditions, e.g. vertical integration and guaranteed employment. From the beginning Barnevik was visible within the organization and his style of management could be characterized as 'hands-on'.

The prompt action was facilitated by the fact that there were numerous people within the organization who immediately, or after some time, agreed with Barnevik. There was in particular one of the vice presidents, Arne Bennborn, who had formulated plans for a matrix organization (that had been presented internally by himself several years earlier but had been rejected). We call this phenomenon the 'Bennborn effect': current members within management contribute well-articulated ideas towards formulating a new strategic orientation and significantly facilitate its implementation.[6] Among the managers in the divisions/companies, there were young people who quickly accepted the new ideas, and in the next phase of the change process became important change agents.

Phase 3: International expansion, mainly by organic growth, 1982–1984

At the beginning of 1982, ASEA's performance improved primarily as a result of the internal structuring. However, the Swedish currency was devalued by 10 per cent during the autumn of 1981, and this contributed to the strengthening of ASEA's competitive advantage.

Up to now the large staffs had not been reduced, this was postponed while other more important structuring was done. Barnevik wanted to attain additional benefits from decentralization by transforming each division into a legally-independent subsidiary with its own profit/loss statement and balance sheet. Opposition from trade unions facing new risks in employment security (i.e. each major division would be an employer without backing from the parent company) caused Barnevik to halt halfway, and put the idea 'on the shelf' for a few years. In order to strengthen ASEA's financial operations an additional business area was created by moving the financial function in-house.

ASEA's corporate portfolio strategy, with the exception of the Fläkt (environment protection) consolidation, could be characterized as 'fine-tuning strategy' with emphasis on market and performance orientation. Unlike its competitors, the new ASEA management continued to refrain from unrelated diversifications. CEO/TMT preached the strategic principles of dominance and market leadership within niches. Priority was given to strengthening the international sales and production organization in the industrialized countries and some selectively-chosen developing countries. No large company acquisition had been implemented yet, but negotiations had been initiated.

Towards the end of 1982 and beginning of 1983 trade conditions improved when, among other things, the Swedish currency was further devaluated by 16 per cent. This gave ASEA enough 'wind behind them' to finalize the structuring of the domestic operations. In many cases the excess capacity of mature businesses had been reduced, and those businesses were now profitable. Performance improved rapidly, and prior to ASEA's 100-year anniversary in 1983, Percy Barnevik was the undisputed leader. Internal as well as external criticism had more or less quieted down. The results had occurred relatively quickly and were sufficient. Barnevik took maximum advantage of the anniversary celebrations to profile ASEA by emphasizing spectacular products, e.g. robots and engines. Thousands of international guests arrived in Västerås, Sweden and were able to view closely the successful corporation and its products. A very skilful PR move that bolstered ASEA's international goodwill.

A closing of accounts for the first years of the Barnevik epoch could now be done. Technology still had a leading position, even if R&D operations were more goal-directed and controlled. A certain insecurity still existed with respect to the long-term effects, but on a short-term basis, no catastrophe had occurred. Critics pointed out that priority was not given to technological questions within the executive management and that ASEA, after divisionalization, had extensive technical problems in co-ordinating large plant engineering projects. For example, the earlier centralized works with the development of technical standards had been discontinued. The new ASEA could be characterized as a market- and profit-oriented organization.

*Phase 4: Strategic development from 'The Nordic Strategy' to
'The Multidomestic Company', 1985–1987*

ASEA's positive development at the beginning of the 1980s differed from that of its competitors. The internal structuring, with help from the Swedish devaluation, gave ASEA good results. The general international trade conditions improved steadily but demand within the power industry continued to be weak. The medium-sized companies in particular showed weak profit growth, and many were bought by larger competitors. Despite signals of deregulation, e.g. in the USA and UK, these and many other markets still remained closed for import.

Where geographically could ASEA expand? The strategy within industrialized countries was to become multidomestic by means of acquisitions. The goal of 10 per cent annual sales growth demanded that approximately half of the growth be created through acquisitions. The strategy that ASEA had for the Nordic countries, its home market, was fulfilled during 1986–7 by the purchase of the Finnish firm Strömberg and the Norwegian firm Elektrisk Bureau. The Strömberg deal has been seen as a notable example of an ASEA-managed turnaround.

During this period the financial function became increasingly important from both a profit and competitive point of view. Competence in this area was needed to support the acquisition strategy and the increasing amount of barter trade. Barnevik's visions became more and more influenced by the discussions concerning the EEC's inner market, and the idea of a European company began to take form.

The divisions of the parent company were eventually made into legally-independent companies with separate profit/loss statements and balance sheets. Thereby 'the last 10 per cent of efficiency was squeezed' from the newly built profit centres.

The new organization, with business areas/product subsidiaries and international subsidiaries within the matrix was not free from problems. Internal price negotiations were required between the divisions, an effect of the new structure. According to some, ASEA's ability to co-ordinate large plant engineering projects had also deteriorated, but they were much better at marketing them. There was a great need for co-ordination, and centres of excellence were created to strengthen functional competence.

Phase 5: ABB combined structuring and expansion, 1988–1991

The preparations for creating ABB began in the utmost secrecy in the spring of 1987. The structures of Brown Boveri Company (BBC) and the ASEA model 1980 were very similar, both were driven by technology while market and profit orientation was weak. Furthermore, each had a small domestic market and was typically dependent on exports. The 1980s were becoming a lost decade for BBC; as compared with ASEA, BBC's position had considerably worsened. In 1980 BBC's turnover was twice as large as that of ASEA and its stock market value was four times larger, but by 1986 the turnover of the companies were approximately comparable while ASEA's value was twice as large as that of BBC. Technological competence was still comparable, and in some areas BBC's technical expertise was even greater. The difference lay in each corporation's management and marketing competence, the degree of decentralization and their international marketing organization.

Percy Barnevik was the undisputed CEO for the newly formed ABB. It has been said that one of BBC's key motives for the merger was its wish to have Barnevik as CEO. The role of chairman in ABB's executive managing committee was shared by Curt Nicolin, ASEA and Fritz Leutwiler, BBC.

The top managers' positions were first divided equally between the managers of ASEA and BBC, but after a short period ASEA's managers took care of the most important positions. Barnevik's change of strategy was primarily the same as with ASEA in 1980. ASEA's record, especially the Strömberg acquisition in 1986, created a sense of trust in the plans. For BBC, the transition to the international matrix, with its extensive rationalizations, co-ordination of production, and cuts in central staffs, was certainly 'bitter medicine'.

Barnevik followed the principles of his previous plan: take all the difficult decisions as early as possible in the change process. As before, the tempo was fast-paced. The link to the Board and also the new TMT was relatively simple compared to ASEA in 1980. On the other hand, the implementation of the changes in the new, multinational environment was essentially more difficult than anticipated. In addition to the issues of national prestige and cultural differences, it is important to note that ABB was five times as large as the ASEA model 1980 both in terms of the number of employees and turnover. ABB's structure consisted of eight business segments, fifty business areas and approximately five thousand profit centres. Also the national trade unions met the plans for change with scepticism and opposition. A Swedish top manager commented on the difference between ASEA and ABB turnarounds as follows: 'They are like comparing a quiet jog with the New York marathon.'

Despite the opposition, ABB's structuring was implemented at a fast pace, and after a couple of years profits from the rationalizations began to be realized. The attitude of the employees and trade unions also became more favourable as results improved. The turnaround put large demands upon the managers' ability, and many were replaced.

According to Barnevik, ABB needed approximately 500 'global managers' who had the ability and the capacity to think multidimensional and who considered the corporation as an integrated entity. These persons should counteract the centrifugal force that is present in an organization with a large number of profit centres. Critics felt that ABB had gone too far in its decentralization efforts, and that the subsequent internal price negotiations were too costly. Furthermore, it was pointed out that disintegration of plant engineering operations risks losing the know-how that comes from centralized competence.

With a turnover of nearly 30 billion USD (approximately 180 billion SEK) in 1990 and approximately 220,000 employees, ABB dominated the heavy electro-technical equipment markets in terms of turnover and market shares. One of the driving forces underlying the merger was Barnevik's wish to obtain a stronger foothold within EC. The Swiss BBC had its largest business in West Germany and saw Italy, Austria and West

Germany as its home markets. ABB's product portfolio was initially more diversified than that of ASEA. Within its core business, ABB had achieved a globally-dominant position. For example, ABB's market share of the global transformer segment in 1988 was 25 per cent, which was three times larger than that of its closest competitor.

ABB's management chose ASEA's strategy 'one more time': focus upon a number of core businesses and avoid unrelated operations. In an area of priority, e.g. energy, rail transportation, and environmental protection, competitiveness was attained through a combination of:

• Being closest to the customer
• Having products with the highest quality and leading technology
• Producing at a low cost

ABB had become a global actor with a widely integrated network of production units in many markets (multidomestic) combined with international sales and service organizations. In this particular respect, ABB differed from its foremost competitors, who typically manufactured in their domestic market and exported to other geographic markets. ABB achieved low cost production via ambitious programmes that rationalized the various production units. The merged specialties of the two corporations soon proved to be complementary to an extensive degree that was unexpected and their competitive power was increased by the shared assortment.

The structuring work was not completed when the opportunity for acquisitions in the USA appeared, e.g. Westinghouse T&D and Combustion Engineering. These opportunities were judged to strengthen further the corporation's globally-dominant position. However, the acquisitions strained the corporation's finances and management's capacity. Profitability diminished, adversely affecting the balance sheet. The most important strategic tasks for the beginning of the 1990s is to structure the operations in North America and consolidate operations in Western Europe. The highest expansion priorities are Eastern Europe and Asia.

Based upon the ABB-phase the hypothesis covering the initiation and first implementation could be supplemented with two more aspects.

Hypothesis 2b

The likelihood for a quick initiation and a successful implementation of a strategic turnaround increases if: (a) the CEO and TMT have had earlier experience and 'blueprints' regarding the course of change; and (b) these earlier experiences have been successful and, thus, give the CEO and TMT credibility.

The hypothesis points to the value of learning from earlier experiences, and how that previous success empowers the CEO and TMT. Compared with the ASEA epoch, the Board's initial support was not as important for Barnevik at ABB.

Finally, let us look at some key success factors for a strategic turnaround.

Hypothesis 3

The likelihood of achieving a successful strategic turnaround increases if: (a) there are visible and 'slumbering' resources that can be activated; (b) top management's first strategy ('grand plan') shows itself, on the whole, to be durable with gradual adjustments and step-wise implementation; (c) there is a productive strategic dialogue between CEO/TMT and SBU managers and a gradual transition of the strategic initiative to the SBU levels; (d) CEO/TMT are able to constructively manage the tension and opposition in the organization, e.g. short- and long-term actions, planned and improvised solutions, centralized and decentralized decision making; (e) the pace is high but at the same time the CEO and TMT have a feeling for 'timing' of important actions and the limits of management capacity.

It can be concluded that ASEA, before the merger (at the end of phase 4), had succeeded with the turnaround after showing radical strategic change – decentralization and internationalization were the main patterns – leading to a good and stable profitability record during a five-year period. Whether the ABB turnaround is a success or not cannot be proven until the mid-1990s but the first four years have been successful. Barnevik was appointed to the European 'Leader of the Year 1991' by a committee with representatives from leading European business media.

What are the key success factors for strategic turnaround of a multibusiness firm? In our attempts to analyse a successful turnaround we find little help in the scarce literature on this subject. One of the few references is Bibeault (1982), who identifies the following explanatory factors which are all important in the evaluation of the ASEA and ABB double turnaround:

1 Improved management processes
2 A viable core business
3 Adequate bridge financing, and
4 Improved motivation

First, we will focus upon the initial situation (pre-turnaround) which corresponds to Bibeault's viable core business and adequate financing factors. How bad was the situation, objectively and as perceived by management? Which 'hidden or slumbering resources' were found and exploited by the new CEO and TMT? Is there something substantial to turnaround?

We agree with Bibeault: the initial situation is critical. In the ASEA and ABB cases there were viable core competences which could be more efficiently exploited.

Situations triggering a turnaround process can differ depending upon one's definition of 'bad performance'. Hofer (1988) differentiates between three various types of 'initial bad performance':

1 Organizational effectiveness or profitability
2 The development of firm size and growth
3 Organizational utilization of resources

Chakravarthy and Lorange (1991) use the term 'turnaround situation' when a multibusiness company perceives 'high portfolio pressure' (lack of growth) as well as 'high financial pressure' (lack of profitability).

Second, there is no room for serious drawbacks in the turnaround process, thus the CEO and TMT must have a grand plan that provides a vision, can be implemented quickly and in an orderly way, but still be flexible. In the ASEA case the CEO and TMT were guided by a rather clear and holistic vision and also had a plan for a step-wise implementation.

If the process loses momentum, and the CEO/TMT lose credibility, the whole turnaround process can fail. In two other turnaround cases (Brandes and Brege, 1990), the companies were forced to go back to the structuring phase which threatened the entire turnaround process and also the power of the CEOs. In one of the cases CEO/TMT missed the 'cleaning up' of the balance sheet and business portfolio. In the other case, however, the CEO also announced overly optimistic goals in a long, general business recession.

Although we believe a turnaround process is very vulnerable to drawbacks, especially in its early phases, strategic change is not just a rational process of sequences of formulation and implementation.[7] Strategies are not formulated in detail by top management and then implemented by the operative managers as assumed by Bourgeouis and Brodwin (1984) in their 'commander model'. In most cases, the CEO's and TMT's strategic visions are broad and have to be interpreted and specified by SBU managers. This is, however, a two-way process, the feedback and other signals from SBU managers are very important. With a time perspective of three to five years, the overall strategic orientation, which could be interpreted in Mintzberg and Waters' (1985) concepts of 'umbrella strategies' and 'process strategies', can be adjusted but not completely reformulated. Barnevik showed political and psychological skill by allowing time for learning and showing openness for emergent opportunities.

The ASEA case shows a series of changes which have been implemented step by step. There are several reasons for this step-by-step logic (cf Quinn, 1978; 1980). A) The managerial capacity to monitor process is limited.

B) Different steps in the process are built upon one another and can therefore not be implemented simultaneously. C) The CEO/TMT must have time to evaluate the outcome and judge the organization's capacity for additional changes. A momentary revolution could lead to chaos and complete inability to act. D) A step-by-step implementation gives faster, more visible results which contribute to strengthening the CEO's position of power as well as motivating the organization to further change.

Thirdly, productive strategic dialogue must be established between the CEO/TMT and SBU management (in another article, Brandes and Brege, 1991, we use the concept of strategy as a dialectic process). Within a frame of strategic dialogue the ASEA/ABB case shows how the strategic initiative moves from the CEO and TMT to SBU management, especially after the structuring phase has been successfully completed. The CEO and TMT, however, must continue to be actively involved.

The ASEA/ABB case also illustrates the momentum (Miller and Friesen, 1980) that is present in divisionalization and decentralization. The number of proposals for expansion tends to increase within a divisionalized organization (e.g. Rumelt, 1974). Without strategic dialogue SBU managers may act too opportunistically, which in turn creates a suboptimizing behaviour from a corporate point of view. This momentum problem, as perceived by Percy Barnevik, was a bigger problem within ABB than the former ASEA. Possible explanations are the multicultural character of the global ABB and increased internal competition.

Fourthly, a turnaround process is complex, and tensions arise between conflicting parties within the organization (Pettigrew, 1985). Short- and long-term actions must be balanced as well as contraction and expansion. Other balancing problems are between global visions and local adaptation (Pralahad and Doz, 1987) and stability versus change in different parts of the organization. The hardest conflicts we have found in the ASEA/ABB case were in the crossings of the international matrix, especially during the first few years after its introduction. When product division managers took their worldwide responsibility, they often came into conflict with the subsidiary managers in different countries. In the beginning, the PCRs (parent company responsible, i.e. the CEO and TMT of ASEA and ABB) had to intervene, but they expected all managers to learn to solve their own conflicts in the crossings. If they did not succeed or came back to their PCR several times, they were replaced, in most cases, by younger executives. After a year or two the international matrix functioned properly.

A final factor for a successful turnaround process is the pace. We have been convinced by our cases, ASEA and ABB, and also four others reported in Brandes and Brege, 1990) that a fast pace, in combination with a sensitive feeling for timing, can, among other effects, motivate employees and confer power on the CEO and TMT.

Summary and Discussion

In the section above we discussed the third research question of this article key success factors in a strategic turnaround. In this section we will summarize and discuss our answers to the two first questions pertaining to the description of a strategic turnaround and CEO/TMT involvement.

Phase model

In our empirical description of the ASEA/ABB double turnaround, we choose to split the process into five phases along the timescale. We would now like to go one step further and present a more general phase model, inductively based on the case presented in this article and the four other turnaround cases that we have researched.

Each phase has its own critical issues, strategic activities and results. Of course, a phase model is a stereotypical way of describing a complex strategic turnaround process *ex post*. The lines between the different phases are, to some extent, arbitrarily chosen.

Phase 1: Change of CEO

The initial phase's focus is upon the Board's decision to replace the CEO in order to solve a crisis situation. The more severe the performance gap identified, the higher the probability of changing CEOs and recuiting the new CEO externally. The mandate given to or negotiated with the new CEO is critical, it defines what corrective action the Board considers acceptable and the Board's criteria for acceptable financial performance.

Phase 2: Structuring with focus on profitability.

During the structuring phase, a company's strategic orientation is changed to take it out of the crisis. Early in the phase, the CEO and TMT, guided by a grand plan, resolve emergency situations and restructure the organization, thereby preparing it for further change. These necessary short-term measures must be balanced against long-term needs. The CEO and TMT must also take the initiative and start to consolidate their power positions through successful short-term operations and the appointments of key personnel in the organization. A fast pace and sensitive timing are required for successful implementation.

The CEO/TMT present a new vision of the future, which details the anticipated outcome of the strategic turnaround. This vision could be expressed both in terms of strategic directions and target positions, and how the company should be organized and function ('umbrella' and 'process' strategies according to Mintzberg and Waters, 1985). The CEO/TMT also start dialogue with the SBU managers. The CEO/TMT initially take the initiative, but as confidence in different SBU managers increases there is a transition towards a more balanced dialogue.

Furthermore, the CEO/TMT initially set the tone for implementation. Contraction (e.g. divestments, closures and extensive reductions of capacity) is emphasized. After a relatively short period of analysis and discussion, priorities are determined by the CEO/TMT and presented to SBU managers. SBUs of high priority are given the resources to expand from the beginning.

Phase 3: Expansion and improved performance

The new strategic orientation is established. Much of the contraction is completed, and expansion is now emphasized. The improved profitability that results from actions of the previous phase supports the activities of this phase. Thus, reaching this phase depends upon a successful structuring.

The CEO/TMT's power positions are consolidated, and the priorities of the business portfolio are accepted within the organization. Most of the strategic initiative now lies with the SBU managers. The CEO/TMT do not abdicate their strategic responsibility but still participate in the dialogue. Occasionally they take the initiative on strategic issues (Dutton and Duncan, 1987) and intervene if a serious problem arises.

Phase 4: Consolidating performance levels

During this phase performance improvements can be documented and targets are reached. Also top management can now claim that the strategy is being realized. New expansion plans may be undertaken, e.g. ASEA's Nordic and ABB's global strategies. There is still some structuring being done.

Comparison of phase models

Our phase model has similarities with other models. Bibeault (1982) discerns the following phases in a turnaround: (1) Change of CEO, (2) evaluation, (3) emergency, (4) stabilization, and (5) back to normal. Gabarro (1987) divides organizational change into: (1) taking hold, (2) immersion, (3) reshaping, (4) consolidation and refinement. Compared to Bibeault's phase model, our starting point is similar, i.e. change of the CEO. Next, we present a structuring phase – a revolutionary phase changing a company's strategic direction (cf. Tushman and Romanelli, 1985) which includes evaluation and emergency in terms of Bibeault, and taking hold, immersion and reshaping in terms of Gabarro.

We find it difficult to split the structuring phase into distinct sub-phases, since there are different processes occurring in parallel, e.g. contraction of some business areas and early expansion in others. The two last phases in our model expansion and consolidation imply continued strategic change, not so much in terms of new directions as establishing new strategic positions and competitive advantages. We include what Gabarro calls consolidation and refinement and what Bibeault calls stabilization back to normal performance levels. A revolutionary pattern, however, may still be present in the expansion phase, e.g. ASEAs repositioning from an exporting Swedish company, to the Nordic strategy, and finally, to a truely global strategy.

CEO/TMT involvement

Our results show that the CEO/TMT have extensive influence upon the strategic turnaround process. Active top management is a necessary but not sufficient condition for a successful strategic turnaround. Other elements of crucial importance are the initial situation and the strategic dialogue between different management levels as well as motivation and consensus in the organization. Positive changes in the environment, independent of top management actions, also influence the company's performance, e.g. the devaluations in the beginning of the 1980s helped ASEA's expansion.

We have come to the opinion that strategic and visionary leadership is to a large degree situationally-determined, as expressed in Pettigrew (1985) and Westley and Mintzberg (1989). The CEO/TMT play important, but somewhat different, roles in each turnaround phase. The most influential role is in the structuring phase, when the vital parts of the new strategic orientation are established. In contrast to Tushman and Romanelli (1985) and others, we do not reduce top management influence to a symbolic role in the following phases. We consider the symbolic role one of several.

During the structuring phase, the CEO/TMT initiate a series of changes, which could not have been easily initiated from the lower levels within the organization. Initially, power is centralized at the top management level. Solution of short-term, emergency problems, development of strategic visions, determination of business portfolio priorities, reorganizations, introduction of new control systems, and appointments of managers are primarily decided upon and controlled by top management.

Contractive and structuring activities are initially in focus and decisions of a contractive nature are typically made and also to a large part implemented by the CEO/TMT. Chakravarthy and Lorange (1991) describe a turnaround situation as guided by central planning or, if the financial pressure is not so high, by corporate portfolio balancing. The ASEA turnaround was a mix of corporate and divisional portfolio balancing, with the focus moving from the corporate to the divisional level. From the beginning, most formal planning activities (e.g. analysis of environment, competitors and internal strengths and weaknesses) were done at the divisional level, but with an intensive strategic dialogue with the top management level.

In the expansion and consolidation phases power is more clearly decentralized, and SBU managers take the initiative. However, an active top management must maintain the dialogue and strategic control to keep a large diversified, decentralized company together. In addition, large acquisitions and business deals are still handled with heavy top management involvement. Furthermore, we would connect to the subtitle of this article and stress the importance of the CEO/TMT getting involved in operational problems via conflicts of interest between division and subsidiary managers, especially in matrix organizations.

Notes

1   This study has been supported by a grant from the Bank of Sweden Tercentenary Foundation.

2   We use Tushman and Romanelli's (1985) concept of strategic orientation but with an extended meaning.

3   This enlarged meaning of strategic turnaround is in line with the definition of 'strategic change' cited in Snow and Hambrick (1980) and Greiner and Bhambri (1989).

4   Core competence is characterized, according to Prahalad and Hamel (1990) in the following way: 'First, a core competence provides a potential access to a wide variety of markets. Second, a core competence should make a significant contribution to the perceived customer benefits of the end product ... Finally, a core competence should be difficult for competitors to imitate'. (pp. 83–4)

5   'Information asymmetry' refers to 'the fact that in the typical principal-agent relationship, the principal has less information than the agent about: (1) the characteristic of the agent, e.g. ability, risk aversion, or propensity to leave an organization and (2) the decisions made and actions taken by the agent'. (Zajac, 1990, p. 220)

6   Tushman and Romanelli (1985) express similar thoughts: 'Reorientations are more frequently initiated through external executive succession of multiple members of an executive team, but are more effectively implemented by internal executive leadership'. (p. 213)

7   This rationalistic perspective is greatly criticized by Mintzberg (1978; 1990). In our opinion Mintzberg is driving his criticism of 'the Design School' and general planning too far. A strategic planning approach to strategic management does not, in our view, exclude visionary and creative thinking, nor learning and adapting to emergent situations.

References

Aldrich H. E. 1979: *Organizations and Environments.* Englewood Cliffs, NJ: Prentice-Hall.

Bibeault, D. B. 1982: *Corporate Turnaround – How Managers Turn Losers into Winners.* New York: McGraw-Hill.

Bourgeois III, L. J. and Brodwin, D. R. 1984: Strategic implementation: five approaches to an elusive phenomenon. *Strategic Management Journal,* 5, pp. 241–64.

Brandes, O. and Brege, S. 1990: *Market Leadership* (in Swedish), Kristianstad: Liber.

Brandes, O. and Brege, S. 1991: Strategic management as a dialectic process. In Mattsson, L.-G. and Stymne B. (eds.) 1991: *Corporate and Industry Strategies for Europe,* Elsevier Science Publishers B. V.

Chakravarthy, B. S. and Lorange, P. 1991: Managing the Strategy Process: A Framework for a Multibusiness Firm. Englewood Cliffs, N. J.: Prentice-Hall.

Chandler, A. 1962: *Strategy and Structure: Chapters in the History of American Industrial Enterprise.* Cambridge: The M.I.T. Press.

Child, J. 1972: Organizational structure, environment and performance: the role of strategic choice, *Sociology,* 6, pp. 2–22.

Cyert, R. M. and March, J. G. 1963: *A Behavioral Theory of the Firm.* Englewood Cliffs, NJ: Prentice-Hall.

Dutton, J. E. and Duncan, R. B. 1987: The creation of momentum for change through the process of strategic issue and diagnosis. *Strategic Management Journal.* 8, 1987, pp. 179–295.

French Jr., J. and Raven, B. 1959: The bases of social power, In D. Cartwright, (ed.), *Studies in Social Power.* Ann Arbor, Institute for Social Research, University of Michigan, pp. 150–67.

Gabarro, J. J. 1987: *The Dynamics of Taking Charge.* Boston, MA: Harvard Business School Press.

Greiner, L. E. 1972: Evolution and revolutions as organizations grow, *Harvard Business Review,* 50, July–August, pp. 37–46.

Greiner, L. E. and A. Bhambri, A. 1989: New CEO intervention and dynamics of deliberate strategic change. *Strategic Management Journal,* 10, pp. 67–89.

Hambrick, D. C. 1981: Environment, strategy and power within top management teams, *Administration Science Quarterly,* 26, pp. 253–71.

Hofer, C. W. 1988: Designing turnaround strategies. In J. B. Quinn, *et al.* (eds), *The Strategy Process Concepts, Contexts and Cases,* Englewood Ciffs, NJ: Prentice-Hall.

Hofer, C. W. 1980: Turnaround strategies. *The Journal of Business Strategy,* 1, pp. 19–31.

Lawrence, P. R. and Lorsch, J. W. 1967: *Organization and Environment,* Boston: Graduate School of Business, Harvard University.

Miller, D. and Mintzberg, H. The case of configuration. In D. Miller and P. H. Friesen (eds). 1984: *Organisations: A Quantum View.* Prentice-Hall Englewood Cliffs, NJ, pp. 10–30.

Miller, D. and Friesen, P. H. 1980: Momentum and revolution in organizational adaptation. *Academy of Management Journal*, 23, pp. 591–614.

Mintzberg, H. 1978: Patterns in strategy formulation. *Management Science*, 24, pp. 934–48.

Mintzberg, H. 1990: The design school: reconsidering the basic premises of strategic management. *Strategic Management Journal*, 11, pp. 171–95.

Mintzerg, H. and Waters, J. A. 1985: Of strategies, deliberate and emergent. *Strategic Management Journal*, 6, pp. 257–73.

Mintzberg, H. 1983: *Power In and Around Organizations*, Prentice-Hall, Englewood Cliffs, N. J.

Pearce II, J. A. and Robinson Jr, R. B. 1987: A measure of CEO social power in strategic decision making. *Strategic Management Journal*, 8, pp. 297–304.

Pettigrew, A. 1985: *The Awakening Giant*, Oxford: Basil Blackwell.

Pfeffer, J. and Salancik, G. R. 1978: *The External Control of Organizations A Resource Dependence Perspective*, New York: Harper & Row.

Pralahad C. K. and Hamel, G. 1990: The core competence of the corporation. *Harvard Business Review*, May–June, pp. 79–91.

Pralahad, C. K. and Doz, Y. 1987: *The Multinational Mission: Balancing Local Demands and Global Vision*. The Free Press: New York.

Quinn, J. B. 1978: Strategic change: logical incrementalism. *Sloan Management Review*, Fall, pp. 7–21.

Quinn, J. B. 1980: *Strategies for Change: Logical Incrementalism*. Richard D. Irwin.: Homewood, IL.

Ross, J. E. and Kami, M. J. 1973: *Corporate Management in Crisis – Why the Mighty Fall*. Prentice-Hall, Englewood Cliffs, NJ.

Rumelt, R. P. 1974: *Strategy, Structure and Economic Performance*, Harvard University Press: Cambridge, Mass.

Snow, C. C. and Hambrick, D. C. 1980: Measuring organizational strategies: some theoretical and methodological problems. *Academy of Management Review*, 5 pp. 527–38.

Starbuck, W. H., Greve, A. and Hedberg, B. 1978: 'Responding to crisis', *Journal of Business Administration*, 9, pp. 111–137.

Tushman, M. L. and Romanelli, E. 1985: Organizational evolution: a metamorphosis model of convergence and reorientation. *Research in Organizational Behavior*, JAI Press: Greenwich, CT, 7, pp. 171–222.

Tushman, M. L. Newman, W. H. and Romanelli, E. 1986: Convergence and upheaval: managing the unsteady pace of organizational evolution. *California Management Review*, XXIX, Fall, pp. 29–44.

Vancil, R. F. 1987: *Passing the Baton*, Harvard Business School Press: Boston, MA.

Westley, F. R. and Mintzberg, H. 1989: Visionary leadership and strategic management. *Strategic Management Journal*, 10, Special issue, pp. 17–32.

Zajac, E. J. 1990: CEO selection, succession, compensation and firm performance: a theoretical integration and empirical analysis. *Strategic Management Journal*, 11, pp. 217–230.

Zald, M. N. 1969: The power and functions of board of directors: a theoretical synthesis, *American Journal of Sociology*, pp. 97–111.

II

Organizational Cognition and Learning

The role of cognition and learning processes in strategic management is explored in the four papers in this section. Cognition is the process of scanning and interpreting environmental events. Levenhagen, Thomas and Porac argue that creating shared cognition is a fundamental skill to a true entrepreneur. The new cognitive categories created by entrepreneurs have to be 'sold' to the market stakeholders before a new market can emerge. The creation of a new market or the diffusion of a new technology calls for shared cognition among market participants.

Learning, on the other hand, is the process of mapping and abstracting knowledge about action-outcome relationships. Learning requires cognition, but cognition can exist without learning. Learning always implies action, whether it be that of the firm (action learning) or that of others (vicarious learning). In contrast, cognition need not call for action. For example, the cognitive categories of entrepreneurs define the domain of future organizational action. These may not be the result of prior organizational actions.

Levenhagen, et al. suggest that the emergence of new markets can be better understood by using a cognition perspective rather than the more typical economics perspective. They challenge the extant prescriptions for entrepreneurship that advocate market research, erecting entry barriers, using multidisciplinary teams, fast operations etc. Instead, the authors propose two critical phases in the market-formation process: (1) novel entrepreneurial conceptualizations that can no longer be understood by market participants in terms of their existing language and (2) concept championing aimed at bringing together resource providers and ensuring the sharing of the new concept by other market stakeholders.

Another concept presented here by Durand is that of cognitive technology maps that can help an organization learn how to manage technology better. The author suggests the use of the so-called 'dual technology tree' (DTT) and 'customer concept tree' (CCT) to come up with novel entrepreneurial conceptualizations of new markets. Staying within a branch of the DTT would be like staying within an existing cognitive domain, while technological changes are depicted as jumping from one branch of the DTT to another. The important point to be noted here is that a technology branch need not be new in order for it to be the source for an entrepreneurial idea.

Bonora and Revang present processes for transforming individual knowledge to organizational knowledge, based on the argument that, in a knowledge-intensive firm, it is the individual knowledge worker who initiates important actions on behalf of the organization. These individual actions result in individual knowledge about successful and unsuccessful actions. These action-outcome pairs can result in heuristic or sometimes even deep knowledge that is resident in the individual. Unless the individual knowledge is shared with other team members or institutionalized as standard operating procedure, it will never become organizational knowledge. If firms cannot establish proper processes for converting individual knowledge to organizational knowledge on a continuing basis, they will be at the mercy of the knowledge worker. Incentive systems, such as economic incentives, as well as providing more intangible incentives like belonging to a valued social structure, are important for retaining the knowledge worker.

A comprehensive framework on organizational learning is provided in the paper by Hedlund and Nonaka, exploring how this process might differ between Japanese and Western firms. The archetypical Japanese firm first captures articulated knowledge from the environment through a process of assimilation. This knowledge is transferred to a group within the organization. The group then engages in intensive reflection and dialogue, internalizing the assimilated knowledge, thus discovering tacit aspects to it. The articulated and tacit dimensions of the knowledge are then extended to other individuals in the organization. In contrast, Western firms are often preoccupied with the process of articulating individual tacit knowledge into articulated knowledge, and its subsequent appropriation by the group, organizational and interorganizational levels.

5

Models of Knowledge Management in the West and Japan[1]

Gunnar Hedlund and Ikujiro Nonaka

It is a commonplace that organizations work with information and knowledge, and that we live in an information society. There is a rich literature emerging on the effects of information and the technologies associated with it for issues such as links to customers and suppliers, the conduct of research and development (R&D), rationalizing logistics, managing multinational firms, and developing new organization structures. Still, more encompassing theories of management and organization have not, in our view, really taken the appreciation of the importance of information, and particularly of knowledge, to heart. This is not the place to review what has and has not been done by authors such as Galbraith (1973), Arrow (1974), Simon (1976), and others. Instead, we shall propose a framework for discussing knowledge management, building on these and other earlier contributions, but also taking a few steps further.

The basic argument builds on the premise that the generation and exploitation of knowledge (cognitive precepts as well as skills and expertise embodied in products or services) in an organizational context revolve around two critical issues: the interplay of articulated and tacit knowledge (Nonaka, 1989; 1990), and the transfer and transformation of knowledge between individuals, organizational units, and the surrounding environment. We argue that a conceptual framework built on these premises captures essential aspects of different models of knowledge management. As the model is explained, we illustrate how it can be used by contrasting 'Western' and 'Japanese' practices, respectively. For Japan, we rely primarily on some recent and well-researched analyses. (Notably Aoki, 1990; Dore, 1987; Kagono *et al.*, 1985; and other works by these authors.)

'Western' here refers mainly to the USA, since European countries constitute too diverse an arena for generalizations. We deliberately focus on and magnify differences between the contexts. Our interest in eliciting differences and contrasts and in developing ideal types rather than representative generalizations necessarily leads to some caricature. As shorthand, we will sometimes refer to 'the J-firm' and 'the W-firm' to denote two types of corporations that represent important alternative institutional solutions to the problem of technological development, and that could be argued to have been differentially 'perfected' in the two national environments (cf. Dore, 1987): the young hi-tech entrepreneurial firm in the West, and the large, mature corporation in Japan.

The characteristics of knowledge management in firms and societies, in turn, have implications for what kind of activities (branches of industry, types of innovation, types of strategies, etc.) an organization or a society is likely to excel in. We conclude the paper by discussing how the proposed framework may throw light on some particular aspects of Japanese industrial specialization.

Implicit in the above is the notion that dealing with knowledge creation, transfer, and exploitation will be increasingly critical to the survival and success of corporations, and of societies. This shifts the focus of those responsible for the strategic health and dynamism of the corporation. It will become apparent in the analysis that 'management' in this context has to do with matters such as: establishing a corporate, and intercorporate, organizational and informational infrastructure; securing investments in search for new knowledge; maintaining steady development of human resources through recruitment, rotation and training; creating channels for dialogue in the corporation; setting up projects and motivating and rewarding their members; allowing for the expression and communication of dormant knowledge, etc. In short, most of these issues are *process* issues, rather than dealing with the content of strategic decisions. Therefore, we feel that the perspective of knowledge management adds to the reasons for paying more attention to strategic processes.

Primary Distinctions in the Model

Our proposed model will be explained conceptually and with Western/Japan exemplification in parallel. However, before this we want to introduce some more general notions. Our model revolves, as indicated above, around two main distinctions. They are often made, although rarely systematically put together. *First*, we need to distinguish between *tacit* and *articulated* knowledge and information. Tacit knowledge (TK) is defined in line with Polanyi (1969), indicating knowledge which is intuitive, non-verbalized and yet unarticulated. Articulated knowledge (AK) is specified either verbally or in writing, computer programmes and the like.

	INDIVIDUAL	GROUP	ORGANIZATION	INTERORGANIZATIONAL DOMAIN
ARTICULATED KNOWLEDGE/INFORMATION				
Cognitive Skills Embodied Syntactic Semantic Pragmatic	Knowing calculus	Data on group performance	Organization chart	Suppliers' patents and documented practices
TACIT KNOWLEDGE/INFORMATION				
Cognitive Skills Embodied Syntactic Semantic Pragmatic	Cross-cultural negotiation skills	Team co-ordination in complex work	Corporate culture	Customers' attitudes to products and expectations of future products

Figure 5.1 A model of knowledge categories and transformation processes: types of knowledge

Second, we need to distinguish between different carriers, or agents, of knowledge. We discuss four different levels: *the individual, the small group, the organization* and *the interorganizational domain.* Both TK and AK exist at all levels. See figure 5.1 for examples of the eight types of knowledge following from our taxonomy. The rationale for some of the examples as well as for the figure as a whole will be clarified later.

The notion of organizational knowledge surfaces in many contemporary analyses. Although no full review is intended, a few recent contributions may be mentioned. One step in introducing cognitive categories in management research is to pay attention to managers' cognitions, 'mental maps', etc. (Stubbart, 1989, provides a review and critique of strategy research from this perspective.) From a sociological viewpoint, Wolfe (1991) argues with Mead (1934) that 'mind' is a social category, drawing analogies between ideas in artificial intelligence research concerning 'connectionism' and the structure of human societies. March (1991) models and simulates the mutual learning in organizations and individuals. Seely Brown and Duguid (1991) insist on the communal context of learning. Nelson and Winter (1982) very clearly refer to organizational routines. Like Pavitt (1980), they also stress the large doses of tacitness in the routines. Stiglitz (1987) emphasizes localized (to the organization) knowledge and the intricacies of individual incentives to learn.

Our model introduces the small groups as an intermediate level, since – as much of the literature referred to above shows – this is where most communication, learning and knowledge transfer actually take place. Empirical research also demonstrates the importance of organic as well as administered team formation for knowledge creation (see Takeuchi and Nonaka, 1986). The model also includes what we have termed the 'interorganizational domain', capturing suppliers, customers, subcontractors, collaborating organizations, etc. These are units outside the firm which may play important parts in, for example, product development (see von Hippel, 1976). Also the characteristics of the wider, contextual environment may be interpreted in terms of categories of knowledge and information. Boisot and Child (1988) provide a model of information structure and distribution at the level of entire societies. Our model refers to the organizational rather than the societal level, but it is interesting to note that also Boisot and Child point the degree of articulation (in their language: 'codification') as critical.

Introducing the group and the surrounding organizational landscape allows a more precise discussion of how knowledge travels and changes between individuals and organization. It is not a matter of reifying the organization, rather it is a matter of analysing how emergent properties of organizations as a whole arise out of the interaction between individuals. Also, starting with knowledge rather than 'learning', which is the more common strategy, in our view makes it more natural to posit supra-individual levels. The organization clearly has knowledge filed in its cabinets. Whether it, rather than its members, learns becomes a more problematical question, particularly as the notion of learning itself is problematical in this context (cf. Weick, 1991). Whatever the starting point, it seems clear that it is necessary to deal more explicitly than in most literature with the problems and reality of shifting levels of analysis. (See Kogut and Zander, 1991, for a related discussion.)

Aspects of Knowledge

In addition to the two fundamental distinctions suggested, a number of other terms and distinctions are used in the discussion below and are necessary for a richer theory of knowledge management. We cannot discuss them all more than rudimentarily here. The most important are outlined below.

Knowledge as cognition, skill, and embodied in artefacts

Thus, we distinguish between three forms – or, better, aspects – of knowledge and information, whether tacit or articulated; namely, *cognitive knowl-*

edge in the form of mental constructs, *skills or competencies*, and *embodied* in products, services or artefacts. In this way, an aptitude for a certain form of action is defined as knowledge, which is not obvious in other uses of the concept. For example, a firm's expertise in the manufacturing of precision machinery is thus seen as a form of knowledge. This is well in line with Polanyi's discussion, a large part of which really focuses on tacit skills, and the difficulties of articulating them. It is also appropriate for an analysis of organizational knowledge management, since to restrict oneself to purely cognitive aspects would mean stretching the abstractions very far, perhaps too far. It is hard to imagine a firm as solely a thinking entity, but much easier to see how it develops practical skills on the basis of knowledge. The inclusion of skill as a knowledge category seems reasonable also in the light of analyses such as by Nelson and Winter (1982) and others. It is also etymologically sound, as 'know', among OED's fourteen other listed meanings, also encompasses 'to understand the way, to be able'.[2]

Space does not allow a full discussion of how the three knowledge forms differ in terms of our model. One important consideration is in terms of transfer ease and transfer mode. Embodied knowledge is probably easiest to transfer between agents, whereas skills are the most difficult. The latter tend to involve tacit knowledge and require communication at this level, whereas a product can be explicitly articulated. Cognitive knowledge falls in between in both respects.[3]

Knowledge and information

Concerning *knowledge* and *information*, it is impossible here to review all uses of the two concepts. Social scientists of various persuasions wrestle with the terms, but we have not been able to extract clear or commonly shared definitions.[4] Information almost becomes a primitive concept, parallel to energy and mass, and the discussion proceeds rather by stating attributes and peculiarities of information. *Knowledge* in our model refers to highly structured, complex assemblages of data, whereas *information* is reserved for simple and more discrete data (or components of skills, or single parts of the output of the organization).[5]

Degree of structured complexity, in the case of articulated cognitive knowledge, could be measured in terms such as: number of simple data items; number of data categories; number of organizing principles the data set is subjected to; complexity and multi-dimensionality of causal connections between data; depth of hierarchical system of classification of data. The case of tacit knowledge is more difficult, but some suggestions, in this case for skills, are: the number of separate subskills involved; the difficulty of integrating subskills with each other; the number of task and environmental contingencies the skill has to be adapted to; the complexity of interaction between cognitive and practical aspects of the skill; degree of discernment and 'fine tuning' required in the performance.

We will use the words 'information' and 'knowledge' somewhat loosely. The context should indicate the degree of structuring implied. (As in the case of tacitness, of course we are really confronted with a continuum rather than with nominal categories.)

Syntax, semantics and pragmatics of knowledge

All information or knowledge could be looked at from at least three different aspects: *syntactic*, *semantic* and *pragmatic*. Syntax has to do with how information is structured and rules for its manipulation and development. Semantics concern the meaning of information. Pragmatics involve the uses of information. It is interesting to consider the differences between tacit and articulated information in the light of the three aspects. Tacit knowledge is probably very important semantically, in that it provides integration and meaning to large fields of data. Deeper meaning can perhaps only be coded tacitly, elicited in complex symbols and rituals but not reducible to these. Articulation is usually, but not always, necessary for the pragmatic aspect of knowledge to become clear, since without articulation it is difficult to communicate precisely how knowledge is to be used in an organizational context. The case of syntax seems to offer the most interesting arena for discussing differences between tacit and articulated knowledge, wherefore we concentrate the discussion on this.

The syntax of articulated information is usually basically some sort of hierarchical classification system, often complemented with cause-effect relations (cf. Stubbart, 1989). Tacit knowledge, we propose, shows a much richer array of syntactical principles, which is one reason for it remaining tacit. Its syntax is more *experimental*, revealed only in and created for specific situations, like when a good tennis player mobilizes whole sets of skills and continuously changes the interpretation of the situation as he runs towards the net.

The syntax of tacitness furthermore, we hypothesize, relies more than articulated knowledge on *prototypical precepts*, with rich and holistically or holographically coded meaning. The tacit component of being a US marine soldier is probably encoded in role models, such as John Wayne's rendering on the archetypical good marine in *Iwo Jima*. This example is provided by Stubbart (1989) concerning cognition in general. We would argue that the mechanism of stereotyping and *idolization* is particularly active in syntactically structuring tacit knowledge. Hero myths are important parts of the largely unconscious culture of many organizations. In learning complex skills requiring tacit knowledge, *imagining* that you are your idol often helps.

A related phenomenon is the importance of *stories* as carriers of information and as educational and socializing tools in organizations. Orr (1990, quoted in Seely Brown and Duguid, 1991) analyses how computer repairmen circulate 'war stories' and thereby effectively learn to master a large number of problems not easily treated in manuals. We would hypothesize that stories more generally figure prominently in tacit syntax, particularly with regard to organizational level skills.

'Aesthetic' consonance also seems to structure tacit knowledge. You, 'just know' what is appropriate because tacit knowledge operates through rules, but not by matching situations and rules one-to-one. Rather, the action selected is tested for consistency with a larger system of norms and previous experiences. The *negative* check is very strong; it is obvious in most organizations what you must *not* do, what is not appropriate. In the same way, it is very easy to recognize a disharmony in a piece of music, but much more difficult to say which of several possible harmonies is the 'best'. Tacit knowledge, we would argue, is structured more like an opera or great novel than like a house or a computer programme. That is why stories, myths, great personalities, ceremonies, etc. are so important in communicating tacit knowledge.

The indirect and symbolic references between knowledge items and the holistic framing of information in tacit syntax make for a certain conservatism. It is easier to change an articulated strategic statement – 'Yesterday we went for market share, today we must differentiate products more' – than to change an almost unconscious, ingrained way of thinking or doing.[6] In companies, such 'shifts of tacit frame' are often accompanied by the change of leading managers, and of, as it were, rewriting the corporate history. Old procedures, such as location and form of board meetings may also change. Thus: new idols, new stories, new rituals. In political systems, the overthrow of *statues* is a sure sign of a challenge to whole complexes of knowing and being.

Knowledge as a stock, as a flow in transfer, and in transformation to new types of knowledge

We distinguish between *storage* of knowledge and *transfer* of knowledge. The former indicates that a stock of knowledge 'resides' in a particular agent. The latter refers to knowledge communicated from one agent to another, such as from one individual to another, or from a group to the entire organization. We furthermore introduce the concept of *knowledge transformation* to indicate processes through which knowledge is added, restructured, recontextualized, reinterpreted, etc., or through which new knowledge is generated. Transformation ranges from simple additions of single data to the invention of totally new concepts or products. We shall use *knowledge/information creation* for the more complex case, reserving *information processing* for the simpler (cf. Nonaka, 1987; 1989). Subcategories of information processing are registration, addition, sorting or classifying, simple manipulation according to given rules, and combining. The sequence indicates a continuous progression from simple and basic to more complex processing. Creation involves the introduction of new kinds of data, reinterpretation of old knowledge, recombination of data, and new holistic conceptions or tangible outputs.[7]

Some of the examples in figure 5.1 are more orthodox, referring to cognitive categories. Others indicate practical competences and skills. Naturally, in most cases knowledge involves both tacit and articulated components, but their relative weights vary. For the sake of clarity, most examples are at a relatively low level of structuring; i.e., rather referring to information than to knowledge. Note that the two dimensions of congnitive/practical/embodied and syntactic/semantic/pragmatic are independent of each other. *All* types of knowledge have all three of the latter aspects.

The Primary Distinctions Applied to the West and Japan

Do the two ideal types of firms/environments differ in terms that can be related to our two primary dimensions? This is critical for a first assessment of the usefulness of the framework.

Concerning *articulation and tacitness*, most descriptions of Japanese management indicate relatively strong tolerance for tacitness. A Japanese company requires employees to understand without being told exactly what to do. The epistemological strategy furthermore builds on induction and experiential learning, which tends to accumulate knowledge in tacit form more than in the case of deductive reasoning. Also business practices rely more on tacit understanding, so that, for example, written contracts are kept simple or do not even exist in cases where a Western firm expects such articulation. It is crucial also to be able to 'read' social situations with great precision, and behave differently according to nuances of composition of the group one is in. Thus, both on the cognitive and on the social plane, tacitness and the talent for working with tacit knowledge are important.[8]

The Western firm is uncomfortable with purely tacit knowledge[9] as is the Western individual. Products are specified, recipes and blueprints produced, principles are enunciated, etc. The latter, in particular, is an important aspect also of the success of Western science. It is significant that the lack of development of Chinese science to a large extent can be attributed to weaknesses of articulating *why* their inventions worked (Needham, 1954).[10] Causal specification is a dominant method of articulation. Mere description and listing is only a first step of articulation of information.

The roles and relative importance of the various agency levels proposed – *individual, group, organization, and interorganizational* – also seem to differ substantially between the W-firm and the J-firm, and between the two social environments. In the West, there is a focus on intensive reflection at the individual level. The statue of the Greek thinker stands as a monument to this continued strong property of the Western conception of knowledge. Rich and varied knowledge at the individual level is highly valued. Child rearing and education emphasize broad familiarity with a number of fields, and deep roots in history. This is an idealized version of the Western model, but still valid to a large extent. After entering working life, the Western individual continues to receive a wide range of inputs, both in articulated and in tacit form. The importance of 'free time' guarantees a sector of life where new perspectives can enter and become internalized.

The individual in the West also has an important role in the creation of new firms which have an important role in knowledge creation in society. A typical model of innovation is its birth in an individual, who starts a new company to exploit it rather than, for example, joins a large firm with large resources to put such ideas into action.

In the J-firm, the primacy is at the organizational and group level. Quality circles, ring systems, long working hours followed by collegial after-hours talk and drinking are all mechanisms to encourage sharing of knowledge. Tacit components are brought to the surface through intensive interaction, allowing transfer and expansion also of information and skills which are difficult to articulate. Learning and thinking are closely associated with normal work and action, rather than taking place in isolation (cf. Starbuck, 1984 and Seely Brown and Duguid, 1991).

Individual education is in Japan primarily seen as certification. At least up to university level, education is heavily influenced by pressure to pass tests of specific knowledge and skills. The broader, humanistic ideal of Western education is not so prevalent, even if today many voices are raised to reform schools in this direction. The university system historically has not had the same importance for knowledge creation as in the West. Universities are, however, crucial as embodiments of prestige and belonging to an élite, and many universities effectively predestine students for particular types of careers. Relations with university friends are often kept up and used intensively in working life.

The Japanese case also puts more emphasis on the interorganizational domain in knowledge management. Relationships with surrounding organizations are imbued with mutual learning. In the West, typical (but this is changing recently, and the portrayal is almost a caricature) supplier contracts are well specified and build on complementarity rather than mutuality. Subcontractors are treated, historically, more on arm's-length basis. Little knowledge is transferred in either direction. In 'strategic alliances', the Western firm often has a hard time appropriating information from the partner (cf. Doz, Hamel and Prahalad, 1990). Joint ventures are also looked upon more in terms of complementarity than in terms of mutual learning through dialogue. In Japan, dialogue with suppliers and customers is extremely time-consuming and rich in terms of information sharing. Also, through this and other channels, knowledge about competitors is transferred. This is seen as quite normal and unavoidable, and means that knowledge superiority is normally extremely short-lived. Foreign companies in Japan often see this as the most important obstacle to rapid growth in Japan.

Geographical proximity reinforces interaction and learning, somewhat as in the case of Silicon Valley in the US. This applies horizontally as well as vertically, where subcontractors are often located within minutes of their main customer. It is important to note the often quoted vertical 'quasi-integration' in Japan. This expresses a closeness necessary for fruitful dialogue. It also, however, indicates that integration is not total, so that the parties have different things to contribute. One should not exaggerate the benevolence of the system for the subcontractors. It remains true that they learn a lot from their large customers.

Processes of Knowledge Transfer and Transformation

Thus, the two main dimensions seem to be relevant for our comparison in terms of flows and interactions in the model. In figure 5.2, we define some more detailed processes of knowledge transfer and transformation. There are four main sets of concepts:

- *Articulation* and *internalization*, the interplay of which we term *reflection* (these processes are depicted as vertical arrows in figure 5.2)
- *Extension* and *appropriation*, with *dialogue* as a result of interaction (horizontal arrows)
- *Assimilation* and *dissemination*, referring to imports and exports of knowledge from the wider environment
- *Expansion*, indicating additions to or changes in knowledge 'within a cell' in the model

Articulation refers to tacit knowledge being articulated. It can occur at all agency levels, not only the individual one. For example, an organization might make its corporate culture explicit by rules of conduct and ethical principles, thus transforming it from TK to AK. Articulation is a crucial process, since it significantly increases the potential for critique, testing and most importantly here – for sharing through transfer of knowledge.

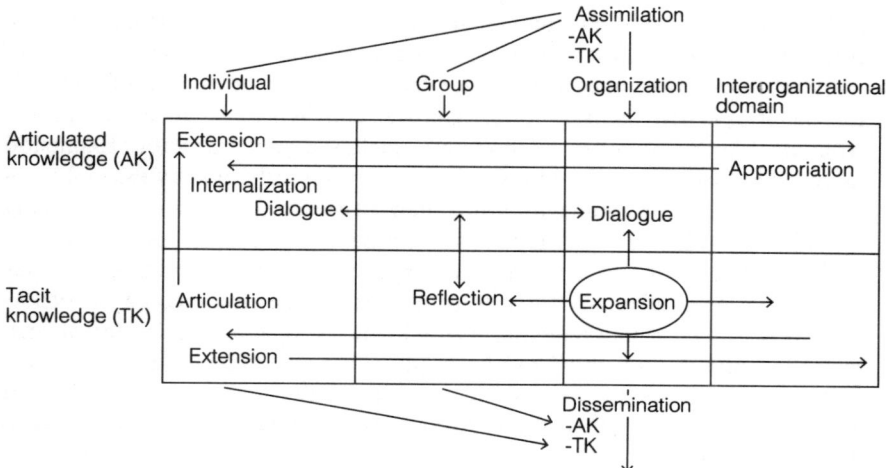

Figure 5.2   A model of knowledge categories and transformation processes: Types of transfer and transformation

When articulated knowledge becomes tacit, we speak of *internalization*, again at all levels of analysis. Internalization is critical in order to use limited cognitive resources economically. An organizaction develops routines, which it unconsciously follows, in order to relieve, or at least with the effect of relieving, its analytical and synthetic capabilities for the most important work (cf. Nelson and Winter, 1982). Of course, this also has negative consequences. Internalization withdraws knowledge from open, critical scrutiny and may thus hinder later adaptation to new circumstances.

To capture the dynamics of articulated and tacit knowledge transformation, a third term has to be introduced. This is the principle of *reflection*, implying a dialectic between tacit and articulated forms of knowledge. Again, this takes place at all levels, but individuals are always involved. The process of successively specifying and improving an idea through articulating it in writing, reassessing it, and rewriting it is an example of the process of reflection. The explication of corporate culture similarly requires an interplay between, and successive expansion of, both tacit and articulated knowledge.

We have indicated above that articulation is stressed in the Western firm, and that tacitness is prevalent in Japan. The most important difference, however, is probably the relative strength of reflection at the supra-individual level in the J-firm. Organizational and social mechanisms (quality circles, long working hours, internalized labour markets, after-hours drinking, group and project organization) encourage the elicitation of both tacit and explicit knowledge, and there is enough permanence and intensity of interaction to allow organizational level reflection.

Extension refers to transfer of knowledge from left to right in figure 5.2, for instance when an individual tells his colleagues, or an entire group, what he knows, or when a company teaches a subcontractor. Extension takes place at the articulated level, but not exclusively SO. By example, observation, imitation, and emulation, knowledge can spread without being articulated. This is perhaps the primary mode of extension for craftsmanlike skills, and for artistic expression and appreciation. It may also be the most effective mode of propagating a desired change in corporate culture from a CEO to the entire firm. (Note that the organizational level does *not* denote the CEO or imply the higher levels of a hierarchy. When the CEO acts or knows, we put him to the left in our model, with everybody else. Only when something is widely shared in (or at least accessible to) the wider organization, do we refer to 'organizational knowledge'.)

Appropriation is transfer from right to left in figure 5.2, when knowledge at higher agency levels is accepted at lower ones. For example: when a new salesman learns the corporate bag of tricks – some articulated and some tacit – in pushing the company's wares onto the customers; or when a component supplier teaches the firm about its technology.

As in the case of tacit/articulate interaction, we need a third category to signify the interplay between extension and appropriation. We refer to *dialogue* as communication between units at a given level and between levels. For example; product concepts are discussed between groups; specific individuals are consulted; the established product assortment of the organization is taken into account; subcontractors' views are ascertained, etc. Dialogue is mostly articulated, but not always so. A football team practising is largely a matter of tacit dialogue. Much of management training is also really a dialogue at this level, where corporate priorities are communicated, checked, refined, and changed as a result of intensive interaction, also at the tacit, subconscious level. Consulting skills and other 'knowledge occupations' are probably learnt to a large extent through tacit dialogue.

The Western firm exhibits a primacy of extension over appropriation (see figure 5.3). Commercialization of technology usually takes the form, at least historically, of individuals forming companies around ideas. The level of the group is subordinated in this process; as it were, skipped over and only engaged as an instrument for carrying out pre-defined tasks. Dialogue is thus chiefly between individual and organization directly. Unavoidably, this requires a standardized and static approach, implying strong specialization of tasks and responsibilities. It is typically difficult for an

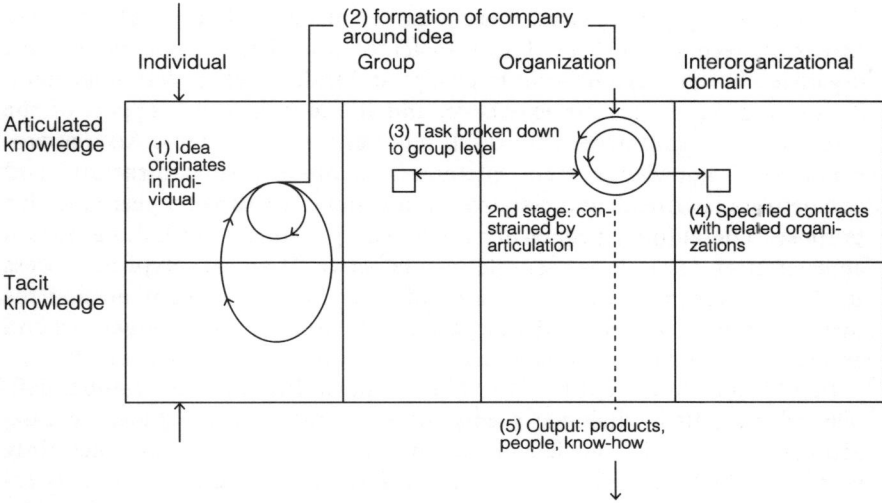

Figure 5.3   Archetypical model of Western knowledge-creation processes

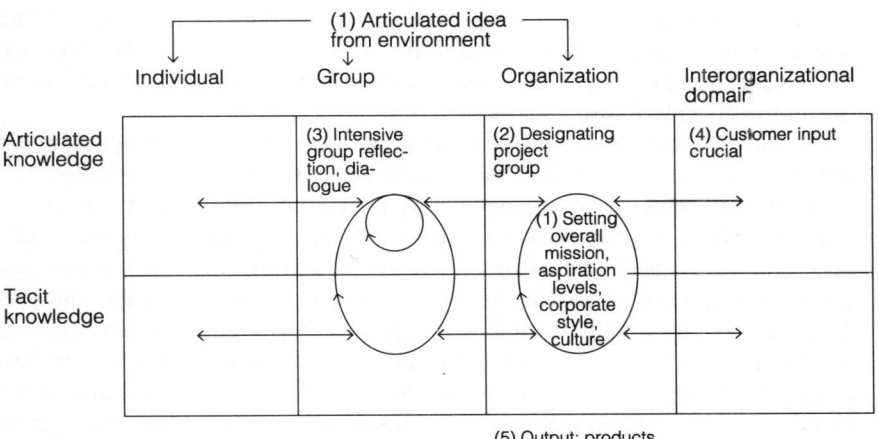

Figure 5.4   Archetypical model of Japanese knowledge-creation processes

existing organization to learn new skills. 'Not invented here', and 'not my table' continue to be problems even when clearly recognized as such and when alternatives are encouraged.

In the large Japanese firm, there is rather primacy of appropriation over extension (see figure 5.4). The transfer of knowledge from, or at least organized by, the organization to groups and individuals is very important. Training programmes are extensive, and life-long learning is part of the career of most employees who reach more elevated positions. Also, appropriation of knowledge from customers, suppliers, subcontractors, and competitors is critical, and resources and systems are directly geared to this purpose. The cultural propensity for listening, rather than talking, makes appropriation (as well as assimilation) effective. If an archetypical process in the Western model is for an individual to form a company around his idea, a Japanese one is for the large company to assign individuals around an idea generated through listening to the environment of the company.

In addition to the 'left-to-right' bias of the W-firm and the 'right-to-left' bias of the J-firm, dialogue seems more intensive in the Japanese case. Mutual sharing of knowledge, possibly with competitors but certainly within the 'own' sphere, is pronounced. Discussion and interaction is extensive as well as intensive, and cross-functional contacts are encouraged by design as well as through the effects of practices such as long careers and rotation within the same firm and the upholding of university ties. The same mechanisms that allow for supra-individual reflection pave the way for dialogue, also for dialogue about ideas outside the immediate work assignment and about non-work matters. Western companies tend to 'instrumentalize' dialogue more. The principle of organization design is to limit the need for mutual co-ordination through dialogue as much as possible, as is obvious from theories in economics and management from Adam Smith over Simon (1976), Galbraith (1973) and onwards. Vertical communication within one's own unit is given priority over lateral communication with other units.[11]

Dialogue is thus the interaction between extension and appropriation, as reflection is the interaction of tacit and articulate forms of knowledge. The quantity and quality of dialogue and reflection largely determines the effectiveness of the organization's knowledge management. It is no coincidence that most pedagogical practices revolve around these two processes: dialogue in the classroom (in theory, in practice rather monologue) and reflection over the textbooks at home (again in theory, in practice more of rote learning and memorization). Teacher geniuses have always known how to inspire dialogue and force the student to reflection by mobilizing his earlier experiences, shocking him, introducing interesting metaphors bridging tacit and articulate content, etc. (See Nonaka, 1989, for a discussion of the important role of metaphors in knowledge creation.)

Assimilation is when knowledge is 'imported' from the extra-organizational environment. Input from related organizations is treated as appropriation. The taxonomy here is a matter of taste and convenience. We prefer to retain appropriation for everything 'within' the model, and assimilation for processes outside the 2 × 4 matrix. Analogous reasoning leads us to include information sent to subcontractors etc. in 'extension' rather than in 'dissemination'.

Dissemination is when knowledge reaches the wider environment from the organization. The result is the output of the organization, which can take the form of statements (such as patents), action (starting manufacturing) or tangible products.

The W- and J-firms, and the Western and Japanese contexts as totalities, differ substantially in terms of assimilation and dissemination. First, the non-firm environment is very important for assimilation in the West. Universities and, to some extent, the political and military systems are primary initiators of novelty, in addition to the corporations. In a way, firms are mainly instruments of exploiting knowledge originating elsewhere – in the brains of geniuses or in research establishments. It is noteworthy that theories of the MNC, for example, start by *assuming* some kind of 'advantage', which is then exploited through 'internalization'. The organization is not primary, and not endowed with the potential for creating. The epistemology of 'organization' (instrument, tool) admirably reflects the implementing, Western conceptions of the institution (cf. Morgan 1986). In Japan, the large firm dominates the knowledge creation landscape, and corporations are seen as much more than instruments.

Second, assimilation of knowledge to a large extent takes place through the selective recruitment of individuals. In rare cases, whole teams (groups) of people are bought over. The firm searches for *specific* talent, and it is assumed that young engineers, for example, have some information useful to the organization. Even more so is this the case for more senior personnel. The Western firm habitually recruits experienced managers from the outside. If a new strategy is to be tried, the board often recruits a new CEO, who is known to stand for such a strategy. There is a market for complex packages of articulated and tacit knowledge (strategic 'recipes') embodied in single, high level executives. The exodus of a talented individual, or sometimes a team of individuals, to form a new firm is also an important mechanism of dissemination. In Japan, the corporation would exploit such opportunities itself. Critical employees rarely leave to form their own company.

Third, the neutral, impersonal view of organizational knowledge in the West also results in assimilation through mergers and acquisitions. Buying another firm is a prime mode of assimilation, and of dissemination. The closeness and continuity necessary for real dialogue often makes this strategy problematical. At best, simple summation of competence is achieved, but more rarely are genuine synergies created or tapped. The result may be very complex information processing rather than knowledge creation. It is well known that acquisitions are rare in Japan.

Fourth, the Western firm is more flexible in terms of form of dissemination. Knowledge is transferred to the environment in all forms: through products and services, in which knowledge is embodied, through personal mobility, by selling cognitive knowledge in licenses, patents, etc., and by selling education services, helping the customer to acquire a certain skill. The talent for articulation, personal mobility, and the propensity for teaching rather than learning (extension rather than appropriation), makes this richness possible.

In contrast, the Japanese firms specialize in embodied dissemination, the output of products (services), rather than in selling licences or transferring know-how through direct investment (or acquisitions). They prefer tight control, through personnel transfer, of foreign units. In our view, one reason for this may be the tacitness of knowledge and management in the Japanese firm. Products are means to package knowledge and make it easily transferable. A fully integrated foreign unit can be managed somewhat organically through personnel flows. Conversely, licences as well as acquired foreign companies require much more articulation.

Fifth, the Japanese firm simply seems to invest more in assimilation, and take a more systematic approach to it. Organizational and group level activities are consciously launched in order to tap the environment for knowledge, and further distribution within the organization is methodically attended to. The Western firm loses much information, since it stays with single individuals and is not seen as requiring conscious management. In Japan, the most straightforward way has been simply to buy patents and licences. Japan's modern development has, to a very large extent, built on effective use of imported technology, as well as of organizational patterns (Westney, 1987). The critical point is that this technology was available, at a low price, to anybody. However, most countries could not benefit from this opportunity. Knowledge has also been assimilated as embodied in products and later copied and improved. There is a tremendous history in this field. An example is the amazing ease with which Japan in the late sixteenth century outpaced Europe in both the quality and quantity of production of firearms, (see Perrin, 1979).

Expansion is the final knowledge process, and the one involving most of the 'value added' and change of knowledge. This refers to knowledge transformation within a cell in the model, such as when a group, through trial and error and discussion, learns how to design its own work process for optimal results. Or, when a lone inventor improves an original idea. Expansion mostly takes place at the tacit and articulate levels simultaneously, and requires interaction with other agency levels. We have indicated this through the two-directional arrows connecting the expansion process vertically and horizontally.

Expansion is, in a way, the final goal of all the other processes, or at least the most ambitious one. Enlarging the discussion somewhat to the character of knowledge creation as a whole, we see an often-noted difference between the two types of firms and systems. In our view, the difference can at least partly be attributed to the underlying logic of the knowledge management models in the two cases.

The Western system typically engages in knowledge creation in large steps, through crisis and external shock. Large organizations do not renew themselves unless seriously challenged to do so. Innovation comes in large, discrete steps, whether it concerns products or internal structure and systems. One reason for this may be the robustness and inflexibility of tightly articulated systems of knowledge and strategies. A Western firm finds it difficult to be inconsistent; that is, to undertake activities not fitting the prevailing notions of what the company is about. In the extreme, the whole company is a systemic plan, where nothing can be changed without upsetting everything else. One solution resorted to is to set up entirely new units, free from the encumbrances of the established structures. (Cf. the literature on innovation in large firms, entrepreneurship, etc., for example Burgelman and Sayles, 1986.) In addition, big deviations from the status quo follow from acquisitions.

Another, related, reason for inertia is that change cannot be initiated at the middle and low level. The subdepartments of the firm are tools for implementing a policy given from the top. Mission statements are generally so vague that they do not indicate any directions for lower level rejuvenation at all, but only financial targets. Alternatively, they constrain developments to rather narrow, prespecified fields, so that departments and groups become processors rather than creators of knowledge.

The Japanese world is not one of giant steps of new innovations. Rather, it is one of a myriad of smaller improvements and incremental development of knowledge. This has to do with the permanence of the staff and the intensive dialogue in the firm. The relative lack of renovation through the birth of new firms leads to a certain kind of conservatism and inertia, different from the one in the West. However, there is also a pronounced willingness to experiment with new combinations of knowledge. The Japanese firm is not tied to supposedly 'consistent' behaviour, but easily introduces elements which to a similar Western firm would seem alien. The relaxed attitude to articulation and systematization may explain this attitude. Reliance on tacit rather than explicit syntax leads to developments which would appear counter-intuitive to a more 'rational' mind. Knowledge is classified, in tacit syntax, more according to context and opportunities, and to perceived role models and perhaps overarching visions (cf. pages 9–11), than according to, for example, science categories, hardware types or professional specializations. The immediate market and competition is of course an important driver of categorization, and it seems that Japanese firms listen very attentively, quickly, and flexibly to customers.[12] Their products combine anything with anything else, as long as there is a market for the combination. This experimental, 'mutational' character justifies characterizing the Japanese model as one of knowledge creation (Nonaka, 1990), its marginalism notwithstanding. Another property of Japanese syntax, in this case of the articulated kind, is the proclivity for working with *lists* of seemingly only vaguely-related items. Agendas for meetings, verbal presentations and research reports display a relaxed attitude to the virtues of architectonically structuring information in hierarchies of classes of different levels of generality. Thus, combination is less constrained, as is also the case when items are clearly articulated (cf. Maruyama, 1978).

Contrasting the Models

It is interesting to note that the gigantic Japanese assimilation of new technology since the Meiji restoration has been undertaken by people in the firms (or government) themselves learning the new technology, not by importing individuals or acquiring companies. This is important in that, probably, this makes it very difficult to assimilate tacit knowledge. This often comes most effectively stored in individuals or work teams, and by definition cannot be put into a patent. Thus, and perhaps a bit paradoxically, the Japanese model builds on articulated input, but on a strong ingredient of tacit organizational throughput. The Western model is almost the opposite: tacit knowledge is imported through high-level recruiting and acquisitions, but throughput processes are highly articulated. Dissemination follows a similar logic (cf. pages 19–20). In summary, the Japanese model is one of importing articulated knowledge, transforming it through largely tacit processes, and again exporting something articulated. The process thus can be summarized as:

$$AK \rightarrow TK \rightarrow AK.$$

The Western case, analogously, is rather to import complex packages of tacit and articulated knowledge, transform it through as articulated means as possible, and export in forms less restricted than in the Japanese case:

$$AK + TK \rightarrow AK \rightarrow AK + TK.$$

In both cases, the middle category represents what goes on in the firm. The boundaries of the Japanese corporation are set largely through the demands for communication of tacit knowledge. This also affects many of the organizational practices. In the Western model other aspects take precedence. It is interesting to note the efforts of Western economists and sociologists to formulate a theory of the firm building heavily on problems of moral hazard and incentive compatibility. (For example, Williamson, 1975.) For the case of MNCs, a number of authors contribute similar models (Buckley and Casson, 1976; Dunning, 1977; Hennart, 1982; Teece, 1977; and Rugman, 1980.) Generally, the fundamental unit of analysis is a given transaction. Aoki (1990) discusses the shortcomings of such models in understanding the Japanese firm, and argues for paying more attention to questions of information processing and decision making. We suggest that our framework is one way of moving in this direction.

We can summarize the core properties of the models in two archetypical processes. Here, we have to emphasize that we speak of two very different things: the birth and early growth of a new corporation on the one hand, and the generation of new knowledge in a large existing firm on the other. The former is depicted in a Western context, the latter in a Japanese. This does not mean that aspects of the new venture firm do not exist at all in Japan, or that Western large corporations may not work as Japanese ones.

In terms of our original model (see figures 5.1 and 5.2), the Western model starts at the left, knowledge moves to the right (from individual to organizational) and upwards (increasing articulation). When an idea has been duly exploited, the firm and its founders have significant difficulty in finding new things to do. They may even leave and form a new company. Often, the firm changes its nature altogether, by being sold or merging with other firms. In a way, the instrument finds itself in lack of a purpose, and becomes a less dynamic force in the economy, living on old advantages and established positions.

The Japanese models starts more to the right (the organization) and on top (assimilation of knowledge from the outside), moves to the left but with much dialogue in the process, and uses both the lower (tacit) and upper (articulate) routes of communication. Note that in this model there is no clear end to the process, since new initiatives start new cycles. This is more likely than in the Western model, since no single individual is indispensable as the source of new ideas.

A particular aspect of the two models is the role of top management. The intensive dialogue inherent in the Japanese model takes place primarily at the middle levels in the organization. The central figure is the 'kacho', or section head. Nothing important happens without active involvement and support at the kacho level. Horizontal interaction between these 'middle managers', often organized in cross-functional projects, is a key ingredient in the Japanese model (see Nonaka, 1988b).

Still, the role of top management entails more involvement in knowledge management than in the West. Four functions seem to be important:

securing the necessary investments in long-term development; formulating challenging visions and aspiration levels; managing the knowledge infrastructure of the company (communication structure, recruitment, rotation, assigning project teams, etc.); and, monitoring progress of projects and contributions by individual employees (Nonaka, 1988a). These functions are also performed by top management in the Western firm. The Japanese peculiarity is in the serious and systematic fashion in which they are carried out, and in the intensity of involvement at the very top of the corporation.

In the West, the catalytic role in knowledge creation is largely unfilled by top management. Its possible role in initiating processes of dialogue, reflection, dissemination and assimilation is not stressed in the West. Rather, the top deals with resource allocation for and between given projects. Somehow, the 'knowledge engineering' is nobody's responsibility or primary interest. Objectives are stated in financial or compititive terms, rather than as encompassing visions with implications for the direction of knowledge creation. Organizational forms are debated mainly from the point of view of optimal structures for information processing, not creation. This means an intensive interest in the design of the optimal corporate hierarchy – by product, by geography, by customer, etc. 'Informal systems' and temporary teams are seen more as oil in the machinery, than as primary parts.[13]

What does the Model Contribute?

We claim that many aspects of reality as documented in the best available empirical research fit our model. For example, tacitness, a trait not discussed in depth in this context heretofore, seems well documented as a Japanese phenomenon. (Brevity of contracts, the importance of tacit social codes, the strong corporate cultures, etc.) Similarly, there is support for the posited differences between the West and Japan with regard to assimilation, the balance between extension and appropriation (teaching versus learning), and the role of top management as a catalyst of knowledge management.

A stronger case for the usefulness of the model is in the identification of organizational and societal requirements for different knowledge transformation processes. For example, if – as we argue – genuine knowledge creation usually requires reflection (i.e., interaction between articulated and tacit knowledge), for an organization to be creative will require processes of *organizational* reflection. Characteristics such as after-hours drinking sessions as well as personnel rotation schemes can be (re)interpreted as such processes, and a partly new explanation for the relative aptitude for rapid innovation in large firms in Japan is arrived at.

We have not pursued the important task of clearly specifying hypotheses of organizational requirements for given processes, but the examples provided hopefully illustrate the usefulness of our scheme for this purpose. It is worth noticing that the model explicitly includes both firm level and society level factors. This is an advantage, since there indeed seem to be very strong societal determinants of the direction of innovation and competitiveness, beyond firm- or industry-specific factors. (See also Porter, 1990, although his analysis is very different from ours.)

Perhaps the strongest support for a new model in the social sciences is if it explains phenomena which previously have not been convincingly explained, or explains them in a new way. ('Explained' here has to be taken in a rather loose sense.) We will confine ourselves mainly to the Japanese case in suggesting how our model throws light on previously ill-understood matters.

Strengths and Weaknesses of Japanese Industry

It is curious how important *pre-existing critical components* are in many showcases of Japanese industry. As we have argued, import of knowledge requires articulated information in Japan. When a patent can be bought this is the case. When the patent results in a clear family of tangible products to use as components, it is even more so. The Japanese success is pronounced in fields building on the transistor, on integrated circuits and on automobile components. As with *output*, we have argued for the embodied, *product* form of output in Japan, which fits empirical reality, and is not convincingly explained in other traditions.

In relation to this, the Japanese are weak in fields where *throughput can be totally articulated*. The basic chemicals and pharmaceuticals field is one such example even if here there certainly are other strong, seemingly paradoxical situations. The strength in complex electronic and mechanical production, with its requirements for mutual co-ordination between employees, is a counter-example. The ideal Japanese industry, according to our model, should be one with *readily-existing and articulated input (components and technology elements), but entailing, a throughput process with strong tacit elements, and requiring much intra- and interorganizational dialogue*. In our view, this prediction seems to fit the real world well.

Much of this implies success in relatively *'mature' technological fields*, or at least fields where results have 'materialized' into components, formulae, etc. The other side of the coin is difficulty in working with knowledge when there is still much interpretation and prototyping to accomplish, and where furthermore *different inputs and outputs are not easily combinative*. The electronics and computer industries, as well as mechanical engineering, are special in the sense that they generate whole systems of combination possibilities. Chemistry or biology is different in this regard, requiring more of new synthesis (and, in our terms, reflection) for every new product. Genetical engineering may change this, making biology and biochemistry more like electronics with large combinative possibilities.

We have related the product orientation of Japan to a bias for embodied, easily transferable output. Fields where sales of products have to be complemented with training, complex service and other non-standardized ingredients are weaker in Japan. Of course, we cannot infer too much from indices of the *volume* of international business here, since such fields tend to be more national everywhere, anyway. However, *relative* competitiveness should be affected as hypothesized. (Unfortunately, trade and investment statistics do not structure data so that the hypothesis can be tested easily. The general impression seems to support our view.)

We have earlier alluded to the *recontextualization of parts*, i.e., putting old parts into new contexts or products, in Japan. This is consistent with an experimental, non-deductive syntax, associated with tacit information processing. Combining slalom skis with tape recorders did not come naturally to Rossignol or Tandberg, but it did to Yamaha. The curious combination of inertia in generating new fundamental components and vigour in combining and recombining existing parts provides, in our view, interesting support for our concepts. The Japanese are able to import the part without buying the whole, instead reinterpreting the function of the part in another totality.

Another interesting fact, and somewhat of an anomaly in other explanations of Japanese strengths, is the difficulty in *integration of very large systems*. For example, in telecommunications the Japanese suppliers have, so far, not made much progress in the West. According to the Western competitors, an important reason is weakness in complex systems design. In computers, software production is also lagging. In spite of a gigantic local market, of leadership in autos and engine technology, and of significant efforts, Japan has not yet given birth to a significant passenger aircraft industry. This weakness in complex systems management is hard to explain in traditional frameworks of analysis. A 'Porterian' view would probably identify the existence of well developed 'diamonds' in all these fields. Likewise, those arguing that the Japanese simply take existing things, improve them and put them in new systems would rather assume that, for example, telecommunications systems design should be a strength of Japan. Furthermore, the defenders of strong customer orientation as a key determinant of Japanese success would say that these fields are exactly those where an ear close to the market is particularly crucial.

In our interpretation, a reason for the weakness in this area is instead that the reliance on internal dialogue, largely at the tacit level, is less effective when very complex tasks have to be co-ordinated. Articulation, systematization, written information and impersonal control become necessary, although not sufficient. The Japanese model of throughput is simply too time-consuming in these fields.

Finally, our analysis may throw some light on the mysteries of *Japanese diversification*. Again, we observe a mixture of apparent contradictions. The relationship inherent in Nippon Steel's venture into electronics and the steel business probably eludes most analysts. Japanese firms are willing to stray relatively far from home, and learn about foreign territories. The stark, articulated scientific syntax of specialized fields and institutions specialized accordingly is not adhered to in a more tacit syntax. Furthermore, tacit syntax is intrinsically *contextually unique*, relative to the firm and its scheme of interpretation. Therefore, we observe varying and idiosyncratic development plans. (But also, as we have noted in connection with the discussion of tacit syntax, liable to fashion.) We do *not* typically observe diversification in the conglomerate style, where the point of the move is to reach territory isolated from the home ground. Japanese diversification, we would argue, is typically related, but 'relation' is defined generously, in a company-specific, experimental, tacit framework (cf. the notion of 'corporate coherence' in Dosi *et al.*, 1990.)

Organizing for Knowledge Creation

Concerning implications for the management of knowledge, we want to suggest that the difficulties of the large Western firm in generating novelty have to do with overemphasizing the instrumental, articulating, exploiting nature of the corporation. The firm loses much of its potential for knowledge creation through the elaboration of complex managerial hierarchies and technical formalism with attendant systems, standardization and, ultimately, loss of overriding purpose. Hedlund (1986, 1991) has suggested *heterarchy* as a fundamental organizing principle for strategies of creation and experimentation, whereas *hierarchy* fits the demands of strategies of exploitation. (See also Hedlund and Rolander, 1990). It is interesting that many properties of heterarchy figure also in Aoki's (1990) description of the 'J-mode' as opposed to the 'H-mode' (Japan versus hierarchy): horizontal rather than vertical co-ordination, distributed storage and utilization of information, decoupling of (hierarchical) incentive schemes from (horizontal) operational schemes, long-term employment and internal promotion, rotation of personnel, informal rather than formal co-ordination, employees' involvement in the situation of the company as a whole and residual claimant status for employees. Dore's (1987) 'community model' of the firm entails similar properties.

The fact that analysis of Western multinational corporations on the one hand, and of the Japanese firm on the other – by authors from quite different backgrounds – lead to similar conceptions suggests that the underlying issues are more general than to do with peculiarities of national culture or organizational history. We hope that our discussion has shown that the interaction between knowledge management processes and the design of organizational systems holds promise both for understanding differences between companies and nations and, ultimately, for suggesting improvements in the practice of innovation and knowledge utilization.

Notes

1   The authors wish to thank Bala Chakravarthy, Yves Doz, Peter Hagström, Bruce Kogut, Jonas Ridderstråle, Johan Roos, and Udo Zander for constructive comments.
Financial support from the Japan Foundation is gratefully acknowledged.
2   Embodied knowledge is a more problematical matter. Rather than treating it as a third form of knowledge, we could regard the various types of embodiment as indicating a separate dimension. Thus, knowledge could be said to be embodied in individuals, in written instructions, in patents, in organizational routines, in production equipment, in computer programs, in final products, etc. (cf. Starbuck, 1984). Here, we want to restrict the meaning to intermediate products/services in the organization and embodiment in the offering to the market and imports to the organization from the environment, capturing other forms of embodiment in other concepts. (For example, our category of articulated individual knowledge is equivalent to knowledge embodied in explicitly communicable form in an individual.) The reason is that knowledge transfer between the organization and its environment relies to such a large extent, although not exclusively and probably to a diminishing extent, on product and relatively standardized service flows.

Perhaps it is best to think of the forms of knowledge as aspects rather than distinct types. Manufacturing of precision machinery can be looked upon from the point of view of cognitive knowledge as well as in terms of practical skills and the results in the form of products. The three aspects imply each other, and the distinctions are not sharp. For example, the manipulation of cognitive knowledge is a skill, and whether we see this as part of the stock of cognitive knowledge or, more dynamically, as a skill, albeit cognitive, depends on the specific problem at hand.

3   It is interesting to note that the three main forms of penetration of foreign markets – 'exports, licensing, and foreign production build on embodiment, articulated cognition, and skills, respectively. Zander (1991) attempts to link characteristics of a given technology, for example its tacitness, to mode and speed of international transfer, and to imitation by competitors.

4   Already in the dictionary, problems appear. The OED regrets that 'the chronology of the senses in English does not agree with the logical order'. The

original sense of 'inform' was to 'give form to', i.e., closer to our notion of knowledge. 'Information' has one sense of 'knowledge communicated concerning some particular fact, subject, or event ...', which is closer to our more atomistic interpretation.

5 It is important to realize that tacitness and structuring are independent dimensions, although tacit knowledge seems to be less structured, and is thus rather of an information character. However, 'packages' of information constitute complexly-structured tacit skills, such as playing a piano or delivering a rousing speech on the corporate culture. Likewise, articulated information is not always very structured, but could consist of single, meaningless bits of data.

6 However, it is not obvious that precise theoretical articulation is less conservative than empirical, 'listlike' articulation. Bloch (1961, Ch. VIII) makes that point the 'customary law' of the kind dominating Anglo-Saxon jurisprudence was *dynamic*, change-prone, since any practice, to be legalized, only had to be common enough. In systems like Roman law, the power of the letter is strong in practice, although it may seem easy just to change it.

7 Obviously, the distinction cannot hinge completely on the implied, parallel distinction between atomistic analysis and holistic synthesis. For example, Gödel's proof is arrived at by manipulation of algebraic axioms and logical rules according to given laws, but it still qualifies as knowledge creation. Some 'new' syntheses are so simple that they could be named information processing rather than creation, even if they involve jumps between sets of meaning. (For example, starting to use financial accounting information in order to build a database of customer information.)

8 It is also tempting to relate these characteristics to the emphasis on the limits of naming and explicitness in some philosophies and religions that have influenced the Orient, and Japan in particular. Taoism and Zen buddhism in particular emphasize such matters, whereas the word and written text are more important in Biblical religions, including Islam. The Japanese model is one of importing articulated knowledge, transforming it through largely tacit processes, and again exporting something articulated.

9 The comparison here is rather between large firms in the West and Japan. Small, young companies, wherever located, are more prone to tacit, organic ways of working. For many of the comparisons below, similar provisos apply.

10 Tacitness goes together with unreflective practice, imitation, and lack of interpretive speculation. Also the Western propensity for constitutional reform, of governments as well as of companies, is related to the emphasis on articulation. Treatises such as Hobbes', Rosseau's, Locke's, de Tocqueville's and Marx's on the nature of society are unknown in most other cultures. So is the systematic questioning of established practices in organizations. Whether more inductive (British empiricism) or more deductive (continental Cartesianism), the Western cognitive style relies heavily on articulation. Hierarchical classification and cause-effect thinking results either way, although more rigorously in the latter tradition.

11 Cf. the very interesting suggestion by Aoki (1990) that his 'J-firm' (not exactly the same as ours) is characterized by *lateral information* processing and *hierarchi-*

cal incentive administration. The 'H-firm' (hierarchical, Western) is the other way around: hierarchical information and lateral (market) incentive mechanisms.

12   A consequence of the propensity for rapid, opportunistic improvement is a certain susceptibility to fashion. Rather than analysing a supposed trend, a Japanese firm assumes there may be something in it and follows by developing products enthusiastically. This neophilia, love of new things, is a characteristic of Japan as a whole. Foreign firms find that they always have to present their newest products, and that it is very important not to seem to be behind the competitors, even if the function of the product is not affected.

13   One way of expressing the bias is in terms of the primacy of programmes of *exploitation* of given resources and knowledge over programmes of *experimentation and creation* of new resources and new knowledge. The distinction is further explored in Hedlund and Rolander (1990), in which the issue of the level at which innovation takes place is also raised. Experimentation at the local or individual level may in each case seem irrational, as when an ant deviates from the scent track left by successful foragers for food sources. However, the system's wisdom is optimized by a certain proportion of ants ignoring the reinforcement cycle of more ants – more scent – more ants, and now and then finding new sources of food. (Example from lecture by Ilya Prigogine and his collaborators. See also Prigogine, 1976.)

The example clearly illustrates that learning and knowledge expansion need not be conscious. However, the design of a system for an optimal balance between exploitation and experimentation requires conscious effort, unless an organization wants to accept the slow process of evolution and natural selection, which will probably leave it dead by the wayside. This catalytic, design-for-learning, function requires quite a different role from top management than the one of the maker of big strategic decisions about the product portfolio, financial risk, etc.

References

Aoki, M., 1990: Toward an economic model of the Japanese firm, *Journal of Economic Literature*, Vol. XXVIII, March, pp. 1–27

Arrow, K., 1974: *The Limits of Organization*. New York: W. W. Norton.

Bloch, M., 1961 *Feudal Society*.

Boisot, M. and Child, J., 1988: The Iron Law of Fiefs: Bureaucratic Failure and the Problem of Governance in the Chinese Economic Reforms, *Administrative Science Quarterly*, 33, pp. 507–27.

Buckley, P. J., and Casson, M. C., 1976: *The Future of the Multinational Enterprise*. London: Macmillan.

Burgelman, R. A. and Sayles, L. R., 1986: *Inside Corporate Innovation: Strategy, Stucture and Managerial Skills*. New York: Free Press.

Dore, R., 1987: *Taking Japan Seriously: a Confucian perspective on leading economic issues*. London: The Athlone Press.

Dosi, G., Teece, D. J., and Winter, S., 1990: Toward a Theory of Corporate Coherence: Preliminary remarks. Unpublished working paper, March.

Doz, Y., Prahalad, C. K., and Hamel, G., 1990: Control, change, and flexibility: the dilemma of transnational collaboration. In Bartlett, C. A., Doz, Y., and Hedlund, G. (eds). 1990: *Managing the Global Firm*. London and New York: Routledge.

Dunning, J. H., 1977: Trade, location of economic activity and the multinational enterprise: A search for an eclectic approach. In Ohlin, B., Hesselborn, P. O., and Wijkman P. M., (eds), *The International Allocation of Economic Activity*. London: Macmillan, pp. 395–418.

Freeman, C., 1984: *Technological Policy and Economic Performance*.

Galbraith, J. R., 1973: *Designing Complex Organizations*. Reading, Mass: Addison-Wesley.

Hedlund, G., 1991: Assumptions of hierarchy and heterarchy: an application to the multinational corporation, in Ghoshal, S. and Westney, E. (eds.), *Organization Theory and the Multinational Corporation*. London: Macmillan, forthcoming.

Hedlund, G., 1986: The hypermodern MNC–a heterarchy?, *Human Resource Management*, No. 25, pp. 9–25.

Hedlund, G. and Rolander, D., 1991: Action in heterarchies: new approaches to managing the MNC, In Bartlett, C. A., Doz, Y. and Hedlund G. (eds.), *Managing the Global Firm*. London and New York: Routledge.

Hennart, J. F., 1982: *A Theory of Multinational Enterprise*. Ann Arbor, MI: University of Michigan Press.

Hippel. E. von, 1976: The dominant role of users in the scientific instrument innovation process, *Research Policy*, Vol. 5, No 3, pp. 212–39.

Kagono, T., Nonaka, I., Sakakibara, K., and Okumura, A., 1985: *Strategic and evolutionary management: a US-Japan comparison of strategy and organization*. Amsterdam: Elsevier Science Publishers.

Kogut, B. and Zander, U., 1991: Knowledge of the firm and the replication of technology. Forthcoming in *Organization Science*.

March, J. G., 1991: Exploitation and exploration in organizational learning, *Organization Science*. Vol. 2, No 1, February, pp. 71–87.

Maruyama, M., 1978: The epistemological revolution. *Futures*. June, pp. 240–2.

Mead, G. H., 1934: *Mind, Self and Society*. Chicago: Univerisity of Chicago Press.

Morgan, G., 1986: *Images of Organization*. Beverly Hills, Ca: Sage.

Needham, J., 1954: *Science and Civilization in China*. Vol, I, Cambridge: Cambridge University Press.

Nelson, R. R., and Winter S. G., 1982: *An evolutionary Theory of Economic Change*. Cambridge, Ma: Harvard University Press.

Nonaka, I., 1987: Managing the firm as an information creation process, Working paper, Institute of Business Research, Hitotsubashi University. Appears in Meindle *et al.* (eds) *Advances in Information Processing in Organizations*, Vol. 4, Connecticut: JAI Press.

Nonaka, I., 1988a: Creating organizational order out of chaos: Self-renewal in Japanese Firms, *California Management Reveiw* (spring).

Nonaka I., 1988b: Toward middle-up-down management: Accelerating information creation, *Sloan Management Review*, (spring).

Nonaka, I., 1989: Organizing innovation as a knowledge-creation process: A suggested paradigm for self-renewing organizations, working paper no. OBIR 41, Walter. A. Haas School of Business, University of California at Berkeley.

Nonaka, I., 1990: *Management of Knowledge Creation: A theory of organizational knowledge creation*. Tokyo: Nippon Keizai Shimbunsha (in Japanese).

Orr, J., 1990: *Talking about Machines: an ethnography of a modern job*. Ph.D. thesis, Cornell University.

Pavitt, K. L. R., 1980: *Technical Innovation and British Economic Performance*. London: Macmillan.

Perrin, N., 1979: *Giving up the Gun: Japan's reversion to the Sword, 1543–1879*. Boulder, Colorado: Shambala Publications.

Polanyi, M., 1969: Knowing and being. London: Routledge and Kegan Paul.

Porter, M. E., 1990: *The Competitive Advantage of Nations*. London and Basingstoke: Macmillan.

Prigogine, I., 1976: Order through fluctuation: self-organization and social system. In Jantsch, E. and Waddington, C. H. (eds.) *Evolution and Consciousness*. Reading, Mass: Addison-Wesley.

Rugman, A. M., 1980: Internalization as a general theory of foreign direct investment: A reappraisal of the literature. *Weltwirtschaftliches Archiv*, VR 116, pp. 365–79.

Seely Brown, J., and Duguid, P., 1991: Organizational learning and communites of practice: toward a unified view of working, learning and innovation, *Organization Science*, Vol. 2, No 1, February, pp. 40–57.

Simon, H. A., 1976: *Administrative Behaviour* (3rd ed). New York: Macmillan.

Starbuck, W. H., 1984: Organizations as action generators. *American Sociological Review*, 48, 91–102.

Stiglitz, J. E., 1987: Learning to learn, localized learning and technological progress. In Dasgupta, P. and Stoneman, P. (ed), *Economic Policy and Technological Performance*. Cambridge: Cambridge University Press.

Stubbart, C. I., 1989: Managerial cognition: a missing link in strategic management research, *Journal of Management Studies*, 26:4, July, pp. 325–47.

Takeuchi, H. and Nonaka, I., 1986: The new product development process. *Harvard Business Review*, February 1986, pp. 137–146.

Teece, D., 1977: Technical transfer by multinational firms: The resource cost of international technological transfer, *Economic Journal* (June), 87, pp. 242–61.

Weick, K. E., 1991: The nontraditional quality of organizational learning. *Organization Science*, Vol 2, No. 1, February.

Westney, D. E., 1987: *Imitation and Innovation: The Transfer of Western Organizational Patterns to Meiji Japan*. Cambridge, Mass: Harvard University Press.

Williamson, O. E., 1975: *Markets and Hierarchies: Analysis and antitrust implications*. New York: Free Press.

Wolfe, A., 1991: Mind, self, society, and computer: Artificial intelligence and the sociology of mind. *American Journal of Sociology*, Vol. 96, No. 5, March, pp. 1073–96.

Zander, U. 1991: *Exploring a Technological Edge – Voluntary and Involuntary Dissemination of Technology*. Stockholm: Stockholm School of Economics.

6

The Formation of Emergent Markets

STRATEGIC INVESTIGATIONS IN THE SOFTWARE INDUSTRY

Michael Levenhagen, Joseph F. Porac and Howard Thomas

Introduction

Recently, an interest in growth and change issues has emerged in management literature along a number of different fronts. Research has examined such issues as strategic change, the management of new-business growth, the strategic management of technology, the management of innovation, entrepreneurship, corporate imagination, and newly de-regulated markets. A common thread which runs throughout this recent writing is the topic of how firms can successfully participate in growth markets.

The nature of markets and the bases for competition are changing rapidly and fundamentally. Prescriptions offered by early strategy theories may no longer apply as they once did. Past strategic thinking arose through functional orientations, to issues of diversification, and to issues of 'strategic management'. Underlying most of these models of strategy were strong assumptions about the nature of markets and, thus, the bases for competition. These models assumed stable economic growth, geographically constrained capital markets and information, mass markets, and rather constrained competitive domains. They also honoured the values of cost, growth, and control. Strategy literature might have been best summed up as a set of prescriptions about how to recognize and properly respond to changes in external environments. These prescriptions were useful because markets and competition changed slowly, and the information-processing demands of managers did not grossly violate the assumptions of rationality.

Current strategic thinking implies that many assumptions no longer seem to hold. Economic growth seems more limited; capital is more fluid; information may be over-abundant; mass markets are fragmenting;

new technologies tear asunder old bases of competition almost overnight; product-life cycles have shortened radically; and competitive domains have become more fluid – and changing at remarkably quick rates. Today, quality, innovation, speed, and service have become more important bases of competition (Stalk and Hout, 1990).

Assumptions underlying market definitions

Substantial market changes affect managers' competitive problem-formulation abilities in three ways. One, firms competing in rapidly changing markets must define increasingly uncertain or ambiguous environments – particularly, the bases of competition, the lists of participants, and the boundaries of competitive spaces. These are significant competitive-definition problems for firms (Abell, 1980). Two, firms must acquire or create new skill sets and assets (Prahalad and Hamel, 1990) to create economic advantage over competitors. Yet, the question is, which ones? Three, significant change (and, thus, growth) is stressful for managers, even more so for organizations. Yet significant change offers opportunity for creative conceptualization and energized engagement (McCaskey, 1982, 1988).

These competitive-definition problems are arguably never resolved until growth markets begin to stabilize. Then firms can objectively define them and make strategic-asset adjustments to them. (But by that time, 'the game' may be over.) Thus, common prescriptions provided by past strategy, entrepreneurship, and technology literature do not apply to participants' strategic tasks in emergent markets. Participants in emergent markets are unsure of their market structures, the breadth of their competitive domains, what skill sets or asset bases should be applied, or even what forms products or services should take.

Mature markets are knowledge domains with strong routines (Nelson and Winter, 1982) and consensual understandings and solutions (Schwenk and Thomas, 1983). Supply and demand are well defined (Porter, 1980), and the structures of markets are assumed known (Hofer and Schendel, 1978). Mature markets assimilate incremental change well (Quinn, 1980). They dampen disruptive events or errant beliefs due to firms' imitative tendencies and institutionalization effects (DiMaggio and Powell, 1983; Meyer and Rowan, 1977; Tolbert and Zucker, 1983). Economics and structure-conduct-performance paradigms (Hay and Morris, 1979) describe these competitive domains very well because bounded-rationality constraints are not violated.

Emergent or fast-changing markets are ill-defined domains. Market knowledge is particularly incomplete, ambiguous, or uncertain – thereby testing participants' bounded-rationality abilities (March and Simon, 1958; Schwenk, 1984). There is little consensus about where economic domains reside, what they contain (cf. Day, Schocker, and Srivastava, 1979), or where competitive or technological trajectories are likely to progress (Davidow, 1986). Efficiency prescriptions are unhelpful because transactions-cost calculations (Williamson, 1975) cannot be ascertained – indeed, they cannot be formulated. In emergent markets, technological development is inconsistent with the prescriptions of economic models because market choices do not always adopt 'the best' technological products (Arthur, 1989), sometimes even over the long run.

Most organizational literature is based upon structural-functionalist assumptions of status-quo regulation and objective epistemologies (Burrell and Morgan, 1979). But these assumptions are incongruent with a description of emergent markets. In emergent markets it may be more productive to assume a participant's viewpoint and an orientation to change. Further below, we make use of these new perspectives.

Questions about emergent-market developments

In emergent or fast-changing markets, three questions stand out. First, how do new market structures evolve? Few economists (Chandler, 1966) or population ecologists (Hannan and Freeman, 1989) have offered detailed explanations of how markets form in their early beginnings. Yet new market formations seem to have substantial economic impact (Chandler, 1990).

Second, what are the successful strategies associated with growth-market development? How is it that certain early players establish dominating positions before market knowledge and structure become well-defined? Do first-movers reap competitive advantages (Lieberman and Montgomery, 1988), or do second movers have the advantage (Baldwin and Childs, 1969; cf. Tang & Zannetos, forthcoming)? Some say (Barney, 1986) or imply (Lippman and Rumelt, 1982) that it is luck, while others argue for stochastic success (Hamel and Prahalad, 1991). Luck or chance seems to beg the theoretical question at hand. Intuitively, unique windows of opportunity lie open very early in emergent markets, perhaps especially so for firms which help to create them. An understanding of early market evolutions may provide deep insights into the conceptual linkages between strategy, entrepreneurship, and technology.

Third, how do firm-level activities link to group activities (McGee and Thomas, 1990) in the process of market formations? Answering this question requires investigations of competition over time (Seth and Thomas, 1990) through longitudinal investigations of many different participants because market infrastructures are enacted by other stakeholders than simply lists of competitors (Hannan and Freeman, 1977). Furthermore, too much recent research in strategy has exhibited a supply-side bias, as though customers and other stakeholders were inconsequential.

Research in an Emergent, Growth Industry: The Software Markets

A team of us have investigated the software markets through a series of studies in the US and UK. Software-development markets offer an almost ideal site to study competition in a dynamic and complex market as it emerges and develops in a process of stops, starts, and technological revolutions. Ambiguous and complex are probably the best words to describe the software industry for the last twenty years or so. The industry has had the markings of a fragmented market, an emergent market, and a growth market. Until just recently, numerous bottlenecks have blocked sophisticated, organizational innovations and market consolidations (Ashe, Jowett, McGee and Thomas, 1986).

Participant's reports in the software industry

Our first research study was exploratory but designed with clear theoretical motivations (Levenhagen and Thomas, 1992). Dissatisfied with the results of empirical research describing entrepreneurship (Wortman, 1987), we agreed with other studies which rejected profit-maximization objectives for start-ups (LaFuente and Salas, 1989; Dubini, 1989). Given our interests in vision, a pilot study of software entrepreneurs was undertaken. Thirteen software entrepreneurs (65 per cent of the population of local software entrepreneurs) were surveyed using unstructured interviewing techniques which focused on the motivations and events leading to their start-ups. Previous theories suggested that external group-identification processes (e.g., Aldrich, 1979; DiMaggio and Powell, 1983) would influence entrepreneurs to form organizations similar in scope and orientation to previous experiences. Instead, the findings contradicted traditional theory and structural-functionalist assumptions. The entrepreneurs relied upon internal and creative competitive conceptualizations in fast-changing markets.

The following themes were also noted: a fascination with core tasks (rejection of profit-maximization), little marketing or competitive analyses, high levels of personal networking, and fluid critical-asset transferability (personnel). The motivations for start-up contradicted external group-identification theories. References were often made to rejections of previous software employers and their competitive definitions. Here are what a few entrepreneurs had to say:

- 'There was not much else to do (but start up)'
- 'No one was "doing it right"'
- '(the previous employer) would not get involved in (a new field of software development)'
- 'It was dumb, they could've had all this (gesturing to the building and organization) for free'
- 'The decision (to start up) was made by default. I had no other choice.'

This first research emphasized the need for more research using participants' points of view. Secondly, it conjectured that emergent markets – for all their ambiguity and uncertainty – encouraged entrepreneurs to create novel businesses, products, and services. Competitive spaces were poorly defined, and the entrepreneurs believed they had no competition, that their offerings were unique. Given the high numbers of firms, the fluidity of personnel transfers, and the level of personal networking, it was surprising that the forces of identification and comparison did not have much impact upon their competitive definitions. There seemed to be an almost infinite number of competitive spaces open for exploitation. The presence of ambiguous competitive spaces may have cognitively encouraged entrepreneurial enactments.

This first research study had methodological faults which did not allow for strong theoretical understandings. A second research study was undertaken using semi-structured interview methodologies drawn from anthropology and using cognitive-science constructs (i.e., cognitive taxonomies – Porac, Thomas, and Baden-Fuller, 1989; Porac and Thomas, 1990; Porac, Thomas, and Emme, 1989). Cognitive taxonomies were elicited from a larger sample (twenty) of local software entrepreneurs as a means to establish how they conceptualized their competitive spaces and the boundaries to their markets and segments. Although many of the software entrepreneurs claimed to be operating within different market segments and niches, high-level industry categorizations (e.g., 'applications software', 'custom software', 'utilities software', 'mass-market software', 'graphical-user interfacing software', etc.) should have been shared cognitively among the software entrepreneurs. This was not the case. No 'composite map' could be generalized even at the superordinate levels. They did not agree to definitions or boundaries of broad industry segments, much less to specific niches.

Entrepreneurs had difficulties articulating the definitions of the software markets. They would reconceptualize competitive-space boundaries and categorizations midway through the interview in preference for new categorizations and boundaries: they would create new taxonomic maps. Or they would indicate multiple perspectives on the competitive space and confound hierarchical organization in preference for more multidimensional structuring of competitive spaces.

> There are many ways to categorize software firms in such a complex industry .... (T)here's no simple way. It's not difficult; it's just that you have to categorize them in various ways. (Software company chairman, seventy-five employees.)

There must have been cognitive conceptualizations acting as models for actions in the minds of entrepreneurs (De Geus, 1988). But, the articulation difficulties suggest that the competitive spaces were very complex or ambiguous. (Or, hierarchical taxonomic structures cannot model them – Grinyer, 1991). Bounded-rationality or articulation limits had been reached or surpassed. Yet competitive definitions and classifications were one of their paramount competitive issues. Entrepreneurs often noted technological standardizations and organizational exemplars as benchmarks in their explanations of what they were trying to achieve. They called the critical tasks leading to organizational success, 'legitimization', 'credibility,' or 'reputation'.

> (We are) trying to get some essentially lateral advertising for the product, because it adds to our credibility immensely when you have someone like a major instrumentation manufacturer featuring your software for their system. You know, we're ..., our name is not Lotus, our name is not Microsoft, and so you have a credibility problem .... And so you have to buy credibility .... And the only way to prove that a company exists in a year or two is, one, either be a company who's been around a long time, or to be linked to a company who's been around for a long time. (Software president, thirty-five employees.)

> (Concerning how to diversify) well, we're hoping to build a reputation for one. Certainly building experience, the ability to say when you go to some new vendor, 'see that product, that vendor, we put that together for them.' (Software president, seven employees.)

Entrepreneurial firms with new technological competitive definitions first sold their visions to other market stakeholders. Customers, suppliers, investors, the press, and others needed to recognize and socially legitimate firms' novel conceptualizations because they needed to distinguish them from the myriad of products, technologies, and firms in a complex and ambiguous set of competitive spaces (Aldrich, 1991). The entrepreneurs had to create new cognitive categorizations for market participants, or they had to fit within pre-existing cognitive categories. Legitimization, defined as shared categorization among market participants, was a key to a technological diffusion.

> I think that – what one has seen happening in the software industry ... is a tremendous tendency on the part of the trade press and the investment community and the industry analysts to kind of pigeon hole everything that happens into some fixed number of boxes .... What's tended to happen is that, in fact, there is a kind of self-fulfilling prophesy. As soon as these pigeon hole things start to exist ... people more and more want to make sure that their software is centrally addressing one of these definite pigeon holes that have been identified. (Software president, one hundred employees.)

These findings stand in contrast to Porac, Thomas, and Baden-Fuller's (1989) findings in the mature Scottish Knitwear industry (also in retailing – Porac, Thomas, and Emme, 1989). Whereas knitwear strategists were cognitively maintaining competitive definitions and boundaries (exhibiting a strong in-group/out-group bias), software strategists were establishing them. Software strategists were creating shared competitive-definition interpretations with other market stakeholders.

> You think software company, what do you need? You just need a PC and a lot of sweat equity. Well that's fine and dandy. You may have a product or a piece of software at the end of that period of time with relatively low investment. *But* to really market it, which is the key to the success in the software industry, you have tremendous marketing costs. (Software president, fifteen employees.)

The ability to established new competitive conceptualizations was accommodated primarily by rapid technological changes which undercut the basis of earlier competitive definitions. Yet, entrepreneurs were aware that the driver which constantly underlay market ambiguity and revolution also offered them competitive opportunities. It was something to be used to establish strategic advantages.

> The main way I want to keep my competitors off balance, as a sustainable differentiator, (is in) my industry it is important to be able to move, move, move, move, move. Mine is an attack industry. So I want to make sure I have got an ability to evolve my product – and we dance, and we dance, and we dance, and we dance. Every time my competitor looks around, I've just done something that just kinda blew him away. And he's gotta respond to it. (Software president, thirty-five employees.)

> The languages have improved so dramatically in the last three years, it is astounding what they will do now, compared to what they did. Unfortunately, the technology has progressed at a rate faster than the learning curve (of) the programmers. (Software president, eight employees.)

This second research was even more suggestive than the first. It suggested that software entrepreneurs engaged in particularly cognitive and social strategic tasks. However, the research had a decidedly supply-side bias to it. The question which arose was, what did the rest of the market pay attention to? What did advisers, customers, distributors, consultants, and expert industry observers think? Were entrepreneurs' interpretations shared with other members in the software value-chain system (cf. Porter, 1985)?

A third research study was undertaken. Varied market participants were interviewed using open-ended interviewing methods with a focus on their definition of 'key factors of success' in the software-development industry. Fifty market participants were interviewed at three locales (Silicon Valley, Chicago, and New York), and they confirmed the initial research findings. The interviewees further fleshed out pictures of competition in fast-changing and ambiguous technological environments. But, the pictures of the software industry were becoming extremely complex, so much so that we began to experience the same bounded-rationality problems we had theoretically ascribed to the participants. The industry seemed very unstructured.

The industry not only progresses rapidly; it is also extremely fluid. Firms change positions within value systems: suppliers become customers, customers become suppliers, and firms' lists of competitors depend upon which set of participants are considered. Diverse arrangements of relationships and networks are pervasive. The industry is deeply incestuous and personally connected more than it is organizationally connected. Participants expose themselves to the same media, but none believe these publications offer much more than promotional hype. Yet, they pay quite close attention to product/service evaluations to determine which way the technological developments are progressing. They believe that few market developments are technologically or competitively inexorable. They believe that 'when the market has made up its mind', then those cumulative market decisions would define the opportunities, trends, and standards. Such 'market decisions' would then indicate where their personal and organizational efforts should be focused.

Participants rarely conversed about specific product features, benefits, functions, or performance characteristics, nor compared products or services one-on-one with other products. Those characteristics seem unimportant. Expertise in the software industry seems more of a question of knowing what the other market participants are thinking and doing, and how they are faring. Successful firms are referent points of industry attractiveness and opportunity, and other firms are attracted to those competitive definitions and market spaces. Technological trends are only significant inasmuch as they reflect market trends.

Attention is next turned to a theoretical presentation suggested by these three research sudies and by another research project presently underway. Specifically, the data acquired thus far has begun to suggest how markets form. A full description of a developed market-formation model is not suggested here (cf. Levenhagen, Porac, and Thomas, 1990). Instead, two critical phases of the model are discussed.

Phases in the Formation of Markets

It is assumed that knowledge and environments change or progress somewhat along the lines of Dosi's (1982) conceptualizations of technological trajectories. Thus, in some sense, there are always gaps (or incongruities) in knowledge within all environments – be they cultural, technological, political, or economic environments. Gaps in knowledge developments provide entrepreneurial opportunities inasmuch as they limit or constrain other environmental developments. Gaps in knowledge are filled with uncertainty.

Phase I: novel entrepreneurial conceptualizations

Schumpeterian entrepreneurs initiate technological revolutions. Rather than following the main body of literature in entrepreneurship (Wortman, 1987), Schumpeterian theory (1934) implies entrepreneurs are cognitive agents who first perceive of uncertain (or poorly formulated) knowledge spaces (cf. Drucker, 1985). Entrepreneurs may predict a future direction for a technology stream, or they may imagine conceptual linkages (intersections) between independent technology streams.

> How do you rise above the din (chaos, ambiguity, technological design proliferation) in the market? What's special? What's distinctive – category creating? Today, you need new twists on things – something that's radically different. (Venture capitalist.)

Next, Schumpeterian entrepreneurs conceive of frame-making (and frame-breaking) ideas. They also conceive of new resource configurations (Dierickx and Cool, 1989; Penrose, 1959; Wernerfelt, 1984) to enact new, commercial ideas.

> Look for a segment to emerge; identify an explosion to occur; identify a product, get it to market, inform the customers and find the right distribution channel, with the right price, right people, promotion .... (Director of consulting firm; oversees accounts for 260+ high-technology firms.)

Frame-making ideas must be genuinely novel. Market-creating ideas must not be simple, incremental modifications based upon existing, competitive definitions found in pre-existing markets. In line with finance precepts, market-creating ideas must reduce (cognitive) uncertainty significantly and thus increase economic value. A good measurement of entrepreneurs' market-creating ideas is the extent to which entrepreneurial ideas can be expressed within existing languages. A market-creating, competitive defi-nition (a novel idea and its attendant resource configuration) must be dis-similar to other competitive definitions, otherwise existing languages would be able to articulate the entrepreneurial idea. Existing market participants might easily expand their conceptual boundaries or redirect their technological skills to subsume incremental innovations. Incremental ideas cannot create new cognitive domains, as they might soon be found incor-porated into prefigured, competitive definitions already enacted.

For example, the independent technological developments of audion tubes, binary theory, Jacquard punchcards, and symbolic logic were cognitively brought together (an intersection) to create the first conceptualization of a computer. The intersection gave rise to new terms and a language which articulated the four, independent knowledge streams. No previous language could adequately describe the concept of a computer. From this frame-making conceptualization, hardware- and software-knowledge streams developed and were later distinguished as new, independent knowledge streams. New, cognitive concepts developed, new sets of languages were articulated, and software became a distinct industry itself.

Phase II: concept championing: cognitive market infrastructures

It is not enough for Schumpeterian entrepreneurs to conceive of economic, value-creating insights. They must bring together markets of resource providers. The process is a multi-stepped cognitive activity which also involves feedback among market participants. First, market-creating entrepreneurs must flesh out their new concepts and languages clearly and consistently in order to articulate their market-creating ideas to themselves and to others (Levenhagen and Hill 1989). New languages will allow entrepreneurs to communicate the degree of their ideas' novelty and to dis-tinguish them significantly from other, existing languages and concepts – and, thus, other economic domains. (The frame-marking conceptualization and its language probably arise simultaneously, informing and changing one another iteratively.) Articulation of a frame-making concept and its language is no simple or brief task. A general understanding of research de-velopment makes clear that the process can be fraught with cognitive, social, and political difficulties (Kuhn, 1970).

What is oftentimes missing at this juncture of market development is the material establishment of the novel concept – viz., the new product or ser-vice. At times, there are no prototypes to evaluate because it may take resources to produce them. Or market-creating ideas may remain strictly conceptual and result in a market which remains almost strictly cognitive (e.g., theoretical, academic research). In either event, as there may be no products or services for the entrepreneurs to show and sell, the novel concepts themselves will have to be sold.

Market-creating entrepreneurs must, therefore, sell their visions to interested parties. Selling visions to potential stakeholders may require cycling back to the previous phase (concept creation). The novel concept must be made to appear important to potential stakeholders (a design problem). Great care must be taken in formulating frame-making ideas to ensure that they link to stakeholders' most critical mental models and viewpoints. The critical mental models of stakeholders are generally those most suffused with ambiguity and uncertainty. The functional purpose of frame-making ideas is that they increase stakeholders' economic value (Rappaport, 1986) by orders of magnitude (Tushman and Anderson, 1986).

> The key factor of success number one is: find a market where you change the functionality in how people do their jobs; it must make their lives dramatically easier. (Software securities analyst.)

For frame-making entrepreneurs, the critical resource to be acquired is organizational legitimacy. Although legitimacy can be assumed to arise from extensive or stable material transactions in well-established markets, legitimacy is also acquired through persuasive efforts aimed at creating consensus among potential stakeholders. A very strong consensus in the mental models of stakeholders constructs social realities (here, markets). It reduces novel ideas' uncertainty through increased understanding of market definition and reinforcement of those definitions through repeated, social behaviours based upon beliefs in the mental models. From cognitions come actions, which in turn reinforce or alter the cognitions – until equilibrium occurs.[1] Market-creating entrepreneurs must sell their visions to potential stakeholders who – by their vote of confidence in novel mental models – will in turn influence others. Once enough stakeholders are cognitively brought together to complete a potential value system, entrepreneurs can then begin to barter for goods and services to establish value systems and their own value chains materially. But first, entrepreneurs must create shared and positive understandings about their frame-making ideas. Shared mental models of new competitive definitions will bring markets together cognitively and provide cognitive bases for material transactions. Consensus of competitive definitions among potential stakeholders will provide cognitive infrastructures, upon which material infrastructures of new markets will be based.

Truly new ideas, and the products and services which embody them, are unknown quantities. Usually, they must be adopted by stakeholders to some extent for the stakeholders to understand their full value. At one extreme are products like software. The value of a software package cannot be fully known until it is used and learned. Its value increases with its use and learning up to some level where learning is exhausted (Arthur, 1989). Furthermore, switching costs are quite significant. (What would it take for the reader to change to a new word-processing system?) Buyers are generally cognizant of the fact they do not truly know what they are buying until after products are bought and used, and they purchase new software with care. Moreover, these buying decisions are exacerbated and constrained by bounded rationality (highly fragmented markets with thousands of different offerings), time, money, accurate information, and oftentimes the projected future of new products or services (technology streams). As a result, few buyers feel secure enough to buy a new product or service without inter-subjective signals from others that the product or service is legitimate (and thus worthy) in the eyes of others.

In high-technology markets, like software, buyers use a number of surrogate indicators to establish the worth of products and services – many of which are not transmitted directly through the value system of distributors, original-equipment manufacturers, value-added resellers, franchises, direct-sales forces, and the like. For example, the quantity of the venture-capital funding and the *quality* of venture-capital providers are often evaluated by buyers. The reviews of products in the trade magazines, what industry luminaries say about directions of technological developments, what key competitors have bought, capital resources available to new ventures, suppliers' market shares, how well packages or services (purportedly) tie to other packages or services (again, a kind of legitimization) are important indicators. As well, venture teams' perceived skill sets, ventures' strategies and marketing plans, ventures' competitive viability against competitors, and the ventures' alliances with key partners are all important non-value-system indicators stakeholders use to judge novel ideas' worth.

As a software company, you must lobby the biggies (to succeed in this business). (Software securities analyst.)

The evaluations of the products follow these points: (1) look at the company, look at the annual reports, financials, size. When they tend to be large, then you know if they're legitimate – e.g., Lotus, IBM, etc. You have to know if they're going to be around next year. Is their distributor network up and running? Do they have venture capital? Do they at least have a channel plan? (2) Look at their financial stability. (3) Do they have the size to support the product? (4) What about the servicing of stores? (5) Can they ship in quantities? (6) What is the likelihood that a new product will sell in volume? Will it create enough 'pull through?...' We do take a chance on 'hot' products, but only if they address certain categories. Do they address a new niche? They can't be 'me-too' products too much. Usually, our response (to the software company) is, 'no, not now – give it six months.' *It's a quest.*[2] (Product evaluator for a US software distributor.)

The more stakeholders who 'buy into' entrepreneurs' frame-making, mental models, the more legitimate and credible the mental models are in the eyes of other stakeholders. The more legitimate and credible visions are, the more they are likely to succeed economically.

Different stakeholders will commit and cognitively position themselves into rudimentary value-system patterns. They will draw together and establish a cognitive infrastructure to support a new value system when they think they recognize a new value-creating product *and when* they see that other stakeholders think so, too. In sum, cognitive conceptualizations and belief structures tend to precede material infrastructures (cf. Porter, 1980) in new markets. New-venture success is critically dependent upon inter-subjective signals of positive belief and confidence between different kinds of stakeholders.

Other research has noted similar observations, even though the studies have investigated intra-corporate innovation processes. Schon (1962) first noted that valid, technical ideas need active, internal sales efforts. No new idea could rely upon technical excellence alone. Successful product champions actively promote new ideas more through informal networks of personal contacts than through formal investment-evaluation processes. Indeed, networks of personal contacts were considered 'cherished resources' of the product champion by Schon. Bower (1970) reiterated Schon's finding by adding that truly new investment decisions can only become accepted through intermediate championing by division managers who filter new ideas from below and sell them to higher organizational levels (cf. Maidique and Zirger, 1985; Science Policy Research Unit, 1972). Kanter's (1982, 1983) and Burgelman's (1983, 1985) works further emphasized the importance of intermediate management (and resource) positions. In innovative organizations, intermediate-level managers husband innovative, autonomous behaviours in order to manage them within corporate strategic contexts, or they manage the strategic contexts in such a way as to accommodate autonomous behaviours. The process is one of a translation of conceptual meaning from one context to another, or one group to another (Bijker, Hughes, and Pinch, 1987).

Formal, profit-maximization calculations are impossible to perform when future variables, their relationships, and their market settings have yet to be created and established: the consensual frameworks of market structures and technologies are lacking. Relying upon strong, technological visions, software entrepreneurs focus their initial efforts within consensually ambiguous, cognitive environments with themselves as central characters – at the centres of new organizations, new markets, and new social structures. Without an ambiguous or uncertain environmental setting – as all emergent, technological competitive environments are – their visions and intense convictions would not find cognitive spaces open for creative, competitive definition and enactment. Novel competitive definitions and highly ill-structured market domains complement and accommodate one another. Indeed, it is questionable whether 'rational actors' with – microeconomic assumptions of perfect information, unlimited processing power, and well-defined decision tools – can figure their ways into novel, cognitive and competitive spaces by means of formalized, profit-maximization objectives alone (Levenhagen & Thomas, 1992).[3]

A by-product of Phase II processes is that the process of concept championing by the entrepreneur may give rise to cognitive, first-mover advantages. Research into competitive groups (McGee and Thomas, 1986; Porac, Thomas and Baden-Fuller, 1989) and category-identification processes (Mervis and Rosch, 1981; Rosch and Mervis, 1975) suggest that prototypes and exemplars are powerful framing devices used for comparisons of individuals' similarities and differences. Assuming that market-creating entrepreneurs properly choose the right areas of uncertainty and correctly formulate frame-making ideas so that they link centrally to potential stakeholders' existing mental models, then cognitive first-movers will force early stakeholders to compare all later entrants attributionally (Aldrich, 1979) to the first-movers – not only cognitively but also materially. New, potential competitors who consider entry must do likewise; they will consider the market exemplars and be forced – cognitively and socially – to position themselves against first-movers in product categories. (Indeed, the same can be said for many research environments: researchers focus on 'more legitimate' areas of stakeholder interest.) If cognitive first-movers properly conceptualize and position their ventures and offerings into the centre of stakeholders' cognitive spaces of uncertainty, then any later entrant will be cognitively disadvantaged in much the same way that competitors can be disadvantaged spatially (cf. Hotelling, 1929; Tang and Thomas, forthcoming). In addition, later entrants can also be materially disadvantaged. The height of the material and cognitive barriers to entry depends upon how quickly cognitive first-movers appropriate new competitive spaces.

Discussion

Much of the strategic analysis presented here has been based upon conjecture and exploratory discovery. It could hardly be any other way. The issues investigated are very large and encompassing. Moreover, a number of new approaches have been employed in the research studies reported here. All need to be tested rigorously and verified by other researchers. Yet the research studies seem fruitful, timely, important, and suggestive of some areas for further investigation.

Emergent-market formations are important topics for discussion. Their impacts are fundamental and far-reaching. Very few, if any, research studies have theoretically or empirically attempted to explicate them precisely because (we suspect) the competitive spaces are not neat. They are confusing, highly ill-structured, and ambiguous. Such competitive arenas will not submit to quick and easy research reports, especially at first – perhaps no early research in a new knowledge domain will. Researchers will have to invest large efforts in industry contextualization just to understand the languages and concepts market participants use.

The mental modelling of industry participants also looks very promising. But this too is a relatively new approach to the study of management issues (Stubbart, 1989). Mental modelling of managers' perceptions can provide the theoretical and empirical underpinnings of market transactions between members in markets, and aggregated transactions can provide the basis of market structures (Williamson, 1975). Industrial-organizational theories, systems theory, marketing, economics, organizational-behaviour theories, and strategy constructs in game theory, competitive rivalry, industry analysis, etc. can be linked at more fundamental levels of analysis through the use of managers' mental models by stipulating why firms trade with some firms rather than others. Socio-cognitive analyses can complement more materially-oriented analyses (e.g., product or service flows, inputs, outputs, cash, paperwork, etc.) and paint more complete pictures of dynamic markets, niches, and competition than are presently available. Moreover, socio-cognitive and materialist perspectives *together* can link managers' beliefs and behaviours to firms' beliefs and behaviours, and those of the firms to group dynamics and activities.

Both of these points suggest new ways of looking at markets. There are good reasons to believe that markets are socially constructed realities as much as they are also the results of matches between supply and demand schedules. As noted, the two perspectives inform one another. Most research in strategy has tended to be static and unidimensional, and it has tended to present strategy as an issue only of concern to competitors. These research studies here suggest otherwise for early market formations. That it could be similar for more mature markets beyond Scottish Knitwear or retailing should not strain the imagination. More research could adopt a purview beyond strict supply-side orientations.

Differing levels of consensus in markets are very likely to be important measurements of market evolution and structure. Yet, what constitutes a 'consensus'? For example, a current research study by the authors is empirically measuring competitive definitions of buyers and suppliers in a software segment. Preliminary analyses of the customers have shown there is no significant consensus concerning the attributes of products or market boundaries. If this conclusion continues with additional observations, then marketing's most basic assumptions cannot be easily supported: i.e., that customers know who suppliers are, suppliers know who customers are, and both agree upon the nature of products transacted between them. Again, the most basic of strategic questions (and the beginning of strategy formulation) lies in competitive definitions – the who, what, and where of competition. In more mature and stable markets, those questions are probably well-understood and agreed upon by market participants. Indeed, most of strategy literature has been devoted to mature-market activities. But today the focus and issues seem to be shifting to rather immature competitive domains found in emergent, growth, technological, and fast-changing markets.

To conclude, there is a need for an increased emphasis upon process studies in strategy – but in such a way as to include content issues. Bromiley (1981), Churchman (1979), Kotovsky & Simon (1990), Mason & Mitroff (1981), Mintzberg, Raisinghani and Theoret (1976), Senge (1990), and others have suggested that highly-defined (or assumed highly-defined) problem domains are really not very problematical after all. Highly-structured systems generally constrain behaviour to predictable outcomes. Markets, however, are social phenomena. As such, they are open to significant influence by human actors because they are the result of behaviours. This means that process sets content, just as contextuality can limit process. The most opportune times to set processes are in the initial stages of development (e.g., the 'new game' phase). Early firms can influence the constraints of competitive spaces by stipulating the rules of the game within newly staked territories. Given that participants recognize a new game as a good one, then the places, times, and rules can become established socio-cognitively. Moves made in an established competitive space, in turn, accede to those rules, times, and places. Hence, industrial-evolution processes are about learning, learning to learn, and unlearning. In the software industry, market participants learn about technological change, fluid competitive spaces, shifting lists of customers, suppliers, partners, and personnel. Perhaps what they are learning most is what each other thinks and believes. For what one believes enough, eventually happens. It is the process of setting a content, and the content of process. To speak of one without the other is rather meaningless and empty.

Notes

1   This interactive model assumes no discontinuous environmental changes, and it relies upon negative-feedback loops. Positive-feedback loops, on the other hand, can give rise to dynamically unstable or discontinuous system changes (cf. Arthur, 1989; Gleick, 1987).

2   It should be noted in this quote *no* mention is made of any functional product characteristic; all the criteria measure legitimacy. Moreover, the quote is quite suggestive of an 'appropriate' choice of categorization – perhaps an intermediate category (cf. Porac and Thomas, 1990).

3   Hayes & Abernathy (1980) have clearly shown that profit-maximization objectives such as ROI goals can result in corporate self-destructions through disinvestment – unless corporations have visions, missions, or purposes by which they relate themselves to their external constituencies and their competitive environments (cf. Campbell and Tawadey, 1990). There is no substitute for a competitive definition (Abell, 1980; Hamel and Prahalad, 1989; Prahalad and Hamel, 1990).

References

Abell, D. F. 1980: *Defining the Business: The starting point of strategic planning.* Englewood Cliffs, NJ: Prentice Hall.

Aldrich, H. E. 1979: *Organizations and Environments.* Englewood Cliffs, NJ: Prentice Hall.

Aldrich, H. E. 1991: Fools rush in? Conditions affecting entrepreneurial strategies in new organizational populations. Paper presented at the Conference on Entrepreneurship Theory, University of Illinois, Beckman Institute, October 18–19.

Arthur, B. 1989: Competing technologies, increasing returns, and lock-in by historical events. *Economic Journal*, 99, pp. 116–31.

Ashe, G., Jowett, P., McGee J. and Thomas H. 1986: The International Software Industry. Alvey Directorate, Department of Trade and Industry, London & London Business School, London.

Baldwin, W. L. and Childs, G. L. 1969: The fast second and rivalry in research and development. *Southern Economic Journal*, July, pp. 18–24.

Barney, J. B. 1986 Strategic factor markets: expectations, luck, and business strategy. *Management Science*, 32 (10), pp. 1231–41.

Bijker, W. E., Hughes T. P. and Pinch, T. 1987: *The Social Construction of Technological Systems.* Cambridge, MA: MIT Press.

Bower, J. L. 1970: *Managing the Resource Allocation Process.* Boston, MA: Harvard.

Bromiley, P. 1981: Task environments and budgetary decision making. *Academy of Management Review*, 6 (2), pp. 277–88.

Burgelman, R. A. 1985: Managing the new venture division: research findings and implications for strategic management, *Strategic Management Journal*, 6, pp. 39–54.

Burgelman, R. A. 1983: A process model of internal corporate venturing in the diversified major firm. *Administrative Science Quarterly*, pp. 223–44.

Burrell, G. and Morgan, G. 1979: *Sociological Paradigms and Organizational Analysis.* Portsmouth, NH: Heinemann.

Campbell, A. and Tawadey, K. 1990: *Missions and Business Philosophy.* Hailey Court, Jordan Hill, Oxford: Heinemann.

Chandler, A. D. 1990: The enduring logic of industrial success. *Harvard Business Review*, March–April, pp. 130–40.

Chandler, A. D. Jr 1966: *Strategy and Structure*, New York: Anchor Books.

Churchman, C. W. 1979: *The Systems Approach and Its Enemies*. New York, NY: Basic Books.

Davidow, W. H. 1986: *Marketing High Technology*, New York: Free Press.

Day, G. S. Shocker, A. D. and Srivastava, R. K. 1979: Customer-oriented approaches to identifying product markets. *Journal of Marketing*, 43, pp. 8–19.

De Geus, A. P. 1988: Planning as learning. *Harvard Business Review*, March–April, pp. 70–74.

Dierickx, I. and Cool, K. 1989: Asset stock accumulation and sustainability of competitive strategy. *Management Science*, 35 (12), pp. 1504–11.

DiMaggio, P. D. and Powell, W. W. 1983: The iron cage revisited: institutional isomorphism and collective rationality in organizational fields. *American Sociological Review*, 48, pp. 147–60.

Dubini, P. 1989: The influence of motivations and environment on business start-ups: some hints for public policies. *Journal of Business Venturing*, 4 (1), pp. 11–26.

Dosi, G. 1982: Technological paradigms and technological trajectories: A suggested interpretation of the determinants and directions of technical change. *Research Policy*, 11, pp. 147–62.

Drucker, P. F. 1985: *Innovation and Entrepreneurship*, New York: Harper Row.

Gleick, J. 1987: *Chaos*, New York: Viking.

Grinyer, P. H. 1991: A cognitive approach to facilitating group strategic decision taking: analysis to practice and a theoretical interpretation. Presented to the Strategy and Policy Group at the University of Illinois at Urbana-Champaign, Champaign, IL, October 30.

Hamel, G. and Prahalad, C. K. 1989: Strategic intent. *Harvard Business Review*, May–June, pp. 63–76.

Hamel, G. and Prahalad C. K. 1991: Corporate imaginaton and expeditionary marketing. *Harvard Business Review*, July–August, 1991, pp. 81–92.

Hannan, M. T. and Freeman, J. 1977: The population ecology of organizations. *American Journal of Sociology*, 82, pp. 929–64.

Hannan, M. T. and Freeman, J. 1989: *Organizational Ecology*. Cambridge: Harvard University Press.

Hay, D. A. and Morris, D. J. 1979: *Industrial Economics*. Oxford: Oxford University Press.

Hayes, R. H. and Abernathy, W. J. 1980: Managing our way to economic decline. *Harvard Business Review*, July–August, pp. 67–77.

Hofer, C. W. and Schendel, D. 1978: *Strategy Formulation: Analytical Concepts*. St Paul, MN: West Publishing Company.

Hotelling, H. 1929: Stability in competition. *Economic Journal*, 39, March, pp. 41–57.

Kanter, R. M. 1982: The middle manager as innovator. *Harvard Business Review*, July–August, pp. 95–105.

Kanter, R. M. 1983: *The Change Masters*, New York: Simon & Schuster.

Kotovsky, K. and Simon, H. A. 1990: What makes some problems really hard: explorations in the problem space of difficulty. *Cognitive Psychology*, 22, pp. 143–83.

Kuhn, T. S. 1970: *The Structure of Scientific Revolutions*, 2nd Ed. Chicago: University of Chicago Press.

LaFuente, A. and Salas, V. 1989: Types of entrepreneurs and firms: the case of new Spanish firms. *Strategic Management Journal*, 10 (1), pp. 17–30.

Levenhagen, M. and Hill, R. 1989: Metaphor and ambiguity: a cognitive approach to understanding the enactment of entrepreneurial activity. Paper Presented at The Annual Meeting of the Academy of Management, Washington, D. C., August.

Levenhagen, M. J., Porac, J. F., and Thomas, H. 1990: Emergent industry leadership and the selling of technological visions: a social constructionist view. Paper presented at the SMS Workshop on Leadership and Management of Strategic Change, Robinson College, Cambridge, England. December 12–14.

Levenhagen, M. and Thomas, H. 1992: Entrepreneurship, cognition and framing complex environments: Evidence from computer software start-ups. In H. Klandt (ed) *Recent Research in Entrepreneurship*. Aldershot, England: Avebury of Ashgate.

Lieberman, M. B. and Montgomery, D. B. 1988: First-mover advantages. *Strategic Management Journal*, 9 (Special Issue), pp. 41–58.

Lippman, S. A. and Rumelt, R. P. 1982: Uncertain inimitability: an analysis of interfirm differences in efficiency under competition. *Bell Journal of Economics*, 13, pp. 418–38.

McCaskey, M. B. 1988: The challenge of managing ambiguity and change. In L. R. Pondy, R. J. Boland, Jr. and H. Thomas (eds.), *Managing Ambiguity and Change*. London: John Wiley.

McCaskey, M. B. 1982: *The Executive Challenge*, Marshfield, MA: Pitman.

McGee, J. and Thomas H. 1986: Strategic groups: theory, research, and taxonomy. *Strategic Management Journal*, 7, pp. 141–160.

McGee, J. and Thomas, H. 1990: Strategic groups and intra-industry competition. In H. Glass (ed.), *Handbook in Business Strategy*. New York: Warren, Gorham, & Lamont.

Maidique, M. A. and Zirger, B. J. 1985: The new product learning cycle. *Research Policy*, 14 (6), pp. 299–313.

March, J. G. and Simon, H. A. 1958: *Organizations*, New York: Wiley.

Mason, R. O. and Mitroff, I. I. 1981: *Challenging Strategic Planning Assumptions*. New York: Wiley.

Mervis, C. B. and Rosch, E. 1981: Categorization of natural objects. *Annual Review of Psychology*, pp. 89–115.

Meyer, J. W. and Rowan, B. 1977: Institutionalized organizations: formal structure as myth and ceremony. *American Journal of Sociology*, 83, 340–63.

Mintzberg, H., Raisinghani, D. and Theoret, A. 1976: The structure of 'unstructured' decision processes. *Administrative Science Quarterly*, 21, pp. 246–75.

Nelson, R. R. and Winter, S. G. 1982: *An Evolutionary Theory of Economic Change*. Cambridge, MA: Belknap Press.

Penrose, E. 1959: *The Theory of the Growth of the Firm*, New York: Wiley.

Porac, J. F., Thomas, H. and Emme, B. 1989: Knowing the competition: the mental models of retailing strategists. In G. N. Johnson (ed.) *Business Strategy and Retailing*. New York: Wiley & Sons.

Porac, J. F. and Thomas, H. 1990: Taxonomic mental models in competitor definition. *Academy of Management Review*, 15 (2), pp. 224–40.

Porac, J. F., Thomas, H. and Baden-Fuller, C. 1989: Competitive groups as cognitive communities: the case of Scottish Knitwear Manufacturers. *Journal of Management Studies*, 26, 4, pp. 397–416.

Porter, M. E. 1980: *Competitive Strategy*, New York: Free Press.

Porter, M. E. 1985: *Competitive Advantage*, New York: Free Press.

Prahalad, C. K. and Hamel, G. 1990: The core competence of the corporation, *Harvard Business Review*, May–June, pp. 79–91.

Quinn, J. B. 1980: *Strategies for Change*, Homewood, IL: Irwin.

Rappaport, A. 1986: *Creating Shareholder Value*, New York: Free Press.

Rosch, E. and Mervis, C. B. 1975: Family resemblances: studies in the internal structures of categories. *Cognitive Psychology*, 7, pp. 573–603.

Schon, D. A. 1962: Champions for radical new inventions. *Harvard Business Review*, March–April, pp. 77–86.

Schumpeter, J. A. 1934: *The Theory of Economic Development*. Cambridge, MA: Harvard University Press.

Schwenk, C. and Thomas, H. 1983: Formulating the mess: the role of decision aids in problem formulation. *Omega*, 11 (3) pp. 239–52.

Schwenk, C. R. 1984: Cognitive simplification processes in strategic decision-making. *Strategic Management Journal*, 5, pp. 111–128.

Science Policy Research Unit. 1972: *Success & Failure in Industrial Innovation*. London: Centre for the Study of Industrial Innovation.

Senge, P. M. 1990: *The Fifth Discipline*, New York: Doubleday.

Seth, A. and Thomas, H. 1990: Theories of the firm: implications for strategy research. Paper Presented at The Conference for Theory and Theory Building in Strategy, University of Illinois, Urbana-Champaign, IL. April.

Stalk, G. Jr. and Hout, T. M. 1990: *Competing Against Time*, New York: The Free Press.

Stubbart, C. 1989: Managerial cognition: a missing link in strategic management research. *Journal of Management Studies*, 26 (4), pp. 325–47.

Tang, M. and Thomas, H. forthcoming: The concept of strategic groups: theoretical construct or analytical convenience. *Managerial and Decision Economics*.

Tang, M. and Zannetos, Z. forthcoming: Competition under continuous technological change. *Managerial & Decision Economics*.

Tolbert, P. and Zucker, L. G. 1983: Institutional sources of change in the formal structure of organizations. *Administrative Science Quarterly*, 28, pp. 22–39.

Tushman, M. L. and Anderson, P. 1986: Technological discontinuities and organizational environments. *Administrative Science Quarterly*, 31, pp. 439–65.

Wernerfelt, B. 1984: A resource-based view of the firm. *Strategic Management Journal*, 5, pp. 171–80.

Williamson, O. E. 1975: *Markets and Hierarchies*. New York: Free Press.

Wortman, M. S. 1987: Entrepreneurship: an integrating typology and evaluation of the empirical research in the field. *Journal of Management*, 13 (2), pp. 259–79.

7

The Dynamics of Cognitive Technological Maps

THE STRATEGIC PROCESS OF THINKING ABOUT INDETERMINATE FUTURE TECHNOLOGICAL OPTIONS WHICH ADAPT TO UNSPECIFIED MARKET DEMANDS.

Thomas Durand

Introduction

Technological innovations affecting competitive dynamics in industry have been studied extensively in strategic management literature over the last twenty years. Several models have been put forward to describe the pattern of industrial innovation. Cooper and Schendell (1976), Abernathy and Utterback (1978), Dosi (1982), Clark (1985), Abernathy and Clark (1985), Durand (1991) and many others have all addressed the same issues from different perspectives.

An interesting aspect of this literature, which in our opinion has been insufficiently developed, deals with cognitive representations of future technological options.

How can organizations draw cognitive maps about uncharted technological territory? How do they adapt their maps as they explore the new land, uncovering on the way new technological options and suboptions, reassessing old possibilities, reviewing the agenda in the search for new dominant technologies?

At some point in the history of the exploration of the western part of the North American continent, some Spaniard *conquistadores* landed on the coast of what was to become northern California.

We are told that they started their exploration carrying their boats with them on land all across northern California.

What led them to bear such a load?

They happened to have a map from Holland. Dutch cartographers of the period had drawn a major body of water east of this future northern California. No one knows where this inaccurate information came from. But as a result, the Spanish explorers had in mind that they would need their boats again further east, and dragged their heavy ships for miles and miles inland; as one might guess they found no such body of water.

Later, testimony of the survivors from the expedition certainly helped to modify inaccurate maps of the time.

Firms need cognitive strategic maps. As a matter of fact they do have maps, whether explicit or implicit. In the field of the management of technology, managers need and use technological maps. The format of the maps may be diverse: visual (i.e., graphical) or conceptual, well-structured or ill-organized, clearly defined or fuzzy and shadowy. They may not be aware of it but managers have, if not a complete view, at least some understanding of what technology could look like tomorrow. Sometimes they may even have a feel, a strategic technological vision, for how their firm should be headed.

We shall call this understanding a cognitive technological map (however poor and foggy it may be) and this vision a technological strategy or a route in the unexplored territory.

More often, they may simply let the firm go for a search process in the technological territory, suggesting no specific direction to follow. Clearly directed by a charismatic leader or a technology guru, or let loose due to an insufficient cognitive representation, the search process will in any case help improve and modify the cognitive technological map.

The main focus of the present paper is to discuss the process by which firms may draw, then modify and thus improve cognitive technological maps as they search unexplored technological territory.

However it should be stressed at this point that any representation of future technological options is at best an inadequate map of new territory to be explored. Indeed, one should not have a deterministic view of technology since past experience has often shown that technology usually unfolds in its own unexpected way.

It is thus by no means suggested that one may draw deterministic maps of technology. Instead we recognize the complex and unpredictable nature of technology and essentially suggest considering the various major technological options and suboptions that one would think plausible at the present time, keeping in mind that technology will end up finding its own peculiar ways.

This paper deals with the processing of technological and market information in organizations: how firms do/can assemble and integrate elementary pieces of information into a structured, organized format.

A simple model to view the way in which strategic information is processed may be presented as follows:

$$Data \rightarrow Information \rightarrow Knowledge \rightarrow Expertise$$
$$(a) \qquad\qquad (b) \qquad\qquad (c)$$

1 Data must be enacted by the firm before it may be regarded as information that pertains to the organization.
2 Elementary pieces of information need to be integrated, assembled in a meaningful, reasonable way to yield a framework – a comprehensive understanding of the jigsaw puzzle – what one may call knowledge.
3 Knowledge itself must somehow be transcended to lead to expertise. Knowledge is not enough to stand as a vision. Expertise is an articulated set of complementary, complex visions. These visions may partially conflict with each other but they result in a unique ability to comprehend a wide variety of problems.

In the sense of this model, cognitive technological maps have the status of knowledge. The paper thus addresses the process described as step (1) primarily and to a lesser extent as step (2), i.e. how technological information is processed by firms, how organizations do/can shape their understanding of future technologies.

Two different perspectives on cognitive technological maps may be adopted at this stage. The first one would assume that firms actually have cognitive technological maps, whether implicit or explicit, since they do have some understanding of what technology could look like tomorrow. The main process issues would then be to understand how firms actually 'draw' and modify these maps, i.e. how they shape their understanding of technological options.

A second perspective would postulate that most firms do not draw explicit technological maps, as they seldom organize and formalize technological information into structured, comprehensive frameworks. In turn, the main process issues would then be to analyse how could organizations draw cognitive maps about uncharted technological territories. We chose to adopt both perspectives in this paper: how firms do/can draw cognitive technological maps.

In order to discuss cognitive technological maps in context, the second section will address the issue of the dynamic interaction of technological options on the supply side with market concept specifications on the demand side, adopting an evolutionary perspective and relating this process –

which takes place at the industry level – to the mapping process within firms. The third section will then be devoted to an attempt to visualize cognitive technological maps in practice and to discuss the process of drawing maps. The fourth section will then explore some of the implications of the conceptual framework presented, raise some issues and formulate and discuss hypotheses. A brief conclusion drawing some implications for management ends the paper.

Technological Options and Market Concept Formation

An evolutionary perspective

As firms search among technological options, they interact with customers' demand on the market place. As Teubal, quoted by Clark (1985), puts it: 'Consumers learn about what they want or need and producers learn to innovate.'

Clark (1985) actually develops in detail the interactions between design options and market concepts. He builds upon Alexander (1964): 'Every design problem begins with an effort to achieve fitness between two entities: the form in question and its context.' He analyses the evolutionary pattern of technological innovation arguing that it is 'the result of two related processes: the first is the logic of problem-solving in design; the second is the formation of concepts that underlie customer choice'.

This in turn leads to the idea that when thinking about cognitive technological maps one should also deal with cognitive customer concept maps. Stated differently, market concept formation and technological choices obviously take place simultaneously through a dynamic interaction.

This dynamic interaction between technological options on the supply side and customer specifications on the demand side may be described as an evolutionary process taking place more or less as follows:

• Some generic functional need on a certain broad market was historically fulfilled by a certain technology, which became dominant. As this technology established itself as dominant, the market turned out to be progressively subdivided into submarkets with more specific functional needs through a segmentation process. This was a maturation process.
• Then, at some point, a new technological paradigm [Dosi (1982)] appears. A certain technological trajectory, or seam [Durand (1991)], is adopted to fulfill the needs of a given market segment associated with a specific customer concept representing a certain expression of the generic, functional need. This may be regarded as a dematuration process. Some firms, possibly new entrants including start-ups, decide to pursue this new technology.

- On that market segment, the new technology evolves, as it is improved and adapted through trial and error. A cumulative search mechanism thus operates to exploit the new seam. Followers enter the race for the new technology.
- The new technology is then adopted for other market segments. It thus spreads out over a larger part of the market, possibly extending it, while at the same time being adapted to specific functional needs on some of the market segments. Previous market leaders attempt to catch up in the race.
- In the meantime the market segmentation also evolves as the market borders vary and as customer concepts are being formed, refined and modified, thus looping back on the technological design choices. A new maturation process thus takes place.

This actually needs to be explored and discussed in more detail because it deals with the most fascinating – and poorly understood – aspect of technology. This is the issue of the key market mechanism that governs the search for a match between technological possibilities on the supply side and market concepts/customer needs on the demand side.

Selective device

Larue de Tournemine (1988) suggests that technological innovation takes place as a changing set of market needs faces a varying set of elementary technologies. These may be combined in many different and changing ways to yield new products and processes. Dosi is also working along the same lines. He suggests that 'economic forces operate as a selective device (the focusing device of Rosenberg, 1976)' in order to choose technological paths 'in a much bigger set of possible ones'. He views technology as 'a perception of a limited set of possible technological alternatives and of notional future developments'. He argues that the selective device draws upon multi-dimensional trade-offs among both technological and socio-economic variables. One may recognize in this description a segmentation process with buying criteria – and similar variables synthesizing the customer behaviour – together with the firms' technical searching process operating as the selective device among technological alternatives.

Irreversibilities

The question of the *relevance* of the choice that comes out of the selective device operating between technological possibilities and customer concepts is an interesting one. There is a recent body of literature on the economics of technical change that addresses this issue.

The nexus of this matter lies in empirical evidence showing that in several sectors it is often not the 'best' technology that becomes dominant. In other words the selective device fails to operate properly as an efficient filtering mechanism among technological options. The concept put forward to explain this phenomenon is called 'increasing rate of adoption', meaning that early accumulation of experience on a certain technological option may make it more competitive than other options at any time, while its technical and/or socio-economic potential is in fact very limited. For more on this idea of lock-in situation, and the underlying concept of irreversibility, see Foray (1989) or Cowan (1990).

In a thorough discussion of Williamson's transaction cost theory (1975) Gaffard (1990) actually suggests that the firm may be seen as an organization designed to:

1 Explore technological options through scanning on the market of technologies thus using a market transaction mode.
2 Adopt specific technological options and suboptions and then adapt them to serve certain market needs, thus using a hierarchical mode to focus on options, with, to a certain extent, irreversibility in the choices.
3 Enter alliances to become part of networks, thus making it possible to tap external sources of technologies in a third intermediary mode – neither purely market nor purely hierarchical.

The firm – as it explores technological options, adopts specific options and suboptions and enters alliances to tap external sources of technologies – will need some form of a technological map to organize the process. At the same time it is the very same process which will help the firm gain more understanding of what is technologically feasible and thus will permit the organization to draw and modify technological maps.

We recognize that cognitive technological maps are social constructs. However, we also argue that a map i.e., a framework, a knowledge – emerges as a result of various cumulative learning processes. These learning processes take place within the organization as the firm experiences in its own ways an evolutionary process occurring at the industry level. It is thus necessary to further discuss these learning mechanisms.

Cumulative learning mechanisms

After Goedert (1990), and building up on Arthur (1988) and Dosi (1988), we believe that four major forms of cumulative learning mechanisms appear to be at work behind our description of the dynamic interaction between technological options and customer specification:

• 'Learning by doing' within the hierarchies i.e., within the firms, Arrow (1962) or Atkinson and Stiglitz. (1969)

- 'Learning by using' for the customer, Rosenberg (1982)
- 'Learning by interacting' in the form of continuous feedback between the designers-producers and the users, von Hippel (1976) or Lundvall (1988)
- learning by searching as the firm conducts research and development and thus builds up its competence base and learns more about technological options and suboptions
- We would add to this list a fifth form of learning which was suggested to us by Jacques De Bandt – 'learning by unlearning' to stress that organizations need to remain capable of adapting to change by loosening up the rigidity formed by their past learning

All these forms of cumulative learning are important. The concept of irreversibility mentioned above is based upon the idea of self-reinforcement of early adoption of a particular technological option through cumulative learning. Although this stands as a rather unsatisfactory view, 'small unknown events' or chance (Arthur, 1983), are traditionally blamed in the literature for early choices. Note in passing that there seems to be quite a debate in the literature on the economics of technical change between Arthur's competing technologies model – increasing rate of adoption – and Dosi's evolutionist's view – technological paradigms and trajectories. Our own understanding is that these two models are not contradictory but rather complementary.

Setting aside this debate among economists and coming back to the main theme of this paper, we must recognize that the different forms of cumulative learning mentioned above, as well as the concept of irreversibility, are far-reaching. They are clearly related to our mapping issue and provide an interesting basis for our analysis.

The dynamic interaction between technological options and customer specification as it takes place over time was described above. It can now be characterized. The cumulative learning mechanisms mentioned above operate in sequence through a maturation/dematuration/maturation evolutionary process more or less as shown in figure 7.1.

In a certain market, maturation has led to a dominant technology with continuous improvements through the triple effect of learning by doing, using, and interacting. Over the years searching has thus become less important. Yet research still goes on. As a result, a new paradigm then appears, 'reopening the agenda' as Clark (1985) puts it; the search is unleashed with renewed vigour. A small unknown event, contingency, or any other more convincing cause leads to the adoption of a specific technological option within the new paradigm.

Learning by using and interacting starts operating again – a fluid stage of Abernathy and Utterback (1978) – as well as learning by doing, soon yielding increasing return and thus irreversibility. Submarkets, i.e. market

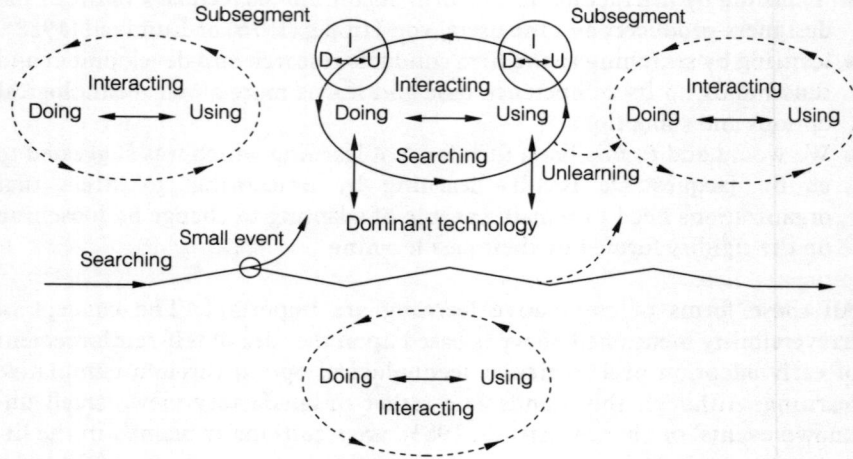

Figure 7.1   Cumulative learning mechanisms and technology dynamics

segments, progressively adopt some specific, adapted forms of the now emerging new dominant technology. The cumulative doing-using-interacting (D-U-I) learning is fully at work, operating as a self-reinforcing mechanism. In the meantime open searching still goes on but at slower pace. This lasts until dematuration strikes again.

This description of the evolutionary process that takes place on technology at the industry level can now be linked to technological mapping within the firms.

The evolutionary process perspective and cognitive maps

Cognitive mapping is obviously a social process within the organization. Informational filters communication channels, past experiences, structures of beliefs, internal politics and cultural values are all factors which play a major role in the process. Personal and organizational biases are fully at work. Cognitive maps are social constructs. The fourth section will discuss cognitive technological maps adopting this perspective.

However, we also argue that this social process takes place as the firm experiences in its own ways an evolutionary process occurring at the industry level in the form of the maturation/dematuration/maturation sequence discussed above. The social process is nurtured and strongly influenced by the technological evolutionary process.

Note, in passing, that we clearly recognized earlier that the technological dynamics at the industry level are also influenced in turn by decision making and other social processes taking place within firms, e.g. the early adoption of a technological option creating a new seam or trajectory.

Let us be more specific about how the social process of mapping rides the waves of the evolutionary process, i.e., how the process by which firms build and then adapt their cognitive technological maps is related to the technological dynamics described above.

In a dematuration phase, learning by searching is fully at work. The searching part, i.e. broadly research oriented, tends to organize the global structure of the map. At that stage the research agenda is wide open as firms are ready to envision many different options because they do not want to jump too soon onto a wrong horse. They thus concentrate on structuring the overall map without paying too much attention to detailed suboptions. It is a time of feasibility studies, gross cost versus performance assessments for the major options, intense and open-minded scanning of the technologically and economically possible. The mapping process is wide and open.

Conversely in a maturation phase, the D-U-I learning processes concentrate on a specific new trajectory to explore the new technological paradigm. The D-U-I learning processes thus help deepen the exploration, the understanding, hence the representation – i.e. the mapping – of these specific options and suboptions on which they are at work. Other options associated with other trajectories are increasingly ignored. Central research labs, which may be at this stage the only part of the organization still interested in other options, are increasingly regarded as insufficiently market-driven by the divisions focusing on the dominant technology.

Open technological scanning is no longer a priority. As more competitors tend to adopt the same technology, more resources are allocated on the same options and thus innovations tend to be focused.

As a result the enhanced understanding of these specific technological options under close scrutiny leads to considerable refinements of the maps. However, these refinements are focused on the specific zone of the technological territory currently being explored and exploited.

In other words the process by which a firm modifies its cognitive representation of potential future technologies heavily depends upon the stage in which the industry happens to be in exploring the set of technological options available at that time.

As an illustration of this idea, one should not expect firms in 'lock-in' situations to alter their overall map much as they essentially focus on the specific trajectory that they are following. They improve and reinforce their understanding of the options and suboptions they adopted and tend to pay much less attention to other options. It is too often left to other players in the industry – including public research centres or new entrants – to keep redrawing their cognitive technological maps, integrating new options and suboptions into the map and continuously reassessing all the options represented. Car manufacturers do not have technological maps for electric cars as precise as they have for standard four-wheel drive cars, with internal combustion engines.

Along these lines Henderson and Clark (1990) show how firms tend to be trapped in the rigidity of a given architecture for a product design, losing the ability to think of other options, i.e. not considering alternatives in the map and instead focusing on suboptions on which they currently work.

This section presented a rather abstract description of the dynamic interaction between indeterminate future technological options and unspecified market demands. This evolutionist perspective of technology dynamics in industry was adopted to help understand how a social process taking place in a firm is influenced by an overall maturation/dematuration process occurring at the industry level.

Before the fourth section which will analyse the various factors influencing the process of technological mapping in an organization, the next section aims at presenting some vizualized technological maps, suggesting some concrete tools and organizational procedures for explicit cognitive mapping.

Cognitive Technological Maps in Practice

We first turn to an attempt to give examples of visual representations of cognitive maps. In this section we thus look at cognitive maps as real visual maps, not just conceptual frameworks or knowledge about future options.

Examples of various mapping formats

Figures 7.2 and 7.3 each show a map for various existing and prospective technologies for heat exchangers. This representation includes four half-axis: (a) the maximum pressure that the equipment may bear; (b) the maximum temperature of the fluids/solids exchanging heat; (c) the number of functions which the equipment fulfills, namely heat exchange in any of the following six combinations liquid-liquid, liquid-gas, gas-gas, gas-solid, evaporation or condensation; and (d) the efficiency of the equipment measured in number of thermal transfer units (NTU). On this map a technology is shown as a rectangle.

The current dominant technology, i.e. tubular exchangers, turns out to withstand very high pressure and temperature conditions (800°C 90 bars) in five functions, i.e. in all of the six possible functions but one. Tubular technologies, however, have a rather low performance in terms of NTUs. In contrast, sealed plates technologies provide much more efficient heat

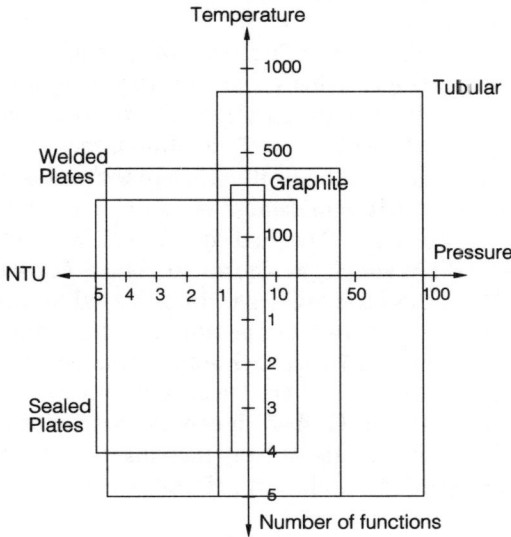

Figure 7.2   Heat exchangers existing technologies

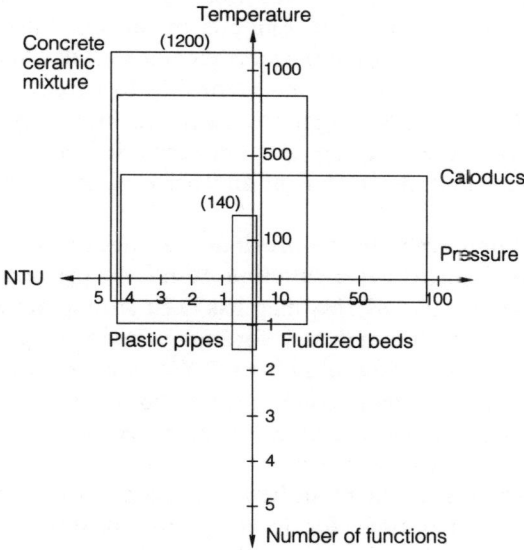

Figure 7.3   Heat exchangers emerging technologies

exchangers, but they can hold under only low pressure and temperature conditions in four of the six exchange situations. Other technologies are shown in a similar way.

Figure 7.2 shows a map of existing technologies while figure 7.3 shows emerging or prospective technologies, most being currently under development. We argue that these representations clearly illustrate the cognitive mapping concept. Technical as well as functional characteristics are combined to provide a map of the heat exchange technologies.

The format of this map was presented to us by an entrepreneur who had innovated in this business. He had developed a welded plates heat exchanger, a technology which, as shown in figure 7.3, has as much performance in NTUs as the sealed plates technology, while withstanding considerably higher pressures and temperatures. This innovator had thus fruitfully explored a new area in the technological territory.

His venture turned out to be very successful and he used his map as a sales communicating device. He had drawn the map himself as a result of his own cumulative learning about heat exchangers, incorporating various pieces of what he regarded as relevant information into a visualized framework.

Note here that our discussions with this innovator led him to accept that a fifth variable should somehow be included in the map, namely product prices: we suggested drawing a price axis vertically out of the plane shown on figures 7.2 and 7.3.

A second example stems from the electronics. Figure 7.4 shows a very common diagram in the field of computer memories. This diagram relates the unit cost of Dynamic random access memories (DRAMs) as it evolved – and is expected to evolve – in time according to successive technological generations, each corresponding to increasing memory capacities. Again we argue that this representation may be regarded as a cognitive map. This map format includes technical and price variables as well as a time dimension.

The major difference with the previous map lies in the diffusion and acceptation of the cognitive representation. While the heat exchanger map belonged to one man, this DRAMs map has been around among analysts and players in the electronic industry for many years. Both maps view the technological territory of their industry. Yet only the second one can be regarded as an industry map. Note that this does not mean that some may not use other maps to view the DRAMs future technological options with a different, complementary perspective.

A third map format is shown in figures 7.5 and 7.6. The maps aim to represent technological options for future public switching technologies in telecommunications. The function to be fulfilled is shown as the starting point of a branching tree. Two major seams or trajectories for future

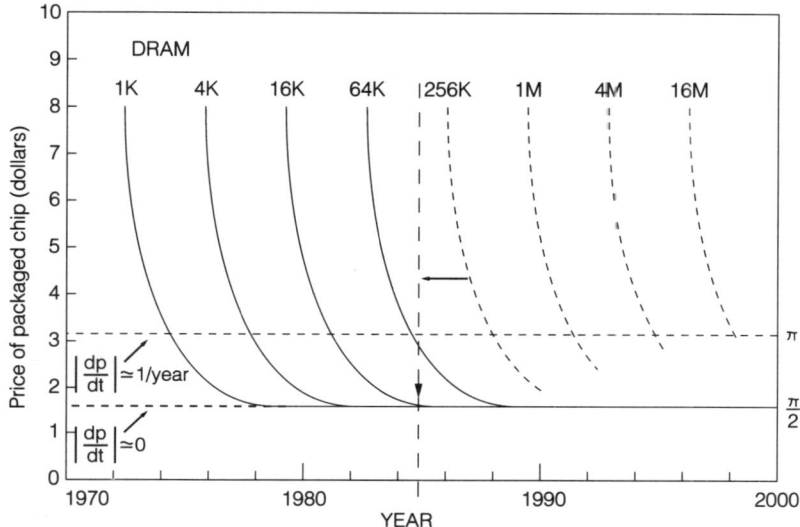

Figure 7.4   DRAM pricing trends – the π rule
M.P. Lepseller and S.M. Sze

switching are identified, digital wideband electronic or optical. Suboptions are shown as branches of a tree.

We drew these maps as part of an industry analysis of technological evolution in public switching. The mapping process was thus conducted by an analyst, an outsider to the industry, collecting and compiling data through review of industry material and interviews. It should be noted that iteration on the mapping was made possible through interaction with technology experts within manufacturing firms and the PTT operators.

After a 'one man-one firm' map (heat exchangers), and a widely accepted map in industry (DRAMs), this third example provides a cognitive technological map as it may be drawn by an industry outsider. All three formats of the maps presented above are clearly different but all illustrate the idea of cognitive technological mapping.

The next section aims at suggesting a specific format for the maps as well as a methodology i.e. a procedure for the mapping process.

Dual technology trees

Clark (1985) suggested that technological design options are in essence hierarchical, as are technological manufacturing processes. He further argued that market concept formation has a similar hierarchical nature.

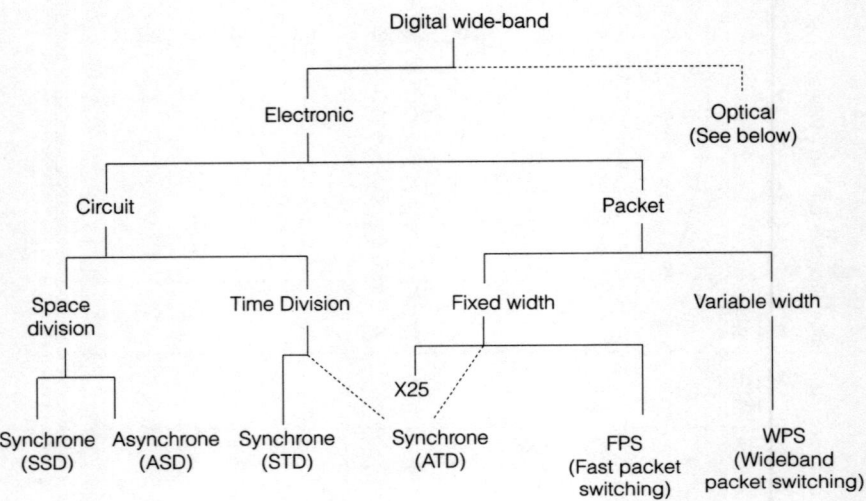

Figure 7.5   Technological tree for wideband switching

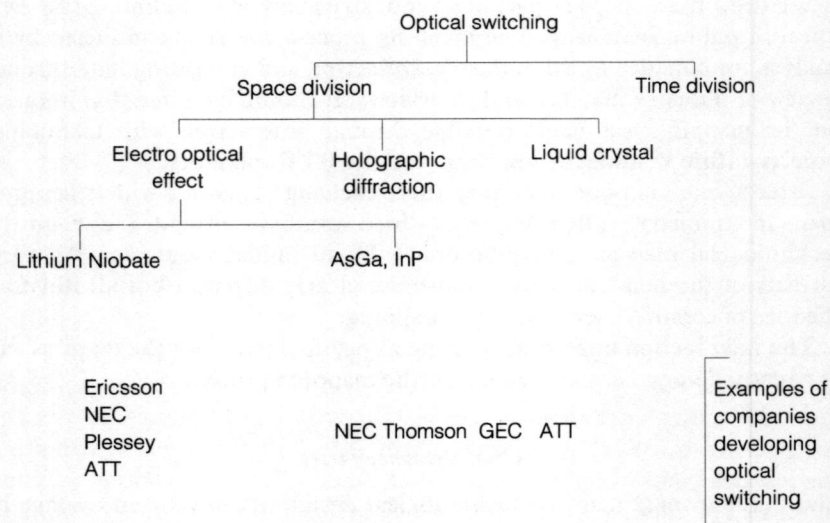

Figure 7.6   Technological tree for optical switching

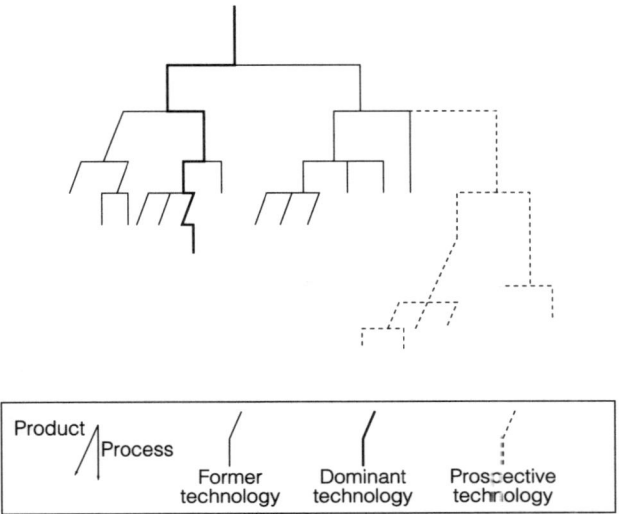

Figure 7.7   Dual technology tree (1)

We in turn suggested visualizing the technological design and process hierarchies by mapping them out as dual technological trees (DTTs). A DTT organizes technological choices in the product/process duality, as shown in figure 7.7. One technology is shown as a path in the tree from the top (the function to be satisfied on the marketplace) down to one branch at the bottom. Horizontal branches represent product designs while vertical branches show process technologies.

Starting from the function to be satisfied, the tree organizes the major technological choices that one would face when redesigning products from scratch to fulfill the particular market need and the processes to manufacture them. Former, existing (dominant or not) as well as prospective technologies must be considered. A former technology appears as a continuous line, the current, dominant technologies appear in **bold** while a prospective technology is shown as a dotted line.

We argue that while the set of technological options may be unlimited, i.e. with unknown boundaries, at least it is possible to grasp part of it by structuring the wide spectrum of the technically possible into potential seams and plausible trajectories, what Dosi calls 'some notional technical future'. The idea is to sort out and visualize the *current* understanding of how technological seams and trajectories might look like in the future, even though we should expect innovations to follow other, unanticipated paths.

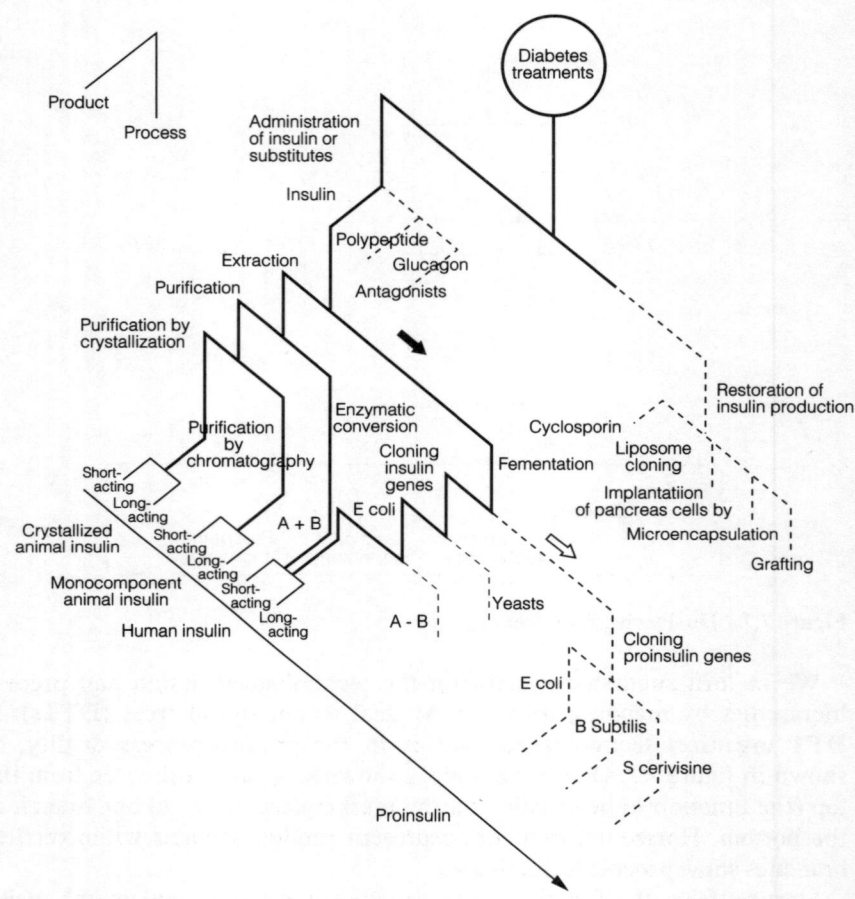

Figure 7.8   Dual technology tree (2)

Figure 7.8 presents a DTT for the case of insulin in pharmaceuticals. The tree is built according to the principle of 'technical competence relatedness': the closer the branches, the more common the competencies required and thus the smaller the change from one technology to the other.

This relates to Abernathy and Clark's (1985) concept of transilience: 'the significance of innovation for competition depends on its capacity to influence the firm's existing resources, skills and knowledge – what we shall call its transilience'.

Technological change thus appears as a jump from one branch to another. The jump may be small or large, meaning that the competence disruption will be small or large. The further and the more unrelated the branches are from one another, the more intense the change from one technology to the other since more competencies will have to be renewed. Branches are unrelated in the sense that one has to go back rather high in the tree to connect them together.

Closely linked branches low in the tree represent slightly different versions of the same technology and share most of the same competence requirements. Branches far from one another, with no close links, in most cases share little competence in common. The most basic design options are thus considered first, generating the earlier major branches in the upper part of the tree. The smaller variations around one particular technological design are presented at the bottom of the branches.

It should be stressed again at this point that future technologies are not known in advance as they will essentially result from the combination of a great number of technical variables, some of them being still unforeseen and unforeseeable.

It was thus by no means suggested above that one may adopt a deterministic view of technology. Instead we recognize the complex and unpredictable nature of technology and essentially suggest mapping the various major technological options and suboptions that one would think plausible at the present time, keeping in mind that technology will end up finding its own peculiar ways.

In some sense the DTT visualizes Clark's technological design and process hierarchies. A DTT may be regarded as a cognitive technological map summarizing the current vision which an organization or part of an organization has of future potential technological options.

Note that in drawing DTTs we actually had to build an upstream tree in some situations, to define and organize the customer functions to be satisfied around certain needs in order to focus on the construction of several DTTS, each of them for a clearly specified function.

This leads in turn to the idea of customer concept tree (CCT). We believe that a CCT should also be visualized. It should start from what DOSI calls 'some generic technological tasks or generic "needs"', i.e., an upstream function to be satisfied on the marketplace, e.g., the treatment of diabetes, switching or transportation.

It should then organize the different combinations of specific needs (characteristics, performance, price etc.) that may be expressed (explicitly or not) on what would thus appear as market segments at a certain time. In this sense, each market segment would then represent a specific customer concept.

However, it should be stressed again that any representation of future technological options is at best an inadequate map of new territory to be explored. Therefore any attempt to describe the dynamic interaction between what we suggest to be a dual technology tree and a customer concept tree is tantamount to charting and locating future settlements in new territory with a 'best guess' map.

Drawing and using a cognitive technological map within the firm

Whether an outsider to the firm or member of the organization, the intervention of any individual or group of individuals to draw some kind of a cognitive representation of technological or market future inevitably introduces some biases. Maps are social constructs.

The mapping process is an iterative, interactive one. It may build upon teamwork as well as upon material compiling and face-to-face interviews with internal specialists including Allen's gatekeepers (1977) and external experts. It starts with a conceptualization of the technologies which will fulfil future market needs. Structuring some understanding of future market segmentation, i.e. customer concept formation, is thus a key part of the process. This mapping process is not just a matter for researchers, engineers and technicians. Marketing help is required.

The iterative part appears when the first tentative maps are drawn; these may then be presented throughout the organization for discussion and suggestion. It should be recognized that the early version of the maps may in turn influence the internal experts and other members of the organization, limiting them within the format adopted for the maps. However, the experts may also expand the structure of the mapping by suggesting other possible modes of representation which they may feel more adequate. A good way to ensure that they do so is to provide them with many different formats right from the beginning so that they feel encouraged to play with the mapping format.

The process which we refer to in this section is that of consensus building, trying to integrate into the maps all pieces of information existing within the firm. The available relevant information may not always be reconciled into a single vision. The only way is then to accept contradicting maps coexisting until more information is available. In turn unreconcilable views about future technological options may help focus the searching process on sensitive matters; still it may be the objective of the mapping process to converge towards a widely accepted structure of the firm's currently available knowledge on future technologies.

In the case of the insulin map shown above as a DTT on figure 7.8, seventeen different versions were needed before reaching a wide acceptance among experts in the industry. Note that this iterative process among experts, in a way similar to some aspects of a Delphi technique, tends to promote a shared vision among interviewees. This means that the process, when conducted within one organization or part of an organization, may help bridge some informational gaps among parts of the organization. This will be discussed in the fourth section.

Key Mapping Issues

This section results from various discussions with Yves Doz. It deals with a number of questions about the conceptual framework and illustrations presented above. It also aims at formulating hypotheses yet to be tested empirically. It draws upon preliminary results stemming from a feasibility study conducted as part of an extensive empirical research project, intended to test the model presented as well as some of the issues discussed below. The feasibility study served as hypothesis building.

Many questions may be raised about cognitive maps: why and when should one expect maps to be fuzzy or well-defined, implicit or more explicit, comprehensive or partial, static or dynamic, singular or plural? Also, how and when do organizations modify, adapt and use their maps?

We suggest grouping these questions into three major sets of issues.

1 The format of the maps clearly raises a first set of difficult complex issues. Two preliminary comments should be made at this stage.

First, note that inasmuch as technological maps are rarely formalized in real life, from a methodological point of view it is not necessarily easy to find ways to extract from an organization – or part of an organization – an explicit representation of its vision(s) for future technological options and market demands. Some of the aspects of the discussion of the third section illustrated this difficulty.

Second, a clear distinction has to be made between:

- Technological options that are already developed and market specifications that are already fulfilled
- Technological options or market specifications that are perceived while not being already feasible or expressed.

Our interest lies primarily in the broader second category as we concentrate here on cognitive technological maps, i.e., the existing vision for future technologies and functionalities regardless of whether they are already developed.

It should be a fair hypothesis to expect that the map formats would vary greatly depending on a set of contextual and organizational factors. One would expect that the format would depend heavily upon the industry, the technologies and their rate of change. The second section of this paper discussed at length the influence of technological dynamics in the industry on the mapping process.

Clearly defined situations, e.g. DRAM technology in microelectronics, may be grasped through rather well defined cognitive maps. However, some fuzzy, uncertain situations may require a compass more than anything else. In such instances, the time required to properly analyse and explore the options as well as the paralysing ambiguity that may come out of systematic, cartesian analyses may not permit much *ex ante* strategic thinking and pondering. Action may count most. 'Caminante no hay camino, se hace el camino al andar' Antonio Machado. (When you walk there is no path, you make your path as you walk.) In such situations, it is not so much an accurate map that is required as a managerial process to search a way through unknown territory.

Eisenhardt (1989) describes a situation in microcomputer firms where some firms cope with the high velocity environment of the industry by making fast strategic decisions based on more information and developing more alternatives than do slow decision makers. These results would tend to indicate that dynamic mapping would in that context be more important than accurate mapping.

Yet another situation may be encountered. Some fluid, emerging industries turn out to be structured by those very companies that surf the fluidity of the technology/market interaction. The territory is wide open without major obstacles. Any direction is permitted; in following a direction, a path will be created. No specific map is thus required ahead of time. In these situations the key issue for firms is to constantly redefine market niches around the specific technological options that they adopt, i.e. the products and services they offer. In these instances, it is not the territory that counts most and therefore not the map but the path followed which in turn will shape the territory.

One may actually formulate the idea that a map for the very same territory would look different for the military general, the farmer, the geologist, or for the tourist. This leads to the hypothesis that the map is heavily dependent upon its basic purpose.

Where the rate of technical change is high, in a fast moving industry with many different small players with entrepreneurial behaviour, one would expect cognitive technological maps to remain mostly fuzzy implicit and often partial. Many different maps may coexist; the probable key there would be to adapt constantly and use the maps in a dynamic way.

In more stable environments with larger firms, fairly organized with central research and development labs and structured 'technology-monitoring departments, with a slower rate of technological change, one should expect more defined, rather comprehensive, possibly explicit maps which in turn may be rather static, not being updated very often or very rapidly. This in turn leads to the issue of the plurality of maps within the same organization and of their comprehensiveness.

2 Can different maps representing the same technologies exist within the same organization? How different can they be?

Our preliminary empirical results in the case of mobile telephony show evidence of diverging cognitive maps existing at the same time in the same organization. The disagreements clearly went across the firm as well as across functions, with part of the organization favouring certain views of technology and market potential futures with the rest of the organization simply ignoring them. Furthermore, empirical data show clearly that the position of national PTTs prevented transparency between market demand and the equipment manufacturers. This led to a situation where the operators' cognitive maps strongly influenced (and sometimes even opposed) the manufacturers' views of technology and future market options. We would argue that in these 'sheltered culture' environments as Derian (1990) calls them, the problem for the firms is not so much to build and use their own maps but, instead, to guess, understand and possibly influence the maps developed by their powerful government-controlled clients.

Regarding what happens within any one organization, there is no reason why a unified monolithic vision should prevail even within a firm. Future technological options are indeterminate and so leave enough room for diversity in the ways various parts of the organization map and read the technological future. One should thus regard this diversity as a source of creativity and adaptability for the organization, especially in the early exploration of new technological paradigms.

However, one might formulate the hypothesis that too much diversity among the maps – whatever their format and status – within the same organization would make co-ordination difficult, hindering technical choices and developments. One would thus expect diversity of cognitive technological representations within the same organization to prove fruitful as long as it does not reach a point of chaotic, generalized misunderstanding. Indeed, the issue for a firm is not so much to impose a common dogmatic map but to prepare for the variety of possible futures and to choose an appropriate path to follow, i.e. technological strategies, to face tomorrow's technological challenges.

Along similar lines, but from a different perspective, Schneider (1991) suggests analysing the 'coverage' versus 'coherence' issue. Should the organization aim at covering the entire territory by many different maps or should it work on its internal coherence by promoting only one map, at the cost of not being comprehensive in its vision of the territory?

Also, inasmuch as a map is nothing but an image of the way the firm views future technologies and markets, are maps within the same organization all structured in the same way? Is there some kind of organizational inertia attached to the firm's capability to envision any new territory?

One may indeed expect to find similar structures of maps transferred from a situation to another within the same organizations. As collective or individual experience heavily influences the ability of an organization to grasp future options, it should be stated that history matters.

3 This in turn leads to the issue of the process by which firms modify, adapt and use the maps. How do organizations modify their maps? How quickly and easily do they incorporate new pieces of information into their technological and marketing vision? How do technological strategy implementation and maps interact?

One would expect to find some form of organizational inertia against modification. The literature on organizational behaviour would clearly lead to the hypothesis of a high level of stability of beliefs, perspectives on the firm's environment and thus on technological options and market demands.

Similarly the literature on the theory of information and decision making processes would indicate that new pieces of information either fit into the existing maps or tend to be distorted, ignored or even rejected if they cannot be adapted to the map.

An illustration of this idea can be found with Pointel, a new telephony mobile concept first developed in the UK in the late 1980s as a way to deal with the problem of vandalism of phone booths. Pointel soon appeared to be a much broader concept, including wireless home phone and wireless PBX as well as a cheap mobile telephone. Yet it took time for mobile telephony players to integrate the Pointel options and suboptions into their cognitive representation as they tended to regard it primarily as an entirely different concept, having nothing to do with mobile telephony.

Again, however, one would expect some of the contextual factors discussed earlier to influence the ability of the firm to adapt and modify its maps. Fast decision makers described by Eisenhardt (1989) in high velocity environments would typically tend to adapt their maps in real time while one may expect players in the DRAM's industry to stick to their map of an ongoing industry, repeatedly yielding new product generation with quadrupled capacity every three years or so. One may expect the latter to react more slowly than the former to unexpected change, i.e. to an unexpected obstacle in the territory.

Conclusion and Implications for Management

Cognitive strategic representations are important to avoid uselessly carrying boats on land as some Spaniard *conquistadores* are said to have done. Firms do use cognitive technological maps, whether implicit or explicit. The paper has presented a conceptual framework designed to follow the dynamic cognitive process of drawing maps of future technological options as the firm explores the technological territory.

In so doing it turned out to be necessary to discuss the dynamic interaction between technological options on the supply side and customer concept formation on the demand side. An evolutionary perspective was adopted to relate the process which takes place at the industry level to the mapping process within the firms as the organizations build up some specific cumulative learnings.

A discussion of the selective device that operates at the interface between designers and users led to the various forms of cumulative learning and to the concept of irreversibilities.

Several examples of vizualized maps were presented to illustrate the mapping concept graphically. The DTT was presented as a tool to provide a visual representation of a cognitive technological map. Nevertheless it was stressed that the DTT is at best a visualization of the current understanding of how indeterminate future technological options may look tomorrow, as technology usually unfolds in its own unexpected way.

Three major issues were finally raised stemming from the framework presented. They dealt with: (1) the format of the maps; (2) the differences among maps representing the same the technologies within the same organization; and (3) the process by which firms modify, adapt and use the maps.

From a managerial perspective, the mapping process as well as the resulting maps can help achieve several objectives. The maps may be used as communicating devices to help structure discussions between functions as well as between top management and the departments. The whole process may help to generate some congruence in the way various groups within the organization view future technological options.

In addition a cognitive technological map may be used to closely monitor the technological environment and competition. A cognitive technological map as discussed in the third section may thus be regarded as a visual aid illustrating a framework and giving substance to a strategic thinking process about technology. Competitors' choices and investments may be shown; research and development budgets, patents filed, and co-operative agreements may be traced and located in the map, thus improving the way the organization views and thinks about technological options.

The whole process is a dynamic mapping since maps evolve in time as new pieces of information are gathered and incorporated into the picture.

References

Abernathy, W. J. and Clark, K. B. 1985: Innovation: mapping the winds of creative destruction. *Research Policy* 14, 3–22.

Abernathy, W. J. and Utterback, J. M. 1978: Patterns of industrial innovation. *Technology Review 50*, June–July, 41–47.

Allen, Th. 1977 *Managing the Flow of Technology*. Cambridge, MA: MIT Press.

Arrow 1962: Economic welfare and the allocation of resources for invention. In Nelson (ed.), *The Rate and Direction of Inventive Activity*, Princeton University Press.

Arthur, W. B. 1983: Competing technologies and lock-in by historical events: the dynamics of allocation under increasing returns. International Institute for Applied systems Analysis, *Paper W. P 83–90*, Laxenburg, Austria.

Arthur, W. B 1988: Competing technologies: an overview in DG. *et al., Technical Change and Economic Theory*, London: Francis Pinter, N. Y. Columbia University Press.

Atkinson, A. B and Stiglitz, J. E. 1969: A new view of technological change, *Economic Journal*, no 76, pp. 573–578.

Clark, K. B. 1985: The interaction of design hierarchies and Market concepts in technological evolution. *Research Policy* 4, 235–251.

Cooper, A. C. and Schendell, D. 1976: Strategic responses to technological threats. *Business Horizons.*

Cowan 1990: Backing the wrong horse: choice among technologies of unknown merit, Forthcoming, *The Economic Journal*.

De Bandt, J. private communication.

de Tournemine, Larue 1988: Comment evaluer les stratègies technologiques. *Revue Francaise de Gestion*. June–July 1988.

Derian, Jean-Claude 1990: *America's struggle for leadership in technology*, MIT Press.

DG. 1982: Technological paradigms and technological trajectories. *Research Policy* 11, 147–162.

DG. 1988: Sources, procedures and microeconomic effects of innovation, *Journal of Economic Literature*, Vol. 26, pp. 1120–1171.

Doz, Yves. private communication.

Durand, Thomas 1991: Dual technological tree: assessing the intensity and strategic significance of technological change. Forthcoming, *Research Policy*.

Eisenhardt 1989: Making fast strategic decisions in high-velocity environments, *Academy of Management Journal*, Vol. 32.

Foray, Dominique 1989: Les modèles de compétition technologique, *Revue d'Economie Industrielle*, no 49.

Gaffard 1990: *Economie industrielle et de l'innovation*, Dalloz.

Goedert, Marie-Françoise 1990: Modèles de compétition technologique versus paradigmes et trajectoires technologiques, Séminaire PIRTTEM.

Henderson, R. and Clark, K. 1990: Architectural innovation: the reconfiguration of existing product technologies and the failure of established firms. *Administrative Science Quarterly*, 35.

Lundvall, B. A 1988: *Innovation as an interactive process: from user-producer interaction to the national system of innovation.*

Rosenberg, 1976: *Perspectives on Technology.* Cambridge: Cambridge University Press.

Rosenberg, 1982: *Inside the black box.* Cambridge University Press.

Schneider, Suzan 1991: *Organizational sensemaking: 1992*, Working paper, INSEAD.

Sigismund Huff, Anne 1990: *Mapping strategic thought*, Wiley.

Von Hippel, E. 1988: The dominant role of users in the scientific instrument innovation process, *Research Policy*, Vol. 5.

Von Hippel, E. 1976: The dominant role of users in the scientific instrument innovation process. *Research Policy.* Vol. 5.

Williamson, O. E. 1975: *Markets and hierarchies*, The Free Press: New York.

8

A Framework for Analysing the Storage and Protection of Knowledge in Organizations

STRATEGIC IMPLICATIONS AND STRUCTURAL ARRANGEMENTS

Elda A. Bonora and Øivind Revang

Introduction

The economic evolution of society is often seen as going through various stages. One speaks about the agrarian society, the industrial age and the service economy. The latter is also sometimes called the information economy or the post-industrial society.

There were two main factors that affected productivity in agriculture. One, the quality of the land, which was the main production factor, and two, the weather. The quality of the land determined the potential efficiency in operations while the weather created uncertainty for the natural process of growing. The main strategy for effective production was that of acquiring the best fertile land in sizes that gave economy in operations. For the farmer, the main uncertainty with respect to economic results was created by the weather but there was little he could do to protect himself from the changes and fluctuations in this environment. The emergence of the industrial age led to a division of labour inside organizations and a specialization of production between companies. The output from one firm became the input for another. The uncertainty facing the production manager of an industrial firm was in acquiring input resources so that the firm's operating core could continue efficiently (Thompson, 1967). The dependency upon input from others increased management's attention towards the firm's external relations. Managing effectiveness became as important as managing efficiency.

The escalating attention on a firm's task environment led to theoretical frameworks for analysing organizations by means of external factors and/or conditions. No one accomplished this task more extensively than Pfeffer and Salancik (1978) in what they called a resource dependence perspective.

However, with the ever-increasing emphasis towards a service economy today, not only has a new, major production factor emerged, a new, major source of uncertainty and dependency has evolved as well. Alongside the capital-intensive and labour intensive organizations of the past, we see the emergence of the 'knowledge-intensive' organization or firm (KIF). As a result of the growing importance of knowledge as a resource, the recognition of knowledge-intensive industries as distinct from capital- or labour-intensive industries as well as the key role played by 'knowledge' workers such as scientists, engineers, computer programmers and certainly, in the context at hand, managers as well, has increased.

One of the main uncertainties facing the leaders of firms where knowledge mainly appears in labour is the loss of competence through the loss of key individuals. This is particularly profound in professional service firms, such as lawyers and consultants, firms that actually do little else than sell knowledge. There are examples of firms that have lost their future in a matter of days through the organized exit of several key persons. In many of these cases, they do not only take their knowledge away from the firm, they may also take the customers with them. For obvious reasons then, competence needs to be nurtured and protected as the knowledge underlying this competence may very well fade if not integrated. Thus as we enter the post-industrial society, the issue of ownership and control of knowledge and information as a source of power in society has become increasingly important.

Despite the growing importance of knowledge in organizations, the management of intellectual capital is still uncharted territory in most companies. Knowledge must be managed so as to create a differential advantage. To do this managers need conceptual frameworks and generic strategies.

Knowledge-Intensive Firms — What exactly are they?

The existing literature is populated with different factors and variables for drawing borderlines between KIFs and 'ordinary firms' (Sadler, 1988; Sveiby and Risling, 1987; Sveiby, 1990; and Starbuck, 1990). However, the term 'Knowledge-intensive firms' (KIFs) itself has generally been used in an indeterminate manner. For example, some view high-tech firms as knowledge-intensive due to the sophistication of the products produced. For others, the growing element of service implies that the knowledge factor is becoming increasingly important in organizations. However, a service-intensive firm is not necessarily the same as a knowledge-intensive firm. Yet still, others see KIFs as firms where employees, holding university degrees, exceed 50 per cent or two-thirds of those employed (Sadler, 1988; Sveiby and Risling, 1987; and Starbuck, 1990). These individuals undergo an educational process which also entails a socialization that creates what can be described as a 'professional corps' which implies that a set of norms and values, as well as models, knowledge, and a professional language have been internalized. At the same time, they are trained to turn information and experience into knowledge. These are major elements that, combined, create the core competence of a KIF (Prahalad and Hamel, 1990).

According to Starbuck (1990), a great problem exists in comparing KIFs with each other, mainly due to the fact that knowledge appears in many different domains. At the very least, we can distinguish between six: (1) in labour; (2) in capital such as machines, plant or equipment; (3) in organizational systems; (4) in organizational processes; (5) in organizational cultures; and finally (6) in products. In view of the fact that knowledge is a mixture of the above factors, comparing such firms is not like comparing apples and oranges but rather like comparing bowls of fruit salad.

Knowledge as an input resource

This chapter focuses primarily on a particular group of knowledge-intensive firms – those where knowledge mainly rests in labour. By using such firms as examples we are able to observe processes and strategies that may take place in more traditional firms as they become increasingly knowledge-dependent.

In view of the fact that the service production in KIFs is usually performed through an interaction between the professional and clients, this process facilitates the growth of skills and knowledge. The main uncertainty with respect to economic results is the professional knowledge embedded in individuals. The individual's knowledge is an invisible asset (Itami, 1987) that determines how successfully one firm can solve its clients' problems in comparison to another.

Therefore, in contrast to the organization of yesteryear, where the major source of control was found external to the firm, we see the emergence of a new and major source of control, namely internal. As a resource, people are important; not just as participants in the labour force, but as accumulators and producers of invisible assets. Thus, to cover the new reality that these firms represent, we can re-title the perspective developed by Pfeffer and Salancik to read 'The Internal Control of Organizations, a Knowledge-Dependence Perspective'.

Purpose

Despite the growing forest of criteria for defining KIFs, it seems to be a reasonable conjecture that the underlying vulnerability of these firms' existence, both on a short- and long-term basis, is the presence of and/or withdrawal of its primary resource, i.e. the knowledge of its employees, which in itself is the fundamental essence upon which the firm prevails. These individuals are, more often than not, the initiators of the firm's business concept and by means of this knowledge, control the knowledge capital of the firm. Several have their own, larger network apart from their employer's organization and are therefore not dependent upon the firm.

Because knowledge differs from traditional resources in dimensions like storing, ownership and development, situations where knowledge is the determinant resource call for the development of a resource dependence perspective in order to cover this reality.

We are primarily concerned about conceptualizing and structuring the strategies that firms may use to avoid uncertainty and balance dependency created by the mobility of knowledge workers.

Despite the fact that it is increasingly obvious to many writers within the field of management that we are in a process of transition towards a knowledge-based society, few have constructed the concept itself. As a result, it becomes difficult to see consequences at the strategic management level.

As a step in this direction, we search to gain a deeper understanding of the resource itself, considering its different concretizations which, as the following sections will show, also provide a deeper understanding of the nature of knowledge in professional service firms. At the same time, we adopt from literature dealing with the sociology of knowledge and philosophy of knowledge, concepts and useful views about the resource which facilitates the differentiation between the concepts of knowledge and skill, which in turn lie at the base of our knowledge dependence perspective.

The mobility of knowledge workers as a source of power

The individual then, is, more than ever, placed at the centre not financial capital or production process. Unlike their comrades during the industrial revolution, these human beings, in many cases and seen from many aspects, hold the very essence of the firm captive. With the emergence of the knowledge-intensive firm and with its main core activity stored within the human brain, the mobility of this primary resource becomes a key element when discussing strategies for the storage and/or protection of knowledge.

The loss of knowledge workers in firms that produce products embedded with knowledge is not an urgent crisis. The problem manifests itself in the next generation of products insomuch as they become delayed, changed or cancelled altogether such as research programmes that are terminated. In the meantime, the firm produces and sells existing products. However, in a law or consulting firm, the exit of several individuals is more likely to create an immediate crisis for the ongoing business and will in turn, have consequences for the firm's sustained performance. To maintain the business and to continue as an organization, such firms must use management techniques purposefully aimed at keeping knowledge workers within the firm.

Thus, the mobility of knowledge workers gives them power. If they are not satisfied with their working conditions, they can leave or start their own business. Due to the fact that their skills are standardized through their education and profession, the costs of establishing a new firm are relatively low. Thus, the rising power of educated brains within organizations in many industries is creating organizations that are internally controlled.

This internal control can be exemplified by the many situations found in, for example, law firms, consulting and accounting businesses where, after a period as employees, the best skills are offered partnerships. This is in sharp contrast to industries where the assets include machinery, products and other capital and where the ownership is regulated through the ownership of shares.

In industries heavily dependent on research and development, such as the computer business and biotechnology, share programmes for employees are one kind of material benefit but seldom give the power or influence that a partnership allows. The type of firms we refer to have invisible assets that, more often than not, are impossible to own or patent.

The phenomenon of internal control can even be found in the world of education, where professors are sought after and bargained for. The institution offering the most prestigious and/or advantageous conditions will often be accepted. Furthermore, entrance as a member to the university staff is decided by committees that control the quality of knowledge acceptable and thus the applying knowledge worker. This is an indication of how the focus shifts when organizations have knowledge as their main resource for performing operations.

Different faces of knowledge

The importance of knowledge as an input in the production process is often mentioned, but seldom defined. Few have systematically and seriously addressed the question of how the information that is produced 'gets established as recognized knowledge, and how its development and utilization become organized, evaluated, and controlled' (Freideson, 1970:28). Popper (1972) approaches the subject of knowledge by penetrating the argument that many philosophers with special interests in theories about knowledge also are very concerned about; namely, beliefs. According to Popper they characterize knowledge as a special type of belief – a belief we have reason to have, and that we can be sure about.

Popper himself draws a line between objective and subjective knowledge. Human knowledge and scientific knowledge consist of, to a large extent, theories formulated in language. Subjective knowledge, or, in Popper's terminology, subjective belief, are part of the subject (me, another human or an animal). This knowledge cannot be shared or validated before it is expressed in words or symbols which are further interrelated in language. Once formulated and written they belong to the world of ideas created by us as professional textbooks, monographs and research papers. Popper defines this as World 3. Knowledge in this sense is knowledge without a knowing subject, It is a piece of formulated material that can be shared and understood by individual subjects.

Popper's World 2 is populated with knowledge that can be called 'I know' knowledge. It is the world where the subjects carry their knowledge, formulated or not. The 'I know' inhabitants are the catalysts who convert information into communication. It is impossible to both produce World 3 information and to understand/use it without the subjective knowledge of World 2. In the production process of a service firm, individual bearers of subjective knowledge give meaning to the task, they perform sense-giving and sense-reading activities. Sometimes this experience rests in World 2, at other times firms have developed tools for abstraction of this experience.

Seen from a business point of view Popper's three worlds are populated with knowledge as precepts, recipes, theories and similarities; knowledge as human skills; and World 1 with the data as facts, things and objects in the 'objective world'. By information, we mean here, structured data. The written knowledge in World 3 represents a form of information that is structured, formulated and written where relationships are established. World 1 data can be both structured and written. In fact, it is often structured into data elements such as customer and product files, but at the same time is not formulated into meanings as logical progressions, relationships, or statements about 'how things really are' or 'how they should be'.

These three forms of knowledge are stored in different forms. Inhabitants of Worlds 3 and 1 can be stored in registers, libraries and documentation. Furthermore, restrictions can be enforced, as in the armed forces, where information is classified into different grades for security reasons and where only individuals who have the equivalent security classification can gain access to the material. The existence of industrial espionage shows that the protection of this kind of instant knowledge can be important to firms for strategic reasons. However, knowledge embodied in individuals cannot be used in more than one place. As property, such knowledge is much harder to protect than other types of resources as it is controlled by possession. An individual possesses his knowledge in a direct and absolute manner. He is the sole arbiter of its use by others (Pfeffer and Salancik, 1978:48).

However, our main concern is the difference between the traditional industrial organization and the emerging mass of knowledge-intensive firms and institutions such as law firms, consulting bureaux of various types and universities. The professionals' capabilities are not just input into the production process(es) of the firm, because the experience gained through acting adds to their existing knowledge, they are simultaneously outputs of the same process(es). Therefore, a production process in professional service firms has two distinctive and different outputs. One, the consulting done for the customer and two, the knowledge added to the individual firm member's existing stock of knowledge as well as development in the person's skills.

The art of doing

Polyani (1958) uses the concepts skill and connoisseurship to understand the nature of World 2. He sees the exact sciences as a set of formulae which have a bearing on experience. In accrediting this bearing, we must rely upon varying degrees of our powers of personal knowledge. Because science is operated by the skill of the scientist and it is through the exercise of his skill that he shapes his scientific knowledge, we may grasp the nature of the scientist's personal participation by examining the structure of skills (Polyani, 1958:49). Knowledge in the context of World 3 can be seen as a set of rules, a set of guidelines on how to solve certain problems based on the knowledge of how things and relationships really are.

Polyani notes that a skilful performance is achieved by the observance of a set of rules which is not known as such by the person following them. For him rules of an art can be useful, but they do not determine the practice of an art. They can serve as a guide to an art only if they can be integrated into the practical knowledge (the skill) of an art. They cannot replace this knowledge. An art which cannot be specified in detail cannot be transmitted by prescription since no prescription exists. It can be developed by practising and personal learning, and it can be passed on by example from master to apprentice (Polyani, 1958:53). 'The medical diagnostician's skill is as much an art of doing as it is an art of knowing. The skill of testing and tasting is continuous with the more actively muscular skills like swimming or riding a bike' (ibid:54).

According to Polyani then, skill can only be communicated by example, not by precept. In the consulting business, we see this phenomenon through the establishment of senior and junior consultants. The junior consultant follows the senior master in order to develop their skills. In some firms we see mentors taking care of younger colleagues. In the education of craftsmen we see it through formal requirement about relevant practice in addition to the internalization of knowledge read. In management education, we develop skills through the use of case analysis and project reports. The large amount of time spent by students of chemistry, biology and medicine in their practical courses shows how greatly these sciences rely on the transmission of skills and connoisseurship from master to apprentice. It offers an impressive demonstration of the extent to which the art of knowing has remained unspecifiable at the very heart of the exact sciences (Polyani, 1958:55). All such training is geared to one goal – the internalization of standards that serve the client and co-ordinate the professional work (Mintzberg, 1983:190).

We do not delve into Popper's arguments about the conditions for knowledge being scientific or not. For our purpose, it is the differentiation of three different categories or worlds that is important. In any event, firms are not concerned about whether or not knowledge is scientific nor from which standpoint knowledge is scientific and in which perspective knowledge is non-scientific. This question of importance is left to some scientists and most philosophers.

This structure is important from a knowledge-management point of view insomuch as that knowledge is hard to get at because it belongs in people's heads and is unstructured. Knowledge is, more than ever before, determinant for business. Therefore, as organizations become increasingly dependent upon educated brains, Popper's three worlds help management to distinguish and understand different forms of knowledge, that is, how and where knowledge is stored. In understanding this, management may be more readily able to conceive the nature of the organization's situations at hand, and increase management's ability towards capturing, capitalizing and leveraging the knowledge possessed by their rare, talented, self-made assets through, among other things, creating inter-personal/social-based relations and creating an organization where knowledge can be shared.

Framework

Knowledge – organic vs. mechanical

The previous discussion concerning the nature of knowledge constitutes an axis upon which knowledge can be placed. At the one end of the horizontal axis, we have skills which we define as personal, subjective knowledge, we call this organically stored knowledge and is covered by the concept of World 2. At the other end of the axis, we have the rules, the precepts, the standardization of behaviour, what we have called information or 'objective knowledge'. We call this mechanical knowledge to emphasize its characteristics of storage and structure. The organizations in question cover the storage of knowledge varying from organic to mechanical in different portions. Firms heavily dependent on organic knowledge to perform their operations, are what are frequently referred to as KIFs or professional bureaucracies (Mintzberg, 1983).

We see educated skilled workers and knowledge workers, as cognitive beings. Their education and experience is the core of the company's latent knowledge because it steers the process or act of thinking and the products of thinking, the ideas or the notions as well as giving meanings to their environment and as such bears the latent knowledge of a company. This knowledge is seen as organic by nature.

It is not the knowledge belonging to World 3 that is critical for the success and survival of the firm but the company's relevant knowledge of World 2 stored in subjects as latent knowledge or skills, and the knowledge workers' ability to set theory into practice applying World 3 in everyday life. World 3 knowledge is, in principle, open to everyone. It can be protected by patents and then owned by someone, but in such a case the knowledge can be viewed as a resource in the traditional sense and analysed within our models for resource dependence (ex. Thompson, 1967; and Pfeffer and Salancik, 1978). It is due to the fact that knowledge, as viewed in World 2, differs from a traditional resource in such a way that it cannot be acquired as an object but only as and through living subjects, that we develop our framework.

Fragmentation and integration — the logic of managerial levels

In the industrial organization labour is specialized to perform narrow tasks with great efficiency. Managerial levels and span of control are designed to co-ordinate the fragmented tasks, central building blocks in the hierarchical organizational design. It has been stated that when tasks are more unstructured and labour more educated, such as the case of research laboratories, flatter structures have greater advantages (Lawrence and Lorsch, 1967). Professional service firms are usually characteristic of having a large variation in the projects undertaken. Accounting firms however, have, to a greater extent, more repetitive, standardized tasks than do professional business consultants. In the latter case, analyses and diagnoses of the customer are needed in order to define which course of action to take. The production process is more often a process between customer and producer, than that of a producer alone. Mintzberg (1983:192) sees the core activity of professional firms as 'pigeon-holing'. That is, the process of categorizing the client's need in terms of a contingency which indicates the standard programme to use (a task often called diagnosis).

Knowledge cannot be separated from the process of knowing, they are identical; knowledge is a process (Zeleny, 1989). Or as formulated by Maturana and Varela (1987), 'all doing is knowing, and all knowing is doing'. The division of labour that is so common in the industrial organization, based on the premise that knowing and doing can be separated is thus outmoded in the knowledge-intensive firm. However, the tendency to use the division of labour as division of skills and division of contact with clients can be identified.

The managerial levels in the classical hierarchical co-ordinates dispersed information and limited skills. When knowledge rests in the individual subject, this kind of co-ordination is performed through team building around projects, the dynamic structuring of a project and the mechanisms for sharing experience within the firm. Due to the fact that the concentration of control over resources and the importance of the resources to the organization determine the focal organization's dependence on any given group or individual knowledge worker, dependence reduction can be achieved through doubling knowledge suppliers, for instance having more than one individual with the same speciality.

Going along the vertical axis from the bottom to the top indicates an increasing co-ordination of fragmented items as standard operation procedures and individual skills. In a summary, the above discussion can be illustrated in a conceptual model such as that illustrated figure 8.1. The model developed shows how knowledge is both stored and co-ordinated by illustrating the framework's major axes, quadrants and concepts.

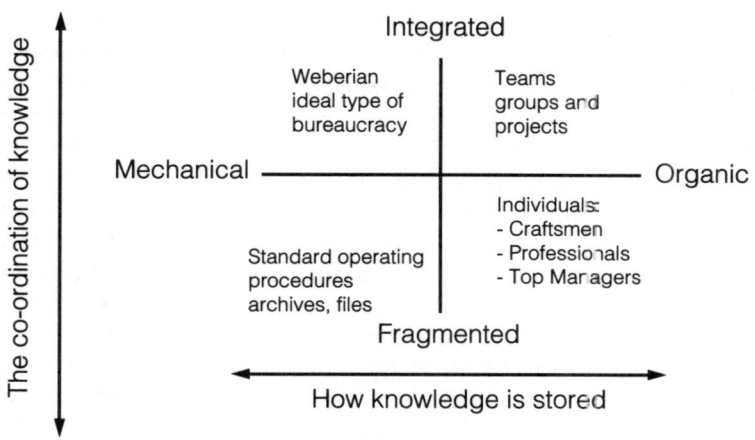

Figure 8.1   Core framework and quadrants

As shown in figure 8.1, the model consists of four quadrants, each having its own particular characteristics. Below, the model is discussed from a more holistic perspective by highlighting these four quadrants in part.

The four quadrants

Our two axes form four modes of potentially storeable knowledge. In the lower right-hand quadrant of figure 8.1, we find professionals on an independent basis. Their professional knowledge is not only organic, i.e. highly personal, it is also both individualized and specialized. Their skills are standardized through their profession and education. However, despite this standardization, no two lawyers, consultants or doctors ever apply their skills in exactly the same way. Many judgements are required (Mintzberg, 1983:191). They learn from their experience, developing variations from the behaviour due to secondary socialization. In this context, and due to the fact that the knowledge is stored independently within each individual, its storage is, from a company's point of view, highly fragmented.

We can think of two modes of operational characteristics. One, if the firm does not integrate the knowledge held by the different subjects, it operates, in essence, as a cluster of singly-independent individuals who share certain facilities such as computers, secretaries and overhead costs. The level of work created by each subject is far too low to legitimatize individual investments in office equipment and staff. Two, if they integrate different knowledge into teams, line-up departments, etc., firms can afford to create economy of scale and scope. However, as soon as a firm develops in this direction, it becomes dependent on knowledge workers.

In the upper right-hand quadrant we find teams and projects in the interests of achieving overall goals. Individuals, with individualized and specialized knowledge, grouped together on a team for the purpose of working with projects of varying sizes. The knowledge that was once specialized and individualized becomes diffused, general and integrated. The knowledge inherent in each individual on the team contributes to solving problems and creating solutions. This is an important step in consolidating the resource of individual knowledge and in turn the effectiveness of internal control. Important decisions about entering new markets, building new plants, or acquiring new businesses are often made in groups. The advantages achieved by forming teams and projects are accessibility to the individual's knowledge as well as the synergy effects achieved by such a working form. Team members learn from each other. Hereby the dependence on one particular skilled person is reduced. Hedlund and Nonaka (1992) suggest that this strategy is used more often in Japanese firms than in Western firms.

Teams must be used when solving projects that are too large for one individual. Size, of both the organization and the task, are of the greatest importance. For example, some auditing firms, lawyers and consultants are too small to have large industrial companies as clients. For those large enough to compete for gigantic companies as clients, allocating individuals to projects and project management can be the central competence that creates a competitive advantage in the marketplace.

In the upper left-hand quadrant we find Weber's ideal type of bureaucracy where rationality rests in the structure. Considerable emphasis is put on control, authority, rules and procedures and standardization, but which also emphasizes co-ordination of effort in the direction of achieving the organization's overall tasks or goals. This is the type of organization where the rules for each job are so well defined that, in actual fact, you can place any individual you wish in any position and achieve the same results from the working processes. This is a structural form where the organization's dependence on specific individuals is minimal. By forming the rules for operation, the written standards, or the handbooks, the organization structure and tasks have become knowledge.

In the lower left-hand quadrant we find standard operating procedures as well as files – fragmented information about the historic development in and around the organization, product files, information about markets etc. Almost every organization stores memos, letters, invoices and reports. This is mechanical storage, storage without a knowing subject. They are also an asset to the firm, but cannot be capitalized upon without a knowing subject. As the use of computers and electronic storage escalates, an enormous amount of data can be stored in company files. The challenge facing companies becomes turning information into knowledge (Hopper, 1990). In many cases this calls for new skills.

In the lower right-hand corner we have the skills stored in individuals. A company without any integrative or mechanical processes will be exposed to a high uncertainty regarding the departure of people when compared to one that does have formalized, ongoing processes of this kind. It is important to remember that we are just discussing strategies for keeping knowledge within the firm. To stay in tune with their environments, organizations have to develop a strategy for a skill-formation process for this quadrant. What encouragement is provided for updating skills, phasing out obsolete skills, and bringing in new ones? (Adler and Shenbar, 1990; Åström, 1990).

Strategies for reducing firms' dependence on the subjective knowledge resource

With reference to our framework of categories, highlighting how knowledge of different types is stored in organizations, we develop a set of uncertainty- and dependence-reducing strategies.

First, we must distinguish between two sets of generic strategies:

1 Reducing dependence on individuals by 'building' knowledge into the organization. In this case, three processes are available:
   a   Diffusion of knowledge among organizational members
   b   Abstraction of knowledge/skill
   c   Institutionalization of knowledge
   Moving along the horizontal axis from organic to mechanical is a process of moving from tacit knowledge to articulated knowledge, turning personal knowledge into form as information for World 3. Movement along the vertical axis from fragmented to integrated is moving from individual to organizational knowledge. We assume that this movement can be achieved either as socialization and internalization through teamwork, or as formalization of the organizational structure and operational tasks.
2 Building exit barriers for knowledge workers. Here, we can distinguish between two different groups:
   a   Material-based exit barriers
   b   Social-based exit barriers

In a broad sense this means that material benefits or social relations are used systematically to lower the uncertainty connected to the mobility of core knowledge workers.

Strategic processes for building knowledge

Our first main class of strategies cover how an organization can transfer knowledge from World 2 to World 3. That is, how firms can lower their dependence on individuals by organizational arrangements. It should be noted that skilled individuals are likely to prefer a great deal of freedom in performing their professional tasks. Applying strategies that reduce their freedom in work can result in unintended behaviour. Therefore one must seek for 'win-win' situations where both the individual and the firm gain some surplus.

Reducing dependence through knowledge diffusion

Organizations can take a number of actions to avoid dependencies that result from reliance on a single critical resource exchange, like buffering, taking control over demand and supply or taking control over the organizations which either provide the needed resource or absorb the output (Pfeffer and Salancik, 1978:108–9). When a professional service firm becomes heavily dependent on a few persons in the company it can become less dependent by diffusing the knowledge of these persons among all members. In many ways, this process shares similarities with obtaining

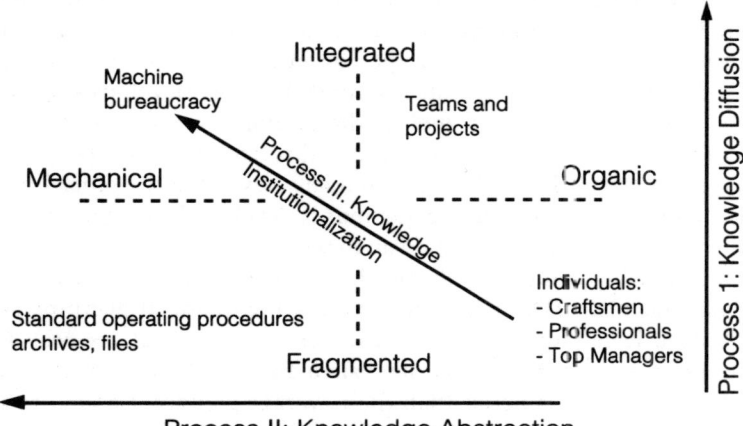

Figure 8.2   Three processes for reducing organizational dependence on skilled knowledge workers

more suppliers of the same resource in an industrial firm. The process does not remove the basic source of the vulnerability, but rather the dependence upon one or a few resource suppliers is reduced.

Knowledge diffusion can take many forms. It can be achieved by forming teams and allocating people to tasks or projects. Assignments to task-forces are another means of fostering professionalism. The use of mentors and differentiating between junior and senior consultants are also among the structural arrangements that can be utilized. If the company deals with homogeneous customers, teams can be used as a mechanism to transfer values between different professions and as a field of training for new employees. One other mechanism is by means of company education – learning how things are done in a specific company.

This process of diffusion requires a basis of generated company-specific World 3 knowledge. Thus the existence of this process very often relies on abstraction processes taking place. Knowledge diffusion can be viewed as World 2 subjects learning either from experience or from teaching.

Reducing dependence through knowledge abstraction

One option available to firms that become too dependent on a resource supplier in the environment is to incorporate the production of the resource into the organization (Thompson, 1967). For an internally controlled firm, a similar option is to extract knowledge from the source of dependence and uncertainty, i.e. the individual professional member. By doing this, the organization becomes less dependent on the individual. This process implies that the behaviour of skilled individuals is brought from World 2 to World 3. That is, from being part of one or more individuals' unconscious cognitive maps to becoming recipes or guidelines for performing operations. An example is an accounting controller who develops a spreadsheet template on his computer to analyse the economic situations and performance of the firm's clients. Once done, this template can be distributed among other controllers within the company. By using the procedure developed, a more united pattern of behaviour is developed and it becomes easier to train new controllers how to do analyses. Due to the development of this tool, the auditing company becomes less dependent on the skills of the individual controller. IDS Financial Services, the financial planning subsidiary of American Express Co., codified the expertise of its best account managers in a software programme called Insight. Now even the worst of their 6,500 planners is better than their average planner used to be. The result is that in four years the percentage of clients who leave has dropped by more than a half (Fortune, June, 1991).

This process may also involve the creation of checklists, the first step towards standardizing behaviour and output. In a broad sense, the outcome of this process is standard programmes or repertoires that the professional can use in the pigeon-holing process. They may well be models that give the firm status within the profession. We are all familiar with examples such as the BCG matrix and McKinsey's 7-s framework. Another example can be found in professional law firms that save their contracts electronically. Through a review process some contracts are classified as 're-petitive' and stored in what they call an experience file. When facing similar customer needs, the lawyer starts his work on the basis of the contract from the experience file. Given the fact that these contracts often are large (sixty to eighty pages) and often in a foreign language, this knowledge base saves a lot of professional work and at the same time lowers the dependency on individuals as it becomes 'mechanical' stored 'knowledge'.

A process such as this will require that some of the members of the firm are devoted to systematizing and categorizing behaviour and reviewing experience, like creating company specific models, norms and guidelines for the members. The effect of not having a process like this is that individuals can easily become atoms of knowledge in the firm, and the firm just the sum of individuals; implying no synergy, no social life, no formal processes for systemizing experience and no company identity. For a small firm it can be difficult implementing such a process because the expertise needed to do such tasks is usually expensive and the work cannot be billed directly to their customers. In the short run they only see costs, but it creates new tools for the individual which at the same time can offer them more adequate means in a changing environment.

Institutionalization: storing knowledge in the organizational structure

In the broadest sense, social structures are always knowledge-containing systems in that they are simultaneously determined by social categories and positions; orientations, knowledge and belief systems (Gurvitch, 1971). Moving along the axis from the bottom right-hand corner up towards the upper left-hand corner indicates a process where the formalization of these variables plays a major part. The highly formalized structure is a neat one and it appeals to people who like to see things in an orderly way. The process can be said to represent a bureaucratization of knowledge. By formalizing individual roles, positions and work prescriptions, behaviour becomes standardized and thus it is easier to replace individuals while maintaining the role they played. This implies reducing the dependence on the individual members, but at the same time lowers the possibilities of innovation and flexibility within the organization. For obvious reasons, this may have very negative effects in a competitive environment. From this point of view this process can be said to represent a movement from World 2 to World 1, where the organization becomes an object, a machine or a part of 'nature'.

The use of this process is dangerous in professional service firms because it is based on norms that are not wholly compatible with such values as individual freedom in decision making and autonomy in work that knowledge workers very often have. As a result, the administrative component grows. This in turn results in less potential for high wages to knowledge workers, and thereby increases the probability of spin-offs and/or departure of core personnel. In addition, the probability of lower creativity in relationships with customers is heightened as preferences for standardized solutions are adopted. It might as well lead to an increase in the organization's conflict level because of administrative personnel who do not share the norms of the professionals (Raelin, 1986).

In situations where great damage can be done if knowledge workers 'break out' and take the customers or clients with them, this process can be used to fragment or hinder the contact with those who pay their wages. In some law firms this is manifested in a division of labour between those who are partners in the firm and those who are employees. Only partners are allowed to have contact with the clients of the firm. Employees can be grouped in specialist departments such as contracting, taxes etc., these departments deliver input to the partner that is the one with the overall knowledge of the task to be solved.

Creating barriers to exit for knowledge workers

The second generic class of strategies cover barriers to exit. The knowledge can be held inside the focal organization by constructing barriers that motivate the individual to stay. Such barriers can work in addition to the processes just explored. Two classes can be identified, one based on material incentives and one based on social ties and relations.

Material-based exit barriers

In industry, wages are monitored and compared as an important input for political decisions to be made by government. For the individuals, the level of remuneration plays an important role in the total quality of their lives. One can change employers if the wage difference seems worth the cost of moving. For knowledge-based companies, where knowledge rests in labour, the existence of a free market for these workers is undermined by offering them something additional, including various forms of fringe benefits, resources available for conferences, courses, sabbaticals, etc. However, it would seem that the mechanism used most widely by professional service firms is partnership.

In firms where lawyers, auditors and business consultants practise we see two categories of knowledge workers, one group works as employees and one group has positions as partners. Very little empirical research seems to have been done on the role and forms of partnership in knowledge-intensive organizations. An exception can be found in Gilson and Mnookin (1985), who investigated profit-splitting in law firms. Others who also have some reflections upon the subject include Gilson and Mnookin, (1990); Sveiby and Risling (1987); and Alvesson (1989).

Partnerships have to be seen as both an instrument for power and as an investment. As firms grow older and their financial capital increases, it becomes more and more expensive to attain the same power for each head if it shall be based on how much of the company assets each partner owns. This can result in a situation where the 'old' hierarchy rules the firm, which in turn results in a decline in motivation and innovation. Attention then has to be paid on how to achieve equal power among partners, even if the size of their investments differ. At least two conditions have to be fulfilled in order to be made a partner. One, the existing partners must agree upon the person in question becoming a partner and two, the new partner has to 'buy' a part of the company. This has been called the 'up or out' system (Gilson and Mnookin, 1990).

A partnership functions as an exit barrier for the accepted partners and as a motivation factor for employees to work hard within the firm to become accepted as a partner. Some firms divide the wages into two parts, one part is a fixed sum while the second part varies with how much the individual has billed the customers. Another form of material exit barrier is the knowledge and information access a firm can provide its employees. Because the amount of work done and the quality of it is dependent on access to information and knowledge, a firm with well developed systems for sharing knowledge and experience as well as access to files, archives and books, gives the individual possibilities for a higher income which he or she may not acquire working for a competitor with less developed systems for supporting subjective knowledge.

Social-based barriers

Mintzberg (1983:195) asks why professionals bother to join organizations in the first place. One reason is that the organization is a place where they can share resources, another is that some services, such as in the case of a MBA programme or hospital care, cannot be offered by one individual alone. More importantly however, organizing also brings professionals together to learn from each other as well as presenting opportunities for humans to act as social beings insomuch as what people do in organizations constitutes interacting with each other. Thus, organizations as collective entities cannot be disputed as they embody and involve collective action.

Of equal importance however, and with even deeper consequences, is the answer or answers to the question why professionals, who join organizations in the first place, choose to remain?

At the risk of professional individuals becoming just atoms of knowledge within the firm, the firm runs the risk itself of just becoming the sum of these individuals. This implies the absence of synergy, social life as well as formal processes for systemizing experience and perhaps most importantly, company identity. Implicit in this risk is the inability of management to understand as well as manage problems in the organization which may very well result in a loss of performance and even complete failure, regardless of market opportunities. Two premises are therefore important in this context. One, that clues for future success lie within the organization and evolving states of development in themselves, and two, that the outcome of favourable work – and perhaps even more important in this case, the propensity of individuals to remain within the firm – is determinant of how well these individuals' needs and personalities are matched by a number of work-environment variables.

The task of management is to make people capable of joint performance, to bring into focus and to make people's strengths effective and their weaknesses inconsequential. This is what organizing is all about and the main reason why management is the one critical, determining factor. Thus, it is management and management alone that makes knowledge and these knowledgeable people we refer to here, effective. Although collective knowledge is hard to identify and even harder to develop and spread, the greatest challenge facing management today is the creation of organizations that can share knowledge.

Insomuch as management deals with the integration of people in a common venture, the management of knowledge is deeply embedded in culture, that is, a system of shared values and beliefs that produce norms of behaviour and establish an organizational way of life. A firm's identity and image projected outwards is in essence a manifestation of the firm's culture inasmuch as it shapes behaviour by conveying a sense of identity to workers. More importantly however, especially in professional service firms, is that it encourages commitment beyond self. Furthermore, it increases the stability of the social system and gives recognized and accepted premises for decision making. In short, it defines the ways in which an organization conducts its business. In this context then, it is not just the knowledge itself but the way it is applied that will give organizations skills beyond the talent of its knowledgeable assets.

Norms, customs and laws in society can be referred to as the 'working rules of collective action' on a macro level. Similarly, the norms, customs and rules within an organization can be seen as the working rules of collective action on a micro level. The notion of working rules of collective action in itself, is based on the legal concept of a 'reasonable person'. Accordingly, the reasonable man must meet some uniform, collective standard of conduct which, in turn, is determined with reference to a community valuation and, in consequence, is the same for all persons. Reasonable behaviour provides an institutional framework within which it can work. Individuals may very well pursue their own goals and attempt to maximize their self-interests as best they can, but they do so under given conditions.

Normative patterns of interaction become instilled with a sense of morality (Etzioni, 1988) rather than sheer pragmatism, affecting individuals in such a way that they feel compelled to abide by them. By establishing stable patterns of collective association, e.g. the individual to the team and team members, it frees the individual and the organization from the need to create new patterns of acting in each situation they encounter. Compliance with norms is therefore voluntary and not coerced. This moral dimension signifies the adoption of a collective orientation with which individuals and organizations identify.

Norms stabilize the collective functioning of interpersonal relations. At the same time, they do not completely suppress autonomy or the pursuit of localized interest nor cause the emergence of conflict between organizational members. Instead, they facilitate mutual adjustment among multiple partisan interests.

Thus, the professional individual can be seen as a cognitive being bounded by their internalization of social practices and social relations which is initiated by the instrumental socialization via primary and secondary groups, and which they bear inherent as cognitive beings. This implies that they select means, not just goals, first and foremost on the basis of values and emotions and furthermore, that decision making often reflects collective attributes and processes. Individual decisions are made, but often within the context set by various collectivities, that is, objective social practices and social relations constitute the form and the content of thought which in turn participates in the maintenance of those very social objectives.

Human thinking is therefore not simply something inside the head of an individual, it is a social and historical product of collective endeavour. Not only is there a world apart between behaviour that is value-rational in the Weberian sense, i.e. behaviour guided by conventional norms or sanctioned legal rules, and behaviour that is purely expressive of overwhelming emotions, but the consequential effects of these differences are also important as socially-based barriers.

The fact that organizations represent a social setting for humans to act as social beings as well as that individuals are bounded by moral commitment illustrate the importance of social-based strategies where social ties and commitment lay the foundation for barriers to exit, and in turn shed light upon the reason why professionals remain within the organizations they join.

Important then in the aforementioned context is the so-called social capital embedded in the relationship between the professional and the firm (Coleman, 1988); that is, the manner in which obligations and expectations, as well as information channels and social norms, affect the roles of the KIF and its primary resource – individuals. The function identified by the concept of 'social capital' is the value of certain aspects identified in the social structure, as resources that actors can use to achieve their interests.

Physical capital, embodied in observable material form, is wholly tangible. Human capital is less tangible as it is embodied In the skills and knowledge acquired by an individual. Less tangible still is social capital as it exists in the relations among persons.

Social capital, like other forms of capital, is productive and facilitates the achievement of certain ends that in its absence would not be possible. However, unlike other forms of capital, social capital is inherent in the structure of relations between and among actors. It does not disappear if some individuals leave, but may do so if a significant proportion of the knowledge workers leave at the same time. It is like social culture, those who live in it do not even see it (Ekstedt, 1990). Social capital then can be seen both as knowledge embedded in the organization and as a structure in which individuals can develop as humans and learn. It shares characteristics with an internal network of people exchanging information, ideas, skills and experience (Tichy and Fombrun, 1979:927). Cultivating social capital can be an important strategy in reducing knowledge workers' preferences for leaving – offering them something that is impossible to reach alone.

Successful firms then will demonstrate a system of management in which there is a combined bonding set of beliefs of values or as expressed by

Kanter (1989) 'a clear culture' – combined together with the facility within the organization to challenge existing assumptions; identify individuals or groups with problems rather than ready-made solutions; and the willingness to progress in the management of those problems.

Applying the strategies

We have sketched out two generic strategies that can be used to reduce the dependency on knowledge workers or the uncertainty grounded in the mobility potential of knowledge workers. The first class of strategic processes covers balancing the dependence on individuals with dependence on other knowledge systems. Some of these substitutes reduce the ability of the organization to adapt rapidly to environmental changes, due to the fact that systems, processes or structures have to be changed. Hence, a careful judgement of environmental characteristics is necessary before applying our strategies, balancing the need for rapid change against the need for reducing dependence on knowledge workers. The second is highlighting ties between the organization and the individual through material and social exit barriers.

A professional firm of some size will have ingredients from both strategies in operation. The degree to which KIFs can develop dependence upon structure and process as well as information or supporting systems will be determined by the characteristics of the working tasks.

If there is little repetition in work tasks, and the tasks to be done are not too huge (just needing one or a few individuals) or when tasks demand creativity and innovative behaviour to get solved, the firm will be heavily dependent on individual skills. In such a situation the second strategy will be most appropriate, creating material- and social-based barriers to exit for the individual subject.

When some of the tasks or parts of operations can be formulated and standardized the company may rely on Process II: knowledge abstraction substituting dependence on individuals with dependence on technical systems, information and standard operation procedures. Creative use of such a process can also create a competitive advantage in the marketplace, due to such factors as rapid solutions and standard of quality.

For firms solving problems that are very repetitive and where there exist a number of different task categories, Process III comes to use. By dividing between different professions and adopting a division of labour, the firm lessens the need for educated individuals to perform the total operation. Hospitals are one example of such a knowledge-dependent organization with these characteristics. Another is law firms that grow from being a group of individuals to a 'lawyer factory' characterized by numerous specialities. During their development they create functional departments, management structure and new set of roles (Gilson and Mnookin, 1990).

Firms facing task structures that have some degree of repetitiveness in operations, as well as where the tasks to be done are complex and so extensive that they cannot be solved by an informal group organization will be very concerned about the diffusion of knowledge, ensuring that they can perform all operations required for the project to develop. To perform well, such firms are dependent on adequate processes of allocating people and resources to tasks or projects.

Summary

The transition towards a knowledge-based society implies great changes for individuals and firms alike. Change, without a doubt, is one of the most interesting phenomena to study. Its very essence touches our everyday existence. Change is so fundamental yet so subtle that we, as human beings, either refuse to acknowledge it, or if we do, see it as unimportant and disregard its relevance.

If we do not understand the fundamental changes that are in our midst, that are in the process of completely restructuring society, then our actions remain based on outdated assumptions. Therefore, the emergence of the new era discussed here is the one most important reality today. There is a pending risk that our way of thinking, our attitudes and thereby decisions are not in sense with how things really are related.

Developing the resource dependence perspective, and constructing the concept knowledge as well as conceptualizing a framework from which strategies and processes are used to avoid uncertainty and balance dependency upon knowledge as a resource are all efforts towards a better understanding of the new reality we face. We have discussed how the face of knowledge shifts in the organization when our strategies are used. In so doing we have also indicated relevant situational characteristics for the use of the strategies.

References

Åström, L., 1990: När blir kunskap obsolent? in *Kunskap som kritisk resurs, en artikelsamling om kunskapsföretag* Lindmark, L., (Ed.), Handelshögskolan i Umeå, Umeå University, pp. 65–83.

Adler, P. S. and Shenbar, A. 1990: Adapting your technological base: The organizational challenge, *Sloan Management Review*, Fall, pp. 25–37.

Alvesson, M. 1989: *Ledning av kunnskapsföretag, eksempelet ENATOR*. Norstedts Förlag: Stockholm.

Coleman, J. S., 1988: Social capital in the creation of human capital, American Journal of Sociology, 94 supplement, pp. 95–120.

Ekstedt, E. 1990: Knowledge Renewal and Knowledge Companies. In *Kunskap som kritisk resurs, en artikelsamling om kunskapsföretag* Lindmark, L. (Ed.), Handelshögskolan i Umeå: Umeå University, pp. 21–35.

Etzioni, A. 1988: *The Moral Dimension – Toward A New Economics*. The Free Press: New York.

Freideson, E. 1970: *Profession of Medicine – A Study of the Sociology of Applied Knowledge*. Dodd, Mead: New York.

Gilson, R. J. and Mnookin R. H. 1985: Sharing Among the Human Capitalists: An Economic Inquiry into the Corporate Law Firm and How Partners Split Profits. *Stanford Law Review*, 37.

Gilson, R. J. and Mnookin R. H. 1990: The Implicit Contract for Corporate Law Firm Associates: Ex Post Opportunism and Ex Ante Bounding. In *The Firm as a Nexus of Treaties* Aoki, M., B. Gustafsson and O. E. Williamson (Eds.), Sage Publications: London, pp. 209–236.

Gurvitch, G. 1971: *The Social Frameworks of Knowledge*. Basil Blackwell and Harper and Row: Oxford.

Hedlund, G. and I. Nonaka, Models of Knowledge Management in the West and Japan. In *Strategic Processes: Learning, Adaption and Innovation* Lorange, P., *et al.*, (Eds.), Basil Blackwell London.

Hopper, M. D. 1990: Rattling SABRE – New Ways to Compete on Information. *Harvard Business Review*, May–June, pp. 118–125.

Itami, H. 1987: *Mobilizing Invisible Assets*. Harvard University Press, Cambridge, Massachusetts, 1987.

Kanter, R. M. 1989: *When Giants Learn to Dance*. Simon & Schuster: London.

Lawrence, P. R. and Lorsch J. W. 1967: *Organization and Environment*. Richard D. Irwin: Homewood, Ill.

Maturana, H. R. and Varela J. F. 1987: *The Tree of Knowledge*. Boston: Shambhala Publications, Inc.

Mintzberg, H. 1983: *Structure in Fives: Designing Effective Organizations*. Prentice-Hall International Editions: Englewood Cliffs, N. J.

Pfeffer, J. and Salancik G. R. 1978: *The External Control of Organizations – A Resource Dependence Perspective*. Harper & Row: New York.

Polyani, M. 1958: *Personal Knowledge – Towards a Post – Critical Philosophy*. London: Routledge & Kegan Paul.

Popper, K. 1972: *Objective Knowledge*. Oxford University Press: Oxford.

Prahalad, C. K. and Hamel G. 1990: The core competence of the corporation. *Harvard Business Review*, May –June, pp. 79–91.

Raelin, J. A. 1986: *The Clash of Cultures*. Harvard Business School Press: Boston.

Sadler, P. 1988: *Managerial Leadership in the Post-Industrial Society*. Gower Publishing Company: Aldershot, Hants.

Starbuck, W. H. 1990: Knowledge-intensive firms: learning to survive in strange environment. In *Kunskap som kritisk resurs, en artikelsamling om kunskapsföretag* Lindmark, L., (Ed.), Handelshögskolan i Umeå: Umeå University, pp. 10–20.

Sveiby, K. E. 1990: Kunnskapsföretaget och årsredovisningen. In *Kunskap som kritisk resurs, en artikelsamling om kunskapsföretag*. Lindmark, L., (Ed.), Handelshögskolan i Umeå: Umeå University, pp. 210–239.

Sveiby, K. E. and Risling A., 1987: Kunnskapsbedriften – Århundrets største lederutfordring? Cappelen, Oslo, *Kunnskapsföretaget*, Liber Förlag.

Thompson, J. D. 1967: *Organizations in Action*. McGraw-Hill Book Company: New York.

Tichy, N. M. and Fombrun C. 1979: Network Analysis in Organizational Setting. *Human relations*, 32, 11, pp. 923–965.

Zeleny, M. 1989: Knowledge as a New Form of Capital. *Human Systems Management*. 8, pp. part 1: 45–58, part 2: 129–143.

III

Co-operation in Networks

The three papers in this section define aspects of the strategy process in a co-operative context: the role and behaviour of brokers in network creation; the relationship between managerial cognitions and the perceived competitive structure within an interorganizational network; and the partner selection processes in a network context.

An attempt to link the strategy process and subsequent performance or, more precisely, the role and behaviour of managers in building and sustaining networks, results in what Snow and Thomas call the 'network broker'. Three types of networks can be delineated: (1) the internal network, in which most assets associated with a particular business are owned by the firm itself; (2) the stable network, in which such assets are owned by several firms; and (3) the dynamic network, in which a lead firm drives asset configurations among several firms. Similarly three broker roles can emerge; architect, lead operator, and caretaker. The most important role broker for the performance of the network is in the creation of the network, that is, the architect.

The boundaries of competition and co-operation within an industry are looked at by Porac, Thomas, Carroll, *et al.* in their study of the Scottish knitwear industry. They specifically address the question of how one can understand a firm's position in an industry that may be characterized as an interorganizational network. Traditionally there have been two ways to approach this question; through supply- and demand-side explanations. The former approach classifies firms according to organizational characteristics, on the assumption that similar firms require similar resources, which can result in industry rivalry. The latter approach classifies firms based on similarities in customer preferences on the assumption of substitutable outputs due to homogeneously-distributed resources, which can lead to interdependence stemming from revenue. The authors here break with this past tradition by taking an explicitly cognitive approach to rivalry. They suggest that interfirm rivalry is structured by shared managerial beliefs about boundaries and groups which they term the 'subjective organization'.

There has been much research on co-operative strategies from many different theoretical and practical perspectives, and, although some aspects of partner selection have been researched, the actual processes by which a partner is selected are still unclear. Geringer and Frayne show that the same process-based issues arise repeatedly across firms. A model consisting of seven subsequent processes emerges: (1) consideration of a joint venture as an investment alternative; (2) development of a selection criterion; (3) identification of prospective partners; (4) evaluation of prospective partners; (5) decision regarding prospects' qualification; (6) negotiations; and (7) final decision. The authors underscore that although these represent fundamental processes they need not necessarily be sequential. Rather, these processes are overlapping in nature and involve feedback loops.

9

Building Networks
BROKER ROLES AND BEHAVIOURS

Charles C. Snow and James B. Thomas

Historically, the strategic management literature has been dominated by studies of the 'content' of strategy. A large number of content studies have focused on the types of strategies that are effective in various industrial settings. Conversely, research on strategic processes – that is, how strategies are formulated and implemented – has tended to be modest and only normative or descriptive (Fredrickson, 1983). Moreover, process studies have seldom addressed organization performance.

In the last decade, however, research emphasis on strategic decision making processes has increased substantially (cf. Janis, 1989). The present study is part of this trend, and it explores the relationship between process and performance in a particular type of organization, the network. The network form of organization has been used increasingly by a wide variety of firms at both the national and international levels (Hakansson and Johansson, 1988), and its growth is likely to continue. Three types of networks were observed, with a specific focus on how key executives called 'brokers' manage the process of formation and development. The overall conclusion is that 'broker' behaviour has a major impact on network performance.

Background

Competitive pressures brought on by globalization, technology transfer and advances in communications forced many US companies in the 1980s to adopt a new equation for running their businesses. Instead of advocating continual resource accumulation and control, the new equation links business success to doing 'fewer things, better, with less' (Kanter, 1989).

Firms that do business this way frequently find themselves organized more like a network than a pyramidical hierarchy (Miles and Snow, 1986). For example, a single firm may handle research and design, while a second assembles and distributes finished products from components produced by

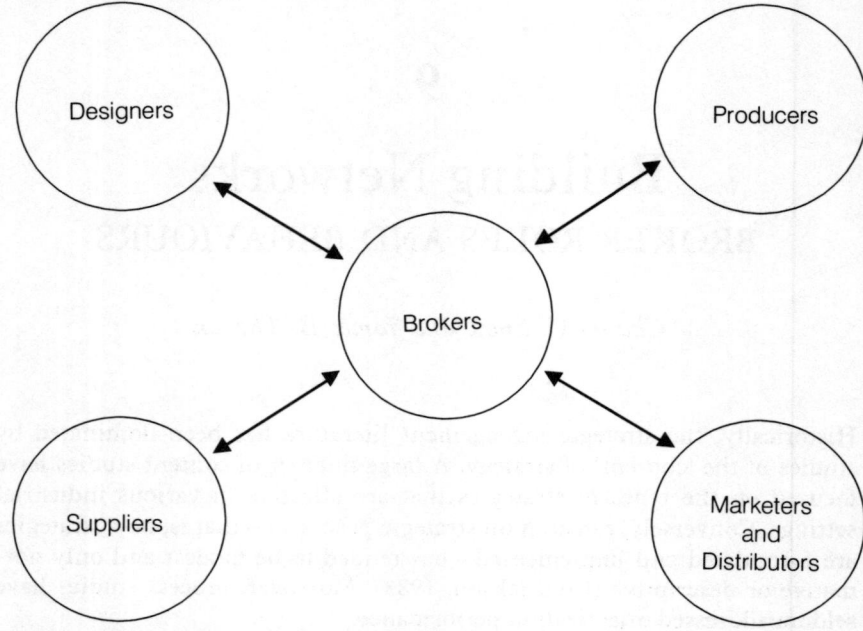

Figure 9.1   Network organization structure

a third firm, and so on. Any given firm linked to a network can fully utilize its core skills while maintaining flexibility through outsourcing. Outsourcing relationships are arranged by managers who act as brokers. Thus, the overall network is a configuration of more or less independent business units. (See figure 9.1.)

Types of networks

Networks have been created within as well as across firms, and three major types have been identified: internal, stable, and dynamic (Snow, Miles, and Coleman, 1992). An internal network is typically created to obtain the benefits of a market without engaging in much outsourcing. (See figure 9.2.). The internal network firm owns most or all of the assets associated with a particular business. Managers who control these assets are encouraged or required to expose them to the discipline of the market. The basic logic of the internal network is that if internal units have to operate with market prices instead of administratively-determined transfer prices, then they will constantly seek innovations that improve their performance.

The stable network uses partial outsourcing in a relatively predictable competitive environment. In the stable network, assets are owned by several firms but are dedicated to a particular business. Typically, a set of vendors

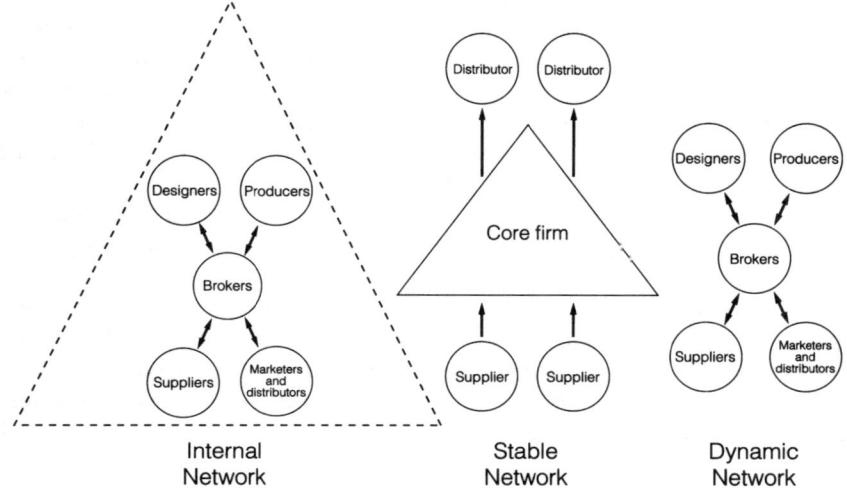

Figure 9.2   Common network types

is nestled around a large core firm, either providing inputs to the firm or distributing its outputs. (See figure 9.2.)

In faster-paced competitive environments, some firms have pushed the network form to the limits of its capabilities. This type of network can be very dynamic. Businesses such as fashions, toys, publishing, movies, and biotechnology may require or allow firms to outsource extensively. In such circumstances, the lead firm essentially identifies and assembles assets owned by others. Lead firms in dynamic networks may have as their prime competence marketing, research and development, design, and even manufacturing. However, in some cases, the lead firm acts solely as a broker. (See figure 9.2.)

The broker's role

In hierarchically organized firms, the fundamental role of management is to plan, organize, and control resources that are held in-house. In many network firms, however, key managers operate across rather than within hierarchies, assembling resources controlled by outside parties. These managers, therefore, can be thought of as brokers. Three broker roles are especially important to the success of network organizations: architect, lead operator and caretaker (Snow, Miles, and Coleman, 1992).

Managers who act as architects facilitate the emergence of specific operating networks. This process seldom proceeds straightforwardly. In some cases, the architect may design a network by conceiving how resources can be assembled into a brand-new configuration. Most likely, however, the architect has in mind only a vague concept of the product or service as well as the value chain required to offer it. This business concept is then brought into clearer focus as the broker seeks out firms with desirable expertise, takes an equity position in a firm to coax it into the value chain, helps to create new groups that are needed in specialized support roles and so on.

Once a set of potential network partners has been identified, emphasis shifts from design to decisions about operation. Managers who act primarily as lead operators take advantage of the conditions previously created by manager-architects (though the two roles may overlap considerably and may be played by the same person). Essentially, this means that the lead operator formally connects specific firms together into an operating network. Although the lead operator role may require a manager to work with several different firms, the same function can be performed entirely within a single firm.

Once in place, networks require continual enhancement if they are to operate smoothly and effectively. Thus, the process of network development is ongoing. Managers who focus on enhancement activity can be called caretakers. The caretaker role is multifaceted and may be just as important as the architect and lead operator roles to the ultimate success of a network organization. A caretaker must frequently monitor a large number of relationships and be prepared to engage in a variety of behaviours, including sharing information, nurturing smaller or newer network members, and disciplining members who act in ways that are harmful to the network's common good.

Ultimately, given the widespread and growing use of network organizations, it is important to achieve a better understanding of how the broker's behaviour during the network building process is linked to network performance.

Method

Research sites and sample

Network creation and development processes were explored in the health care industry. For many reasons, including soaring costs and changing reimbursement patterns, all health care providers have come under increasing pressure to integrate services and reduce costs while improving quality (D'Aunno and Zuckerman, 1987; Goldsmith, 1989). A major means of realizing these goals is the development and maintenance of effective health care networks (Longest, 1990). Therefore, the health care industry was seen as an ideal arena for studying network organizations.

Research sites were selected through consultation with a large northeastern state's hospital association. Three main selection criteria were employed: (a) the site must permit observation of the network development process so as to avoid sole reliance on retrospective accounts; (b) key brokers must be accessible for multiple interviews and observation; and (c) all of the sites combined must represent the three major network types discussed earlier (internal, stable, and dynamic).

The first site chosen consisted of two hospitals and a number of other health care institutions (physician groups, a rehabilitation centre, several ambulatory care centres, etc.). At the time of the study, these various organizations were attempting to form a single health care firm. The intent of the alliance was to create a central administrative organization that would provide performance standards and system-wide policies. A new legal entity was formed, and the chief administrator of one of the two collaborating hospitals became its president. Although the participating physician groups retained substantial autonomy in their respective medical specialities, the various components of this network firm wished to offer an integrated package of health care services. Thus, the structure exhibited the characteristics of an *internal network*. (See figure 9.3.)

The second research site took the form of a *stable network*. In this type of network, assets are owned by several firms but are dedicated to a particular business. Typically, a set of vendors is nestled around a large core firm. (See figure 9.3.) At the beginning of the study, the chief administrator of a large regional hospital was in the final stages of formalizing an alliance with a large physician group (representing a wide variety of medical specialities), a small out-patient surgery centre, and several other health care providers (a rehabilitation hospital, nutrition centre, pharmacy, medical laboratories, etc.). The core firm in this alliance was a facility referred to by its members as a 'medical mall'. The medical mall enhanced the market power of all the organizations involved with it through a steady flow of patient referrals. The lead broker in this network, the chief administrator of the regional hospital, played a key role in developing both the medical mall and the network.

The third health care alliance was a *dynamic network*. (See figure 9.3.) In its extreme form, a dynamic network may be constructed by a broker who commits few (if any) physical or financial assets to the network. The broker essentially identifies and assembles assets owned by other firms. In this case, the lead broker was the former director of strategic planning at a large urban hospital who formed his own firm to co-ordinate the provision of health care services across a dozen independent health care institutions. At this site, the study focused on the process used by the lead broker to add a new member to the network.

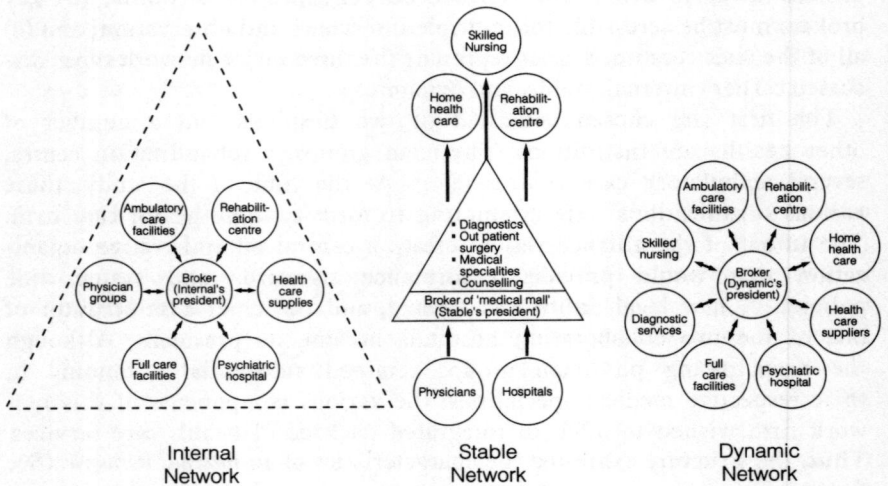

Figure 9.3   Three health care networks

Data and respondents

Given the paucity of detailed, systematic observation of network development processes, a multiple case format was used (Eisenhardt, 1989; Yin, 1989). Comparative case studies provided the best vehicle for building an understanding of the complexity and richness of network formation and development processes.

The multiple case approach requires that data and theory be compared and contrasted throughout the data collection and analysis process (Isabella, 1990). As constructs, perspectives, and relationships were identified, a model of the network development process, and the role of the network broker, gradually evolved.

The unit of analysis was the network. In addition to multiple interviews with the three lead brokers, other individuals involved in the development of each network provided confirmatory information. These individuals included both physicians and executives (e.g., vice president of medical affairs, chief financial officer, and chief operating officer). Where appropriate, interviews were held with decision makers who were no longer with the institutions that formed the network but who had been involved in the early stages of its development. These respondents offered insight into the history of the network's relationships.

The study consisted of three phases. The first phase involved: (a) an extensive interviewing process; (b) observation of various events (e.g., executive meetings, consultant presentations, and informal interactions among network participants); and (c) the gathering of appropriate documents (e.g., contracts, reports, memoranda, and other written analyses). Analysis of the interview, observation, and archival data provided an initial understanding of the network formation process and the role of the network broker. (See Thomas and Trevino, forthcoming, for details)

During phase one, twenty-four interviews were conducted with brokers, other decision makers, and major network stakeholders (n = 7, 8, and 9 across the three sites). The same interview procedure was used with all respondents. Each interview lasted from $1\frac{1}{2}$ to $2\frac{1}{2}$ hours and was conducted by two interviewers. The interview schedule contained both structured and open-ended questions. Interviews were audiotaped and later transcribed. Interview notes and impressions were discussed and analyzed within one day of the interview in accordance with the twenty-four-hour rule (Yin, 1989).

The second research phase was an in-depth analysis of the interview data obtained during phase one. Transcripts were analysed by different researchers in an attempt to verify the accuracy and reliability of the results. For example, one analysis was performed by nine analysts who were not involved in the data collection process. Following Miles and Huberman (1984) and Spradley (1979), they identified themes in the interview data obtained from the three lead brokers. According to the theme analysis, brokers' observations about network creation and development emphasized areas such an leadership, politics, and conflict management. Another analysis, performed by the two researchers who conducted the interviews, identified themes in the observations made by other network participants (n = 21). These additional themes included momentum, information processing, history, and performance. Together, these qualitative analyses helped greatly to identify important aspects of broker behaviour.

The third phase of the study involved the construction of a survey questionnaire based on the qualitative analyses. The questionnaire was pretested with five hospital executives not included in the study and then mailed to all twenty-four interviewees; seventeen responded (71 per cent). Responses from the three sites (n = 6, 6, and 5) were combined to provide a description of the network development process at each site as well as perceptions of the roles and behaviours of each network's lead broker.

Variables and measures

The questionnaire contained items about five variables: (a) network performance; (b) network politics; (c) information processing structure, (d) the broker's conflict management style; and (e) the leadership style of the broker. With the exception of conflict management, which employed single-item measures, all variables were measured with multi-item, seven-point Likert scales. For each variable scale, item scores were averaged to calculate a variable score. Cronbach alphas for all scales were greater than D.74. The survey questions are shown in the Appendix.

Network performance

It is difficult to measure objectively the performance of a network organization during its creation and development. Therefore, a perceptual measure of network performance similar to that of Fornell, Lorange, and Roos (1990) was used. The specific performance factors were adapted from Fottler's (1987) discussion of health care organization performance, including: (1) financial performance (short- and long-term profitability, growth, market share); (2) innovation, prestige, and service range; and (3) satisfaction of physician needs and concerns. An additional item reflected what network participants themselves looked for in judging success: service to the community. Lastly, all of the measures were combined to represent overall network performance (short and long run).

Respondents were asked first to indicate the importance of each factor in determining network performance. All factors measured greater than four on a seven-point scale. Then respondents were asked to what extent these performance factors had been met in their network. All questions were posed twice. The first measurement occurred soon after each network had been put into operation. The second measurement was taken approximately eighteen months later by telephoning previous respondents.

Network politics

Politics in organizations refers to conflicts that emerge among various groups due to their different perspectives and preferences (Cyert and March, 1963). Politics is especially important to network organizations because the various members of the network must work together as well as pursue their own self-interests. Network political activity was operationalized along six dimensions: goals and preferences, decision process, rules and norms, information requirements, information use, and decision outcomes (Pfeffer, 1981: 31). The six items were scaled so that a higher score indicated greater pursuit of self-interest among network participants.

Information processing structure

Information processing structure refers to the degree of formality, interaction, and participation among the managers associated with the network development process. The eleven-item scale used to measure information processing structure was based on Thomas and McDaniel (1990). The items were scaled so that higher scores represented low formality, high interaction, and high participation, indicating a large processing capacity (Galbraith, 1973).

Conflict management style

The broker's style of managing conflict was measured by four items that asked to what extent disagreements over network creation issues were resolved by (a) executive order, (b) debate, (c) compromise, and (d) accommodation. An executive order approach to conflict management indicates autocratic behaviour on the part of the broker, while the debate, compromise, and accommodation styles indicate more collaborative conflict management approaches. These latter styles have been identified as collaborative approaches used at the interorganizational level (Brown, 1982).

Leadership style

The broker's leadership style was measured along four dimensions: task orientation, people orientation, facilitation, and supportiveness (Bass, 1981: 331). The ten items were scaled so that higher scores indicated that the broker's leadership style was oriented more toward people than tasks.

Findings

The findings reported below reflect both the qualitative and quantitative analyses and are organized into three categories: (a) network performance, (b) broker roles, and (c) broker behaviours.

Network performance

The longitudinal performance measures for all three networks are shown in table 9.1. As indicated, each network experienced a different performance pattern. For example, Stable Network, in which a variety of health care groups were organized in a medical mall, was successful from the beginning. It met community health-care needs (5.3 on a seven-point scale), was perceived as a prestigious service operation (5.3), and its initial financial performance was good (4.9). The network also satisfied the needs and concerns of its physician groups (4.2). Overall, Stable Network showed solid performance for a newly-created organization (4.9). Eighteen months later, all of these performance indicators either stayed the same or increased, and Stable Network's overall performance improved to 5.2 at the end of the study period.

Internal Network and Dynamic Network both started poorly relative to Stable Network. However, Dynamic Network, the health care alliance of

Table 9.1   Network performance

	Internal Network		Stable Network		Dynamic Network	
	1988	*1990*	*1988*	*1990*	*1988*	*1990*
Service to the community	2.1	na	5.3	6.0	2.5	5.5
Innovation, prestige, and range of services	2.5	na	5.3	5.5	2.0	4.5
Financial performance	1.3	na	4.9	5.2	2.9	4.0
Satisfaction of physician needs	2.0	na	4.2	4.2	2.8	6.0
Overall performance	1.9	na	4.9	5.2	2.6	5.0

Note: All scores are averages based on a scale of 1 = very low to 7 = very high. Sample size = 17.

twelve organizations led by a small broker firm, was able to improve its performance on every dimension examined. At the end of the study, its overall performance was almost as high as that of Stable Network (5.0 versus 5.2). Internal Network, on the other hand, was not able to correct its initial poor performance. After a trial period lasting approximately one year, Internal Network disbanded the firm it had created specifically for this health care alliance.

Broker roles

Internal network

Internal's lead broker had been a hospital administrator for thirty-five years prior to becoming the president of the firm specifically created for this health-care venture. This individual's health-care experience was rooted in a previous era in which alliances were infrequent, cost increases could be passed along to patients or third-party payers, and so on. Although he was a respected administrator, it soon became apparent that he was not well suited to performing certain aspects of the broker role.

Internal's president got the idea of forming a network in his region by observing the success of health-care alliances in other communities. He prepared a lengthy fact sheet that contained the data and reasons supporting the need for a network of health-care services. Relying on his reputation as the administrator of the region's largest hospital, he was able to convince physician groups and other health-care providers to form the network for a trial period. When he resigned as hospital administrator to become Internal's president, he was replaced as the chief administrator at his hospital (which remained in the network).

The president established clear performance measures for each of the member institutions so that their behaviour could be legitimately compared within the network as well as to the behaviour of non-network providers. Generally, this meant viewing each facility as a business unit and encouraging it to sell its products or services on the open market. Also, each facility was assigned (or retained) an area of expertise such as the provision of ambulatory care, skilled nursing, or specific medical focus (oncology, obstetrics, etc.). Each network component was expected to be known as the expert at providing its product or service and to co-operate with other members of the network wherever appropriate.

However, during the course of this standardization process, network members became disaffected with the president's unilateral directives and ever-present fact sheets. The culmination of these internal problems came when an anonymous complaint was filed with the Federal Trade Commission alleging that the network was restraining trade in the region. After a series of stormy discussions, Internal's board of directors decided not to fight the complaint, the president resigned shortly thereafter, and the network dissolved within a month.

With respect to the broker's role, Internal's president seemed to make three major mistakes. First, his leadership style emphasized the tasks to be accomplished (e.g., setting goals and formulating policies) instead of the relationships to be formed and managed. In general, the president was not perceived as a people person. Second, the president conceived of the network as belonging to him rather than to the member institutions. As a result, his method of handling problems and conflicts was primarily that of executive fiat. Seldom did he genuinely collaborate with network members to resolve issues that they had raised. Third, the president focused only on the architect and operator roles of the broker; he performed very few caretaker activities. When he did act as a caretaker, he often used inappropriate approaches to conflict management and information processing. (See table 9.2 for a summary of the three lead brokers' roles.)

Stable network

Stable Network was born out of a geographic as well as a business need. The chief administrator of a large regional hospital realized that he could not easily expand his facility because of its physical location. At the time, out-patient surgery as a percentage of all surgery was expanding dramatically and the hospital's operating rooms could no longer accommodate the

Table 9.2 Broker roles

	Internal's President	Stable's President	Dynamic's President
Overall Image Within Network	Autocratic, task and quantitatively oriented, power seeker	Professional, well-respected leader	Relations oriented, consensus builder, patient
Architect	**Pioneered first health care network in the region**	Originated 'one stop health care' idea as the focus of the network	Original idea to expand network came from a previous broker
	Identified appropriate members	Developed with the physician leader the concept of a 'medical mall'	
Lead Operator	**Formed new firm**	Implemented medical mall concept including design and construction of physical facility	**In charge of all analyses required to add a new node onto the network**
	Developed standard policies and performance measures		
Caretaker	Was not aware of the importance of this role and basically ignored it	Managed information and politics extremely well	**Spent over half of his time resolving process issues**
		Shared this role with newly hired manager of the medical mall	

Note: Boldface type indicates role(s) emphasized by the lead broker.

demand. He was worried that some outside health-care provider would enter the region and take away the hospital's out-patient business. Therefore, he initiated some preliminary discussions about an ambulatory surgery centre with two individuals: (a) the head of a small ambulatory surgery facility located nearby; and (b) the leader of a group of physicians who used the hospital for much of their surgery.

The leader of the physician group was particularly intrigued with the concept of an out-patient surgery centre because, among other reasons, his group owned some land that could serve as the proposed centre's site. In a subsequent conversation, the hospital administrator and the physician leader hit upon the idea of 'one-stop health-care' offered in a 'medical mall'. The hospital administrator pursued this idea, ultimately becoming the president of Stable Network.

Not long after it was agreed that the medical mall was a viable concept, all of the initial participants, at the suggestion of Stable's president, decided to bring in a general manager to run the mall. The individual who was hired, a young administrator from a small psychiatric hospital, was brought in early enough to oversee the mall's construction, arrange for financing, and so on. Stable's president then retired, but stayed in the area and served as a consultant to the network.

An a broker, Stable's president appeared to do three things very well. First, he involved key people in both the planning and implementation of the network. He shared information as it became available, and he encouraged certain individuals to head up committees to resolve issues that were important to network members. Second, he managed network politics carefully and effectively. There were many opportunities for a particular group to obtain a disproportionate share of the business or to have things done its way. The president was adept at maintaining a balance in the interests of members by diplomatically resolving concerns at meetings, social events, and over the telephone. Third, Stable's president demonstrated that broker responsibilities can be shared. on many occasions, for example, the leader of the physician group acted as an architect and caretaker of the network. Further, the president, long before he retired, began to share the operator role with the administrator who was brought in to run the medical mall.

Dynamic network

The lead broker at Dynamic Network was the director of strategic planning at a large regional hospital located on the west bank of a river that dissected a metropolitan area. He worked for the hospital's chief administrator, a veteran in the health-care field. On several occasions the chief administrator had expressed the idea of aligning with another hospital located across the river in a more affluent area. This smaller hospital was doing poorly financially, staff morale was low, and the surrounding community did not perceive the hospital to be a high-quality health-care provider. By coupling this struggling hospital to the network of health-care relationships that the large hospital already had on its side of the river, the administrator thought that he could create a service system that would dominate the entire region.

The chief administrator assigned his strategic planning director the task of exploring the desirability of forging this link. After a thorough examination of the hospital's two main alternatives, either building a new facility across the river or aligning with one or more larger hospitals in the area, the decision was made to ally with the target hospital. At that point, the strategic planning director resigned and formed his own management firm to lead the expansion 'across the river'.

The lead broker, now Dynamic Network's president, spent virtually all of his time managing the incorporation of the new network member. He estimated that he devoted 'seventeen meals a week' to this process – talking to recalcitrant members of the target hospital's board, resolving conflicts, building consensus in the community, and so on. He was very patient in his attempts to influence network stakeholders. He worked hard at creating solid relationships, using quantitative data only when requested. For example, he hired an independent health care consulting firm to present its analysis of the region's business opportunities to the target hospital.

Thus, except for some early studies, Dynamic's president worked full-time at the caretaker role during the network development process. Three aspects of his performance of this role were notable. First, he was adept at handling people and politics – he was much like Stable's president in this regard. However, he was even more patient in letting ideas percolate and consensus evolve. Second, he was good at managing momentum. The addition of this particular hospital to the network required, in the president's opinion, a careful, deliberate pace. However, his skill in sensing when to push the process forward, or to follow its natural tempo, was so apparent to network participants that it seemed he could alter his style to fit the pace of any organization development process. Third, he used a long-term perspective in all of his dealings with network members. He was willing to forego solutions to problems unless they appeared to have a lasting quality. This perspective paid off in that Dynamic Network had much higher performance at the end of the study period than at the beginning.

Broker behaviours

Four main broker behaviours were observed: conflict management style, leadership style, information processing approaches, and methods of managing political activity among network members. The results are shown in table 9.3.

Table 9.3   Broker behaviours

	Internal Network	Stable Network	Dynamic Network
Conflict Management:			
Executive order	4.3	1.8	2.5
Accommodation	2.3	4.2	4.2
Compromise	2.3	4.8	3.5
Debate	2.6	5.0	4.3
Leadership Style	3.2	4.8	4.4
Network Politics	4.3	3.9	3.7
Information Processing Structure	4.1	5.2	4.8

Note: All scores are averages based on a scale of 1 = very low through 7 = very high (except for network politics which was reverse scored). Sample size = 17.

The findings on broker behaviours in large part mirrored the findings on network performance and broker roles. That is, Internal Network was quite different from both Stable Network and Dynamic Network, which shared many similarities. Specifically, Internal's president relied mostly on executive orders to respond to conflict (4.3) and focused more on tasks than people in his leadership style (3.2). These approaches were unsuccessful in establishing productive long-term relationships among the network's participants. Although the differences were not large, Internal Network's members tended to act more in their own self-interest than in the interest of the network as a whole (4.3 versus 3.9 and 3.7 on a reverse-scored scale). Lastly, less information was shared in Internal Network than in the other two networks (4.1 versus 5.2 and 4.8). Ultimately, although Internal's president can be credited with creating and assembling a potentially viable network (see the architect and lead operator roles in table 9.2), his management of the network development process was widely regarded as poor.

Conversely, the lead brokers in Stable Network and Dynamic Network behaved similarly even though their networks developed from very different starting points (the creation of a complete medical mall versus the incorporation of one new network participant). When conflicts arose, Stable's president encouraged the affected parties to debate them (5.0) and compromise if necessary (4.8). Dynamic's president also encouraged debate (4.3) and urged conflicting parties to be willing to accommodate other groups' interests (4.2). In neither case did these brokers focus their resolution of conflict on executive fiat (1.8 and 2.5).

The presidents of Stable and Dynamic were also similar in their leadership style (4.8 and 4.4), which was very people-oriented. They managed network politics similarly, such that there was somewhat less self-interest behaviour evident in these two networks than was the case with Internal Network (3.9 and 3.7 versus 4.3). Lastly, due to their respective brokers' approaches to managing information, Stable Network and Dynamic Network had larger information processing capacities than Internal Network (5.2 and 4.8 versus 4.1).

Discussion

Based on all of the interview, observation, and archival data, it appeared that the success of all three networks was heavily dependent on the process used for building the network. Four critical factors were controlled for during the study that strengthen this assertion. First, the study controlled for industry effects by examining only health-care networks. Second, each network had a well-conceived strategy for conducting its business – in the sense that appropriate analyses had been performed, consultants had been retained, and so on. Consequently, the content of each network's strategy appeared to be sound. Third, the size of each network, as measured by the number of members, was approximately the same. Lastly, given the demand for health-care services in the respective regions, the regions' similar economic health, and the same state-mandated regulations, each of the networks had a similar chance of being successful.

The fact that Internal Network failed, while Stable Network and Dynamic Network succeeded, provided additional support for the proposition that process is important to outcome. By drawing comparisons and contrasts across the three evolutionary processes, it is possible to specify some of the major factors associated with building a successful network. (See figure 9.4.)

Formational phase

The primary broker role to be played in the formation of a network organization is that of the architect. The presidents of both Stable Network and Internal Network performed the architect's role well. Based on their approaches, it appears that three strategic decisions are critical to the successful completion of this phase of network evolution. First, the architect must establish a business need for the network. The prime motive for any firm to join a network is an opportunity for financial gain. It is the architect's challenge to articulate the vision of the network and to demonstrate to potential members the advantages of joining the network.

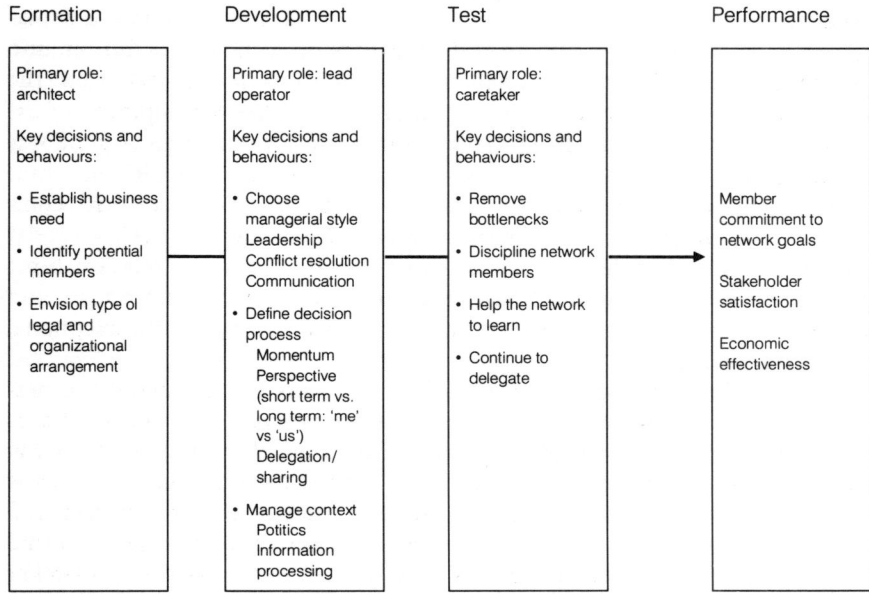

Formation	Development	Test	Performance
Primary role: architect	Primary role: lead operator	Primary role: caretaker	
Key decisions and behaviours:	Key decisions and behaviours:	Key decisions and behaviours:	
• Establish business need	• Choose managerial style Leadership Conflict resolution Communication	• Remove bottlenecks	Member commitment to network goals
• Identify potential members		• Discipline network members	Stakeholder satisfaction
• Envision type ol legal and organizational arrangement	• Define decision process Momentum Perspective (short term vs. long term: 'me' vs 'us') Delegation/ sharing	• Help the network to learn	Economic effectiveness
		• Continue to delegate	
	• Manage context Potitics Information processing		

Figure 9.4 Relationships among network phase, broker roles and behaviours, and performance

Second, the architect identifies network members. In the case of Internal Network, all of the potential participants were easily identified. At Stable Network, on the other hand, considerable effort was spent by the broker to identify firms appropriate for inclusion in the medical mall. After identifying a potential member, the architect must anticipate the issues that are likely to arise if this firm becomes part of the network and begin to resolve these issues early.

Third, the broker as architect must envision the type of legal and organizational arrangements by which network members will be linked. Internal's president started a new firm for this purpose while Stable's president created a core firm (the medical mall) around which several other health-care providers were organized. A key part of the process of choosing a legal and organizational scheme is a risk assessment of each member, including the perceived fit of its expertise, its ability to perform consistently, and any liabilities that the member may pose upon joining the network.

Developmental phase

As a network moves into the developmental phase, the broker's emphasis shifts from design to operation. The presidents of all three networks devoted considerable time to the lead operator role, and three areas seemed to demand most of their attention. First, the broker must choose a managerial style, particularly with regard to leadership, conflict resolution, and communications. Internal's president used a very different style than the other two presidents, one which appeared to harm the development of his network from the outset. In particular, his ineffective managerial style was characterized by a task orientation (to the exclusion of people), an autocratic approach to conflict resolution, and the use of impersonal communications media such an memoranda, fact sheets, and so on. Conversely, the other two presidents were oriented toward building relationships; handling conflicts through debate, accommodation, and compromise; and communicating through media such as informal meetings, the telephone, and social events.

Second, the lead operator must define a process for managing the network as relationships formalize. This includes proceeding at a pace that is comfortable to all parties. Momentum can be nudged or simply allowed to proceed, but the broker must be aware of how the evolutionary process is unfolding for each network participant. Also, though the broker may deal with many short-run problems, he or she must keep the long view in mind at all times. Otherwise, agreements may later unravel. Lastly, the broker may decide to delegate or share the operator role during the developmental phase. Doing so builds more knowledge and management expertise into the network. Among the three brokers, Stable's president relied most heavily on role sharing, and all of his network members believed that this was effective.

Third, compared to traditional organizations, networks pose special problems of political activity and information processing. The presidents of Stable Network and Dynamic Network recognized this distinctive context and deliberately managed it; Internal's president did neither. Each network member has a dual allegiance – to itself and to the network. The broker must be sensitive to managing the developmental process in such a way that individual as well as collective interests are taken into account. Otherwise, as in the case of Internal Network, members may choose to return to independent status or perhaps join another network. Similarly, network members have varying capacities to absorb and digest information before making decisions. The broker must provide information, in form and amount, that is suitable for the information-processing capacity of each network member.

Test phase

The final phase of network evolution consists of testing. This is a trial period where the network begins to offer its product or service to customers. In order for this phase to be successful, the broker's emphasis must shift heavily to the role of caretaker. Of the three network brokers, Dynamic's president spent by far the most time playing the caretaker role.

As a caretaker, the broker must engage in at least four specific behaviours. First, the caretaker must remove any bottlenecks that have a negative impact on the network. Bottlenecks can include previous issues that have not been fully resolved, or new issues that arise in the course of running the network. In either case, the caretaker must take action with the goal of smoothing the flow of operations.

Second, the caretaker may have to discipline a network member. Given the centrality of the role, the broker is perhaps the only person (or group) who can spot inimical behaviour within the network. On one occasion, for example, Dynamic's president hinted diplomatically that he might have to recall a loan made to one of the network's firms if it continued to spend money on resources outside the originally agreed upon scope. This mild warning was all that was needed to bring the offending member back into alignment with the other network participants.

Third, the broker as caretaker helps the newly operational network to learn. This is accomplished by pointing out to all members those things that are helpful to the network's progress and by motivating the members to improve. The caretaker serves as a critical feedback loop to all members until formal and permanent mechanisms are in place.

Finally, as operations stabilize, the caretaker may decide to share or delegate the caretaker role. Just as Stable Network's president shared the architect and lead operator roles, Dynamic's president began to look for ways of spreading caretaking responsibility among more people in the system so that the entire network did not have to rely solely on him to perform these activities in the long run.

Conclusion

This study contributes to the strategic management literature in three main ways. First, it identifies empirically the major process variables related to performance in newly formed and evolving network organizations. Second, the primary focus of the study was on broker roles and behaviours. In the future, as more firms adopt the network structure, managers will find themselves increasingly called upon to act as brokers. This study provides insights into the process issues facing network brokers. Lastly, by examining both successful and unsuccessful networks, the study generated several prescriptions that brokers can use to manage more effectively. Future research should examine the roles, behaviours, and relationships described here in larger-scale studies of the process-performance link.

Appendix
Survey Questions

Network performance

To what extent have each of the following performance objectives of the network been met?

1 Long-term profitability
2 Net profit for the coming year
3 Growth
4 Market share
5 Prestige of network participants
6 Innovation of medical care and delivery
7 Increasing range of services offered
8 Service to the community
9 Meeting the needs of physicians

Leadership style
To what extent do the following words accurately describe _____'s leadership style during the formation process?

1 Negotiating
2 Sharing
3 Participative
4 Supportive
5 Commanding
6 Cooperative
7 Directive
8 Resolute
9 Autocratic
10 Authoritative

Network politics
To what extent:

1 Did coalitions form and change among decision makers during the formation process?
2 Was strategic decision making during the development process characterized by the 'push and pull' of different interests?
3 Was conflict an accepted action during the process?
4 Was information used to influence decisions during the formation process?
5 Was there a systematic search for information during the development process?
6 Can the development process be characterized as an exercise in bargaining, negotiation, and compromise?

Information processing structure
During the development process, to what extent:

1 Did you feel you had the opportunity to express your ideas about the relationship?
2 Did you feel that your views were included in the decision process?
3 Did you feel that others' ideas were imposed upon you?
4 Were written rules and procedures followed?
5 Did individuals interact with each other on an informal basis?
6 Did committees, such as ad hoc task groups, form to deal with strategic issues?
7 Did one or two people dominate the handling of the development process?
8 Was there a free and open exchange of ideas?

To what extent can the development process be characterized as:
9 Formal and rule-oriented?
10 Participative?
11 Interactive?

References

Bass, B. M., 1981: *Stogdill's Handbook of Leadership*. The Free Press: New York.
Brown, L. D. 1982: *Managing Conflict at Organizational Interfaces*. Addison-Wesley: Reading, Massachusetts.
Cyert, R. N. and March, J. G., 1963: *A Behavioral Theory of the Firm*. Prentice-Hall: Englewood Cliffs, New Jersey.
D'Aunno, T. A. and Zuckerman, H. S. 1987: A life cycle model of organizational federations: The case of hospitals. *Academy of Management Review*, pp. 534–545.
Eisenhardt, K. M. 1989: Building theories from case study research. *Academy of Management Review*. pp. 532–550.
Fornell, C., Lorange, P. and Roos, J. 1990: The cooperative venture formation process: A latent variable structural modeling approach. *Management Science*, pp. 1246–1255.
Fottler, M. D. 1987: Health care organizational performance: Present and future performance. *Journal of Management*, pp. 367–391.
Fredrickson, J. W. 1983: Strategic process research: Questions and recommendations. *Academy of Management Review*. pp. 565–575.
Galbraith, J. R. 1973: *Designing Complex Organizations*, Addison-Wesley: Reading, Massachusetts.
Goldsmith, J. 1989: A radical prescription for hospitals. *Harvard Business Review*. pp. 104–111.
Hakansson, H. and Johansson, J. 1988: Formal and informal cooperation strategies in international industrial networks. In F. Contractor and P. Lorange (eds). *Cooperative strategies in international business*, Lexington Books: Lexington, MA, pp. 369–379.

Isabella, L. A. 1990: Evolving interpretations as a change unfolds: How managers construe key organizational events. *Academy of Management Journal*, pp. 7–41.

Janis, I. L. 1989: *Crucial Decisions: Leadership in Policy Making and Crisis Management.* The Free Press: New York.

Kanter, R. M. 1989: Becoming PALs: Pooling, allying, and linking across companies. *Academy of Management Executive.* pp. 183–193.

Longest, B. B. 1990: Interorganizational linkages in the health sector. *Health Care Management Review.* pp. 17–28.

Miles, M. B. and Huberman, A. M. 1984: *Qualitative Data Analysis: A Sourcebook of New Methods,* Sage Publications: Beverly Hills, California.

Miles, R. E. and Snow, C. C. 1986: Network organizations: New concepts for new forms. *California Management Review*, pp. 62–73.

Pfeffer, J. 1981 *Power in Organizations,* Pitman: Marshfield, Massachusetts.

Snow, C. C., Miles, R. E. and Coleman, Jr. H. J. 1992: Managing 21st century network organizations. *Organizational Dynamics*, pp. 5–20.

Spradley, J. P. 1979: *The Ethnographic Interview.* Holt, Rinehart and Winston: New York.

Thomas, J. B. and McDaniel R. E. 1990: Interpreting strategic issues: Effects of strategy and the information-processing structure of top management teams. *Academy of Management Journal*, pp. 286–306.

Thomas, J. B. and Trevino, L. K. forthcoming: Information Processing in Strategic Alliance Building: A Multiple Case Approach. *Journal of Management Studies.*

Yin, R. K. 1989: *Case Study Research: Design and Methods.* Sage Publications: Beverly Hills, California.

10

The Subjective Organization of the Scottish Knitwear Industry

Joseph F. Porac, Howard Thomas, Charles Carroll, Fiona Wilson and Douglas Paton

Delineating the boundaries of competition among firms has historically been one of the most intractable issues in the study of economic organizations. The problem entails describing a very complex interorganizational reality by showing that interfirm rivalry is discontinuous across an organizational field. Showing that competitive relationships 'cluster' within subsets of firms reduces the complexity of the organizational field by dividing firms into relatively homogeneous subgroups of rivals. These subgroups allow researchers and analysts to develop group-specific predictive models of firm behaviour. Moreover, competitive grouping provides managers with a ready-made classification for understanding a firm's position in an interorganizational network. For these reasons, many attempts have been made to develop logical and consistent criteria for identifying interfirm boundaries and for forming industrial groups.

In this paper, we report some of the preliminary results of an ongoing study to map competitive relationships within the Scottish knitwear industry. Although our approach draws from previous classification models, the point of the research is to break with past traditions by taking an explicitly *cognitive* approach to rivalry. The research is based upon the straightforward assumption that competitive relationships among firms are mediated by complex patterns of managerial inferences and decisions. Working backwards from this assumption to the information-processing mechanisms underlying managerial thinking, we suggest that the pattern of rivalry among firms is structured by shared managerial beliefs about interfirm boundaries and groups. These beliefs we term the 'subjective organization' of an industry, and the purpose of the present research is to uncover the subjective organization of Scottish knitwear firms.

A Closer Look at the Competitive Boundary Problem

In general, previous efforts to assess competitive boundaries among firms have proceeded in two directions. So called 'supply-side' approaches have attempted to classify firms on the basis of similarities and differences in organizational characteristics. Supply-side classifications rest upon the assumption that a firm's characteristics determine its resource requirements. Thus, similar firms will require similar resources and be strategically interdependent. This interdependence will ultimately be reflected in rivalry. So called 'demand-side' organizational groupings divide the actual resource space in which a firm's activities are embedded. Demand-side classifications rest upon the assumption that scarce resources flowing equally well to two or more organizations imply strategic interdependence among those organizations.

As many writers have noted, neither supply-side nor demand-side attempts to cluster organizations have been completely successful (e.g., Robinson, 1952; Nightengale, 1978; Auerbach, 1988; McKelvey, 1982). Numerous criticisms have been levelled against both approaches over the years, but for purposes of the present research two issues are especially pertinent. First, there has been persistent confusion over the theoretical status of such supply-side terms as 'industries', 'strategic groups', and 'organizational species'. Because organizational classifications have been developed to describe discontinuous clusterings of rivalry among firms, there is a clear implication that firms within a cluster are cognizant of their interdependence and engage in interfirm sensemaking when formulating business strategies. Rivalry implies strategic intent, and clusters of firms developed from supply-side similarities are most useful when they describe the social reality of member firms. In this view, a label such as the 'steel industry' should represent an organizational community of firms who have at least some knowledge of each other's existence and who engage in reciprocal sensemaking to reduce the uncertainty of market transactions. Unfortunately, however, many supply-side classifications seem to be more the analytical abstractions of outside observers than the social reality of member firms. Technological similarity only imperfectly predicts patterns of interfirm relationships, making groupings such as the Standard Industrial Classification suspect. Multidimensional classifications have attempted to overcome this limitation, but many of these efforts have given insufficient attention to choosing organizational dimensions that accurately reflect strategic awareness and intent. In the end, despite much research on organizational classification, the status of industrial groupings as consensually understood communities of organizations is still more conjecture than established fact.

Unlike supply-side advocates, many demand-side researchers have attempted to establish the social reality of organizational groupings by taking an explicitly cognitive approach to mapping interfirm boundaries. In particular, marketing researchers have assessed customer product classifications and brand switching behaviour as a way of establishing the substitutability (and, hence, rivalry) of two or more firms' outputs (e.g., Day, Shocker, and Srivastava, 1979). However, mapping demand-side substitutability, even cognitively, fails to take into account the inherent relationship between supply-side strategies and demand-side equivalencies. Products are similar in the eyes of customers because the organizations supplying those products have selected similar product strategies. These strategies are embedded within a series of ongoing interfirm comparisons during which managers adjust the characteristics of their firm's products according to the perceived characteristics of products supplied by the other companies. Because output substitutability is a consequence of supply-side strategic intent, demand-side classifications are imperfect and indirect assessments of strategic interdependence among organizations (Auerbach, 1988).

These issues suggest that classifying organizations is a particularly difficult problem. In the end, probably no single grouping criteria will be satisfactory for all purposes, making it imperative to decide upon the purposes of the classification before choosing any specific taxonomic method. However, to the extent that organizational groupings are meant to reflect the strategic intent of firms, it is necessary to: (a) develop taxonomic criteria that are consistent with the social reality of managers within those firms; (b) describe the structure of an organizational field as these managers define it; and (c) show that this structure influences patterns of interfirm rivalry. In short, it is necessary to describe the 'subjective organization of an industry'. We use this term to mean the consensually-held cognitive categories which describe, for managers, the salient similarities and differences among firms, and which psychologically organize strategic networks of interfirm rivalry.

The Present Research

The present study attempted to accomplish the three objectives stated above by mapping the subjective organization of interfirm boundaries within the Scottish knitwear industry. The study is an extension of earlier work by Porac, Thomas and Baden-Fuller (1989). Porac et al. investigated how managers of firms in one segment of the Scottish knitwear industry (firms located in the Borders region of the country) socially constructed the boundaries of their subgroup. Porac et al. found evidence for strong consensually-shared beliefs which created for managers a sense of belonging to a distinct group of firms within the industry. These beliefs were associated with strong competitive ties within the group and weak ties with firms outside the group, both domestic and foreign. Porac *et al.* suggest that these strong perceived boundaries have encouraged managers of firms within the group to look inward and formulate ways of competing among themselves. A well-formed competitive recipe has emerged to facilitate intergroup competition, but according to Porac *et al.*, the recipe may retard the firms' responsiveness to outside threats from other domestic and foreign firms.

The present research expands the Porac *et al.* study by examining the subjective organization of the Scottish knitwear industry as a whole. Managers interviewed by Porac *et al.* made reference to various other segments of the domestic knitwear industry, and described the strategic differences between their own firms and these other groups. The comments of these managers suggested that a reasonably well-understood language existed among them for characterizing intra-industry stratification. The purpose of the present research was to describe this language and map its relationships with the pattern of rivalry among knitwear firms. The general hypothesis tested in the research was that consensually understood strategic subgroups within the Scottish knitwear industry structure the network of perceived rivalry among firms within that industry. Each subgroup within the industry should be a set of firms who are aware of each other, who understand that their firms are similar, and who consider each other rivals.

Method

In order to achieve our research objectives, the study was conducted in three stages:

Stage 1

Knitwear has been produced in Scotland for 400 years, and well-developed strategic recipes have evolved to cope with product and process uncertainties. Archival data sources were exploited to assess the general structure of the industry and to capture the key issues facing managers of knitwear firms. In addition, several directories of Scottish knitwear producers were consulted to compile a master directory of firms known to be in business at the time of the research. The master directory eventually consisted of 260 firms located throughout the country.

Stage 2

Semi-structured interviews were conducted with the managing directors or proprietors of twenty-one firms selected to represent the entire range of knitwear production in Scotland. These interviews had two objectives. First, respondents were taken through a series of questions designed to elicit a description of their company's value-added activities. Managers were asked to describe how their company organized its activities, starting with supplier relationships, progressing through production and distribution processes, and ending with a description of major customer markets. These descriptions were quite detailed, and permitted an assessment of the variation of business and organizational structures across the industry. Second, an effort was made to assess each respondent's 'mental model' of the Scottish knitwear industry. Using a structured taxonomic interview (Porac and Thomas, 1987), respondents were asked to begin with the Scottish knitwear industry as a whole, and segment the industry into the major subtypes of firms existing within the knitwear sector. Taxonomic interviews of this sort capture the mental categories that individuals use to describe perceived variation in a given environmental domain. Usable cognitive taxonomies were obtained from twenty respondents. Stage 2 interviews were tape recorded and subsequently analysed to generate items for the mail questionnaire administered in Stage 3.

Stage 3

The central purpose of the research was to assess the relationship between the cognitive categories of managers and the network of competitive relationships among knitwear firms. The cognitive taxonomies elicited in Stage 2 were examined and the categories mentioned by respondents were coded into a standard classification. Table 10.1 lists seven categories of firms that were derived from the taxonomic interviews. These seven intra-industry categories were taken to be the hypothesized subjective

Table 10.1 Seven managerial categories of knitwear firms in Scotland

---

Handknitters
  Traditional
  Designer

Handframe knitters
  Traditional
  Designer

Upmarket fully-fashioned producers

Middle-market fully-fashioned or cut-and-sew niche specialists

Mass-market contract knitters

---

organization of the Scottish knitwear industry. That is, they were considered to be the major categories of firms which managers perceived to exist within the knitwear sector.

The managerial interviews were also used to derive the key dimensions along which variations among knitwear firms exist. Table 10.2 outlines the major dimensions of variation that were evident: knitting methods, yarn fibres, dyeing, assembly methods, product styles, knitting gauges, customer markets, product categories, order types and distribution channels.

Using the seven categories of firms and dimensions of variation derived from the managerial interviews, a questionnaire was constructed to examine the relationship between subjective organization and competitive structure. 'Competitive structure' was defined as the network of perceived competitive relationships among firms. Firm A competes with firm B to the extent that firm A's managers view firm B as a competitor and use firm B as a benchmark for pricing and product decisions. For an industry of N firms, then, an N × N matrix can be constructed where any given cell (A, B) contains a '1' if the manager of firm A considers firm B to be a competitor, and a '0' if this is not the case. Within the matrix, no firm is considered a competitor of itself. Since it is possible that A sees B as a competitor but not vice versa, the resulting competitive 'network' is a square and non-symmetric binary matrix. Using this definition of competitive structure, the Stage 3 questionnaire examined the relationships between the seven subjective categories of firms listed in table 10.1, variation among firms on the organizational dimensions listed in table 10.2, and an N × N matrix of competitive ties generated from managerial respondents.

Questionnaire structure

The Stage 3 questionnaire was mailed to the managing directors or proprietors of all 260 firms in the composite directory compiled for firms in the industry. The questionnaire requested information about the firm, asked the manager to categorize the firm using the table 10.1 categories, describe the firm using table 10.2 dimensions, and denote which of the other 259 firms in the industry were competitors of the manager's own firm. Usable questionnaires were obtained from 89 of the 260 firms.

The Stage 3 questionnaire operationalized the above variables in the following way:

Categories

Respondents were asked to rate the extent to which their own firm fitted into each of the seven table 10.1 categories on 5-point scales ranging from 1 = 'My company does not fit into this category at all' to 5 = 'My company fits into this category extremely well'.

Table 10.2   Company characteristics derived from managerial interviews

Knitting Methods:
  Handknitting with pins
  Handframe knitting
  Knitting on fully fashioned machines
  Cut-and-sew knitting

Yarn Fibres:

Cashmere	Mohair
Shetland Wool	Natural/synthetic blends
Camel hair	Cotton
Synthetics	Silk
Angora	
Lambswool	

Yarn Dyeing:

  Top dyed
  Hank or package dyed
  Piece dyed

Assembly methods:

  Hand sewing
  Linking
  Cup seaming
  Overlocking

Product styles:

  Traditional knits such as Fair Isles and Nordics
  Classic knits such as plain or intarsia V-necks
  High fashion knits with unique knit structures,
    shapes, and colours

Knitting gauges:

2.5	14
3	15
4.5	21
5	24
7	30
8	
9	
10	
12	

Customer markets:

  Direct exports to foreign countries
  Tourists travelling in the UK
  UK domestic markets

246   Co-operation in Networks

Product categories:

Women's:

Dresses/skirts
Pullovers/cardigans
Suits
Hosiery
Shirts
Accessories

Men's:

Pullovers/cardigans
Shirts
Jackets/blazers
Trousers
Hosiery
Accessories

Children's:

Pullovers/cardigans
Hosiery
Other clothes
Accessories

Cut and sew blanks

Order types:

Special one-off designs
Make to order items from a company range
Orders for stock service items from a company range
Contract orders using retailer designs

Selling and distribution methods:

Direct contacts with retailers at trade fairs
Phone orders from retailers
Company sales personnel
Agents in the UK
Agents outside the UK
Buying houses
Factory or home shop
Company showrooms in London or other large cities
Direct consumer mail orders
Wholesalers in the UK or elsewhere
Company owned retail shops
Market stalls

Company characteristics

Each of the seventy-five table 10.2 characteristics was rated for how important that characteristic was to the respondent's firm on 5-point scales
ranging from 1 = 'Has not been a part of our business at all' to 5 = 'Has been
a very large part of our business (over 30% of our sales)'.

Competitive networks

Respondents were presented with the list of 260 knitwear firms compiled in
the composite directory for the study. They were asked to check off the
firms which they considered to be competitors of their own company.
Competitors were defined as 'other Scottish knitwear producers that might
affect your own company's business and who you often consider when setting prices, developing products, and marketing your knitwear'. They were
also asked to note any other Scottish, UK, and foreign knitwear firms not
on the list that they would consider to be competitors of their company.

Other variables

In addition to the above, respondents were requested to provide information on company ownership structure, date of incorporation, annual
sales, and number of employees. Finally, respondents were asked to rate the
extent to which they personally engaged in a number of activity categories,
and to rate how often they used each of several information sources to keep
track of market trends.

Results

We will address two general questions suggested by the research design. Do
the table 10.1 cognitive categories map on to specific combinations of the
seventy-five table 10.2 company characteristics? If distinguishable cognitive
groupings do exist within the Scottish knitwear industry, how do such
groupings influence the structure of the competitive network as represented
by the N x N competitive matrix?

Cognitive categories and company characteristics

Each manager rated the applicability of each of the category labels to their
firm. One assessment of the degree to which these labels represent distinct
cognitive categories for describing firms in the industry are the intercorrelations among the seven category variables. These are shown in
table 10.3. Table 10.3 suggests that the two hand knitting categories were

Table 10.3   Intercorrelations of category label ratings

Category	1	2	3	4	5	6	7
HKTRAD	1.00	0.73**	0.13	−0.09	−0.27	−0.31*	−0.24
HKDESN	0.73**	1.00	0.01	−0.03	−0.26	−0.35**	−0.28*
FKTRAD	0.13	0.00	1.00	0.33*	0.09	−0.21	−0.23
FKDESN	−0.09	−0.03	0.33*	1.00	−0.02	−0.23	−0.29*
UPMARKT	−0.27	−0.27	0.09	−0.02	1.00	0.04	−0.15
MIDMARKT	−0.31*	−0.35**	−0.21	−0.23	0.04	1.00	0.31*
MASSMKT	−0.23	−0.28*	−0.23	−0.29*	−0.15	0.31*	1.00

Note of cases: 87   2-tailed Signif: * −0.01   ** −0.001

very highly correlated, sharing approximately 50 per cent of their variation. This suggests that managers made few distinctions between these two categories. The two handframe categories were moderately correlated, as were the mass and mid-market categories. However, only about 9 per cent overlap existed, suggesting that these categories were relatively distinct. All other significant correlations were negative, suggesting that the distinctiveness among the category labels was high. On the basis of these correlations, the seven cognitive categories were reduced to six: hand knitters, designer handframers, traditional handframers, upmarket fully-fashioned, mid-market niche companies, and mass-market cut-and-sew.

Company characteristics

To validate the above six categories, the seventy-five company characteristics listed in table 10.2 were cluster analysed using a hypothesized six cluster Ward's solution (Lorr, 1983). If the six category labels represent valid cognitive categories, the perceived company characteristics should cluster into relatively separable groups that correspond to the category ratings. To test this correspondence, groups were extracted with the six cluster solution, and mean ratings on each of the seven category ratings were computed for each of the six cluster groups. Significant differences in category ratings should be apparent across the six groups, with each group being significantly higher than the others on one category rating.

Table 10.4   Mean ratings of each cluster group on seven category labels

			Category Label				
Cluster	*HKTRAD*	*HKDESN*	*HFTRAD*	*HFDESN*	*UPMARKT*	*MIDMARKT*	*MASSMKT*
1	1.00	1.10	1.85	2.10	4.75	2.20	1.65
2	2.27	2.37	3.30	2.67	2.30	1.23	1.04
3	1.15	1.69	1.23	4.77	1.54	1.08	1.00
4	3.33	3.00	1.22	1.00	1.11	1.00	1.00
5	1.00	1.00	1.00	1.00	1.00	3.45	3.36
6	1.00	1.00	1.66	1.66	1.66	5.00	2.66

The six resulting clusters had membership N's of 20, 29, 13, 10, 11, and 6 for cluster groups 1 through 6 respectively. Table 10.4 shows the mean ratings for each group on the seven category variables in table 10.1. Cluster 1 fitted most closely the 'upmarket' category, cluster 2 was equally distributed across handknitting and handframe knitting categories, but had the highest score on the 'handframe traditional' category. Cluster 3 members categorized themselves most strongly into the 'handframe designer' category. Cluster 4 managers rated their firms highest on the 'handknit designer' category, but also rated themselves as fitting the 'handknit traditional' category. Cluster 5 was split evenly between the 'mid-market' and 'mass-market' categories, while cluster 6 managers rated themselves as fitting most closely the 'mid-market' category.

In general, the above results provide reasonable support for the validity of the six groups formed by clustering the company characteristic variables. As a further check, however, clusters formed with 5, 7, 8, 9 group Ward's solutions were compared to the six cluster solution. None of these other solutions fitted the category labels as well as the Ward's six cluster solution, further supporting the basic validity of the six intra-industry groups extracted from the data.

Competitive networks

The basic purpose of the research was to show that intra-industry cognitive categories structure the network of perceived competitive relationships among firms. Since questionnaires were received from eighty-nine firms, with each respondent checking off which of the other 259 knitwear

Table 10.5   Competitive densities for six cluster groups

Cluster	1	2	3	4	5	6
1	0.37	0.01	0.00	0.00	0.02	0.00
2	0.03	0.03	0.02	0.01	0.00	0.01
3	0.00	0.00	0.14	0.01	0.00	0.00
4	0.00	0.02	0.06	0.10	0.00	0.02
5	0.00	0.00	0.00	0.00	0.14	0.00
6	0.03	0.02	0.01	0.00	0.02	0.47

companies were competitors, the complete competitive network available for analysis consisted of a binary 89 × 260 rectangular matrix. Only the 89 × 89 square submatrix consisting of all possible pairs of respondent companies was analysed for the present research.

The basic hypothesis to be examined in this paper was whether the density of competitive relationships was stronger within each of the derived company clusters than between clusters. Density can be defined as the percentage of non-zero cells to total cells in a matrix or submatrix. In order to examine this question, the 89 × 89 matrix of perceived competitive ties was divided into six submatrices corresponding to the six company groups. Thus, the six submatrices were square, nonsymmetric, binary matrices with 20, 29, 13, 10, 11, and 6 rows/columns for groups 1 to 6 respectively. Densities were computed within each submatrix by dividing the number of non-zero cells by the total number of cells. Between-group densities were computed by taking the ratio of number of perceived competitive ties between pairs of companies in two different groups and the total possible links between these two groups. Table 10.5 shows the results of these analyses. Off-diagonal elements in table 10.5 are between-group densities, right diagonal elements are within-group densities. In all but one case (group 2), within-group densities are substantially higher than between-group densities, lending support for the argument that perceived competitive relationships are structured by category membership.

This conclusion is further bolstered by examining the number of competitive linkages reported by individual respondents. On average, each manager reported 3.3 competitive ties to other knitwear firms in Scotland. Of these, 2.6, on average, were perceived competitive relationships with firms within the same industry cluster. Only 0.75 linkages, on average, were reported with firms outside the cluster by each respondent. By a paired t-test, the difference between these two means is highly significant ($\underline{t}$ (88) = 4.72, p $\leq$ 0.001).

Discussion

The present study reinforces the cognitive view of competitive boundaries and competition that has begun to appear in the strategy and organizations literature (e.g., Porac *et al.*, 1989; Porac and Thomas, 1990; Zajac and Bazerman, 1991; Spender, 1990). Such a view entails the recognition that rivalry is an inherently cognitive process in which managers from different firms attempt to make sense of the marketplace. The results of the present research suggest that one important aspect of this sensemaking process is the construction of competitive boundaries among firms. Consensual categories of firms were found to relate significantly to the pattern of perceived competitive relationships. A cognitive approach complements more traditional attempts to delineate competitive boundaries by locating the source of rivalry not in the material conditions of the firm, but in the minds of those individuals who are charged with managing those conditions.

The practical implication of such a view, of course, is that it places interfirm rivalry in the 'eye of the beholder'. Two firms with highly similar asset endowments may or may not be strong rivals depending upon whether the firms' managers perceive a competitive relationship to exist. From a strategic point of view, this implication has two side effects. One, it suggests that a key strategic problem is understanding the implicit competitive definitions that have been constructed within an industrial community. Knowing that two firms have similar asset configurations is less important than knowing whether their managers are using each other as competitive referents. Much of the tacit knowledge underlying competitive strategy probably pertains to the implicit competitive orderings that exist within a community of firms. Two, a cognitive view of rivalry also suggests that competitive strategy can be decoupled from immediate physical assets and reconceptualized on the basis of the evolving mental models of a firm's strategists. Such would be the case, for example, during strategic metamorphoses when competitive strategies are being reconstructed by projecting a new competitive mental model (or strategic 'vision') forward in time. This allows the decision maker to go beyond the physical and financial constraints of a current business situation and project new competitive referents and a new business definition as future objectives. We suspect that decoupling the material and cognitive aspects of business rivalry is the generative motor of creative responses to changing business conditions.

References

Auerbach, P. 1988: *Competition: The economics of industrial change*. Oxford: Basil Blackwell.

Day, G., Shocker, A., and Srivastava, R.K. 1979: Customer-oriented approaches to identifying product markets. *Journal of Marketing*, 43, 8–19.

Hannan, M. and Freeman, J. 1988: *Organizational ecology*. Cambridge, MA: Harvard University Press.

Lorr, M. 1983: *Cluster analysis for social scientists*. San Francisco: Jossey-Bass.

McGee, J. and Thomas, H. 1986: Strategic groups: Theory, research, and taxonomy. *Strategic Management Journal*, 7, 141–160.

McKelvey, B. 1982: *Organizational systematics*. Berkeley, CA: University of California Press.

Nightengale, J. 1978: On the definition of industry and market. *Journal of Industrial Economics*, 27, 31–40.

Porac, J. and Thomas, H. 1987: Cognitive taxonomies and cognitive systematics. Paper presented at the annual convention of the Academy of Management, New Orleans, LA.

Porac, J. and Thomas, H. 1990: Taxonomic mental models in competitor definition. *Academy of Management Review*, 15, 224–240.

Porac, J., Thomas, H., and Baden-Fuller, C. 1989: Competitive groups as cognitive communities: The case of Scottish knitwear manufacturers. *Journal of Management Studies*, 26, 397–416.

Robinson, J. T. 1952: The industry and the market. *Economic Journal*, 66, 360–361.

Scherer, F. M. 1980: *Industrial market structure and economic performance* (2nd. Ed.). Chicago, IL: Rand-McNally.

Spender, J. C. 1990: *Industry recipes*. Oxford: Basil Blackwell.

Zajac, E. & Bazerman, M. 1991: Blind spots in industry and competitor analysis: Implications of interfirm (mis)perceptions for strategic decisions. *Academy of Management Review*, 16, 37–56.

11

The Joint Venture Partner Selection Process

J. Michael Geringer and Colette A. Frayne

Joint ventures (JVs) are one of several organizational types available to managers in their efforts to attain corporate objectives, and lately they appear to be enjoying a resurgence of interest. These ventures involve two or more distinct organizations (the partners), each of which participates in the decision-making activities of the jointly owned entity (Geringer & Hebert, 1989). Although a relatively extensive literature on JVs exists, there is very little published information on one specific facet of this topic: the *process* by which organizations select, or are selected by, their partners. The choice of a specific partner may critically impact prospects for effective implementation of JV strategy because it influences the operating policies and procedures which will be employed, along with the overall mix of skills and resources which will be available to the JV. While a number of JV studies have addressed one or a few issues central to partner selection, including motivations for JV formation, partner selection criteria, or negotiations, prior studies have not engaged in concerted efforts to link these issues in a processual manner.

This paper's objective is to help bridge this gap in the literature by presenting a framework of the JV partner selection process (PSP). Using published case data from the business and academic press, literature on decision making models, and interviews with senior executives with extensive JV experience, a preliminary framework of the PSP was constructed. This framework was subsequently refined on the basis of data collected in semi-structured interviews involving over 150 senior executives from North American parent firms involved with 132 randomly selected JVs. Each executive had been intimately involved in the formation of their firm's JV, and all of the ventures were formed during the 1980s. Interviews took place in the executives' offices and lasted an average of $1\frac{1}{2}$ hours apiece. The interviews were structured by asking each executive to provide a chronological description of the formation process for individual JVs, beginning with the initial decision to consider investment in a particular project and concluding with either signing of the final JV agreement or termination of the formation efforts.

Although the participants focused on the unique circumstances of their particular JV, we found that the same process-based issues and components arose repeatedly across the individual interviews. A revised framework was subsequently constructed. This framework includes seven component subprocesses and several contingency-based feedback loops which may comprise the PSP, as discussed below.

Component Subprocesses in the Partner Selection Process

The JV partner selection process may be conceptualized as consisting of seven different subprocesses. Beginning at the point an organization decides to consider involvement in a particular project or series of projects (e.g., development of a new product line, or entry into a new market), the principal subprocesses are as follows:

1.   Consideration of a joint venture as an investment option

In this framework, the PSP is considered to begin at that point when the organization first initiates formal or informal consideration of involvement in a JV. Possible use of the JV form of organization may be examined simultaneously with other structural options, such as a wholly-owned venture or licensing, or it may be the sole alternative under consideration. A number of variables may influence the outcome of this subprocess, including legal and tax considerations as well as the specific competitive conditions which confront the firm (Contractor and Lorange, 1988). In some cases, use of the JV form of organization is mandatory in order to make an investment (e.g., local government fiat regarding the allowable mode for foreign investment), while in other instances the organization is free to choose which organizational form to employ.

This first subprocess has two possible outcomes: either the JV option is rejected (which leads to either rejection of participation in the proposed project, or to examination of other forms of investment exclusive of JV), or else the JV option is perceived to have some potential viability (either as the only option or as one of several potential alternatives) and the PSP continues to evolve through the following subprocesses.

2.   Development of selection criteria

The second subprocess involves the development and refinement of decision criteria which will be employed when evaluating and selecting the prospective partner organization(s). The degree of explicitness and thoroughness employed in the development of these criteria may vary immensely between organizations or between different JVs involving the same organization. Nevertheless, the existence of such criteria is, by definition, a prerequisite for the selection decision (Geringer, 1991).

Prior JV research supports conceptualization of two broad categories of partner selection criteria. In particular, it appears possible to distinguish between criteria associated with the operational skills and resources which a JV requires for its competitive success (i.e., 'task-related' criteria) and criteria associated with the efficiency and effectiveness of partners' co-operation (i.e., 'partner-related' criteria) (Geringer, 1991). More specifically, task-related criteria refer to those variables which are intimately related to the viability of a proposed JV's operations *regardless* of whether the chosen investment mode involves multiple partners. The variables could be tangible or intangible, human or nonhuman in nature. Examples include patents or technical know-how, financial resources, experienced managerial personnel, and access to marketing and distribution systems (Geringer, 1988a). The relative importance managers place on a particular task-related criterion appears to be a function of the perceived critical success factors which confront the proposed JV, as well as the firm's current and anticipated future competitive position *vis-à-vis* these factors (Geringer, 1991). In general, firms appear to seek partners evidencing asymmetry on task-related dimensions, i.e., the desired partner will evidence strengths where the firm is weak, and vice versa (Geringer, 1988a; Harrigan, 1988).

The concept of partner-related criteria refers to those variables which become relevant *only if* the chosen investment mode involves the presence of multiple partners. Examples include a partner's national or corporate culture, the degree of favourable past association between the partners, compatibility of and trust between partners' top management teams, perceived mutual need or dependence between partners' top management teams, and a partner's organizational size or structure. In contrast to the case for task-related criteria, it appears that firms generally seek partners evidencing symmetry on partner-related dimensions: i.e., the desired partner will evidence similarity on individual dimensions, such as corporate culture or relative size of business units (Daniels, 1971; de Hoghton, 1966; Geringer, 1988c; Killing, 1983; Tomlinson, 1970). Such similarity can serve to enhance the efficiency and effectiveness of interactions among the partner organizations. In fact, to the extent that substantial imbalance may exist between partners in terms of organizational size or other resource-based factors, concerns with overdependency may severely impede efforts to establish a satisfactory collaborative relationship among prospective partner organizations (Adler and Hlavacek, 1976; Dymsza, 1988; Geringer, 1988b).

3.   Identification of prospective partners

The third subprocess involves generation of a list of one or more prospective partner organizations which appear to satisfy the prerequisites
established by the selection criteria. Again, the thoroughness of the identification process may exhibit substantial variation between organizations,
or between different investments of a single organization. Indeed, the resource requirements (e.g., the technology which will be involved in the JV)
may be so specific that the range of prospective partners is very limited.
However, initial efforts to identify prospects usually emphasize the
perceived ability of a potential partner to satisfy task-related requirements
of the JV (Geringer, 1988a). Thus, initial prospects are typically identified
by examining firms with either a horizontal (e.g., competitors in the same
or related product-markets) or a vertical relationship (e.g., suppliers or
buyers) with the firm seeking a partner. For example, an examination of
over 3200 JVs operating in Canada during the 1980s revealed that over 85
per cent were in the same industry as one or more of the parent firms.
Further, for over 98 per cent of these JVs, two or more of the parents
competed in the same industry (Geringer and Woodcock, 1989). Purely
conglomerate relationships are seldom pursued (Porter and Fuller, 1986)
and the rationale for their choice has been strongly argued against (e.g.,
Lasserre, 1984).

Substantial amounts of time and other resources must frequently be
expended in identifying potentially suitable partner organizations. This is
particularly the case when an organization's managers have limited experience with the proposed JV's products or markets, although the costs can be
substantial even if management already has a thorough knowledge of the
JV's industry. Despite the task's importance, managers often hesitate to devote a significant amount of corporate resources to the process of
identifying an extensive list of viable partner prospects. This is particularly
the case when a partner with the minimum technical requirements appears
to have been found. The first candidate is often discovered in a rather ad
hoc manner, such as through contacts established by bankers or other
agents, by business colleagues in the market or industry under consideration, or through chance encounters (Geringer, 1988a; Lasserre, 1984;
Tomlinson, 1970). Often, partners appear to have been chosen for reasons
not fully relevant to the organization's objectives and without a stringent
comparison of alternatives (Geringer, 1988c). Many partners seem to have
been identified almost by accident, or at least without full consideration of
how they might influence the JV's operations. In many cases, particularly
in developing country JVs, when the firm already has a distributor or other
agent in the proposed JV's industry or country, the distributorship is often
transformed into an industrial JV with this agent as the partner (Lasserre,

1984; Tomlinson, 1970). Under these circumstances, little or no screening is typically conducted for generating alternative prospects who might be more appropriate in the expanded role of being a partner in a JV. This apparent disregard for thorough planning and evaluation may help account for the widespread perception that JVs tend to be fraught with problems and that they commonly 'fail' within a relatively short period of time.

As with many other aspects of the PSP, identification of viable partner prospects is in many respects a research task. This is particularly true if the JV is to include local partners from an unfamiliar region. As noted above, at a minimum the partners should be able to provide the additional capabilities which, in both the short and the longer-term, are necessary to enable the JV to be competitive. This means the firm must analyse the JV's anticipated target market, as well as the businesses which prospective partners are currently in or likely to enter in the relatively near future, in order to identify possible synergies. However, unless a manager has a thorough knowledge of the JV's industry and the potential players, reliance on superficial scanning efforts is unlikely to result in identification of an optimal partner. Particularly for fast-moving technologies, such as telecommunications, biotechnology, or semiconductors, managers should be cautious about making assumptions regarding other firms' capabilities. Reputations may be misleading, and several executives reported that they felt blind-sided when they belatedly discovered that a firm they identified as being a strong partner prospect did not actually have the skills necessary for the JV's success.

When identifying partners, there was no single approach which would be preferable in all situations. However, the evaluation should consider such factors as the peculiar characteristics of the industry, the firm's competitive position, and the JV's anticipated requirements for capital and other resources. Typically, among the first potential partners to be identified are the distributors, suppliers, and customers for the industry of the proposed JV. Yet, even these companies must be examined to see which ones are available for venturing and which might be pre-empted from participation due to prior agreements with competitors, sociopolitical biases, or similar reasons.

Of course, extensive search and screening efforts are not always feasible. Sometimes the nature of the proposed investment dictates a limited range of prospective partners. For instance, there might be only one firm with access to the technology or raw materials needed by the JV. In other cases, government fiat or regulations regarding foreign ownership may sharply limit the number of available partner prospects. However, even if only one or a few viable partner prospects exist, identifying which of these companies would be a potentially suitable JV partner is still a critical task.

In our sample, 70 per cent of the organizations perceived that four or less qualified partners existed. Indeed, 44 per cent of the participants responded that there was only one qualified potential partner firm, 15 per cent felt there were only two qualified prospects, and an additional 11 per cent perceived that three to four qualifying organizations existed. In contrast, 19 per cent of respondents perceived five to six qualifying partners existed, 7 per cent perceived seven to ten qualifying partners, and 2 per cent responded that over ten qualifying organizations existed.

4.   Evaluation of prospective partners

The fourth subprocess entails evaluation of each previously identified prospective partner organization for suitability as a partner in the proposed collaborative project. A key component of this phase is an assessment of the likelihood of reaching an arrangement to collaborate with the prospective partner(s), at least on terms which will be mutually beneficial. This may be of particular concern when there is no previous history of interaction among the parties and thus no precedent which may be referred to. Concerns regarding a prospect's suitability may also arise if the prospective partner has previously been involved in other similar ventures, not necessarily with the evaluating organization itself, and it has benefited at the expense of its partners.

This evaluation may include direct prenegotiation or initial 'feeling out' contacts with one or more of the prospective partner organizations. Prior research also suggests that, in many cases, little or no screening is done for seriously comparing alternative partner prospects, nor is there an in depth investigation of the motives and capabilities of the candidate (Geringer, 1988a, 1988b; Lasserre, 1984).

Because of the technical complexity of the required analyses, the number of tasks to be accomplished, and the frequent lack of requisite expertise and JV experience among in-house personnel, it was often difficult for the JV champions and their principal colleagues to maintain a generalist's grasp of the evaluation process. The potential problem of integrating a variety of overspecialized and fragmented views on the deal was recognized by many respondents, and indeed was used by several executives to justify their decision not to pursue a thorough and systematic process for identifying and evaluating prospective partner organizations. Such practices seemed widespread. In our study, 65 per cent of the participants reported that their firms formally evaluated only one prospective partner firm, 9 per cent evaluated two firms, 15 per cent formally evaluated three to four prospective partners, 7 per cent evaluated five to six firms, and 4 per cent evaluated seven to ten prospective partners.

Consistent with these findings, prior research suggests that many of the problems confronting JVs originate from a lack of deep prior understanding of the intentions of the prospective partner, its capabilities and its management style (e.g., Lasserre, 1984). This appears to be a result of the nature of the evaluation process itself. Among the individuals involved in the formal evaluation, only a few of these people typically have worked together before, and the entire process lasts only a relatively short time. (As noted later in this paper, the time from the initial idea to the final JV agreement averaged six to twelve months in length.) People who have not previously worked together closely or who do not share a common expertise and jargon can communicate only the most standardized information quickly and effectively. Within a given speciality, people tend to gather similar data and produce comparable analyses. As larger groups of people with different specialities get involved, decision makers have more difficulty comparing and integrating analyses. Although specialization is an inherent part of decision making in many organizational settings, the resulting isolation of specialists within and between the various subprocesses of the PSP leads to a lack of integration in their analyses. As a result, the managers, and particularly the analysts involved in the evaluation, often focus their attention on more easily and quickly communicated issues of strategic fit and quantitative, 'objective' components that tend to characterize task-related dimensions rather than the more subtle and qualitative concerns of organizational fit which characterize partner-related dimensions (Geringer, 1988a). This dynamic occurs for several reasons. First, task-related and strategic issues directly reflect the espoused purpose of the JV. The focus on these dimensions may also be supported by arguments of Renforth (1974) and Harrigan (1987), who claimed that relationship traits are less important in determining effectiveness of co-operative alliances than are industry traits and other task-related factors, and that venturing firms should concentrate principally on the competitive needs of a JV (Harrigan, 1988). Second, these issues often lend themselves to standardized analytical approaches that organizations use to assess markets, products, industries or technologies (Geringer, 1991). In contrast, issues of organizational fit are more ambiguous, more subjective, and therefore more open to challenge. Third, few channels of communication exist to exchange information among the various groups of analysts who perform their work in different time periods or subprocesses.

There is also an observable tendency for firms to conduct evaluations of these two types of criteria in a hierarchical manner, beginning with task-related evaluations, which may introduce bias into the evaluative process through technocratic tunnel vision. Initial evaluation of a prospect typically emphasizes task-related dimensions of criteria and is largely delegated to functional specialists at lower or middle-management levels of the organization (Geringer, 1988a). In contrast, partner-related dimensions of compatibility are more commonly evaluated by general managers at more senior echelons of a firm. Although evaluation of task- and partner-related dimensions of compatibility may be undertaken simultaneously, it is more common for the evaluation of the latter dimensions to lag behind examination of task-related dimensions. This observed lag does *not* necessarily reflect managers' perceptions of the relative importance of task-related as opposed to partner-related criteria to JV success. On the contrary, research indicates that while overcoming deficiencies along task-related dimensions may be a *necessary* condition for selecting a complementary partner, it may not be *sufficient* (Geringer, 1988a). Indeed complementarity on partner-related dimensions also appears to be a critical determinant of JV performance since it can influence the efficiency and effectiveness of co-operation between partners (Geringer, 1988a, 1988b, 1991; Sullivan and Peterson, 1982; Tomlinson, 1970). Nevertheless, as a result of this process, certain prospective partner organizations which may rank very highly on partner-related dimensions, yet which may rank marginally lower on the more 'objective' task-related dimensions, may be eliminated from further consideration after completion of the initial, task-related phase of the evaluation process.

Lasserre (1984) proposed that the process of assessing partnership consists of two phases: an analysis of the strategic fit and an analysis of the resource fit. During the first phase, each party tries to assess whether the strategy of the partner with regard to the project under study is compatible with its own. This requires accumulation and analysis of data regarding the competitive position of the partner, its strategic objectives and its portfolio of activities. An assessment is made in terms of which of the parties' interests are likely to be the same, which will be opposing, and which are unique or different. This provides a basis for evaluating the likelihood of identifying a common purpose or direction between the organizations, and the prospect that at least some of the desired ends may be realized. This analysis may involve formal or informal inquiries to help develop a realistic understanding of how the other prospective partners view the issues and what their interests are. This permits an assessment of how likely it would be that a relationship with each alternative partner prospect will satisfy the parties' joint and individual interests. The objective is to determine the extent to which the project truly represents an important component of the partner's overall strategy or simply an opportunistic move, and whether it involves the partner's main line of activities or represents a diversification effort. In this regard, prior research suggests that the JVs which will have the best chance of survival and success are those that are most central to a company's business (Woodcock and Geringer, 1990).

During the second phase, each partner tries to determine whether, given its own resource base and the resource requirements of the proposed project, the prospective partner's resources are adequate to complement its own. At this point, many firms have found it to also be of value to evaluate the previous JV experiences of the prospective partner, to ascertain whether their track record suggests they are able to form successful JVs and whether prior ventures involved technologies or markets related to those involved in the proposed venture.

Yet, organizations often find it necessary to go beyond the largely task-related aspects of the two-phase approach outlined above. Particularly for those organizations with prior JV experience (Lyles, 1988), there is also an assessment of partner-related dimensions of inter-partner 'fit'. One important aspect of this is an evaluation of the level of commitment to the proposed JV among the top management of the prospective partner (Lasserre, 1984). In addition, it is necessary to evaluate the extent of mutual need among the prospective partner organizations (Geringer, 1988b). A company that truly needs its partner is argued to be the one that will be most likely to stay with the partnership the longest and devote the attention and resources necessary to make it work. The long-term success of the JV may be less important for a partner investing for opportunistic or diversification reasons, or for which the investment represents a minor component of overall activities (Lasserre, 1984).

5. Decision regarding prospects' qualifications

The fifth subprocess involves efforts to assess the results of the evaluation subprocess described above and decide which, if any, prospective partner organizations have the requisite capabilities to warrant pursuit of further negotiations and, possibly, formation of a JV. The outcome of this decision process may be influenced by a number of variables, including the firm's motivations for engaging in a JV, the explicitness and thoroughness of selection criteria which were employed, the number of partner prospects perceived to exist as well as the number formally evaluated, and the prospects' perceived qualifications. The de facto decision regarding each partner prospect is typically made by the JV champion in conjunction with other key individuals in the process, generally managers from the upper-middle or upper levels of an organization's hierarchy who have been intimately involved throughout the JV formation efforts (Geringer, 1988). Only four of the parent companies in our sample reported that this decision was formally made, rather than merely approved, at the level of the board of directors or a senior management committee (e.g., strategic planning, capital budgeting).

6.   Negotiations to form a joint venture

Efforts to reach a mutually acceptable agreement with the selected partner organization(s) regarding establishment of a JV represents the framework's sixth subprocess. The functioning of this subprocess can evidence substantial variation across JVs, depending on the parties' motives for pursuing the JV, preexisting relationships between prospective partner organizations or their managers, the environment of the proposed JV (e.g. , uncertainties of demand, supply, or technologies to be developed or employed), the number of alternative investment options or prospective partners which are perceived to be available and the number of prospective partners which the respective companies are negotiating with, *inter alia*. In some cases, the process can be quite complex and time-consuming (e.g., the GM-Toyota negotiations for the NUMMI JV, chronicled in Weiss, 1987), while in other instances, such as oil and gas drilling JVs, the negotiations may literally be both initiated and concluded over lunch (Hill, 1987). Negotiations are often initiated informally during the partner evaluation process discussed above (subprocess 4), as part of the organization's efforts to ascertain the extent of strategic and operational fit between itself and the prospective partner organizations. While negotiations can be conducted with a number of different prospective partner organizations, either simultaneously or sequentially, the vast majority of this study's respondents (74 per cent) reported that their firms negotiated with only one prospective partner organization. In contrast, 15 per cent negotiated with two different firms, 7 per cent held formal or informal negotiations with three or four firms, and the remaining 4 per cent reported that their firms negotiated with five or six prospective partners. Furthermore, 91 per cent of the study's participants responded that the organization which they finally chose represented their first choice for a partner.

Several issues are salient during the negotiation phase. First and foremost is achieving a common definition of the nature of the JV being considered. It is essential that the proposed JV be likely to provide substantive benefits to each of the prospective partners, as well as to each of the major stakeholder groups within each of the partner organizations, or subsequent efforts to collaborate are unlikely to succeed. If the basic proposal is defined in a manner which is not satisfactory to one of the partners or a major stakeholder associated with that organization, the latter will have little incentive to collaborate. Indeed, to the extent that the proposed JV would be harmful to the organization or a stakeholder group, it may be in the latter's best interests to attempt to derail the negotiations.

Delicate shuttle diplomacy, especially by the JV champions or liaisons, is frequently necessary in order to identify potential obstacles and tease out a basic proposal which will be sufficiently broad or ambiguous to incorporate the agendas of multiple partner organizations and their key stakeholder groups, and thus to permit the negotiations to proceed. The basis for such a common definition around which the parties can unite is identification of a proposal which recognizes the parties' interdependencies, the recognition that each party's objectives may be better served by pursuing the JV rather than other alternatives, and the confidence that their particular concerns will be addressed and that positive outcomes will be possible.

Another key issue is to determine the appropriate participants in the negotiation process, in order to facilitate efforts at achieving an agreement which will be workable. The skills necessary to negotiate a JV typically differ from those required to run things afterwards. Consequently, specialists in negotiation and analysts skilled in number-crunching may think that operating matters are beyond their competence and may confine themselves to more familiar and easily analysed financial or legal issues. Functionally skilled analysts also tend to view issues of organizational fit as postponable and less prestigious – one does not work with chief executive officers (CEOs) to assess organizational fit, one deals with operating managers. Since resolution of these issues is not perceived as essential to completing the PSP, they are postponed for others to handle. In attempting to identify the relevant stakeholders in each of the prospective partner organizations, it is necessary to determine which of those have a legitimate stake in the problem, i.e., those likely to be significantly impacted by the actions of the other stakeholders. They are likely to become involved in order to enhance positive or moderate negative impacts associated with the proposed venture. For example, when partners are of different sizes, the largest one often tries to assume overall leadership for the JV. While establishing clear responsibility, this arrangement does not guarantee that the partners' resources will be effectively utilized, nor that the interests of the smaller partners or significant subgroups thereof will be protected (Geringer and Frayne, 1990; Moxon and Geringer, 1985). Thus, the involvement of these stakeholders may be through such means as their control of financial or informational resources essential to the process, or their power to nullify a JV through either direct veto action or their inability or unwillingness to carry out the agreement once it is reached.

A third salient issue is the identification of a commonly accepted base of information. Often, stakeholders within or among the different organizations discover they are working from very different sources of data, or that neither side has sufficient data to answer questions that arise during their deliberations. In these circumstances, stakeholders of often undertake a joint search for the 'facts' surrounding the proposed JV. To the extent that the participants base their interpretations on different sets of facts, much time can be spent arguing over whose data is accurate. Mutual examination of relevant data can help the parties to develop a common base for discussion, as well as encouraging the disputants to discriminate among shared, opposing and merely differing interests. This can also help break down mistrust and inhibitions, and promote efforts aimed at developing mutually satisfactory solutions. Further, the joint fact-finding efforts often help the participants to discover that they entered the process with ill-defined goals for the JV, a common malady affecting JVs (Geringer, 1988a). Efforts to identify the underlying facts may help to highlight instances where organizations that appear to agree on generalities differ substantially on specifics. Unless these differences can be resolved, it may be advisable for the organizations to pursue JVs with other parties or to consider other non-JV alternatives, such as licensing or full ownership. Conflicts between the partners are best avoided if anticipated before the JV is established, and to the extent that joint fact-finding can identify such irreconcilable differences, the additional effort expended up front in selecting a compatible partner may repay itself many times over in avoided costs of misunderstandings, delays and 'divorce'.

Unless terminated prematurely, the final step in the negotiation phase of the PSP is reaching agreement and closing the deal to form a JV with a particular partner organization. Ideally, reaching an agreement should include gaining commitment of each of the parties to a single option or to a package of options. For more complex JVs which involve decisions regarding multiple issues, the final agreement may be forged by sequentially negotiating agreement on each individual issue and then combining these various components into a comprehensive agreement. This 'building-block' approach (Carpenter and Kennedy, 1988) permits the parties to break down the overall problem into manageable pieces, which can then be pursued at different locations or on different timeframes. Thus, the negotiators can achieve incremental progress towards the overall agreement as each issue is settled.

Another common approach is to strive for an agreement in principle, sometimes called a memorandum of understanding, that helps provide a general framework for the negotiations and within which the details can subsequently be worked out. This approach permits the parties to experience a sense of accomplishment and to maintain momentum in the negotiations by achieving a preliminary agreement on key issues early in the process. This stage often involves very senior executives from the respective organizations, who then leave negotiation of the details to others. As the negotiations proceed, increasingly specific proposals that fall within the earlier agreement in principle are considered (Moore, 1986).

Throughout the negotiation process, particularly for the more complex and potentially contentious aspects of an agreement, shuttle diplomacy by the JV champions or liaisons can enhance achievement of closure, especially if one or more parties are reluctant to commit themselves to an agreement. If the champion or liaison is involved in private sessions with each of the parties, he or she may be able to identify bases for agreement and make trial proposals to each party individually in order to assess prospects for achieving consensus.

7. *Final decision regarding the joint venture option*

The seventh and final subprocess involves the formal decision regarding whether or not to utilize a JV form of organization for the particular project or series of projects. In addition to judgement of the final agreement resulting from negotiations, this phase may also occur at other key junctures during the negotiations themselves. For example, a decision regarding whether to continue or terminate negotiations may be necessary when a prospective partner requests major concessions or suggests a substantive change in the proposed JV's mission.

Except for very small-scale JVs, the final decision to affirm or reject a proposed partner and JV is almost always formally made at the organizational headquarters level, even in those instances where the key decision maker(s) maintains extensive involvement throughout the negotiations. The final decision phase of the process usually involves a confirmatory vote in key senior management committees (e.g., capital budgeting) and the board of directors. However, except for very large JVs and those which are intimately linked to an organization's core business activities, the *de facto* decisions regarding partner selection and JV formation are typically made by subsidiary or division level management, rather than at the corporate level (Geringer, 1988a). While the partner evaluations, financial projections and overall strategic plans of the JV may be reviewed at corporate headquarters, such review typically is of a summary nature. Instead, JV partner selection and formation decisions are typically delegated to the level of the hierarchy where operational responsibility resides. This fact further reinforces the importance of assigning extremely competent individuals to the partner selection task force, especially those individuals who are expected to function as the JV's champions and as key participants in implementation of the JV.

Representatives to any negotiation have to deal with the back-home or 'two-table' problem (Colosi, 1985). That is, they must persuade their constituencies that the agreement was the best they could achieve. Often, other parties in the negotiations may assist the JV champions and their colleagues in devising a compelling case to present to their various constituencies. If these parties do not now nor have they previously taken the time to ensure that the various stakeholder constituencies understand the rationale for any trade-offs made and gain their support for the final JV agreement, any or all of these stakeholders may respond through overt or covert opposition to the agreement at this phase or at some future date.

There are four possible outcomes of this final subprocess:

Termination of negotiations and rejection of the joint venture option

This option entails the decision to terminate efforts to utilize the JV form of investment as a means of pursuing organizational objectives for a particular project or series of projects.

Termination of negotiations with a particular partner prospect but continued efforts to form a JV

This option involves the decision to terminate negotiations with a particular prospective partner organization, but maintaining the possibility of forming a JV with one or more different prospects.

Continuation of negotiations with a particular partner prospect

This option involves the decision to maintain negotiations with the current partner prospect. It affirms the potential desirability of that organization as a prospective partner, but may involve a modification in such issues as the scale of the JV or the nature of the issues currently under negotiation. Indeed, renegotiations of certain aspects of the agreement may be necessary to accommodate changed circumstances.

Successful negotiation and formation of the joint venture

This option involves the decision to approve a negotiated agreement and thereby pursue a particular project or series of projects through formal establishment of a JV with the partner organization(s).

Of course, the principal participants cannot always control the PSP or its timing. Intermediaries and third parties have their own agendas, while contextual factors may make a quick – even hasty – decision to go ahead with the JV an unavoidable outcome (Jemison and Sitkin, 1986). The amount of time necessary to progress through the PSP may vary enormously, ranging from essentially zero (e.g., if the initial possibility of considering formation of a JV is quickly rejected) to many years. For our sample of JVs, almost all of which had been successfully formed, the length of this process ranged from approximately one week to nearly three years. In fact, for 6 per cent of the JVs, the process took less than three months, 20 per cent took three to six months, 50 per cent took six to twelve months, 20 per cent took one to two years, and 4 per cent took two to three years. These results appeared to be consistent with the participants' overall experiences with such JVs. Indeed, 56 per cent of the participants with other JV experience reported that this JVPSP took about the same amount of time as the firm 'normally' took.

In comparison, 23 per cent viewed it as taking somewhat (19 per cent) or much more (4 per cent) time than normal, and 21 per cent viewed it as taking somewhat less time than normal.

Functioning of the Partner Selection Process: an Overview

The framework presented above is predicated on the assumption that, although certain phases may be more significant for some partner selection efforts than for others, there remains a fundamental set of issues that must be addressed in the course of any JVPSP. Each of the seven component subprocesses described above evidences conceptual uniqueness and they have been presented in the order in which they typically progress. In practice, however, the subprocesses may not necessarily be discrete and sequential steps. Overlaps can, and often do, occur. For example, it is not uncommon for decision criteria to continue to be revised and refined as the subprocesses of identification or evaluation of prospective partners are simultaneously progressing. However, the potential for non-linear progression through the subprocesses does not invalidate the proposed framework. On the contrary, analysis of prior JVs and responses of practitioners reinforces the practical and conceptual usefulness of a distinction between the above subprocesses. The potential for non-linear progression is acknowledged and accounted for via incorporation of contingency-based feedback loops, as discussed below.

Figure 11.1 illustrates the PSP in simplified flowchart form, incorporating the seven principal subprocesses outlined above. This figure highlights the processual nature of partner selection, including the potential for feedback loops to occur at various stages during the process. To clarify the framework, it may be useful to first describe the PSP in its most elementary form. Once this simplified form is discussed, several situations which introduce additional complexity through the use of feedback loops will be subsequently outlined.

Simplified form: absence of feedback loops

The functioning of the PSP in its most elementary form occurs when no contingency-based feedback loops are operative. In this instance, when an organization has considered involving itself in a project (Subprocess 0) and decides to consider a JV as an investment option (Subprocess 1), the process essentially evolves in a linear manner, progressing from development of selection criteria (Subprocess 2), to identification of the prospective partner organization(s) (Subprocess 3), evaluation of each prospect's suitability as a JV partner (Subprocess 4), and determination of which, if any, prospect to

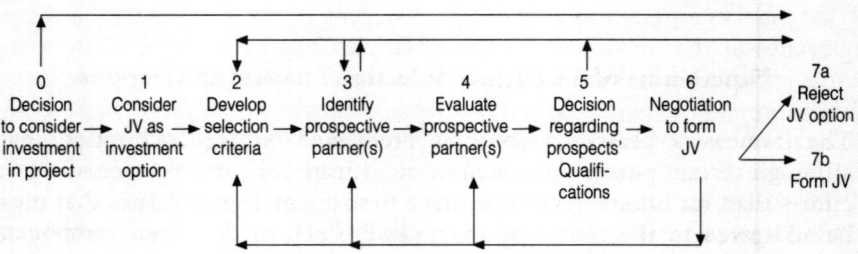

Figure 11.1   The joint venture partner selection process

pursue as a partner (Subprocess 5) and subsequently conduct negotiations with (Subprocess 6). At that point, the simplest case would entail either complete rejection of the JV option and termination of the PSP (Outcome 7a), or else formation of a JV with the prospective partner(s) (Outcome 7b). It is useful to note that this simple, linear, rational process tends to be relatively rarely observed in practice.

Additional complexity: existence of feedback loops

The PSP can, and in practice typically does, demonstrate greater complexity than the simplified version presented above. Contingency-based feedback loops can arise at several junctures within the process, introducing additional complexity. For instance, after conducting initial efforts to generate a list of prospective partners (Subprocess 3), a firm may not be satisfied with the results obtained. If the initial criteria employed were perceived as too strict (e.g., an insufficient number of prospective partners was generated, or potentially satisfactory partners failed to survive the screening) or as not strict enough (e.g., too many prospective partners were identified to permit evaluations to be adequately conducted within the constraints of available resources), or if there is political opposition within the organization to the results of this subprocess, the organization may first return to Subprocess 2 to modify the original selection criteria before continuing forward in the process. Another possible deviation from the simplified case presented above would arise if, after completing Subprocess 3, the firm decided against continuing on to the evaluation stage or returning to Subprocess 2, and instead chose to completely reject the notion of a JV (Outcome 7a).

Feedback loops could also occur after completion of Subprocess 5. At this point, instead of attempting to progress to Subprocess 6, a firm may decide to return to Subprocess 2 (e.g., changes in environmental conditions, such as a dramatic change in world energy prices or the outbreak of war, might have made previously developed criteria seem inadequate), to Subprocess 3 (e.g., changes in environmental circumstances might not have altered the relevance of the firm's selection criteria, but may have rendered the outcome of Subprocess 3 inadequate. For example, deregulation of an industry might expand the population of prospective partner organizations), or to rejection of the notion of a JV (Outcome 7a). The feedback loop from Subprocess 5 to Subprocess 3 could also result if the firm was pursuing a sequential, 'satisficing' approach to the generation and evaluation of prospective partners, which in practice appears to be a more common course of action than undertaking generation of a single comprehensive list of prospective partners followed by their evaluation *in toto*.

The final set of potential feedback loops emanates from Subprocess 6. In these cases, after an unsuccessful attempt to entice a prospective partner organization into formation of a JV, the firm may not choose to reject the notion of a JV outright. Instead, the firm may either return to Subprocess 2 (i.e., to modify the selection criteria which were employed, and thus the set of prospective partners), or return to Subprocess 3 (e.g., to generate a new or expanded list of prospective partners or, in the case of the sequential selection method mentioned in the previous paragraph, to identify the next prospective partner organization).

The inclusion of these feedback loops provides flexibility to the framework presented here, enabling it to incorporate the richness and complexity that characterizes the PSP as it occurs within the often diverse population of JVs.

Conclusions

As discussed earlier, the literature on *process* aspects of JV partner selection has been noticeably sparse. For this reason, one objective of this paper was to outline the essential components necessary for the construction of a framework of the JVPSP, as well as the anticipated relationships which may be observed among these components. The resulting framework may appear rudimentary in form, constrained as it is by the limited data available from prior studies and the difficulty of accessing a sample of sufficient breadth and depth. Nevertheless, this framework appears to have some usefulness for researchers examining JVs and other forms of collaborative alliances.

The conceptual framework presented in this paper is simple, yet quite robust. The framework is dynamic, allowing for contingency-based decisions and feedback. The framework examines the PSP within the context of the traditional business policy literature, emphasizing rationality as a means of formulating and implementing strategies. Yet, although the framework is consistent with the premise of rationality, it does *not* demand the often unrealistic assumption that the entire process is rational or uninfluenced by nonrational factors. Furthermore, although in its most elementary form the process suggests a readily comprehensible linear sequential decision making framework, the incorporation of contingency-based feedback loops provides the basis for an iterative process mirroring the richness and complexity that characterizes JV formation. Moreover, the feedback loops offer a subject focus just as intrinsically interesting, if not more so, than the individual linear stages themselves.

This framework was constructed from interview data collected from executives with intimate experience with the JVPSP. From this data, it was possible to identify seven salient component subprocesses which comprise the JVPSP. The framework also includes several contingency-based feedback loops which may occur among the various subprocesses, providing the basis for an iterative process mirroring the richness and complexity that characterizes JV formation. Key issues to be addressed within each subprocess were identified, along with potential outcomes and variables which influence their likelihood of occurrence.

The conceptual framework discussed in this paper was developed and refined using published case studies as well as interview data on JV formation. However, it should be noted that the framework as presented herein has not yet been subjected to rigorous empirical testing. It has also been based on analysis of JVs principally within the manufacturing, mining, and oil and gas industries, most but not all of which had operations concentrated in developed countries. It has been developed and is presented to enhance researchers' abilities to conceptualize the PSP and its associated complexities, and to suggest avenues for future research.

Undoubtedly, this framework is susceptible to refinement, particularly regarding the individual subprocesses, as well as the relationships between subprocesses and the overall outcomes which are obtained. Nevertheless, the framework offers several possible contributions for researchers examining the topic of interfirm collaboration in general, and JVs in particular. In light of extremely limited prior conceptual or empirical efforts to examine the processual aspects of JV partner selection, this framework provides a base from which further research efforts may be conducted.

References

Adler, L. & Hlavacek, J. D. 1976: *Joint ventures for product innovation*. New York: American Management Association.

Carpenter, S. L. and Kennedy, W. J. D. 1988: *Managing public disputes: A practical guide to handling conflict and reaching agreements*. San Francisco: Josey-Bass.

Colosi, T. 1985: A core model of negotiation. In R. J. Lewicki and J. A. Litterer (eds.), *Negotiation: Readings, exercises and cases.* Homewood, IL: Irwin.

Contractor, F. J. and Lorange, P. 1988: Why should firms cooperate? The strategy and economics basis for cooperative ventures. In F. J. Contractor & P. Lorange (eds.), *Cooperative Strategies in International Business,* Lexington, MA: Lexington Books, 3–30.

Daniels, J. D. 1971: *Recent foreign direct manufacturing investment in the United States.* New York: Praeger.

de Hoghton, C. 1966: *Cross-channel collaboration.* London: PEP.

Dymsza, W. A. 1988: Successes and failures of joint ventures in developing countries: Lessons from experience. In F. J. Contractor & P. Lorange (Eds.), *Cooperative Strategies in International Business,* Lexington, MA: Lexington Books, 403–424.

Geringer, J. M. 1988a: *Joint Venture Partner Selection: Strategies for Developed Countries,* Westport, Conn.: Quorum Books.

Geringer, J. M. 1988b: Selection criteria for developed country joint venture partners. *Business Quarterly,* 53 (1): 55–62.

Geringer, J. M. 1988c: Selection of partners for international joint ventures. *Business Quarterly,* 53 (2): 31–36.

Geringer, J. M. 1991: Strategic determinants of partner selection criteria in international joint ventures. *Journal of International Business Studies,* 22 (1): 41–62.

Geringer, J. M. and Frayne, C. A. 1990: Human Resource Management and International Joint Venture Control: A Parent Company Perspective. *Management International Review,* 30 (Special issue): 103–120.

Geringer, J. M. and Hebert, L. 1989: Control and performance of international joint ventures. *Journal of International Business Studies,* 20 (2): 235–254.

Geringer, J. M. and Woodcock, C. P. 1989: Ownership and control of Canadian joint ventures. *Business Quarterly,* 54 (1): 97–101.

Harrigan, K. R. 1987: Joint ventures: A mechanism for creating strategic change. In A. Pettigrew (Ed.), *The management of strategic change.* London: Basil Blackwell.

Harrigan, K. R. 1988: Strategic alliances and partner asymmetries. In F. Contractor and P. Lorange (Eds.), *Cooperative strategies in international business,* 205–226. Lexington, MA: Lexington Books.

Hill, R. 1987: A Contingency Model of Joint Venture Strategy Formulation and Implementation. Paper presented at Stratgeic Management Society Annual Conference, Boston, October.

Jemison, D. B. and Sitkin, S. B. 1986: Corporate acquisitions: A process perspective. *Academy of Management Review,* 11 (1): 145–163.

Killing, J. P. 1983: *Strategies for joint venture success.* New York: Praeger.

Lasserre, P. 1984: Selecting a foreign partner for technology transfer. *Long Range Planning,* December: 43–49.

Lyles, M. A. 1988: Learning among joint venture-sophisticated firms. In F. J. Contractor & P. Lorange (Eds.), *Cooperative Strategies in International Business,* Lexington, MA: Lexington Books, 301–316.

Moxon, R. W. and Geringer, J. M. 1985: Multinational consortia in high technology industries: Commercial aircraft manufacturing. *Columbia Journal of World*

Business, 20 (2): 55–62.

Moore, C. W. 1986: *The mediation process: Practical strategies for resolving conflict.* San Francisco: Jossey-Bass.

Porter, M. E., and Fuller, M. B. 1986: Coalitions and Global Strategy. In M. E. Porter (Ed.), *Competition in Global Industries*, 315–344. Boston: Harvard Business School Press.

Renforth, W. E. 1974: *A comparative study of joint international business ventures with family firm or non-family firm partners: The Caribbean community experience.* Unpublished doctoral dissertation, Indiana University.

Sullivan, J. J. and Peterson, R. B. 1982: Factors associated with trust in Japanese-American joint ventures. *Management International Review*, 22 (2): 30–40.

Tomlinson, J. W. C. 1970: *The Joint Venture Process in International Business: India and Pakistan*, Cambridge, Mass: MIT Press.

Weiss, S. E. 1987: Creating the GM-Toyota Joint Venture: A Case in Complex Negotiation. *Columbia Journal of World Business*, 22 (2): 23–27.

Woodcock, C. P. and Geringer, J. M. 1990: The relationship of parent strategy, ownership structure and cultural congruity with joint venture performance. *Administrative Sciences Association of Canada Proceedings*, 11 (6): 83–92.

IV

Designing Strategic Systems

In this section we present three papers which give a good overview of strategic management systems designed over time. Traditionally, strategic management systems have been designed on a normative basis, a certain design for planning systems, control systems, incentive systems and so on, proposed by its proponents as the 'best'. In today's situation it should be acknowledged that there is no one best design, rather the design of such strategic management systems will probably have to be based on the particular strategic context of a firm.

According to Rajagopalan, Rasheed and Datta, a thorough study of past empirical research in this area, identifying major patterns and contradictions in past research, has been limited. Future research with implications for theoretical, methodological and managerial points of view includes the need for more theory testing, a consistent operationalization and measurement of research constructs, and a need for a greater orientation to practitioners. The authors hope to see future research enhancing the understanding of the complexities of the strategic decision processes and providing meaningful guidance to managers in their decision making roles.

The paper by Camillus describes a new type of firm which is emerging distinguished by a low degree of hierarchy and a low degree of differentiation between the various internal functions. Future firms will be a synthesis between the dynamics of a super-team and the flexibility of the network, and they will construct their own environments.

Designing strategic management systems for a global firm is truly complex. However, most studies in the past have focused on the internationalization of the firm and not on how firms manage their subsidiaries once they become global. Gupta and Govindarajan show that by studying the information flow between the subsidiary and the head office and the flow from the subsidiary to the other subsidiaries we can begin to make important design choices on strategic management systems.

12

Strategic Decision Processes

AN INTEGRATIVE FRAMEWORK AND FUTURE DIRECTIONS[1]

*Nandini Rajagopalan, Abdul M. A. Rasheed and
Deepak K. Datta*

Research in the area of strategic management has been characterized by a dichotomy between 'content' and 'process' issues. However, content issues such as portfolio management through mergers, acquisitions or divestments, product-market choice, and the alignment of firm strategies with environmental characteristics have dominated the research agenda. Models proposed by Ansoff (1965), Andrews (1971), Grant and King (1980), and others, as well as Porter's (1980) work on generic strategies, have provided content researchers with a common vocabulary and a reasonable level of consensus on underlying theoretical and research questions. To some extent, this has led to the building of cumulative knowledge. On the other hand, there has been less theory-building and empirical research directed at process issues, which focus on the political, informational, and temporal dimensions by which strategic decisions are made and implemented. However, currently there is renewed interest in process research, as well as increased awareness of the critical interrelationships between content and process issues (Huff and Reger, 1987). As suggested by Mintzberg and Waters (1985:269): 'More research is required on the process of strategy formation to complement the extensive work currently taking place on the content of strategies; indeed, we believe that research on the former can significantly influence the direction taken by research on the latter (and vice versa)'.

In order to provide meaningful direction to strategic decision processes research, it is important to identify the crucial patterns and contradictions in extant research. Considerable diversity in the findings of past studies has often made it difficult to arrive at generalizable conclusions. For example, the performance implications of comprehensiveness in decision processes is still not clear, with studies finding both negative (e.g., Fredrickson and Mitchell, 1984) as well as positive (e.g., Eisenhardt, 1989) performance effects of comprehensive decision processes in rapidly changing environments.

The objectives of this paper are threefold. First, to review and synthesize past research on strategic decision processes. Unlike the exhaustive review of the entire body of stategic process research undertaken by Huff and Reger (1987), the focus of our review is strictly limited to empirical research on strategic decision processes. In order to do the review in a systematic manner, we develop a parsimonious integrative framework which identifies critical relationships among key antecedent and outcome variables. This framework seeks to clarify our understanding of the determinants and outcomes of strategic decision processes. Second, the paper uses the framework to identify gaps in the body of research, i.e., areas in which past research has been limited. Finally, based on a review of the literature, the paper suggests several useful directions for future research. These suggestions address theoretical, methodological, and managerial issues.

Theoretical Overview and Integrative Framework

Following Mintzberg, Raisinghani and Theoret (1976) and Schilit and Paine (1987), strategic decisions can be defined as those that utilize an organization's threats and opportunities to enhance its long-term prospects. By their very nature, strategic decision problems are more complicated and ill-defined than other problems (Lyles, 1987). They are also characterized by interconnectedness to other problems, complexity with recursive feedback, uncertainty in a dynamic environment, ambiguity dependent upon viewpoint, and conflicting trade-offs associated with alternative solutions (Mason and Mitroff, 1981). A number of theoretical models of strategic decision processes have been proposed. In the following paragraphs we briefly compare the major models and identify key variables and sets of relationships which form the basis for our integrative model of strategic decision processes.

Strategic decision process models: a comparison

Models that attempt to explain the process of strategic decision making reflect different conceptions of organizations. They range from 'rational' models that present the image of an integrated, well co-ordinated decision making body, making reasoned choices from clearly defined alternatives (e.g., Andrews, 1971; Ansoff, 1965) to political/behavioural models in which decisions are viewed as an outcome of bargaining and negotiations among individuals and organizational subunits with conflicting perceptions, personal stakes and unequal power (Narayanan and Fahey, 1982; Pettigrew, 1973; Tushman, 1977). Different classificatory schemes of strategic decision process models have been suggested by Allison (1971), Chaffee (1985), Mintzberg (1973) and Lyles and Thomas (1988). These models differ substantially in terms of their underlying assumptions, biases, and performance outcomes. This is not surprising, given the models' underlying theoretical grounding in diverse disciplines such as social psychology, and group decision-making (Janis, 1982) on the one hand and political/governmental processes (Lindblom, 1959) on the other.

While a detailed review of the various strategic decision process models is beyond the scope of this paper, we can classify those models under the following four broad categories: (1) rational/analytical; (2) political/power-behavioural; (3) organizational process/bureaucratic; and (4) organizational adaptation/adaptive models. These categories reflect different assumptions about the decision context and different characteristics of the decision process itself. A comparison of the assumptions and characteristics underlying each category is provided in table 12.1. While the table highlights differences across categories, considerable diversity exists even within categories, especially in the conceptualizations used by various authors. For example, while 'logical incrementalism' (Quinn, 1980) and 'disjointed incrementalism' (Braybrooke and Lindblom, 1970) both fall into the category of adaptive models, the former emphasizes the existence of a visionary leader while the latter describes a situation which lacks a central, co-ordinating vision.

The classificatory scheme presented in table 12.1 is by no means exhaustive. Moreover, the paper does not advocate the use of a single model of the strategic decision making process to the exclusion of other models for either normative or descriptive purposes. In fact, much of the richness of process research emanates from the use of multiple conceptualization of the same organizational event (e.g., Allison, 1971; Johnson, 1988). Rather, what is needed is a clarification of the assumptions and attributes of each of the models. In this way, empirical investigations of organizational processes can be guided by a clearer understanding of the model employed and its methodological imperatives, rather than an ad hoc examination of relationships among variables belonging to radically different models.

Strategic decision processes: an integrative framework

Table 12.1 allows us to draw certain broad conclusions. First, strategic decisions are made in the context of two sets of factors: (1) an organization's environment, in terms of its complexity and volatility; and (2) organizational conditions such as the internal power structure, past performance, past strategies, and the extent of organizational slack. Since both sets of factors vary from one organization to another even within the same industry, strategic decisions are likely to follow different patterns in different organizations. Second, even within a single organization, the process varies across decisions. This is due to differences in the impetus for the decision, the urgency associated with the decision, the degree of outcome uncertainty, and the extent of resource commitment. Thus, environmental and organizational factors as well as decision-specific factors determine a wide range of decision process characteristics, such as the duration of the process, the degree of rationality and comprehensiveness, the amount of political activity, and the extent of individual/subunit involvement in the decision process. The decision process, in turn, translates itself into certain process outcomes, namely, the timeliness/speed of the decision (Eisenhardt, 1989), the level of commitment from individual and organizational units (Carter, 1971), and the exent of organizational learning (Dutton and Duncan, 1987). Process characteristics as well as process outcomes in turn influence economic outcomes such as ROI/ROA and sales or profit growth (Eisenhardt and Bourgeois, 1988; Fredrickson and Mitchell, 1984). The interrelationships identified above can be depicted in the form of an integrative strategic decision process framework (figure 12.1). In addition to helping integrate the various perspectives, it serves as an analytical review scheme to summarize past empirical research on strategic decision processes. As noted by Ginsberg and Venkatraman (1985:422), '... an analytic review scheme is necessary for systematically discerning patterns from a widely differing set of studies and evaluating the contributions of a given body of research'. Such a framework also constitutes a broader, more completely specified model which can form the basis for identifying issues for future research.

This framework identifies primary links (I-VI) and secondary links (represented by dotted lines). We shall focus on the primary links since these links directly explore relationships between decision process characteristics, their antecedents, and their outcomes.

Figure 12.1 identifies six primary linkages, with the central role played by strategic decision process characteristics. This framework identifies three sets of antecedent relationships: environmental factors (Link I), organizational factors (Link II), and decision specific factors (Link III) and two sets of outcome relationships: process outcomes (Link IV), and economic outcomes (Link V). It also postulates relationships between process and economic outcomes (Link VI). These six sets of relationships are directly relevant for understanding the antecedents and outcomes of different types of strategic decision processes. It is important to note that our definition of the strategic decision process subsumes all the different steps involved in making strategic decisions, i.e., problem/issue identification,

Table 12.1 Comparison of strategic decision making models

	Model Type			
Characteristics	*Rational/analytical*	*Political/power/behavioral*	*Organizational processes/bureaucratic*	*Organizational adaptation/adaptive*
Classification examples	Allison (1971: Model 1) Chaffee (1985: Linear) Mintzberg (1973: Planning) Lorange & Vancil (1977) Andrews (1965) Ansoff (1965), etc.	Allison (1971: Model III) Tushman (1977) Pettigrew (1973) Narayanan & Fahey (1982)	Allison (1971: Model II) Mazzolini (1981)	Chaffee (1985: Adaptive) Mintzberg (1973: Adaptive) Quinn (1980) Braybrooke & Lindblom (1970) Miles, Snow, Meyer & Coleman (1977), Summer (1980)
Environment of the organization	Closed, certain and relatively predictable	Complex and unpredictable	Largely routine; predictable for sub-units	Complex, relatively unpredictable
Internal power structure	Centralized, integrated power structure	Dispersed bases of power. Existence of groups with conflicting priorities and perceptions	Loosely allied sub-units with parochial priorities. Fractionated power with/without strong leadership	Less centralized and integrated
Organizational norms and traditions	Not vital to strategy formulation. Could be a criterion in alternative evaluation	May/may not exist. Used as a bargaining/negotiating tool	Well established procedures and practices. Rules govern actions	Constitute a constraint in decision making.
Role of top management/leadership	Opportunity/problem identification, co-ordination and communication of alternatives	Coalition management, building commitment, keeping political exposure low and forcing decisions	Initiating force in problem identification, managing the structural context to influence behaviour. Providing approval/commitment to a course of action	problem/opportunity identification. Gearing internal organization to achieve alignment. Building awareness

Time horizon	Brief and timely	Many interruptions, delayed	Quick for routine decisions Delayed for complex decisions spanning many sub-units	Varies from one decision to another
Focus of decision making	Achievement of predetermined goals	Choice of acceptable/workable alternative	Sequential problem solving as per standard operating procedures	Organization-environment alignments. Achievement of organizational goals
Nature of organizational goals	Predetermined and explicit	Determined by conflict/compromise between coalitions	Constraints that limit the choice of alternatives	Changing goals that reflect demands of the environment
Impetus for change	Problem/opportunity	Individual/group initiative	Problem/top management's initiative	Environmental opportunity/threat, internal performance standards, performance failure
Decision process	Linear. Formulation precedes implementation	Iterative. Commitment built prior to choice of alternative	Centralized formulation. Implementation as per standard operating procedures	Co-evolving goals and means for implementation

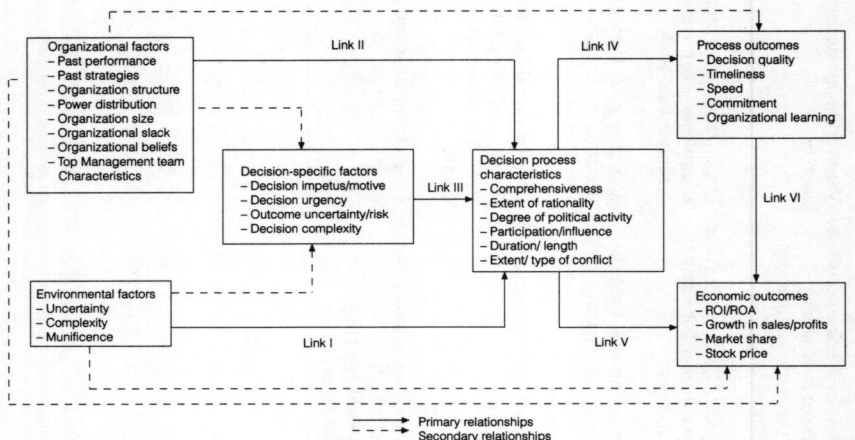

Figure 12.1   Strategic decision processes: an integrative framework

alternative generation, evaluation, and selection (Fredrickson, 1984). While a few studies have examined how strategic decision process characteristics differ across different phases (Fahey, 1981; Nees, 1983; Schilit, 1987) the focus has not been on the strategic decision process as a whole. Moreover, these studies do not identify any consistent or significant pattern in the differences among the various phases. This suggests that there is limited utility in distinguishing among these phases.

Link I in the framework pertains to the relationship between environmental factors and strategic decision process characteristics. The key issue addressed in research related to this link is how environmental factors (e.g., environmental complexity or uncertainty) influence strategic decision process characteristics (e.g., the extent of rationality and comprehensiveness). On the other hand, Link II research has primarily examined how organizational factors such as organizational size, past strategies and performance, structure, top management team characteristics, beliefs, and organizational slack influence decision process characteristics. Research on Link III has examined the relationships between decision-specific factors such as decision urgency, decision impetus, decision complexity, and outcome uncertainty, and process characteristics. Finally, Links IV, V and VI focus on outcomes and attempt to establish some prescriptive relevance for research on strategic decision making by relating it to either process outcomes (IV) or economic outcomes (V) or both (VI). The following section reviews key studies in each linkage as well as emerging patterns and contradictions.

Review of Past Empirical Literature

A systematic search[2] was undertaken to identify empirical studies which examined at least one of the six linkages identified in figure 12.1. Each study was then classified by one of the authors along six key theoretical and methodological dimensions: the underlying theoretical bases of the paper, sample, data sources/methods, measures of key variables (including the controls used), analytic methods and major findings. The classification was independently verified by co-authors for the purpose of validity and consistency. The results of our review are presented in table 12.2. The table is organized in terms of studies which examined a single linkage, followed by studies which examined multiple linkages.

Link I: Relationships between environmental factors and decision process characteristics

As seen in table 12.2, studies pertaining to Link I have focused primarily on one environmental dimension, namely, the extent of environmental uncertainty defined in terms of stability (e.g., Fredrickson, 1984, Fredrickson, 1985, Fredrickson and Iaquinto, 1989) or velocity (e.g., Eisenhardt and Bourgeois, 1988; Eisenhardt, 1989). The findings of studies belonging to this stream are, however, somewhat contradictory. For example, studies conducted by Fredrickson and his colleagues indicate that comprehensive strategic decision processes are associated with superior economic performance in stable environments and inferior performance in unstable environments. In contrast, Eisenhardt's studies found that effective strategic decisions in high velocity environments, though made within a short time duration, are characterized by comprehensiveness. This contradiction may be partly attributable to organizational factors, such as power distribution and information processing systems, which were included in Eisenhardt's studies, but not in Fredrickson's. In addition, Fredrickson and Iaquinto (1989) found significant differences in the levels and types of comprehensiveness across industries, which suggests that industry factors play a crucial moderating role in the relationship considered in Link I. These studies also indicate that there may be important interaction effects between environmental and organizational factors when we consider the performance effects of decision processes. Thus, not only do different combinations of environment and strategic decision process characteristics have different performance effects, but also within a given environment, different combinations of decision processes and organizational contexts may give rise to different performance implications.

Review of Link I studies also revealed certain major gaps in the literature. For example, the effects of two important aspects of the environment,

Table 12.2 Summary of empirical studies on strategic decision processes

Study/links	Theoretical bases	Sample	Data sources/methods	Measures	Analytic methods	Major findings
Welsh & Slusher (1986) Link II	Contingency theory and political models of decision making	40 professional colleges (decision about selection of a dean)	Questionnaires and interviews	*Organizational factors* Task specialization, faculty heterogeneity, centralization, consensus, interdependence *Decision process characteristic* Political activity	Correlations Hierarchical regression	When interdependence is low, increasing consensus leads to more political activity among faculty members.
Duhaime & Baird (1987) Link II	Divestment theory	91 divested units in mail study, 56 personal interviews in Fortune 500 firms	Mail survey, personal interviews	*Organizational factor* Unit sales as a percentage of total firm sales (measure of unit size) *Process characteristic* Unit manager's involvement	Chi-square	Managers of smaller units generally had greater involvement in the decision process than did managers of larger units. Business unit size is an important issue in divestment decision-making.
Langley (1990) Link II	Contingency theory	In-depth analysis at senior levels in three organizations, eight/ten recent strategic issues	80 interviews with senior managers, analysts, professionals and line managers	*Organizational factors* Three structural types (machine bureaucracy, professional bureaucracy, 'adhocracy') *Decision process characteristic* Formal analysis	Content analysis Kruskal-Wallis test Chi-square	Patterns in decision making processes and the use of formal analysis related to organizational structure, leadership style and the nature of issues faced by the organization.

Study	Theory/Focus	Sample	Method	Variables	Analysis	Findings
Schilit (1987) Link III	Rational decision models, socio-political decision models	60 middle-level managers, 329 strategic decisions	Questionnaires, participant records, single informant	*Decision-specific factor* Riskiness/return *Decision process characteristic* Upward influence *Controls* Stage of the process, type and size of organization	Frequencies Tests for proportion differences Multiple regressions	Upward influence activity more likely in i) low risk/return decisions than high risk/return decisions ii) implementation than formulation iii) private organizations than in public organizations.
Schwenk (1984) Link IV	Group decision making	80 undergraduate students	Laboratory experiment, questionnaires	*Decision process characteristics* Decision making approach – Dialectical inquiry, devil's advocacy or consensus *Process outcomes* Number of strategic alternatives, number of functional area alternatives, satisfaction with the process	ANOVA	Subjects using DA & DI reported higher satisfaction than those using expert approach. DI worked better with video presentation and DA with written aids.

Study/links	Theoretical bases	Sample	Data sources/methods	Measures	Analytic methods	Major findings
Schweiger, Sandberg & Ragan (1986) Link IV	Group decision making	120 MBA students	Laboratory experiment, questionnaires	*Decision making characteristics* Decision making approach – DI, DA or consensus *Process outcomes* Number of assumptions, quality of assumptions and recommendations, satisfaction and desire to continue to work in group, acceptance of group decisions	MANOVA, ANOVA	Quality of recommendations DI & DA > C Quality of assumptions surfaced DI > DA Satisfaction with decision and desire to continue to work in group C > DI & DA
Schweiger, Sandberg & Rechner (1989) Link IV	Group decision making	120 middle and upper-middle level managers from three divisions of a Fortune 500 company	Laboratory experiment, questionnaires	*Decision process characteristics* Decision making approach – DI, DA or consensus *Process outcomes* Number, validity, and importance of assumptions, quality of recommendations, satisfaction and desire to continue to work with group, acceptance of group decision, critical evaluation, meeting duration	MANOVA, ANOVA Correlations	Quality of decisions: DI = DA > C Acceptance of decisions: C > DI = DA Experience in using DI, DA & C reduced time required to reach decision and improved decision quality, critical re-evaluation levels and reactions of group members

Study	Theory area	Sample	Method	Variables	Analysis	Findings
Schweiger & Sandberg (1989) Link IV	Group decision making	120 MBA students	Laboratory experiment, questionnaires	*Decision process characteristics* Decision making approach – DI, DA or consensus *Process outcomes* Number, validity and importance of assumptions: quality of recommendations *Other* Utilization of individual capabilities	Construct validity & reliability tests MANOVA, ANOVA	Quality of recommendations DI & DA > C Quality of assumptions DI > DA, C DI yields better group performance on all measures, but does not differ substantially from DA in utilization of individual members' capabilities
Schwenk (1990) Link IV	Group decision making	42 executive MBA students from business and not-for-profit organizations	Questionnaires	*Decision process characteristics* Decision making approach – DI, DA or consensus *Process outcomes* Quality of decision: overall quality, clarity, assertiveness	Factor analysis Correlations	High conflict is associated with high quality in not-for-profit organizations but with low quality in for-profit organizations
Dess (1987) Link V	Organization theory	74 members of the top management team of 19 privately held firms in the paints and allied products industry	On-site interviews and mail questionnaires	*Decision Process characteristics* Consensus on competitive methods *Performance* Sales growth, after tax return on assets, overall firm performance *Controls* Sales	Correlational analysis ANOVA	Consensus on methods/strategies is positively related to organizational performance

(continued)

Study/links	Theoretical bases	Sample	Data sources/methods	Measures	Analytic methods	Major findings
Bourgeois (1980) Link V	Political and behavioural models of decision making	CEO's of 12 non-diversified public corporations plus 67 members of their top management teams	On-site interviews, questionnaires	*Decision process characteristics* Consensus on industry relevant competitive weapons *Performance* Factor score of ROA, growth in capital, growth in net earnings, growth in EPS, improvement in ROS	Analysis of variance	Consensus on means leads to higher performance
Fahey (1989) Links II & III	Rational decision models, behavioural/political decision models	Six multi-divisional firms in diverse industries, strategic energy management decisions in each firm, key executives at corporate and divisional levels	Structured questionnaires, interviews, multiple informants	No a priori constructs/measures: decision process characteristics derived from observations/descriptions	Inductive/descriptive theory building No statistical tests	Strategic decision processes are characterised by both rational and behavioural/political processes: phases in the process are interrelated, interactive, and often characterized by considerable political activity. Also influenced by degree of criticalness, impetus and frequency of occurrence.

Study	Theory	Sample	Method	Variables	Analysis	Findings
Jemison (1981) Links I & II	Strategic contingency theories of intra-organizational power	124 senior executives from 15 firms in 3 industries	Survey questionnaires, multiple respondents	*Organizational factors* 3 types of power bases *Environmental factors* 3 boundary spanning roles *Decision process characteristic* Departmental influence *Controls* Industry type	Construct reliability tests ANOVA Correlation analysis	Environmentally derived sources of strategic decision making have a greater association with departmental influence than organizationally derived sources
Astley, Axelsson, Butler, Hickson & Wilson (1982) Links II & III	Political models of decision making	150 decision topics analysed in 30 organizations	Rating of cases by researchers	*Organizational factor* Cleavage *Decision specific factor* Complexity *Decision process characteristics* Scrutiny, negotiation, discontinuity, centralization, duration *Process outcome* Synopticism, anticipation and acceptability	Generalization based on case studies Cross tabulation of data	Centralization is high when complexity and political cleavage is high. When decision is simple and without cleavage, decision making process is fast. Negotiation is high when political cleavage is high.
Fredrickson & Mitchell (1984) Links I, V	Synoptic and incremental decision making	109 executives in 2/ firms	Structured interviews, questionnaires utilizing decision scenarios	*Decision process characteristic* Comprehensiveness *Performance* ROA, % of sales growth	Partial correlations	Negative relationship between comprehensiveness and performance. Relationship holds for both measures of performance.

(continued)

Study/links	Theoretical bases	Sample	Data sources/ methods	Measures	Analytic methods	Major findings
Fredrickson (1984) Links I, V	Synoptic and incremental decision making	152 executives in 38 firms	Structured interviews, questionnaires utilizing decision scenarios	*Decision process characteristic* Comprehensiveness *Performance* ROA, % of sales growth	Partial correlations	Positive relationship between comprehensiveness and performance (ROA) in a stable environment. However, no significant relationship is observed when performance is operationalized as sales growth.
Fredrickson (1985) Links I, II, III	Organizational decision making	321 MBA students and 116 upper-middle level executives	Laboratory study, questionnaires	*Organizational factors* Past performance *Environmental factors* Opportunity, threat *Decision process characteristic* Comprehensiveness	MANOVA, ANOVA	MBA students were more comprehensive when recommending actions in response to environmental threats and poor performance than to environmental opportunities and excellent performance. Similar results were not observed in the case of executives.

Study	Focus	Sample	Data sources	Constructs/Measures	Analysis	Findings
Shrivastava & Grant (1985) Links I, II, III, IV	Organizational information processing, organizational learning, adaptive decision making models	61 senior executives from 31 firms in diverse industries, computerization decisions	Interviews, organizational records	No a priori measures/ constructs; several organizational, environmental and process characteristics derived from post-facto analysis	Grounded theory and historical analyses Within-case and cross-case comparisons Thematic analyses Frequencies & descriptive statistics	Four models of strategic decision making can be identified: managerial autocracy, systemic bureaucracy, adaptive planning, and political expediency. Each is characterized by different organizational and environmental conditions, process characteristics, and outcomes.
Bourgeois (1985) Links I, II, V	Group decision making	20 nondiversified firms, 99 responses (multiple respondents from each firm including CEO)	Interviews, questionnaires, secondary sources	*Environmental factors* Volatility, perceived environmental uncertainty (PEU) *Decision process characteristic* consensus *Economic outcomes* ROTA, growth in net earnings, EPS, return on sales and capital	Correlations Factor analysis	Consensus on PEU and goals together lead to poor economic performance. Congruence between PEU and volatility is positively related to performance. Diversity in environmental perceptions and goals related positively to performance, but only when it occurs in conjunction with congruence between PEU and volatility.

(continued)

Study/links	Theoretical bases	Sample	Data sources/methods	Measures	Analytic methods	Major findings
Pinfield (1986) Links II, III	Structured and anarchic decision making	A Canadian governmental bureaucratic organization	Participant observation, archival data, interviews	*Decision specific factor* Decision urgency *Decision process characteristic* Participation *Organizational factors* Structural arrangements, organizational goals	Case study/ Qualitative methodology	A partial synthesis of the structured and anarchic decision models can link changes in participation and external variables to decision process.
Miller (1987) Links II, V	Contingency theory	CEOs, VPs or general managers of 97 firms (multiple respondents)	Questionnaires	*Organizational factors* Structure: integration, decentralization, complexity *Process characteristics* Rationality, assertiveness, interaction *Performance* Self reported scores on relative profits, growth in income & ROI	Principal components analysis Multiple regression	Organizational structures and strategy-making processes must be complementary to ensure good performance. Formal integration was found to be positively related to rationality and interaction in strategy making. Decentralization showed a weak positive association with interaction and assertiveness.

Study / Links	Theory base	Sample	Method	Variables	Analysis	Findings
Schilit & Paine (1987) Links III & IV	Rational decision models, group decision making, socio-political models	60 middle-level managers, 329 strategic decisions	Questionnaires, participant records, interviews, single informant	*Decision-specific factors* Information source, riskiness, return *Decision process characteristics* Duration, coalition activity, conflict, rationality *Process outcomes* Speed *Controls* Stage of process, functional background	Factor analysis Chi-square tests	Higher the riskiness/return, greater is the duration of the process, the use of collaborative and incremental techniques, and the level of coalition activity and negotiation.
Segev (1987) Links II, V	Contingency theory, strategic typologies	133 MBA students	Laboratory experiment, questionnaires	*Organizational factors* Strategic type: prospectors, analysers, defenders and reactors *Decision process characteristics* Strategy making mode: entrepreneurial adaptive and planning *Economic outcomes* Market shares, profitability measures	MANOVA, ANOVA Correlations Fisher Exact tests Cronbach Alphas for reliabilities	Strong associations between strategic types and strategy making modes. Fit between strategic type and mode associated with higher market share for prospectors.

Study/links	Theoretical bases	Sample	Data sources/ methods	Measures	Analytic methods	Major findings
Bourgeois & Eisenhardt (1988) Links I, V	Rational, political and incremental models of decision making	4 decisions in 4 microcomputer firms (multiple informants)	Interviews and questionnaires	*Decision process characteristics* Comprehensiveness, newness of alternatives tried *Process outcomes* Decision speed *Economic outcomes* Market acceptance of product, sales and profitability	Embedded multiple case design	In high velocity environments, successful firms do comprehensive analysis but make quick decisions, have powerful CEOs & TMTs, and seek risk and innovation but execute safe, incremental implementation.
Eisenhardt and Bourgeois (1988) Links I, II, IV, V, VI	Political models of decision making	8 firms in microcomputer industry (multiple informants)	Interviews, questionnaires, secondary sources	*Organizational factor* Centralization of power *Decision process characteristics* Political behaviour, conflict, stability of alliances *Process outcomes* Decision speed *Economic outcomes* CEO's ranking relative to other firms in industry, sales growth, return on sales	Grounded theory and historical analyses Within-case and cross-case comparisons Thematic analyses Frequencies and descriptive statistics	Politics arises from power centralization. Politics is organized into stable coalitions based on demographic characteristics. Politics within top management teams are associated with poor firm performance (both in economic and process outcomes).

Study / Links	Theory	Sample	Method	Variables	Analysis	Findings
Miller, Droge, Toulouse (1988) Links I, II	Contingency theory	CEOs, VPs or general managers in 77 firms (multiple respondents)	Questionnaires	*Organizational factors* Structure: integration, formalization, centralization, CEO need for achievement *Environmental factor* Uncertainty *Decision process characteristic* Analysis, interaction	LISREL	Extent of analysis and interaction in strategic processes are positively influenced by CEO need for achievement structural formalization and integration.
Eisenhardt (1989) Links I, II, IV, VI	Synoptic and incremental processes, political model of decision making	8 firms in microcomputer industry (multiple respondents)	CEO interviews, semistructured interviews with each member of a firm's top management team, questionnaires, and secondary sources.	*Decision process characteristics* Consensus, real-time information, multiple simultaneous alternatives, two-tier advice process *Process outcomes* Decision speed, number of alternatives considered, integration among decisions, commitment to decisions *Economic outcomes* Sales growth and profits, CEO self reports	Grounded theory and historical analyses Within-case and cross-case comparisons Thematic analyses Frequencies and descriptive statistics	Fast decision makers in high velocity environments use more information, consider more alternatives, use counsellors, and pursue active conflict resolution strategies. Decisions based on this pattern of behaviours lead to superior performance.

(continued)

Study/links	Theoretical bases	Sample	Data sources/ methods	Measures	Analytic methods	Major findings
Fredrickson, Iaquinto (1989) Links I, II, V	Synoptic and incremental decision making, group decision making	45 firms from 2 industries, 159 executives including CEOs (multiple respondents)	Interviews, questionnaires utilizing decision scenarios	*Environmental factor* Stability/instability *Organizational factors* Change in size, change in executive team intrafirm tenure, executive team continuity *Decision process characteristics* Comprehensiveness, change in comprehensiveness *Economic outcomes* Average after tax return on assets adjusted for extraordinary items	Correlations Multiple regression Analysis of variance	Relationships found in the two 1984 studies continue to hold. Changes in organizational size, executive team-tenure, and level of team continuity were positively associated with changes in comprehensiveness. Comprehensiveness exhibited considerable inertia. Also, significant across-industry differences were found in comprehensiveness.
Wooldridge & Floyd (1990) Links IV, V, VI	Organizational processes, group decision making	11 banks and 9 manufacturing organizations	Semi-structured interviews with CEOs and questionnaires from middle-level managers	*Decision process characteristics* Participation involvement *Process outcomes* Commitment and understanding of strategy *Economic outcomes* competitive position, ROA, efficiency, growth rate	Correlations	Involvement by middle level management in the formation of strategy leads to greater understanding by them and improved economic performance.

Reference	Topic area	Sample	Method	Decision process characteristics	Analysis	Findings
Cray, Mallory, Butler, Hickson & Wilson (1988) No specific links examined	Information processing, political models of decision making, group decision making	30 firms from diverse industries, 150 strategic decisions	Interviews with multiple key executives in each firm, company documents	*Decision process characteristics* Scrutiny, interactions, duration, centrality, gestation time, process time	Content analysis Clustering Discriminant analysis	Three types of decision making processes capture a wide range of decision processes – i) Sporadic: discontinuous, prolonged, highly politicized ii) Fluid: continuous, rational, shorter duration iii) Constricted: procedure-dominated, low involvement and interaction, single/few decision makers.
Nees (1983) No specific links examined	Strategic decision making, divestment decision making	Two separate groups of 25 European middle- to senior-level managers in a management development programme	Simulation experiment with three business cases: observations and video taping	*Decision process characteristics* Time allotted to different stages in the decision process; total time for arriving at decision; number and characteristics of different phases in decision process	No statistical tests *except* for percentages	The divestment process consists of four phases: identification, solution development, selection and implementation; more time spent on solution development and selection than implementation; groups with *more* experience develop *faster* solutions.

namely, complexity and munificence (Dess and Beard, 1984) on decision process characteristics have not been examined. The degree of environmental complexity in a firm's operating environment directly impacts the amount and nature of information that has to be processed by decision makers (Schwenk, 1984; Thomas, 1984). This, in turn, affects strategic decision process characteristics such as comprehensiveness, rationality, and duration. Research on cognitive processes (Schwenk, 1984; Schwenk, 1988) suggests that high environmental complexity may lead to greater use of cognitive simplification processes such as selective perception, heuristics and biases, and the use of analogies. These cognitive simplification processes, in turn, affect the strategic decision process by potentially restricting the range of strategic alternatives considered and the information used to evaluate alternatives. Techniques developed in social and cognitive psychology such as cognitive mapping (Axelrod, 1976), may help researchers understand how decision makers assess interrelationships among environmental factors, which factors they consider important, and how they arrive at particular choices.

In addition to environmental complexity, munificence should also influence strategic decision processes. Munificence refers to an environment's capacity to provide resources which support the organization. Organizations are less likely to be penalized for poor or suboptimal decisions in munificent than in non-munificent environments. Thus, decision processes suited to munificent environments may be inappropriate for less munificent ones. However, past research has failed to address these questions, in spite of the fact that findings would have important normative implications for managers who must formulate strategic decisions in a variety of environmental contexts.

Link II: Relationships between organizational factors and decision process characteristics

Studies pertaining to this link have mostly focused on two sets of organizational factors: power distributions within the decision-making group (Eisenhardt, 1989; Jemison, 1981; Shrivastava and Grant, 1985) and structural aspects such as formalization, integration, and decentralization (Miller, Droge, and Toulouse, 1988). Several theoretical arguments have been made which indicate how these two organizational factors influence strategic decision processes. Provan (1989) argues that managerial perceptions and enactment of the environment are heavily influenced by power distribution within an organization. Powerful individuals and departments are likely to determine the identification of problems and issues (Dutton and Jackson, 1987), the type and extent of information used, and the criteria used to evaluate alternatives (Shrivastava and Grant, 1985). Similarly, organizational structure can influence information flow (Bower, 1970; Fahey, 1981), as well as the extent of analysis and interaction at different organizational levels (Miller, Droge, and Toulouse, 1988).

While a number of empirical studies have been undertaken on relationships identified by Link II, consistent patterns with meaningful implications for practitioners are lacking. For example, Shrivastava and Grant (1985) suggest that formal structures and power centralization are associated with rationality in decision making processes, lower degree of political activity and subunit involvement, and quicker decisions. Similarly, Miller, Droge and Toulouse (1988) and Miller (1987) found positive relationship between structural formalization and integration and also between the extent of rationality and integration in strategic decision processes. In contrast, Eisenhardt (1989) and Eisenhardt and Bourgeois (1988) found that in rapidly changing environments, power centralization is associated with a higher degree of political activity within the top management team and poorer economic performance. As noted earlier in our discussion of Link I studies, this suggests crucial interactions between organizational and environmental factors in the relationship between strategic decision processes and performance. In other words, alternative power distributions and structures may affect strategic decision processes differently in different environments and the outcome effects of different structure/power and strategic decision process combinations may also vary across different environments.

Research relating other organizational factors (identified in figure 12.1) to strategic decision processes is limited. Exceptions include studies by Fredrickson (1984), which examined the role of past performance and Fredrickson and Iaquinto (1989) which examined the effects of changes in organizational size and top management team characteristics on decision process comprehensiveness. In other studies exploring this link, Fahey (1981) and Shrivastava and Grant (1985) examined a wide range of organizational factors through case studies but did not identify the specific effects of these factors except in terms of general propositions. Segev (1987), using laboratory and field experiments, found significant associations between a firm's strategic orientation and strategy making modes. However, because of the small number of studies which examine these relationships, it is difficult to draw any generalizable conclusions or identify consistent patterns.

The review of Link II studies also points to several organizational factors which, though theoretically meaningful, have received little or no attention in past research. These include the role of organizational slack, belief structures, top management team characteristics, and past strategies and performance. Also, our review indicates that past research in this link has predominantly used contingency theories to study relationships. This is appropriate since these studies primarily focus on structure and power. However, other theoretical arguments may be needed to explore the role of the neglected organizational factors in the future. In particular, theories of group decision making and cognition which emanate from a social psychological perspective of decision making are relevant. Bateman and Zeithaml (1989) used the psychology literature on escalation and decision framing to study the effects of past performance and organizational slack on the divestment decision. While their study focused on the content rather than the process of decision making, interesting parallels can be drawn. For example, favourable past performance and high organizational slack can create positive decision frames, and high levels of decision maker confidence which, in turn, can lead to a limited examination of new alternatives, limited information search, and less comprehensive, but faster decision processes. Past strategies can have similar effects on strategic decision processes according to theories of escalating commitment. Cognitive simplification processes such as illusion of control and selective perception, which can restrict the range of strategic alternatives considered, may be associated with favourable past perfomance and the presence of organizational slack. Research into the effects of top management team (TMT) characteristics (such as size, tenure and demography) on strategic decision processes can draw upon theories of group decision making such as polarization (Lamm and Myers, 1978; McGrath, 1984), social comparison (Jellison and Arkin, 1977), and persuasive argumentation (Vinokur and Burnstein, 1974). These theories of intra-group decision processes can constitute relevant theoretical bases for understanding the effects of TMT characteristics on strategic decision processes. For example, the study by Gladstein and Reilly (1985), on group decision making has useful implications for TMT decision making as well.

With regard to methodological perspectives, most studies belonging to this link have utilized field surveys and case studies. Given the number of confounding factors in such settings and the wide variety of factors examined, there are serious concerns of internal validity. In order to improve future theory building, researchers may need to make greater use of laboratory and carefully controlled field settings. These research designs permit the researcher to identify specific effects of each organizational factor while controlling for other factors, as well as possible two-way and three-way interactions (e.g. Bateman and Zeithaml, 1989). Relationships identified in such controlled settings can then be tested among a wide variety of organizations using techniques of stratified sampling which control for one set of factors while varying the others (Harrigan, 1983).

Link III: Relationships between decision-specific factors and decision process characteristics

Our review of the literature indicates that relationships between decision specific factors and decision process characteristics have received very limited attention in past research. Only seven out of the thirty-one studies reviewed in table 12.2 examined Link III. Five of these tested specific hypotheses with the remaining two being case studies. In addition, the available body of research is also fragmented. Given the variety in the types of strategic decisions that managers make, there clearly is a need to examine the influence of decision context on process characteristics. Carter's (1971) pioneering study indicated that decision context, defined in terms of level of technical uncertainty, degree of outcome uncertainty, and criticalness to decision makers, has an important influence on process characteristics. In a more recent study of strategic energy management decisions, Fahey (1981) found that the process characteristics were influenced by factors such as degree of criticalness, impetus, and frequency of occurrence. Also, Schilit's (1987) findings suggest that the risk/return characteristics of a decision impact the extent of upward influence exercised by middle level managers. Other decision specific factors that have been identified as having influence on process characteristics include decision complexity (Astley *et al.* 1982), decision urgency (Pinfield, 1986), decision motive (Frederickson, 1985; Shrivastava and Grant, 1985), information source (Schilit and Paine, 1987), and problem classification (Volkema, 1986). Further empirical evidence supporting the impact of problem characterization on decision processes and outcomes is available in studies by Cowan (1988) and Dutton and Duncan (1987).

   In summary, two factors limit our ability to draw generalizable conclusions about the relationship between various decision specific factors and process characteristics. First, little consensus exists regarding the definition and operationalization of important decision specific factors, leading to loose and inconsistent definitions of key constructs. Further, terms such as decision criticalness, decision urgency, and outcome uncertainty have been used in several studies with little or no attempt to satisfy the requirements of construct validity and reliability. Only one out of the seven studies in this link (Frederickson, 1985) provided tests for construct validity and reliability. Second, very few studies in Link III have simultaneously examined or controlled for the influence of environmental and organizational factors. This clearly limits our ability to draw strong inferences regarding this link or to build theory cumulatively. Perhaps the major contribution of studies in this link is a heightened awareness of the need for closer examination of the interrelationships between decision specific factors and process characteristics.

Links IV, V, & VI: Relationships among decision process characteristics and process/economic outcomes

As Venkatraman and Ramanujam (1986) point out, performance improvement is at the heart of strategic management. Therefore, it is not surprising that a number of empirical studies have examined the relationship between process characteristics and performance outcomes. However, most studies have focused on Links IV (process characteristics and process outcomes) and V (process characteristics and economic outcomes), leaving Link VI (process outcomes and economic outcomes) as the most underresearched link in our model. Of the nineteen studies which examined strategic decision process outcomes, ten studied Link IV, eleven studied Link V, but only three examined Link VI.

Studies in Link V have attempted to establish some prescriptive relevance for strategic decision making research by investigating the relationship between decision process characteristics and economic outcomes. These include studies by Fredrickson (1984) and Fredrickson and Mitchell (1984) which found a positive relationship between decision process comprehensiveness and superior performance in stable environments, and a negative relationship in unstable environments. In a longitudinal extension, it was found that these relationships hold even after several years (Fredrickson and Iaquinto, 1989). However, conflicting results have been reported by Eisenhardt (1989) who found a positive relationship between comprehensiveness and performance in high-velocity environments. This lack of consensus on the relationship between comprehensiveness and performance is very similar to the contradictions encountered in the research on formal planning systems and financial performance (Pearce, Freeman, and Robinson, 1987), since the formality of the planning system may often be indicative of the comprehensiveness of the planning process.

A number of studies belonging to Link V have also investigated the relationship between TMT consensus and economic performance. (See Dess and Origer [1987] for a comprehensive review of these studies.) As with the relationship between the comprehensiveness of the decision process and economic performance, empirical results in this area are conflicting. While Bourgeois (1980), and Dess (1987) found a positive relationships between consensus and firm performance, Bourgeois (1985) and Grinyer and Norburn (1975) found the relationship to be negative. Priem (1990) suggests that a direct relationship between consensus and performance may be too simplistic and that environmental change may strongly moderate such a relationship. Further, he argues that consensus itself may be the outcome of organizational factors or more specifically TMT characteristics such as homogeneity and group structure.

While the impact of decision process characteristics on economic outcomes has been of considerable interest to both researchers and practitioners, it must be recognized that several organizational and environmental factors also affect economic performance. As a result, cause-effect relationships are difficult to establish. Because of the model underspecification which characterizes many of these studies, reported relationships are likely to be confounded by factors extraneous to the research question under investigation.

In contrast, the relationships between process characteristics and process outcomes (Link IV) are more direct and are less likely to be confounded by extraneous factors. Timeliness, speed of decision making, acceptability to organizational members, adaptiveness to change, and the extent of organizational learning appear to be useful indicators of strategic decision process outcomes (Quinn and Rohrbaugh, 1983). Studies belonging to this link include Eisenhardt (1989), who found that speed of decision making is positively related to comprehensiveness and extent of analysis, and Langley (1990), whose study indicated that formal analysis in strategic decisions ensures convergence towards action.

A stream of research that has focused on Link IV relationships consists of several laboratory studies on the relative effectiveness of Dialectical Inquiry (DI) and Devil's Advocacy (DA) on decision performance. Both of these methods are based on inducing cognitive conflict in the decision making process. While these studies provide some evidence that cognitive conflict generally leads to better quality decisions (e.g., Schweiger, Sandberg, and Rechner, 1989; Schweiger, Sandberg, and Ragan, 1986), they do not provide any conclusive evidence as to whether one method is superior to another (Schwenk, 1989). Further, if a broader definition of outcome is adopted, incorporating such factors as satisfaction with the decision and desire to continue to work in the group, the results become even more confusing.

Lastly, empirical studies pertaining to Link VI, i.e., the relationship between process outcomes and economic outcomes, are scarce. Our research identified only three such studies (Eisenhardt, 1989; Eisenhardt and Bourgeois, 1988; Wooldridge and Floyd, 1990). Eisenhardt (1989) found a positive relationship between decision speed and performance. Wooldridge and Floyd (1990) found that involvement and commitment by middle-level managers lead to better performance.

Our review of Link's IV, V, and VI suggests that a number of important questions have remained unanswered. For example, are there patterns in the relationships between different strategic decision making process characteristics and the extent/type of organizational learning that takes place as a consequence of these processes? Also, what are the performance/

outcome implications of these relationships? Since learning is an ongoing process in organizations an important issue is whether we should view it as an outcome variable at all. In other words, while the knowledge base resulting from organizational learning is a process outcome, learning itself could be viewed as a continuous organizational process. Shrivastava and Grant (1985) suggest that different types of organizational learning systems support different types of strategic decision making models. For example, formal learning systems such as strategic planning systems and management information systems support adaptive strategic decision making processes. But do different strategic decision making processes contribute differentially to organizational learning? Mintzberg and Waters (1985) argue that comprehensive, deliberate strategic decision making can often hinder strategic learning since messages from the environment tend to get blocked out. On the other hand, strategies which are characterized by emergent/evolutionary processes may keep the organization open, flexible, and responsive.

Conclusions and Implications for Future Research

Based on the preceding review of empirical research on strategic decision processes, several conclusions and implications for future research can be identified. These are discussed in the following paragraphs grouped along theoretical, methodological, and managerial dimensions.

Theoretical implications

Need for more theory testing

Strategic decision process research to date is based on a very rich and diverse theoretical base. Empirical studies have often used more than one theoretical model to study strategic decision processes, resulting in a much richer description of the process than would have occurred with simpler theoretical models. In particular, the use of both rational and political/behavioural models has been far more prevalent in process research than in content research. However, our review does indicate the importance of utilizing multiple theories in order to develop more testable hypotheses. Given the rich descriptions of the strategic decision process and multiple models used to analyse it, the development of additional descriptive models is likely to result in only limited benefits. More useful would be studies which attempt to test the normative and predictive usefulness of existing models. Such studies would not only permit the identification of the nature of causal relationships but also result in greater cumulation of research findings.

Greater use of cognitive/psychological theories

Past empirical research on strategic decision processes has been dominated by theoretical models which adopt an organizational/macro perspective rather than an individual/micro perspective. This is evident in the number of studies which have utilized contingency theories, rational, socio-political, and organizational process models of decision making. Twenty-one out of the thirty-one studies in our review utilized macro/organizational theoretical perspectives, as opposed to only six studies which adopted a more micro view of the decision process. The latter set of studies typically utilized group decision making theories. Only four studies (Cray *et al.* 1988; Fredrickson and Iaquinto, 1989; Schilit and Paine, 1987; Wooldridge and Floyd, 1990) reflect a combination of the micro and macro perspectives in studying this topic. While a macro perspective is both necessary and useful, the role of the individuals and groups involved in the strategic decision process needs to be acknowledged to a greater extent in future research. In this regard, cognitive psychological theories of decision making (e.g., Axelrod, 1976; Bateman and Zeithaml, 1989: Kahneman and Tversky, 1984) and theories of group decision making (Gladstein and Reilly, 1985) can certainly contribute to a better understanding of the impact of factors such as individual backgrounds, experiences, biases, group composition, and tenure on the strategic decision process. We believe that combining the macro and the micro views of strategic decision making should be particularly important in both future theory building and theory testing. Several specific research questions which can be explored from a micro perspective were identified earlier in our discussion of Links I and II.

Multiple theoretical specifications

Boal and Bryson (1987) identify four underlying theoretical models to represent interrelationships between contextual, process, and outcome variables: independent, intervening, moderating, and interaction effects models. In the intervening effects model, contextual factors (such as environment, organization, and decision-specific factors) impact outcomes through their effects on process-related variables. In the independent effects model, contextual and process variables have independent effects on outcomes. In the moderating effects model, context moderates the effect of process on outcomes. Finally, in the interaction model, context and process jointly determine outcomes. Knowing which theoretical model best describes each link in figure 12.1 could have a number of significant implications for theory testing, as well as for managerial practice. The choice of a model, in itself, raises a number of questions. First, should managers focus on context or process or both? Second, can they influence strategic decision processes in such a way as to realize desired outcomes?

Third, where in the causal sequence should top managers intervene? While a detailed discussion of these models is beyond the scope of this paper (see Boal and Bryson [1987] for a detailed treatment), our review indicates the dominance of the independent/intervening effects models in past research. Although this is appropriate for Link I, II, and III studies, studies examining the outcome-oriented links IV, V, and VI are more likely to benefit from utilizing the moderating/interaction effects models since these specifications will enable researchers to include contextual variables in the process-outcome linkage.

Methodological implications

Research on strategic decision processes reveals rich theory development. However, far less attention has been paid to methodological rigour. Undoubtedly, the complexity of the topic complicates both data collection and analysis. Our review suggests several useful directions and guidelines regarding research methods for future research. These are discussed in the following paragraphs.

Operationalization and measurement of research constructs

As noted earlier in our review of Link III studies, empirical studies have often been plagued by a plethora of definitions and operationalizations, especially in the context of decision-specific antecedent factors and strategic decision process characteristics. More importantly, very little attention has been paid to issues of construct validity and reliability. Utilization of single-item measures in field studies and surveys, and post-facto description of measures by the researcher not only reduce the comparability across studies but also raise questions about the internal validity of the findings. Very few studies in our review made use of multi-item measures, and provided tests for scale reliability and validity. This is a shortcoming which needs to be addressed in future research.

Data sources and data collection methods

Several studies in the past have used survey questionnaires and single respondents for data collection. There are several problems to be noted in this respect. First, questionnaires are subject to respondents' varying interpretations and cognitive orientations and do not establish whether the context is strategic (Fredrickson, 1986). Second, the perceptions of a single individual, notwithstanding the person's organizational status, may not reflect organizational reality. Wolfe and Jackson's (1987) study, for example, found a severe lack of agreement among participants about the nature and details of their own strategic decisions. In their study, subjects disagreed more than half the time on even the most basic elements of their strategic decisions. This suggests that data obtained through survey questionnaires needs to be validated using other data sources (Huber and Power, 1985). Content analyses of transcripts of actual processes, cross-check of recall data, and multiple concurrent self reports can be used in conjunction with survey questionnaires to overcome problems of respondent bias and distortions (Wolfe and Jackson, 1987).

The use of decision scenarios as a research methodology also holds considerable promise (Fredrickson, 1986). Scenarios enable researchers to adopt a decision-based perspective which assumes that strategic decision processes are patterns of behaviour that develop in organizations, with individual decisions being made and integrated into an overall strategy (Mintzberg and Waters, 1985). As demonstrated in studies by Fredrickson and his colleagues, scenarios based on detailed industry knowledge allow the creation of strategic contexts, while providing respondents with standardized stimulus. Scenarios can be tailored to different industry contexts. Moreover, multiple scenarios, when used in a single study, can enable researchers to achieve internal validity as well as generalizability. Scenarios also permit the use of multiple respondents, multi-item indicators of research constructs, and construct development techniques which maximize both agreement within firms and between-firm variance (Fredrickson, 1986). Finally, scenarios can also be used to assess cross-sectional and temporal variances by administering them to the same set of respondents at different points in time and thereby assessing causal patterns of relationships over time. Scenarios appear to combine some of the advantages of controlled laboratory studies (i.e., high internal validity through controlled stimulus) with those of field studies (i.e., realism and generalizability). For this reason, they offer a promising data collection method for future studies.

Greater utilization of longitudinal research designs

Field studies, commonly used in past research on strategic decision processes, have been largely cross-sectional. They pool strategic decisions and respondents from multiple industries and environmental contexts without incorporating adequate controls. Thus, if we are to more fully understand the causal relationships (and their directions) between the antecedent factors and process characteristics and also their impact on outcomes, it is important that longitudinal research designs are emphasized. Van de Ven's (1980 a, b) work in programme planning provides an excellent illustration of how longitudinal studies can explain the relationships among context, process, and outcomes over time. Fredrickson's various studies in the paint and forest products industries reviewed earlier also indicate the usefulness of a longitudinal approach in determining whether certain synoptic/incremental modes of strategic decision making persist over time and their performance implications. While it has been argued that cross-sectional studies permit greater generalizability, longitudinal studies have the advantage that they help eliminate the possibility of reverse causalities among a study's variables, an unavoidable problem associated with cross-sectional studies.

Several options are available, with respect to data collection and analysis, which combine both generalizability and accuracy within certain limits. Samples of firms and industries can be chosen to permit maximum variation on one set of antecedent variables while controlling the others (Harrigan, 1983). For each member within this sample, data on process characteristics and various outcome variables can be collected at different points in time. The effects of cross-sectional variations and temporal effects can then be assessed simultaneously by employing data analytic methods suited for pooled cross-sectional time series data.

Causal modelling and multivariate analysis methods

The most commonly used statistical methods in past empirical studies are bivariate, zero-order, and partial correlations and also analysis of variance techniques which assess main effects and simple interactions. Although these methods are both appropriate and useful in assessing relationships within independent/intervening effects models (Boal and Bryson, 1987), more complex analytic methods will be needed to assess multivariate relationships within moderating/interaction effects models. Moderated regression analysis and subgroup regression analysis are particularly useful for this purpose (Arnold, 1982). Second generation multivariate models such as LISREL could be very useful in testing interaction effects models. Moreover, the model depicted in figure 12.1 suggests the need to examine direct as well as indirect effects through causal modelling techniques such as path analysis (Wright, 1960). For example, path analysis can be used to assess whether process characteristics have a direct impact on economic outcomes or whether the effect is indirect through their effects on process outcomes. Such analysis would also expose the relative strength of these direct and indirect effects.

Managerial implications

Need for greater outcome orientation

Nineteen out of the thirty-one studies in our review included either economic or process outcomes or both. In spite of the large number of studies which have examined the outcomes of strategic decision processes, little by way of useful advice to practising managers can be drawn from these. Two general conclusions seem to emerge from our review. First, the performance effects of strategic decision processes are context specific. Environmental and organizational factors have independent as well as interaction effects, but unequivocal patterns are hard to establish. Second, processes which induce intra-group cognitive conflict appear to improve decision quality, but whether such processes also improve other process outcomes such as decision speed, commitment etc. is unclear. These conclusions point to a rather serious limitation of strategic decision process research, namely, limited prescriptive relevance. Strategic process research should aspire to descriptive accuracy as well as prescriptive relevance. Research to date has been very productive in terms of describing how and why decision process characteristics vary between different contexts. However, it tells us little about whether one set of characteristics is more effective than another and the conditions under which such effectiveness can be realized. It also fails to tell us whether decision processes account for significant variance in performance, economic or otherwise. As suggested by Bateman and Zeithaml (1989), research needs to identify and explicate relationships which are not obvious to managers. To the extent that the outcome effects of strategic decision processes are both non-obvious and extremely complex, studies which examine these links are likely to have considerable practical significance.

Defining relevant outcomes

Variables used to capture outcomes in the strategic decision process research, to a large extent, reflect the economic orientation of content researchers. This research emphasis raises the interesting question as to whether economic measures of performance are the only legitimate outcome variables or whether they reflect the biases imposed by the researcher's cognitive framework (Reger, 1988) and data availability. A broader conceptualization of process effectiveness is needed which incorporates both process-related as well as economic-performance-related measures (Venkatraman and Ramanujam, 1986). Cause-effect relationships are much harder to assess in the study of economic performance outcomes than in the study of process outcomes, because of the variety of organizational and environmental influences on economic performance (as indicated by the secondary links in figure 12.1). Future researchers must also ask themselves whether research is focusing on outcomes which are considered desirable and valuable by top managers and other decision makers. Other topics of relevance to managers are the possibility of trade-offs among different outcomes, their potential benefits, and their long-term and short-term effects. These and several other related questions reflect greater attention to performance implications of strategic decision processes and are likely to be very meaningful from the point of view of practising managers.

In conclusion, while considerable research has been undertaken on strategic decision processes in the last decade by scholars in strategic management, the research has remained fragmented and non-cumulative. Our evaluation of the empirical literature suggests that there are a number of gaps and inconsistencies in past research. It is our hope that the framework proposed in this paper, which is based on a careful assessment of the existing theoretical and empirical literature, will be of help in addressing the many unresolved research issues relating to strategic decision processes. It also suggests several useful directions for future research. As discussed in the preceding paragraphs, we expect such research to not only enhance our understanding of the complexities surrounding strategic decision processes, but also provide meaningful guidance to managers in the making of effective strategic decisions.

Notes

1   The authors wish to thank Anthony Daboub, Gregory G. Dess, Peter Lorange, Johan Roos and V.K. Narayanan for their helpful comments on earlier drafts of this paper.
2   Our review covered empirical work published in Academy of Management Journal, Administrative Science Quarterly, Strategic Management Journal, Journal of Management, Journal of Management Studies, Management Science, Organization Science, and Organization Studies during the period 1981–90.

References

Allison, G. T. 1971: *Essence of decision*, Little, Brown and Co.: Boston, MA.

Andrews, K. R. 1971: *The concept of corporate strategy*. Irwin: Homewood, IL.

Ansoff, H. I. 1965: *Corporate strategy*, McGraw-Hill: New York.

Arnold, H. J. 1982: Moderator variables: A clarification of conceptual, analytic, and psychometric properties, *Organizational Behavior and Human Performance*, 29, pp. 143–174.

Astley, W. G., Axelsson, R., Butler, R. J., Hickson, D. J. and Wilson, D. C. 1982: Complexity and cleavage: Dual explanations of strategic decision-making. *Journal of Management Studies*, 19, pp. 357–375.

Axelrod, R. (Ed.) 1976: *Structure of decision: The cognitive maps of political elites*. Princeton University Press: Princeton, New Jersey.

Bateman, T. S. and Zeithaml, C. P. 1989: The psychological context of strategic decisions: A model and convergent experimental findings. *Strategic Management Journal*, 10, pp. 59–74.

Boal, K. B. and Bryson, J. M. 1987: Representation, testing, and policy implications of planning processes. *Strategic Management Journal*, 8, pp. 211–231.

Bourgeois, L. J. 1980: Performance and consensus. *Strategic Management Journal*, 1, pp. 227–248.

Bourgeois, L. J. 1985: Strategic goals, perceived uncertainty and economic performance. *Academy of Management Journal*, 28, pp. 548–573.

Bourgeois, L. J. and Eisenhardt, K. M. 1988: Strategic decision processes in high velocity environments: Four cases in microcomputer industry. *Management Science*, 34, pp. 816–835.

Bower, J. 1970: *Managing the resource allocation process.* Graduate School of Business Administration, Harvard University Press: Boston.

Braybrooke, D. and Lindblom, C. E. 1970: *A strategy of decisions: Policy evaluation as a social process,* Free Press: New York.

Carter, E. 1971: The behavioral theory of the firm and top level corporate decisions. *Administrative Science Quarterly*, 16, pp. 413–428.

Chaffee, E. E. 1985: Three models of strategy. *Academy of Management Review*, 10, pp. 89–98.

Cowan, D. A. 1988: Executive knowledge of organizational problem types: Applying a contingency perspective. *Journal of Management*, 14, pp. 513–527.

Cray, D., Mallory, G. R., Butler, R. J., Hickson, D. J. and Wilson, D. C. 1988: Sporadic, fluid and constricted processes: Three types of strategic decision making in organizations. *Journal of Management Studies*, 25, pp. 13–39.

Dess, G. G. 1987: Consensus on strategy formulation and organizational performance: Competitors in a fragmented industry. *Strategic Management Journal*, 8, pp. 259–277.

Dess, G. G. and Beard, D. W. 1984: Dimensions of organizational task environments. *Administrative Science Quarterly*, 29, pp. 52–73.

Dess. G. G. and Origer, N. K. 1987: Environment, structure and consensus in strategy formulation: A conceptual integration. *Academy of Management Review*, 12, pp. 313–330.

Dutton, J. E. and Duncan, R. B. 1987: The creation of momentum for change through the process of strategic issue diagnosis. *Strategic Management Journal*, 8, pp. 279–295.

Dutton, J. E. and Jackson, S. 1987: Categorizing strategic issues: Links to organizational action. *Academy of Management Review*, 12, pp. 76–90.

Eisenhardt, K. M. 1989: Making fast strategic decisions in high-velocity environments. *Academy of Management Journal*, 32, pp. 543–576.

Eisenhardt, K. M. and Bourgeois, L. J. 1988: Politics of strategic decision making in high-velocity environments: Toward a midrange theory. *Academy of Management Journal*, 31, pp. 737–770.

Fahey, L. 1981: On strategic management decision processes. *Strategic Management Journal*, 2, pp. 43–60.

Fredrickson, J. W. 1984: The comprehensiveness of strategic decision processes: Extensions, observations, future directions. *Academy of Management Journal*, 27, pp. 445–466.

Fredrickson, J. W. 1985: Effects of decision motive and organizational performance level on strategic decision processes. *Academy of Management Journal*, 28, pp. 821–843.

Fredrickson, J. W. 1986: An exploratory approach to measuring perceptions of strategic decision process constructs, *Strategic Management Journal*, 7, pp. 473–483.

Fredrickson, J. W. and Iaquinto, A. L. 1989: Inertia and creeping rationality in strategic decision processes. *Academy of Management Journal*, 32, pp. 543–576.

Fredrickson, J. W. and Mitchell, T. R. 1984: Strategic decision processes: Comprehensiveness and performance in an industry with an unstable environment. *Academy of Management Journal*, 27, pp. 399–423.

Ginsberg, A. and Venkatraman, N. 1985: Contingency perspectives of organizational strategy: A critical review of the empirical research. *Academy of Management Review*, 10, pp. 421–434.

Gladstein, D. L. and Reilly, N. P. 1985: Group decision making under threat: The tycoon game. *Academy of Management Journal*, 28, pp. 613–627.

Grant, J. H. and King, W. R. 1980: *The logic of strategic planning*. Little, Brown & Co.: Boston.

Grinyer, P. and Norburn D. 1975: Planning for existing markets: Perceptions of executives. *Journal of the Royal Statistical Society*, 138 (1), pp. 70–97.

Harrigan, K. R. 1983: Research methodologies for contingency approaches to business strategy. *Academy of Management Review*, 8, pp. 398–405.

Huber, G. P. and Power, D. J. 1985: Retrospective reports of strategic-level managers: guidelines for increasing their accuracy. *Stategic Management Journal*, 6, pp. 171–180.

Huff A. S. and Reger, R. K. 1987: A review of strategic process research. *Journal of Management*, 13, pp. 211–236.

Janis, I. L. 1982: *Victims of Groupthink*, Houghton-Mifflin: Boston, MA.

Jellison, J. and Arkin, R. 1977: Social comparison of abilities: A self-presentation approach to decision-making in groups. In J. Suls and R. Miller (eds.), *Social comparison processes: Theoretical and empirical processes*, Hemisphere Press. Washington, D. C.

Jemison, D. B. 1981: Organizational versus environmental sources of influence in strategic decision making. *Strategic Management Journal*, 2, pp. 77–89.

Johnson, G. 1988: Rethinking incrementalism. *Strategic Management Journal*, 9, pp. 75–91.

Kahneman, D. and Tversky, A. 1984: Choices, values, and frames. *American Psychologist*, 39, pp. 341–350.

Langley, A. 1990: Patterns in the use of formal analysis in strategic decisions. *Organization Studies*, 11, pp. 17–45.

Lamm, H. and Myers, D. G. 1978: Group induced polarization of attitudes and behavior. In L. Berkowitz (ed.), *Advances in experimental social psychology*, 11, pp. 145–195.

Lindblom, C. E. 1959: The science of muddling through. *Public Administration Review*, 19, pp. 79–88.

Lyles, M. A. 1987: Defining strategic problems: Subjective criteria of executives. *Organization Studies*, 8, pp. 263–279.

Lyles, M. A. and Thomas, H. 1988: Strategic problem formulation. *Journal of Management Studies*, 25, pp. 131–146.

Mason, R. O. and Mitroff, I. I. 1981: *Challenging strategic planning assumptions*. Wiley: New York.

McGrath, J. E. 1984: *Groups: Interaction and performance*, Prentice Hall. New Jersey.

Miller, D. 1987: Strategy making and structure: Analysis and implications for performance. *Academy of Management Journal*, 30, pp. 7–32.

Miller, D., Droge, C. and Toulouse, J. M. 1988: Strategic process and content as mediators between organizational context and structure. *Academy of Management Journal*, 31, pp. 544–569.

Mintzberg, H. 1973: Strategy-making in three modes. *California Management Review*, 16, pp. 44–53.

Mintzberg, H. and Waters, J. A. 1985: Of strategies, deliberate and emergent. *Strategic Management Journal*, 6, pp. 257–272.

Mintzberg, H., Raisinghani, D. and Theoret, A. 1976: The structure of 'unstructured' decision processes. *Administrative Science Quarterly*, 21, pp. 246–75.

Narayanan, V. K. and Fahey, L. 1982: The micro-politics of strategy formulation. *Academy of Management Review*, 7, pp. 25–34.

Nees, D. B. 1983: Simulation: A complementary method for research on strategic decision-making processes. *Strategic Management Journal*, 4, pp. 175–185.

Pearce. J. A. Freeman, E. B. and Robinson, R. B. 1987: The tenuous link between formal strategic planning and financial performance. *Academy of Management Review*, 12, pp. 658–675.

Pettigrew, A. 1973: *The politics of organizational decision making*. London: Tavistock.

Pinfield, L. T. 1986: A field evaluation of perspectives on organizational decision making. *Administrative Science Quarterly*, 31, pp. 365–388.

Porter, M. E. 1980: *Competitive strategy*. Free Press: New York.

Priem, R. L. 1990: Top management team group factors, consensus, and firm performance. *Strategic Management Journal*, 11, pp. 469–478.

Provan, K. G. 1989: Environment, department power, and strategic decision making in organizations: A proposed integration. *Journal of Management*, 15, pp. 21–34.

Quinn, J. B. 1980: *Strategies for change*. Dow-Jones Irwin: Homewood, IL.

Quinn, R. E. and Rohrbaugh, J. 1983: A spatial model for effectiveness criteria: Towards a competing values approach to organizational analysis. *Management Science*, 29, pp. 363–377.

Reger, R. K. 1988: *Competitive positioning in the Chicago banking market: Mapping the mind of the strategists*, Unpublished doctoral dissertation, University of Illinois, Urbana-Champaign.

Schilit, W. K. 1987: An examination of the influence of middle level managers in formulating and implementing strategic decisions. *Journal of Management Studies*, 24, pp. 271–293.

Schilit, W. K. and Paine, F. T. 1987: An examination of the underlying dynamics of strategic decisions subject to upward influence activity. *Journal of Management Studies*, 24, pp. 161–187.

Schweiger, D. M., Sandberg, W. R. and Ragan, J. W. 1988: Group approaches for improving strategic decision making: A comparative analysis of dialectical inquiry, devil's advocacy and consensus. *Academy of Management Journal*, 29, pp. 51–71.

Schweiger, D. M., Sandberg, W. R. and Rechner, P. L. 1989: Experiential effects of dialectical inquiry, devil's advocacy and consensus approaches to strategic decision making. *Academy of Management Journal*, 32, pp. 745–772.

Schweiger, D. M. and Sandberg, W. R. 1989: The utilization of individual capabilities in group approaches to strategic decision-making. *Strategic Management Journal*, 10, pp. 31–43.

Schwenk, C. R. 1984: Effects of planning aids and representation media on performance and affective responses in strategic decision making. *Management Science*, 30, pp. 263–271.

Schwenk, C. R. 1988: Cognitive simplification processes in strategic decision-making. *Strategic Management Journal*, 9, pp. 111–128.

Schwenk, C. R. 1989: A meta-analysis on the comparative effectiveness of devil's advocacy and dialectical inquiry. *Strategic Management Journal*, 10, pp. 303–306.

Schwenk, C. R. 1990: Conflict in organizational decision making: An exploratory study of its effects in for-profit and not-for-profit organizations. *Management Science*, 36, pp. 436–447.

Segev, E. 1987: Strategy, strategy making, and performance in a business game. *Strategic Management Journal*, 8, pp. 565–577.

Shrivastava, P. and Grant, J. H. 1985: Empirically derived models of strategic decision-making processes. *Strategic Management Journal*, 6, pp. 97–113.

Thomas, H. 1984: Strategic decision analysis: Applied decision analysis and its role in the strategic management process. *Strategic Management Journal*, 5, pp. 139–156.

Tushman, M. L. 1977: A political approach to organizations: A review and rationale. *Academy of Management Review*, 2, pp. 206–216.

Van de Ven, A. H. 1980a: Problem solving, planning, and innovation. Part I. Test of the program planning model. *Human Relations*, 33, pp. 711–740.

Van de Ven, A. H. 1980b: Problem solving, planning, and innovation. Part II. Speculations for theory and practice. *Human Relations*, 33, pp. 757–779.

Venkatraman, N. and Ramanujam, V. 1986: Measurement of business performance in strategy research: A comparison of approaches. *Academy of Management Review*, 11, pp. 801–814.

Vinokur, A. and Burnstein, E. 1974: Effects of partially shared persuasive arguments on group induced shifts: A group problem solving approach. *Journal of Personality and Social Psychology*, 29, pp. 305–315.

Volkema, R. J. 1986: Problem formulation as a purposive activity. *Strategic Management Journal*, 7, pp. 267–279.

Wolfe, J. and Jackson, C. 1987: Creating models of the strategic decision making process via participant recall: A free simulation examination. *Journal of Management*, 13, pp. 123–134.

Wooldridge, B. and Floyd, S. W. 1990: Strategy process, middle management involvement and organizational performance. *Strategic Management Journal*, 11, pp. 231–242.

Welsh, M. A. and Slusher, E. A. 1986: Organizational design as a context for political activity. *Administrative Science Quarterly*, 31, pp. 389–402.

Wright, S. 1960: Path coefficients and path regression: alternative or complementary concepts? *Biometrika*, 47, pp. 189–202.

13

Crafting the Competitive Corporation

MANAGEMENT SYSTEMS FOR FUTURE ORGANIZATIONS

John C. Camillus

Designing organizations that are suited for survival and success in the context of turbulent environments is a challenge that is being addressed both in the real world and in the academic arena. Organizations and their managements face a future that is significantly different to the context in which practice and thinking about organizational design and administrative systems have developed. Notions such as 'adhocracies' (Mintzberg, 1979) in organization design and 'logical incrementalism' (Quinn, 1980) in administrative systems have been around for over a decade and do reflect the beginnings of a response to the changing contexts that business organizations are encountering today. Current literature emphasizes swiftness (Tucker, 1991), adaptation (Chakravarthy and Lorange, 1991), knowledge use (Barabba and Zaltman, 1991), learning (Senge, 1990) and vision (Westley and Mintzberg, 1989) as organizations strive to survive and succeed. Traditional organizational forms and administrative systems are not particularly noted for displaying or promoting such characteristics. As management faces the enormous challenge of creating organizations and systems that can respond to the imperatives of the future business environment, an understanding of the forces that are fashioning this future is a necessary prerequisite to a reasoned and effective response. Five of these forces that are commonly cited are:

1 The increasingly rapid and discontinuous nature of change
2 The explosion of information technology
3 The growth of 'knowledge-based' industries
4 The imperative of globalization
5 The increasing professional competence of managers

Each of these forces is briefly discussed below.

Rapid and Discontinuous Change

Toffler (1970, 1980; 1990) is perhaps the best-known chronicler and prophet of the increasing rapidity and magnitude of change being experienced by society in general and business in particular. The transformation of societies that Toffler (1980; 1990) describes impacts greatly on the context in which business organizations function and on the way in which they should be managed. An organization that cannot anticipate or at least respond swiftly to change will not endure long. Ponderous and precise management processes involving several layers of hierarchy are singularly inappropriate to contexts in which technology, markets and competition are in a constant state of flux. What may be needed in such contexts are adaptive and organic processes (Burns and Stalker, 1961; Chakravarthy, 1982), self-designing organizations (Hedberg, Nystrom and Starbuck, 1976), responsiveness to weak signals (Ansoff, 1975), and a structure that promotes communication (Semler, 1989). Many of the emerging responses being adopted by business organizations have been documented in the popular press (Naisbitt and Aburdene, 1985; Dumaine, 1990).

Explosion of Information Technology

A significant driving force behind the 'third wave' (Toffler, 1980) is information technology. Information technology permits new organizational structures and relationships (Camillus and Lederer, 1985) in addition to the more explicit options of: (1) more efficient information storing, retrieval and processing; (2) more effective decision support; and (3) more ways to communicate. The novel organization forms and relationships are alternatives that merit exploring in a changing world, particularly given the availability of these options to the competition.

Information technology as a means of exploiting time as a competitive weapon (Stalk and Hout, 1990) again creates pressures for management systems and competences that can employ such technology.

Growth of 'Knowledge-Based' Industries

While knowledge-based industries (such as consulting, science-based and high technology) have always played a significant role in industrialized societies, an inevitable concomitant of the post-industrial world (Toffler, 1980) is a major increase in the number, variety and importance of knowledge-based industries.

The very nature of such industries depends on the professional, specialized capabilities of their employees. Two-way communication becomes even more important in such a context. Power, stemming from expertise, will be more widely distributed. Professionals have loyalties, relate to peer groups, and espouse aspirations that often lie outside their employing organizations. The egalitarian culture that such organizations would lean toward requires that traditional hierarchical authority, typified in the extreme by the military and certain religious organizations, give way to other means of ensuring a shared organizational purpose.

The Imperative of Globalization

The enhanced differentiation arising from operating in different and distant geographical areas, countries, cultures, markets and legal systems places greater demands on the mechanisms and processes of integration. With globalization being increasingly seen as necessary to foster growth, competitiveness and vitality, strengthening of the integrative aspects of management systems becomes critically important.

Another aspect of the globalization trend is the necessity for organizations to develop the flexibility to operate in vastly different contexts. Self-designing organizations (Hedberg, Nystrom and Starbuck, 1976) would obviously be of value in this regard.

Professional Competence of Managers

With the development of management disciplines, the competence of professionally educated managers has grown at least in areas requiring analytical skills (Porter and McKibbin, 1988). For instance, over the last two decades formal planning and business policy as management disciplines have developed enormously. Decision contexts, once the province of managers who had presumably gained wisdom through experience, are neither alien nor outside the domain of managers with frameworks and skills developed through education rather than experience. Consequently, expert knowledge as a source of authority is reducing in significance while competence possessed by junior managers becomes increasingly relevant to decision contexts previously the exclusive domain of senior managers.

The development of management as a profession also offers executives affiliations with professional associations and peer groups that are external to their employing organizations. Traditional loyalty to an organization may increasingly have to compete with personal commitment to growth in a management discipline or function.

Observed Corporate Responses

Organizations have no option but to respond to these forces if they are to survive, let alone prosper. In looking at how organizations are observed to be changing, it is useful to recall the fundamental characteristics of traditional or classic organizational forms. Classic organizational forms are characterized by a *hierarchy* of management levels and *differentiation* of management functions (Galbraith, 1977). There are indications that these two characteristics are being affected by the changing business context being created by the five forces identified. Two developments, in particular, have been quite extensively documented (Dumaine, 1990; Naisbitt and Aburdene, 1985; Schrage, 1990). The first of these two developments is the emergence of 'networks' (Naisbitt and Aburdene, 1985) of relationships that are different from the formal hierarchical structures of organizations. Secondly, 'superteams' (Dumaine, 1990) that integrate traditionally separate functions are increasingly being employed by a wide variety of organizations.

An important characteristic of networks is that they recognize and emphasize the different competences of individuals in an organization but largely disregard hierarchical structures in terms of who relates to whom. Of the two dominant characteristics of classic organizations, namely hierarchy and differentiation, it appears that networks disregard or discount hierarchy while recognizing or reaffirming differentiation. Networks emerge to take advantage of the differing capabilities, knowledge, resources, perspectives, and locations of their individual participants.

Superteams, in a somewhat different mode, do recognize that their members possess different perspectives or competences, but submerge these differences in the commonality of purpose that created the superteam. Thus, while marketing, manufacturing, design, engineering, and finance experts may be part of a superteam, their backgrounds are subsidiary to the superteam's mission of for example, developing a new product for an organization. The melding of expertise and overlapping of responsibilities intrinsically emphasizes integration while ensuring that the range of competences necessary to accomplish its purpose is available. It does appear, furthermore, that the accepted dimensions (Lawrence and Lorsch, 1967) along which functions in organizations are expected to differ – goals, interpersonal relationships, structure and time horizons – are made consistent for all members of a superteam regardless of their prior functional orientation.

Superteams can be viewed as one form of collateral organization (Zand, 1974), and as such authority must exist to create and disband the team, thus requiring the existence of a hierarchy.

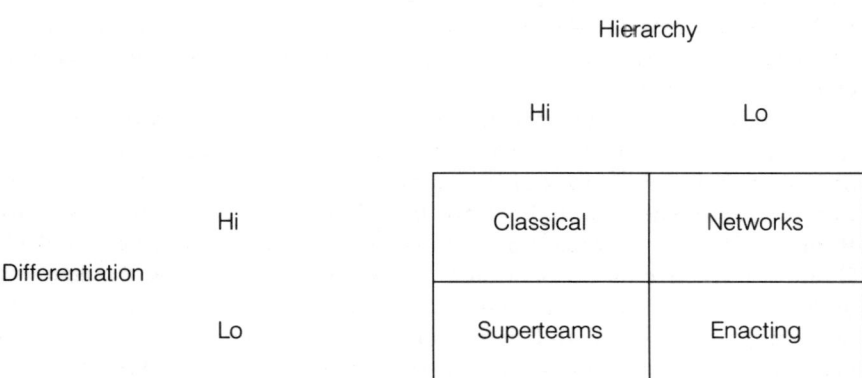

Figure 13.1   Characteristics of emerging organizations

What one observes then are trends in some organizations to create a 'network' of relationships that disregard formal hierarchical structures and in others to form 'superteams', that discount the classical notions of differentiation. If both trends were combined one could hypothesize an 'emerging' organization form in which both hierarchy and differentiation are minimized. These trends and their possible extension are captured in a matrix of possibilities in figure 13.1. The emerging form is labelled 'enacting' in figure 13.1, and its likely characteristics are described below.

The 'Emerging' Organization

The emerging organizational form, labelled as the enacting organization in figure 13.1, is inherently paradoxical in that it lacks the defining, structural elements of hierarchy and differentiation and yet is intended to resist and overcome the pressures and challenges of a turbulent environment. Of obvious relevance to understanding this form of organization are the self-designing tenets of Hedberg, Nystrom and Starbuck (1976) and the interpretive system model of Daft and Weick (1984).

Daft and Weick's (1984) description of the enacting mode of interpretive behaviour is singularly appropriate to the emerging form of organization in that it is a response to an 'unanalysable' environment by an 'active' organization. One related proposition of Daft and Weick (1984) is, however, questionable in that an organization in such a mode cannot be limited to an incremental approach to strategy formulation. Quantum changes in strategy, it can be argued, are needed to address discontinuous changes in the environment. With this single qualification the term 'enacting' as described by Daft and Weick (1984) and Smircich and Stubbart (1985) appears to be particularly relevant to the emerging form of organization and hence is employed as a label.

The term 'enacting' suggests that these emerging organizations are active in character, and that they construct their own environments as a result of acting on their perceptions of the environment. In such a context, the notion of 'creative destruction' defined by Schumpeter (1950) and applied by Barney (1986) to the theory of strategy takes on fresh meaning. Chaffee's (1985) interpretive model of strategy is clearly of relevance to the enacting organization, as the alternative linear and adaptive models require a degree of stability, objectivity and definition of the environment that does not necessarily exist in the context that gives rise to and is addressed by the enacting organization.

Evidence of the existence of 'enacting' organizations is somewhat sparse. Semler (1989) claims to have fashioned such an organization, though in a somewhat unique context in terms of ownership, size and culture. However, critiques of the conventional, classic view of organizations such as those by Schein (1989) and Kanter (1989) do strongly support the possibility and argue for the desirability of this emergent form of organization. Mills' (1991) description of 'cluster organizations', in fact, offers an intriguing approach to organizational design that de-emphasizes both hierarchy and differentiation. Both academics and practitioners appear to be recognizing and responding to the need to develop new forms of organization that would fall into the 'enacting' mode.

The Management Challenge

In the light of the observed and projected trends in organizational forms, it appears logical to define the challenge faced by the management of future organizations as the development of administrative systems appropriate to contexts where hierarchy or differentiation or both are to be minimized. Conventional approaches to the design of administrative systems are based on classic notions of hierarchy and differentiation and are likely to be inappropriate or dysfunctional in these emerging contexts.

The administrative system employed by general managers in organizations can be defined in a variety of ways. The 7-S model popularized by a major consulting firm has been effectively employed in a variety of contexts (e.g., Pascale and Athos, 1981) to identify the range of management practices in organizations. Similar perspectives have been employed by scholars in other countries and cultures such as Germany (Coenenberg and Baum, 1987) and Japan (Kono, 1984).

A more parsimonious view (Camillus, 1986) suggests that competitive strategy, organizational structure, planning and control systems, and management style are the necessary and sufficient elements of administrative systems that must be managed to promote organizational effectiveness. Crafting the competitive corporation therefore requires that the characteristics of these four elements of the administrative systems relate and respond to organizational contexts represented by the three cells of the matrix in figure 13.1 that differ from the classic form.

In exploring the design possibilities and imperatives in these three contexts one can derive some guidance from an appreciation of why low hierarchy and high differentiation may be appropriate in one organization while the reverse – high hierarchy and low differentiation – may be better suited to another organization.

Networks versus Superteams

It can be argued that networks are relevant to organizations that are equipped to or need to cope with four of the five forces identified earlier. These four forces are information technology, 'knowledge-based' competence, globalization and professionalization of management.

Information technology, in particular technology related to communication, can greatly aid the functioning of a network. Networks are needed to share and integrate knowledge which is a characteristic of particular relevance to knowledge-based industries or businesses. Globalization, with the concomitant need to understand and exploit differences and potential (both markets and technology) worldwide, can be seen as demanding the creation of a network. Finally, the different expertise possessed by functionally-oriented or discipline-oriented professional management may argue for a network to provide needed integration and appropriate application of available expertise. It appears logical to argue, therefore, that networks are highly relevant to, and a natural development in, organizations needing to and able to cope with these four forces.

Why then do we encounter the development of superteams in other organizations? It is contended that networks are not particularly suited to respond effectively to the first of the five forces – rapid and discontinuous change. Networks, by their very nature, are oriented toward making incremental changes. They derive a certain stability from being anchored in the knowledge or expertise of the managers who constitute them. Members of the network can, of course, effect significant, quantum changes in their areas of responsibility, but to bring about such changes in the entire organization a sequential rather than simultaneous set of changes is likely to be the path taken.

Superteams on the other hand are consciously separated from traditional organizational moorings. There can and is likely to be a quantum change character to their assignments. Their discrete tasks do not require maintenance of a comprehensive network of relationships with the rest of the organization. Superteams are particularly well suited to effect changes that are significant or quantum developments.

The nature of network-oriented organizations can, if the earlier argument holds, be described as essentially *incremental* in character. In contrast, superteams are suited to tasks that create quantum changes in organizations, that can perhaps be meaningfully described as *inspirational* in character.

It follows that the intriguing if not daunting task of the enacting organization is to combine the incremental and inspirational metaphors in the way it functions. To help visualize the appropriate form of administrative systems for enacting organizations the network and superteam contexts may provide direction, focus and insights. The organizational structure element of administrative systems in the three non-classic forms is implicit in the way they have been defined. Consequently, in looking at the administrative system, it is meaningful initially to address just the three elements of strategy, systems and style.

Strategy and the Emerging Organizational Forms

The most commanding concept in the area of strategy, under which are nested a series of subsidiary concepts, is the organization's mission. The conventional wisdom regarding the nature and focus of the organization's mission, as seen by Abell (1980) and Pearce (1982), is defined by the triad of products, markets and technology (PMT). (For the sake of simplicity this discussion addresses only business strategy as distinct from corporate strategy.) Such a PMT-based mission is of relevance to a superteam context as demonstrated by examples such as IBM's development of the personal computer and Canon's development of the personal copier.

In network contexts, with knowledge sharing being their *raison d'etre*, with their intrinsic diversity of perspectives, with their expected awareness of the organization's core competences, a less constraining construct than a PMT-based mission may be needed to unite the members of that network. Hamel and Prahalad's (1989) description of 'strategic intent' is well-suited to a strategic approach that seeks to employ an organization's core competences without being constrained by transitory and limiting PMT definitions.

In the enacting context, a PMT-based mission's characteristics (Camillus, 1980) appear to be inappropriate. Products change, markets evolve and technology is dynamic. The lack of a hierarchy in enacting organizations suggests that they may find it difficult to keep abreast of rapid developments. The lack of emphasis on differentiation in these organizations also suggests that core competences based on leading-edge knowledge, necessary to forge and give meaning to strategic intent, may not always be present.

When a particular strategic task-orientation or distinctive resource/ knowledge-based competence cannot serve to define an organization's *raison d'etre*, an alternative that merits consideration is that of a 'vision' (Smith, 1989; Westley and Mintzberg, 1989). Chaffee's (1985) interpretive model of strategy demands the existence of such a metaphor or vision. The intensely personal, almost religious and dream-like, character of a vision can be a uniquely powerful, bonding force when it is shared. Visions are influenced by one's beliefs and values which suggests the basis for determining who should belong to a particular emerging organization.

While the mission defines the *raison d'etre* or self-image of the organization, its strategic objectives give it direction. The very nature of the superteam makes the classic notion of 'shocking objectives' (employed by organizations such as Texas Instruments and ITT) particularly relevant. Superteams make possible accomplishments that the organization would otherwise be incapable of, suggesting therefore that shocking objectives can be seen as both a reason for and a result of the existence of superteams.

Networks, given the earlier assertion that they are not oriented toward quantum or inspirational strategies, and given their professional competence orientation would not be readily responsive to shocking objectives. The objective of excellence, primacy or supremacy in the exercise of their perceived competence would fit well with the character and capabilities of networks.

In enacting organizations, the relevance of shocking objectives as well as individually-generated aspirations toward excellence suggests strategic objectives, the character of which can perhaps best be described as heroic. Heroes accomplish ends that are dramatically beyond the accepted norm. Heroes act spontaneously, of their own volition – not because the context forces them to behave in a particular fashion. Heroes demonstrate personal courage, both moral and physical. The shared vision and values of individuals belonging to enacting organizations both facilitate and require strategic objectives that are heroic in character.

Sustainable competitive advantage is at the root of enduring organizational viability and success. The superteam's task orientation seeks such strategic advantage through effectiveness and swiftness of strategy implementation. Networks' access to knowledge and command of the techniques of sharing knowledge are their competitive edge, which finds even more sophisticated expression in the form of strategic alliances (Kanter, 1989). The enacting organization, not necessarily possessing the advantages intrinsic to superteams and networks, being faced with major uncertainties and novel contexts, has to *learn* (DeGeus, 1988; Levitt, 1991; Mintzberg, 1987; Senge, 1990; Toffler, 1990) how to deal with these better and more quickly than its competitors.

The discussion regarding the strategy component of administrative systems as they relate to the non-classic forms of organization is summarized in figure 13.2.

Style and the Emerging Organizational Forms

Figure 13.2 reflects the essence of how the management style in the non-classic organizational contexts reflects the character and imperatives of these contexts. The terminology employed is not uncommon and the logic of the arguments follows the premises articulated in the preceding discussions, so figure 13.2 is presumed to be largely self-explanatory. Three cells, however, reflect ideas that are not necessarily widely shared or commonly understood and are therefore briefly elaborated on below.

The leadership dimension in the superteam context is described as 'inspirational'. The connotations of this term are twofold. First, there is a top-down character to the leadership style. Second, the leader's mental model (Senge, 1990) of the organization and its interaction with its environment is communicated to and accepted by the superteam, and ultimately the rest of the organization.

The empowered form of leadership in the emerging context draws its legitimacy and its power from the members of the organization. This is the reverse of the flow of power in traditional notions of empowerment (Conger and Kanungo, 1988). Effective leaders in these emerging contexts are essentially those who at a particular time represent a confluence of understanding regarding environmental needs and organizational capabilities (Thompson, 1967). In fact one might argue that they are exceptionally capable 'followers' (Kelley, 1988; Smith, 1989).

The 'high-involvement' mode of decision-making is described by Lawler (1988) as one in which lower level employees in organizations are intimately involved in the total organization and its strategy formation, not just in their subset of the organization. A further dimension of high-involvement relevant to the emerging context is that organizational leaders are intimately familiar with the operations of the organization. The concept of high-involvement decision making that is captured in figure 13.2 therefore suggests that individuals in enacting organizations all have simultaneous influence on and understanding of both the strategic and operating domains.

Admin. System Elements \ Organizational context		Superteam	Network	Enacting
STRATEGY	Mission	PMT definition	Strategic intent	Vision
	Objectives	'Shocking'	Primacy/ excellence	Heroic
	Strategic advantage	Implementation/ swiftness	Knowledge util./ alliance	Learning ability
STYLE	Leadership	Inspirational	Expertise-based	Empowered
	Decision making	Top-Down	Consensus	High involvement
	Organizational character	Goal orientation	Professional competence	Shared values
SYSTEMS	Rewards	Performance based	Collaboration oriented	Intrinsic
	Control orientation	Feedforward	Adaptive	Social, feed forward & feedback
	Planning orientation	Synoptic	Incremental	Opportunistic

Figure 13.2   Administrative systems characteristics

Systems and the Emerging Organizational Forms

Figure 13.2 is again substantially self-explanatory with regard to the characteristics of planning and control systems in non-classic contexts. A few brief observations may, however, provide better understanding of what are logical extensions derived from the 'strategy' and 'style' characteristics in these non-classic contexts.

The 'intrinsic' rewards in the enacting organization come from the satisfaction and joy of doing what one desires to do. The test-pilot needs little motivation other than the opportunity to fly the best and most modern aircraft. The missionary needs no reward beyond the opportunity to preach the gospel as he or she sees it. The high-involvement members of an enacting organization are there to actualize their values and realize their aspirations in concert with others who share a common vision.

The feedforward, orientation in the control system is both necessary and feasible in the superteam context. Superteams, when engaging in tasks that have not been accomplished before, have little feedback information on which to base their control. The shared mental models, stemming from the inspirational leadership discussed earlier, provide the cause-effect assumptions necessary (Veliyath, *et al.*, 1986) for the team members to engage in feedforward control.

The incremental, resource-driven, implicitly trial and error approach in the network context is well-matched to the characteristics of adaptive control (Camillus 1980), where an ex post assessment of whether resources were optimally employed during the period under review replaces conventional reviews focusing on actual performance versus an ex ante performance expectation.

In the enacting context, with its emphasis on learning, feedback as a means of learning takes on importance. Feedforward too retains its importance in light of the uncertain, unfamiliar futures that are anticipated. Social controls or clan-type (Ouchi, 1980) controls stemming from shared values and beliefs are also compatible with the enacting context.

With regard to the planning dimension, a synoptic orientation is feasible in the superteam context because of the power and role of senior management. The incremental and opportunistic orientations are consistent with and reinforce the character of the network and enacting contexts respectively, as typified by the preceding style and strategy dimensions. While the incremental approaches to strategy formulation have been extensively researched in the literature (Lindblom, 1959; Quinn, 1980), opportunistic approaches to strategy formulation have not received the same attention. The literature on strategic issue management (Ansoff, 1980; Dutton and Otternsmeyer, 1987; Camillus and Datta, 1991) provides a perspective pertinent to the opportunistic approach suggested in the enacting context. Characteristics of such opportunistic approaches that are suggested by the issue management literature are a continuous (year-round process, a framework (of beliefs and values) that helps identify weak signals, and a task force (superteam) approach to significant issues.

Transforming the Classic Organization

Movement from the classic organizational form towards the superteam and network forms of organization can perhaps be managed effectively by understanding the character and relative significance of the five forces impacting on a particular organization. If the dominant concern is a future marked by changes of a largely unpredictable character and of a substantial magnitude, then the superteam approach suggests itself. Alternatively, if the four other forces are seen to be more pertinent, movement towards the network form can be initiated and supported by investments in highly professional human resources, communications-oriented information technology and recognition that knowledge is the key strategic resource of the organization.

Moving from network and superteam forms to the enacting form suggests the need to add the characteristics of superteams to networks and vice versa. However, the orientations towards hierarchy and differentiation of those two forms are intrinsically incompatible. Consequently, evolutionary changes that reduce the differences and build on the similarities appear to be the logical course to take. The enacting form is essentially self-designing in character and such a capability has to grow in an organic fashion and cannot be added in a mechanistic mode.

Daft and Weick (1984), with their model of organizations as interpretation systems, highlight an approach to unlocking the door to the enacting form if this form is thought to be appropriate or needed for the organization to survive. The network or superteam organization has to engage aggressively in the enacting mode of interpreting itself and the environment. As consciousness builds and learning takes place, coalitions may emerge that identify individuals with shared values and a shared vision, creating the necessary conditions for the enacting form to develop.

Tentative Research Directions

Figure 13.2 provides a framework for identifying the enormous range and potential for research that may help us understand and manage these non-classic forms of organization.

The matrix in figure 13.2 suggests scope for researching, at a descriptive level, the design of elements of the administrative system in non-classic organizations. Studying the fit between these elements, between these elements and environmental characteristics, and between these elements and the anticipated future of the organization may provide significant insights. The existence, and possibly the influence, of shared mental models and values in different contexts is a promising and relatively untapped area for study. Longitudinal studies that explore the transformation of one type of organization to another could provide valuable insights and options for management. The existence of different forms of non-classic organization as subunits within a larger, complex organization, if identified and studied, can prove to be a particularly rich source of understanding.

An intriguing source of understanding that is not suggested in figure 13.2 is the body of research regarding disaster management. Thompson (1967) describes 'synthetic' organizations that emerge in a disaster context. Leaders, in those crucial moments, are those in whom are combined an understanding of what is demanded by the situation and an awareness of what the available resources are.

These disaster situations (Comfort, 1988) appear to embody several of the characteristics of emerging organizations and their contexts – unexpected and dramatic circumstances, transitory leaders who are empowered by others with a similar vision, extraordinary time pressures, high costs of failure and learning while doing. They may, therefore, offer us a glimpse of what the future promises, threatens and demands of organizations and their management.

References

Abell, D. 1980: *Defining the Business*, Prentice-Hall: Englewood Cliffs, NJ.

Ansoff, H. Igor 1975: Managing Strategic Surprise by Response to Weak Signals. *California Management Review*, Winter.

Ansoff, H. I. 1980: Strategic Issues Management. *Strategic Management Journal*, April–June.

Armstrong, W. and Camillus, J. 1989: Strategic Vision and the Real World. *Proceedings of the International Conference of the Planning Forum*.

Barabba, V. P. and Zaltman, G. 1991: *Hearing the Voice of the Market: Competitive Advantage through Creative Use of Market Information*. Harvard Business School Press, Boston.

Barney, J. B. 1986: Types of Competition and the Theory of Strategy: Toward an Integrative Framework. *Academy of Management Review*, October.

Burns, T. and Stalker, G. M. 1961: *The Management of Innovation*. Tavistock Publications: London.

Camillus, J. 1980: Six Approaches to Preventive Management Control. *Financial Executive*, December.

Camillus, J. 1982: Reconciling Logical Incrementalism and Synoptic Formalism. *Strategic Management Journal*, July–September.

Camillus, J. 1986: *Strategic Planning and Management Control*. Lexington Books: Lexington, MA.

Camillus, J. 1988: Strategic Vision and Organizational Performance: Capturing the Dimensions of Strategic Choice. Working Paper No. 684, Katz Graduate School of Business, Pittsburgh, PA.

Camillus, J. and Lederer, A. 1985: Corporate Strategy and the Design of Computerized Information Systems. *Sloan Management Review*, Spring.

Camillus, J. and Datta, D. 1991: Managing Strategic Issues in a Turbulent Environment. *Long Range Planning*, April.

Chaffee, E. E. 1985: Three Models of Strategy. *Academy of Management Review*, January.

Chakravarthy, B. S. 1982: Adaptation: A Promising Metaphor for Strategic Management. *Academy of Management Review*, January.

Chakravarthy, B. S. and Lorange, P. 1991: *Managing the Strategy Process: A Framework for a Multibusiness Firm*, Prentice-Hall: Englewood Cliffs, NJ.

Coenenberg, A. and Baum, H. 1987: *Strategisches Controlling*. Schaffer GMB & Co., Stuttgart.

Comfort, L. K., (ed.) 1988: *Managing Disaster: Strategies and Policy Perspectives*. Duke University Press, Durham, NC.

Conger, J. A. and Kanungo, R. N. 1988: The Empowerment Process: Integrating Theory and Practice. *Academy of Management Review*, July.

Daft, R. L. and Weick, K. E. 1984: Toward a Model of Organizations as Interpretation Systems, *Academy of Management Review*, April.

DeGeus, A. P. 1988: Planning as Learning. *Harvard Business Review* March–April.

Dumaine, B. 1990: Who Needs a Boss? *Fortune*, May 7.

Dutton, J. and Otternsmeyer, E. 1987: Strategic Issue Management Systems. Forms, Functions and Contexts. *Academy of Management Review*, April.

Galbraith, J. R. 1977: *Organization Design*, Addision-Wesley: Reading, MA.

Hamel, G. and Prahalad, C. 1989: Strategic Intent. *Harvard Business Review*, May–June.

Hedberg, B., Nystrom, P. and Starbuck, W. 1976: Camping on Seesaws. *Administrative Science Quarterly*, March.

Kanter, R. 1989: The New Managerial Work. *Harvard Business Review*, November–December.

Kanter, R. *When Giants Learn to Dance*, Simon and Schuster: New York.

Kelley, R. E. 1988: In Praise of Followers. *Harvard Business Review*, November–December.

Kono, T. 1984: *Strategy and Structure of Japanese Enterprises*, Macmillan, London.

Lawler, E. 1988: Choosing an Involvement Strategy. *Academy of Management Executive*, August.

Lawrence, P. R. and Lorsch, J. W. 1967: *Organization and Environment*. Division of Research. Boston: Graduate School of Business Administration.

Levitt, T. 1991: *Thinking About Management*, Free Press: New York.

Lindblom, C. E. 1959: The Science of 'Muddling Through'. *Public Administration Review*, Spring, pp. 79–88.

Lorange, P. 1992: *Implementation of Strategic Planning*, Prentice-Hall: Englewood Cliffs, NJ.

Mills, D. Q. 1991: *Rebirth of the Corporation*. John Wiley: New York, NY.

Mintzberg, H. 1979: *The Structuring of Organizations: A Synthesis of the Research*. Prentice-Hall: Englewood Cliffs, NJ.

Mintzberg, H. 1987: Crafting Strategy. *Harvard Business Review*, July–August.

Naisbitt, J. and Aburdene, P. 1985: *Re-inventing the Corporation*, Warner Books: New York.

Ouchi, W. G. 1980: Markets, Bureaucracies and Clans. *Administrative Science Quarterly*, Vol. 25, March, pp. 129–141.

Pascale, R. and Athos, A. 1981: *The Art of Japanese Management: Applications for American Executives*. Simon and Schuster: New York.

Pearce, J. 1982: The Company Mission as a Strategic Goal. *Sloan Management Review*, Spring.

Porter, L. and McKibben, L. 1988: *Management Education and Development*, McGraw-Hill: New York.

Quinn, J. B. 1980: *Strategies for Change: Logical Incrementalism*. Irwin: Homewood, IL.

Schein, E. 1989: Reassessing the 'Divine Rights' of Managers. *Sloan Management Review*, Winter.

Schrage, M. 1990: The Collaborative Organization. *New York Times*, November 11.

Schumpeter, J. A. 1950: *Capitalism, Socialism and Democracy*, (3rd ed.), Harper, New York.

Semler, R. 1989: Managing Without Managers. *Harvard Business Review*, September–October.

Senge, P. M. 1990: *The Fifth Discipline: The Art and Practice of the Learning Organization*. Doubleday: New York.

Smircich, L. and Stubbart, C. 1985: Strategic Management in an Enacted World. *Academy of Management Review*, October.

Smith, B. 1989: Vison: A Time to Take Stock. *Business Quarterly*, Vol. 54, No. 2, Autumn.

Stalk, G., and Hout, T. 1990: *Competing Against Time*, Free Press: New York.

Thompson, J. D. 1967: *Organizations in Action*. McGraw-Hill: New York.

Toffler, A. 1970: *Future Shock*. Random House: New York.

Toffler, A. 1980: *The Third Wave*. Morrow: New York.

Toffler, A. 1990: *Powershift: Knowledge, Wealth and Violence at the Edge of the 21st Century*, Bantam: New York.

Tucker, R. B. 1991 *Managing the Future: 10 Driving Forces of Change for the '90s* Putnam's Sons: New York.

Veliyath, R., Camillus, J. and Prescott, J. 1986: Feedback and Feedforward in Strategic Management. *Proceedings of the 17th Annual Meeting of the Midwest Decision Sciences Institute*.

Westley, F. and Mintzberg, H. 1989: Visionary Leadership and Strategic Management. *Strategic Management Journal*, Summer, Special Issue.

Zand, D. 1974: Collateral Organization: A New Change Strategy. *Journal of Applied Behavioral Science*, January–March.

14

Coalignment Between Knowledge Flow Patterns and Strategic Systems and Processes within MNCs[1]

Anil K. Gupta and V. Govindarajan

Despite the increasing globalization of most industries, research on multinational corporations (MNCs) has focused far more on the question of why a domestic company becomes a multinational (Caves, 1982; Hymer, 1976) than on the systems and processes that MNCs use to co-ordinate and control their widely disparate and dispersed subsidiaries. As Porter (1986: 17) observed: 'We know more about the problems of becoming a multinational than about strategies for managing an established multinational.'

Our knowledge of how MNCs manage their subsidiaries is constrained also by the fact that, with limited exceptions (Ghoshal and Nohria, 1989; Egelhoff, 1982), research in this area has focused only on broad differences across entire MNCs (e.g., Franko, 1976; Fouraker and Stopford, 1968; Prahalad and Doz, 1981) and not on variations across subsidiaries performing different strategic roles within the same MNC. Thus, while past research provides some clues regarding how the global structure of IBM might differ from that of Fujitsu, it sheds little light on how, *within* an IBM or a Fujitsu, corporate control over one subsidiary might differ from that over another. Conceptualizing subsidiary strategic roles in terms of different patterns of knowledge transactions between a focal subsidiary and the rest of the corporation, this paper hypothesizes and tests for systematic coalignments between a subsidiary's knowledge-flow based strategic role and the systems and processes linking the subsidiary to the rest of the corporation. Data were obtained directly from the presidents of 359 foreign subsidiaries of a cross-section of major US, Japanese, and European corporations. Key measures were also cross-validated with data from the corporate superiors of eighty of these subsidiary presidents.

The MNC as a Network of Transactions

Building on Caves (1982) and Teece (1976), we have suggested elsewhere (Gupta and Govindarajan, 1991) that the multinational corporation can be viewed as a network of three types of inter-subsidiary transactions: (1) capital flows e.g., investments into or dividend repatriations from various subsidiaries; (2) product flows e.g., intracorporate exports to or imports from various subsidiaries; and (3) knowledge flows e.g., technology and/or skill transfer to and from various subsidiaries. We believe that there are many analytical benefits that accrue from such a multi-dimensional network perspective. *One*, since the existing network of capital, product, and knowledge flows within any MNC can be viewed as a concrete manifestation of its 'emergent' global strategy (Mintzberg, 1978), the network perspective allows for a parsimonious way to map accurately and comprehensively the emergent global strategies of different MNCs. *Two*, the multi-dimensional network perspective permits us to adopt a layered approach to the study of MNCs i.e., it allows us to study the antecedents and consequences of across-MNC variations only in capital flow patterns, only in product flow patterns, or only in knowledge flow patterns. Of course, while it would eventually be essential to examine the implications of interactions between all three types of flows, a layered approach may serve as a necessary platform for the conduct of more complex analyses. *Three*, the network perspective also provides us with an obvious and logical way to study the question of internal differentiation in subsidiary strategic roles and co-ordination and control mechanisms within the MNC. All that is required is to allow for the possibility that the magnitude and directionality of capital, product, and knowledge flows may vary across the various nodes (i.e., subsidiaries) of the network (i.e., the MNC).

Given the almost complete absence of prior research on inter-nodal differences within the MNC network in this empirical paper, we have deliberately chosen to pursue a more focused and in-depth examination of such differences along only one – albeit perhaps the most important – of the three types of flows viz., knowledge flows. As is widely accepted in the economics literature, the multinational enterprise – as distinct from international trade among independently owned businesses located in different countries – comes into being predominantly because of a desire to internalize knowledge transfers (Caves, 1982; Hymer, 1976; Teece, 1976). The economic argument is that, in general, knowledge can be transferred more effectively and efficiently through internal organizational rather than external market mechanisms; this is due to the fact that external transactions in knowledge are susceptible to several market imperfections including recognition problems, disclosure problems, and negative externalities.

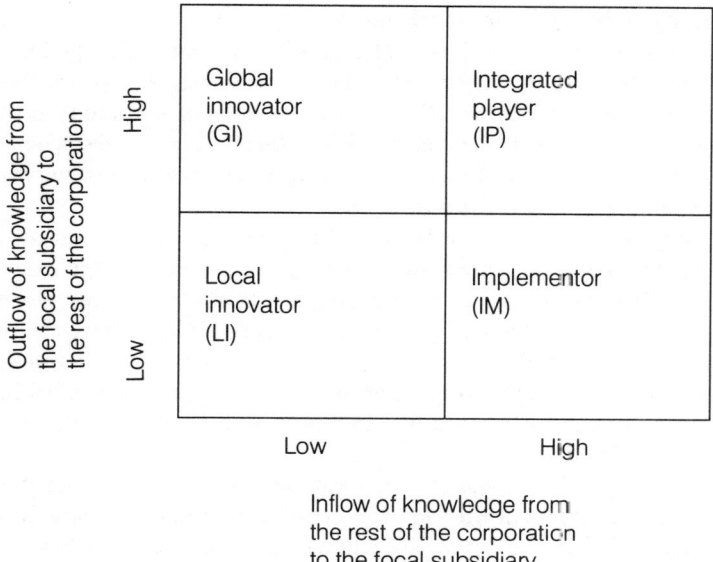

Figure 14.1   Variations in subsidiary strategic contexts: a knowledge-flows based framework

Knowledge Flow Patterns and Subsidiary Strategic Roles

Focusing on variations in knowledge flow patterns, Gupta and Govindarajan (1991) have further proposed that all MNC subsidiaries could be located somewhere along the following two dimensional space: (1) the extent to which a subsidiary engages in knowledge *in*flows from the rest of the corporation; and (2) the extent to which the subsidiary engages in knowledge *out*flows to the rest of the corporation. Thus, in terms of knowledge flow patterns, four generic subsidiary roles can be identified (see figure 14.1): *global innovator* (high outflow, low inflow); *integrated player* (high outflow, high inflow); *implementor* (low outflow, high inflow); and *local innovator* (low outflow, low inflow).

In a *global innovator* (GI) role, the subsidiary serves as the fountainhead of knowledge for other units. This role has traditionally been played only by the domestic units of export-oriented MNCs. However, as technological gaps among countries have declined, some foreign subsidiaries have begun turning into major knowledge creators for the entire corporation (Harrigan, 1984) – e.g., as Bartlett and Ghoshal (1989) have documented, L.M. Ericsson's Italian subsidiary serves as the company's global centre for the development of transmission systems whereas the Finnish subsidiary has the leading global role for mobile telephones.

The *integrated player* (IP) role also implies a responsibility for creating knowledge that can be utilized by other subsidiaries. However, the IP and the GI roles differ in that an IP subsidiary is not self-sufficient in the fulfilment of its own knowledge needs. IBM's Japanese subsidiary, responsible for high levels of both knowledge inflow and knowledge outflow, represents a good example of a unit with an IP role.

The *Implementor* (IM) role is one where the subsidiary engages in little knowledge creation of its own and relies heavily on knowledge inflows from sister subsidiaries. This role is the theoretical obverse of the global innovator role in that, in the early histories of most MNCs where the domestic unit served as the global innovator, the role of foreign units automatically became that of serving as implementors. 3M Corporation's subsidiary in a small country such as Finland would represent a good example of a foreign unit with an IM role.

Finally, the *local innovator* (LI) role implies that the subsidiary has almost complete local responsibility for the creation of relevant know-how in all key functional areas; however, this knowledge is seen as too idiosyncratic to be of much competitive use in other countries. Traditional 'multidomestic' MNCs have consisted almost entirely of subsidiaries with local innovator roles. However, LI subsidiaries can exist also in transnational or simple global MNCs; for instance, a case study on Kentucky Fried Chicken indicates that, within the company's Japanese subsidiary, the architecture and size of each outlet, the menu, as well as the advertising theme are radically different from those in other countries, most of which replicate the US format (Bartlett, 1986).

The rest of this paper advances and provides empirical tests of theoretical propositions linking these four strategic roles to six key co-ordination and control systems and processes. In order to map adequately the richness and complexity of the task facing managers in MNCs, we focus on not just formal administrative systems (e.g., the use of formal committees and the incentive compensation system) but also other informal or quasi-formal organizational processes (e.g., the intensity of communication and the corporate socialization of managers) that shape the decisions and actions of subsidiaries.

Hypotheses

Our hypotheses linking subsidiary strategic roles to intra-corporate control mechanisms are based on the following core arguments: (1) Different subsidiary strategic roles imply systematic differences in the task environments facing subsidiary managers. (2) Different task environments require different behaviours on the part of subsidiary managers. (3) Different control mechanisms induce and support different kinds of managerial behaviours. (4) Therefore, assuming norms of administrative rationality (Thompson, 1967), we can expect systematic associations between subsidiary strategic contexts and the emergence of specific corporate control mechanisms. In particular, in this study, we focus on differences in corporate control mechanisms associated with differences in (1) the extent of lateral interdependence between focal and peer subsidiaries and (2) the need for autonomous initiative on the part of the executives managing the subsidiaries.

Strategic roles and lateral interdependence

As Gupta and Govindarajan (1991) have suggested, on definitional grounds, the extent of lateral interdependence between focal and peer subsidiaries can be expected to a positive function of the extent of both knowledge inflow and knowledge outflow. In other words, the extent of lateral interdependence with peer subsidiaries can be expected to be highest for integrated players (high outflow – high inflow), intermediate for global innovators (high outflow – low inflow) and implementors (low outflow – high inflow), and lowest for local innovators (low outflow – low inflow).

Though not in the context of managing foreign subsidiaries, strategy and organizational research has focused on the management of interdependence at a more general level. Based on an extensive review of this literature, the following emerge as the sum of the key administrative systems and processes that can be used to effectively manage interdependence among peer subsidiaries within an MNC: (1) formal integrative mechanisms (Galbraith, 1973; Nadler and Tushman, 1987); (2) communication linkages (Allen and Cohen, 1969; Tushman, 1979); and (3) intra-corporate socialization of subsidiary managers (Van Maanen and Schein, 1979; Edstrom and Galbraith, 1977). Based on direct one-to-one linkages between these organizational variables and the management of lateral interdependence, the following are some of the specific hypotheses advanced by Gupta and Govindarajan (1991); these hypotheses will be tested empirically in the present study (see figure 14.2 for a pictorial representation):

Hypothesis 1:

The use of lateral inter-subsidiary integrative mechanisms will vary across subsidiary-strategic contexts; on average, the complexity of such mechanisms will be high for integrated players, medium for global innovators and implementors, and low for local innovators.

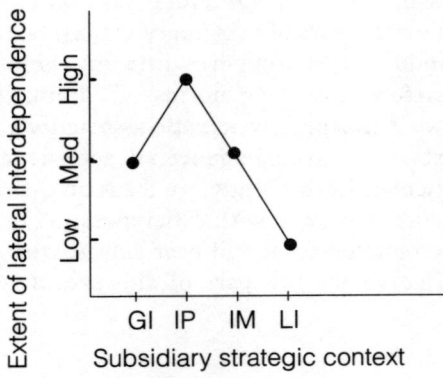

Hypothesized control mechanisms that need
to be aligned to different levels of
'lateral interdependence':

- Formal integrative mechanisms
- Intensity of communication
- Corporate socialization of managers

Figure 14.2   Subsidiary strategic context and lateral interdependence

Hypothesis 2:

The intensity of communication between a focal subsidiary and the rest of the corporation will vary across subsidiary-strategic contexts; on average, it will be high for integrated players, medium for global innovators and implementors, and low for local innovators.

Hypothesis 3:

The global corporate socialization of a subsidiary's top managers will vary across subsidiary-strategic contexts; on average, it will be high for integrated players, medium for global innovators and implementors and low for local innovators.

Strategic roles and need for autonomous initiative

The greater the magnitude and scope of knowledge creation expected from a subsidiary, the greater should be the need for the exercise of autonomous initiative by the subsidiary. Thus, on definitional grounds, expected differences in the need for autonomous initiative can be premised as follows: The need for autonomous initiative will be highest for global innovators, intermediate for integrated players and local innovators, and lowest for implementors.

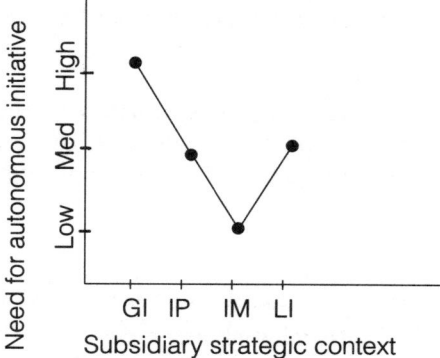

Hypothesized control mechanisms that need
to be aligned to different levels of
'need for autonomous initiative':

- Subsidiary manager's locus of control
- Corporate-subsidiary decentralization
- Size of bonus relative to salary

Figure 14.3   Subsidiary strategic context and need for autonomous initiative

Gupta and Govindarajan (1991) have further argued that, from a corporate control perspective, relevant systems and processes would be those which allow for a differentiation in the extent to which subsidiary managers are intrinsically predisposed to taking initiatives, are given the latitude for the exercise of initiative, and are rewarded for doing so. In this context, an examination of the organization theory literature yields the following as the variables of particular interest: (1) the subsidiary head's locus of control (Rotter, 1966) – a determinant of predisposition to taking initiative; (2) corporate-subsidiary decentralization (Ford and Slocum 1977) – a determinant of the available latitude for autonomous action; and (3) size of bonus relative to salary (Galbraith and Nathanson, 1978; Salter, 1973) – a determinant of the potential reward associated with the exercise of initiative. Based on a theory-based one-to-one linkage between these organizational systems and processes and the fostering of autonomous initiative, the following are some of the hypotheses advanced by Gupta and Govindarajan (1991) which will be empirically tested in the present study (see figure 14.3 for a pictorial representation):

Hypothesis 4:

Managers' locus of control will vary across subsidiary-strategic contexts; on average, managers in charge of global innovators will be high internals, those in charge of integrated players and local innovators will be medium internals, and those in charge of implementors will be low internals.

Hypothesis 5:

The degree of corporate-subsidiary decentralization will vary across subsidiary-strategic contexts; on average, it will be high for global innovators, medium for integrated players and local innovators, and low for implementors.

Hypothesis 6:

The size of bonus relative to salary will vary across subsidiary-strategic contexts; on average, it will be high for global innovators, medium for integrated players and local innovators, and low for implementors.

Method

Sample

Data was collected through a pilot-tested questionnaire survey of the heads (variously titled presidents, managing directors, or general managers) of 359 foreign subsidiaries of major multinational firms headquartered in the US (19 MNCs), Japan (45 MNCs), and Europe (15 British and Scandinavian MNCs). The number of subsidiaries from each of these three regional groups of MNCs in the total sample is 105, 111, and 143 respectively. Every MNC in the sample had sales exceeding US $1 billion and the number of employees per subsidiary averaged 959. In overall terms, participation in this study was sought from the presidents of 997 subsidiaries. Thus, the final sample of 359 represents a response rate of 36 per cent. By geographical region, the response rates were 26 per cent for subsidiaries of US headquartered MNCs, 41 per cent for Japanese MNCs, and 46 per cent for European MNCs. The higher response rates in case of Japanese and European MNCs appear to reflect the fact that, in both cases, subsidiary presidents also received supporting letters from either the head of an industry-sponsored research institute or the corporate CEO. Subsidiary presidents within Japanese MNCs received both an English and a Japanese language questionnaire; initial interviews with the European companies indicated that only the English-language questionnaire would suffice.

Measures

A summary of how the six organizational systems and process variables (lateral integrative mechanisms, intensity of communication, corporate socialization, locus of control, decentralization, and size of bonus relative to salary) were measured is contained in the Appendix. In all cases, we used standard well-established research instruments with minor changes in wording to adapt the instrument to the multinational context. Given below are details pertaining to how the key variable – i.e., classification of subsidiaries in terms of strategic roles based on patterns of knowledge inflow and outflow – was measured.

Each subsidiary head was asked to complete a nine-item instrument for *each* of four knowledge-flow contexts: (1) outflow of knowledge and skills from the focal subsidiary to the parent corporation; (2) outflow of knowledge and skills from the focal to peer subsidiaries; (3) inflow of knowledge and skills from the parent corporation to the focal subsidiary; and (4) inflow of knowledge and skills from peer subsidiaries to the focal one. The nine items pertained to the following different types of knowledge and skills that might be exchanged among various units: (1) market data on customers; (2) market data on competitors; (3) product designs; (4) process designs: (5) marketing know-how; (6) distribution know-how; (7) packaging design/technology; (8) purchasing know-how; and (9) management systems and practices. For each of the 36 items, the respondents were asked to indicate on a Likert-type seven-point scale (ranging from 'not at all' to 'a very great deal') the extent of knowledge flow in which the focal subsidiary was engaged.

Responses were first averaged across the nine items for each type of knowledge-flow context. Then, the two types of knowledge *out*flow measures (to the parent and to peer subsidiaries) were combined to yield a composite measure of knowledge *out*flow from the subsidiary. Similarly, the two types of knowledge *in*flow measures (from the parent and from peer subsidiaries) were combined to yield a composite measure of knowledge *in*flow into the subsidiary. Finally, median splits along these two composite measures were used to identify the knowledge-flow based strategic role that a particular subsidiary can be said to be playing within its parent MNC's global network of subsidiaries. Consistent with our theoretical framework, high outflow – low inflow subsidiaries were termed 'global innovators', high outflow – high inflow subsidiaries were termed 'integrated players', low outflow – high inflow subsidiaries were termed 'implementors', and low outflow – low inflow subsidiaries were termed 'local innovators'.

To test for construct validity, the respondents were also asked to indicate, through a separate question, which *one* of the following four statements best described their subsidiary's strategic context over the recent past:

1 *Primarily a provider of knowledge and skills*: Your subsidiary serves as a major provider of knowledge and skills to other units of the parent corporation; however, the extent of knowledge and skills received from other units is relatively low.

2 *Primarily a receiver of knowledge and skills*: Your subsidiary serves as a major recipient of knowledge and skills from other units of the corporation; however, the extent of knowledge and skills provided to other units is relatively low.

3 *Neither a provider nor a receiver of knowledge and skills*: Your subsidiary is neither a major provider nor a major receiver of knowledge and skills to/from other units of the parent corporation.

4 *Both a provider and a receiver of knowledge and skills*: Your subsidiary is a major provider as well as a major receiver of knowledge and skills to/from other units of the parent corporation.

A Chi-square test across the two classification schemes rejected, at $P < 0.0001$, the possibility that the two classification approaches were different. As an additional check for validity, for 80 subsidiaries in the sample, we were also able to get data on subsidiary knowledge-flow patterns from the immediate corporate-level superiors of the responding subsidiary presidents. For each subsidiary, these superiors completed an 18-item measure (9 pertaining to knowledge outflows from and 9 pertaining to knowledge inflows into the subsidiary). For these 80 subsidiaries, the composite knowledge outflow and inflow measures from corporate superiors correlate positively (at $P < 0.05$) with the corresponding outflow and inflow measures provided by the subsidiary presidents themselves.

For the total sample, the final distribution of subsidiaries across the four strategic roles was as follows: 64 global innovators, 114 integrated players, 63 implementors, and 111 local innovators. It should be noted that the median split approach adopted by us to attribute various strategic roles to specific subsidiaries forces us to recognize 50 per cent all subsidiaries as either global innovators or integrated players. We would speculate that, in reality, the proportion of 'true' global innovators and 'true' integrated players is likely to be lower; thus, to the extent that our approach might have treated some 'true' local innovators and/or 'true' implementors as global innovators or integrated players, there is likely to be some 'noise' in the results. Since this would reduce the likelihood of finding significant differences across cells, it should render the tests reported in this paper as somewhat more, rather than less, conservative.

Results

All variables were standardized prior to testing the hypotheses. Table 14.1 gives zero order correlations among the seven organizational variables of interest (note that, as described in the Appendix, intensity of communication was measured separately for corporate-subsidiary communication

Table 14.1   Zero-order correlation coefficients

	1	2	3	4	5	6	7
1 Lateral integration							
2 Corporate-subsidiary communication	0.07						
3 Inter-subsidiary communication	*** 0.24	*** 0.35					
4 Corporate socialization	** 0.13	−0.06	−0.08				
5 Subsidiary president's locus of control	−0.01	*** 0.29	** 0.12	*** −0.28			
6 Corporate-subsidiary decentralization	−0.04	** 0.13	0.00	0.01	* 0.09		
7 Size of bonus relative to salary	−0.07	** −0.13	−0.07	** 0.14	** −0.23	−0.03	

* one-tail $p < 0.05$
** one-tail $p < 0.01$
*** one-tail $p < 0.001$
(N = 359 subsidiaries)

and inter-subsidiary communication). As can be seen, none of the correlations is so high as to suggest redundancy among the selected organizational variables.

Table 14.2 contains the results of ANOVA tests conducted to check for differences in the mean values of the organizational systems and process variables across the four subgroups of subsidiaries, each subgroup pursuing a different strategic role within the MNC context.

As an overall observation, it should be noted that, for six of the seven systems and process variables, there are significant inter-group differences; significant inter-group differences were not found only in the case of corporate-subsidiary decentralization. These results provide strong reinforcement to the emerging notion of MNCs as networks of differentiated subsidiaries (Bartlett and Ghoshal, 1989; Ghoshal and Nohria, 1989); as can be seen, MNC subsidiaries differ not only in terms of their strategic roles within the network but also in terms of how they are organizationally linked with and controlled by this network. The next question is whether

Table 14.2   Differentiation in control mechanisms across strategic roles

	Mean values across different subsidiary strategic roles				F-statistic (differences between means) and significance
	Global innovator (N = 64)	Integrated player (N = 114)	Imple-mentor (N = 63)	Local innovator (N = 111)	
1 Lateral integration	−0.07	0.40	0.00	−0.40	13.36****
2 Corporate-subsidiary communication	0.19	0.29	−0.13	−0.27	7.65****
3 Inter-subsidiary communication	0.06	0.32	−0.03	−0.34	9.05****
4 Corporate socialization	−0.35	0.08	0.27	−0.04	4.60**
5 Subsidiary president's locus of control	0.07	0.19	−0.27	0.00	3.12*
6 Corporate-subsidiary decentralization	0.04	−0.03	−0.10	0.08	0.54
7 Size of bonus relative to salary	−0.21	−0.17	0.13	0.28	4.43**

Note: All variables were standardized (mean = 0, sd = 1) before conducting these tests.

* $p < 0.05$
** $p < 0.01$
*** $p < 0.001$
**** $p < 0.0001$

or not the differences in organizational variables are linked to those in strategic roles in the theoretically-predicted manner.

Hypotheses 1, 2, and 3 (H 1, 2 and 3) predicted that use of formal lateral integrative mechanisms, intensity of communication, and corporate socialization of the subsidiary president would be highest for integrated players, lowest for local innovators and intermediate for the other two strategic roles. The results pertaining to lateral integration and intensity of corporate-subsidiary as well as inter-subsidiary communication correspond fully with the predictions of H1 and H2. However, in terms of the directionality of differences, the results pertaining to corporate socialization are quite different from the predictions in H3. As per H3, integrated players and local innovators do have an intermediate level of corporate socialization. However, implementors have the highest and global innovators the lowest levels of corporate socialization – exactly the opposite of our predictions. One interpretation of these findings would be that the presidents of global innovators are mavericks within the corporate system who push for and adopt such a strategic role for their subsidiaries largely on their own and not because of a close social and/or value integration with corporate executives; in fact, our results suggest that a high degree of corporate socialization is associated with the implementor role i.e., one requiring the least degree of new knowledge creation within the SBU. Thus, just as the heads of global innovators appear to be corporate 'mavericks', the heads of implementors appear to be corporate 'clones'.

Hypotheses 4, 5, and 6 predicted that internal locus of control, decentralization, and size of bonus relative to salary would be highest for global innovators, lowest for implementors, and intermediate for the other two roles. Results pertaining to locus of control are generally consistent with H4, although the hypothesis had predicted an even higher level of internal locus for global innovators than suggested by the results. As indicated earlier, H5 pertaining to decentralization is not supported at all. One interpretation would be that, because global innovators affect the performance of several subsidiaries, corporate executives deem it essential that they get involved in the decisions and actions of such subsidiaries, even though high decentralization, in general, fosters greater initiative-taking on the part of the subsidiary management. If true, this interpretation would also suggest the possible existence of considerable ambivalence on the part of corporate executives over the question of exactly how global innovators might be managed effectively within the global network. The case for this speculated ambivalence is supported also by the results pertaining to H6 i.e., size of bonus relative to salary. Once again, contrary to predictions, global innovators have the least amount of potential bonus relative to basic salary. We interpret this finding as suggesting that corporate executives seem to believe that the global innovator role needs to be shared and performed by a subsidiary jointly with corporate headquarters rather than on the subsidiary's own autonomous initiative. If true, this speculation, combined with our interpretation of the results pertaining to corporate socialization, suggests that there possibly exists a high degree of conflict between the presidents of global innovators and their corporate superiors. Whether this conflict is constructive or destructive would appear to be an important question – but one that is beyond the scope of this paper.

Discussion

In this paper, we conceptualized the MNC as a network of three types of transactions – capital flows, product flows, and knowledge flows – between units located in different countries, and argued that the nodal strategic roles of subsidiaries within the same MNC can differ significantly in terms of the magnitude and directionality of transactions between the subsidiary and the rest of the corporation. Focusing on one, arguably the most important, of the three transaction types, viz., knowledge flows, we developed a four-cell classification matrix (global innovators, integrated players, implementors, and local innovators) for mapping differences in subsidiaries' nodal positions. Building on this classification scheme, we then advanced hypotheses regarding systematic inter-nodal differences in co-ordination and control mechanisms linking focal subsidiaries to the rest of the corporation. Finally, we tested these hypotheses through the analysis of primary data collected from the presidents of 359 foreign subsidiaries of leading US, Japanese, and European MNCs.

The results strongly reinforce the notion of differentiated subsidiary-strategic roles and differentiated control systems *within* MNCs. Using an instrument validated with data from both subsidiary presidents and their immediate corporate-level superiors, we found significant inter-subsidiary differences in knowledge-flow patterns. We also found that, across the four knowledge-flow based strategic roles, there were significant differences in the use of lateral integrative mechanisms, the intensities of corporate-subsidiary as well as inter-subsidiary communication, corporate socialization of the subsidiary president, size of the subsidiary president's bonus relative to salary, and the subsidiary president's locus of control. On the other hand, we found no significant differences in the level of overall decentralization across the four strategic roles.

Specific findings with respect to variations in systems and processes associated with each of the four strategic roles can be summarized as follows:

1 *Local innovator* subsidiaries are involved minimally in formal lateral integration mechanisms with other subsidiaries and have the lowest intensity of communication with peer subsidiaries as well as with the parent corporation. While the locus of control and corporate socialization of LI presidents is about average, the ratio of their variable-to-fixed compensation tends to be very high.

2 *Implementor* subsidiaries are headed by presidents who exhibit the lowest degree of internal locus of control and have had the highest degree of corporate socialization. On other systems and process characteristics, IM subsidiaries tend to be about average.

3 *Integrated player* subsidiaries exhibit the maximum use of formal lateral integration mechanisms and also have the highest intensity of communication with peer subsidiaries as well as the parent corporation. Also, they are headed by presidents who are very high on internal locus of control and, for whom, the ratio of variable-to-fixed compensation is quite low. On other systems and process characteristics, IM subsidiaries are about average.

4 *Global innovator* subsidiaries exhibit moderately high intensity of communication with the parent corporation – but not with sister subsidiaries. In addition, these subsidiaries tend to be headed by presidents who are high on internal locus of control and who have had the lowest degree of corporate socialization. Also, for these executives, the ratio of variable-to-fixed compensation is the lowest.

The findings pertaining to global innovators are particularly interesting. Note that, by definition, these subsidiaries engage in high knowledge outflows to the rest of the corporation while receiving low knowledge inflows. In other words, they are serving as crucial sources of creativity and innovation not just for their own local markets but also for the whole corporation. Yet, in terms of systems and processes, the presidents of these subsidiaries emerge as having had the lowest degree of corporate socialization. Coupled with the fact that these executives also are high on internal locus of control, we are inclined to conclude that, *un*like our hypothesized prediction, the global innovator role is not assigned from corporate headquarters as part of top-down 'induced strategic processes' (Burgelman, 1991); instead, it seems that the global innovator role is carved out by enterprising subsidiary managers as part of bottom-up 'autonomous strategic processes'. In suggesting the presence and criticality of autonomous bottom-up processes within MNCs, this study also reinforces the notion that, if researchers' intent is to understand strategic processes within MNCs, then focusing only on corporate 'induced' (i.e., centrally managed) processes would run the risk of overlooking important and directly relevant phenomena. Further, it would seem that the study of autonomous processes would need to be conducted first at the level of the subsidiary and only secondarily at the level of the parent corporation.

Note

1 Partial funding support for this project was provided by the Center for International Business Education and Research of The University of Maryland at College Park, The Tuck School at Dartmouth College, and The International Management Research Institute, Tokyo. Portions of this paper were presented at and published in the proceedings of the annual national meeting of The Academy of Management, Miami, August 1991.

Appendix

Measurement of Organizational Variables

Lateral integrative mechanisms

Based on Galbraith (1973), Nadler and Tushman (1987), and Miller, Kets de Vries, and Toulouse (1982), this variable was measured through a 3-item Likert-type 7-point scale (ranging from 'used rarely' to 'used very frequently') that asked respondents to indicate the extent to which their subsidiary used liaison personnel, temporary task forces, and permanent teams to co-ordinate decisions and actions with sister subsidiaries. The final measure was a weighted average of responses to the three items where the most complex mechanism (permanent teams) was given a weight of 3, the intermediately complex mechanism (temporary task forces) was given a weight of 2, and the least complex mechanism (liaison personnel) was given a weight of 1.

Intensity of communication

This measure was adapted fron Van de Ven and Ferry (1979). For each of four modes of communication (face-to-face, over the telephone, routine and periodic formal reports, and electronic or paper-based letters or memos), the respondents were asked to indicate the frequency of a communication first between (1) their subsidiary and parent corporation executives, and then between (2) their subsidiary and peer subsidiaries. Respondents were provided with a 7-item scale ranging from '1 = daily' to '7 = less often than once a year'. In each of the two cases, responses were reverse scored and averaged across the four items to yield composite measures of intensity of communication. Chronbach alphas exceeded 0.80 in both cases.

Corporate socialization

This measure was adapted from Bartlett and Ghoshal (1989). Respondents were asked to provide 'yes' or 'no' answers to the following four questions: (1) Have you worked for one or more years at corporate headquarters in this corporation? (2) Have you worked for one or more years in other subsidiaries of this corporation? (3) Have you participated in executive development programs involving participants from several subsidiaries? and (4) Do you have a mentor at corporate headquarters? For each respondent, the number of 'yes' responses was treated as a measure of corporate socialization.

Subsidiary manager's locus of control

This variable was measured through 11 items taken from Rotter's (1966) standard instrument for locus of control. It was scored in such a way that high values on this measure reflect a more 'internal' and low values a more 'external' locus of control.

Corporate-subsidiary decentralization

This variable was measured through a 9-item instrument patterned after Vancil (1980) and Tannenbaum (1968). For each of nine different strategically relevant decisions the respondents were asked to indicate, on a Likert-type 5-point scale, the degree of their authority in making the decision. Responses across the nine items were averaged to yield a composite measure of corporate-subsidiary decentralization (Cronbach alpha = 0.86). High values on this measure indicate higher decentralization.

Size of bonus relative to salary

This variable was measured through a straightforward question to the respondents: 'Many incentive bonus programmes limit the maximum amount of bonus that an individual can receive. If you were to receive the maximum bonus possible, what approximate percentage of your basic salary (excluding bonus) would it be?'

References

Allen, T. J., and Cohen, S. 1969: Information flow in R&D laboratories. *Administrative Science Quarterly*, 14, 12–19.

Bartlett, C. A., and Ghoshal, S. 1989: *Managing across borders: The transnational solution*. Boston, MA: Harvard Business School Press.

Bartlett, C. A. 1986: Kentucky Fried Chicken (Japan) Limited. Case No. 9-387-043. Boston, MA: Harvard Business School Case Services.

Burgelman, R. A. 1991: Intraorganizational ecology of strategy making and organizational adaptation: Theory and field research. *Organization Science*, 2: 239–262.

Caves, R. E. 1982: *Multinational enterprise and economic analysis*. Cambridge, U.K.: Cambridge University Press.

Edstrom, A. and Galbraith, J. R. 1977: Transfer of managers as a coordination and control strategy in multinational organizations. *Administrative Science Quarterly*, 22, 248–263.

Egelhoff, W. G. 1982. Strategy and structure in multinational corporations. *Administrative Science Quarterly*, 27: 433–458.

Ford, J. D., and Slocum, J. W. 1977: Size, technology, environment, and the structure of organizations. *Academy of Management Review*, 2, 561–575.

Fouraker, L. E., and Stopford, J. M. 1968: Organizational structure and multinational strategy. *Administrative Science Quarterly*, 13, 47–64.

Franko, L. G. 1976: *The European multinationals: A renewed challenge to American and British big business*. Stamford, CT: Greylock.

Galbraith, J. R. 1973: *Designing complex organizations*. Reading, MA: Addison-Wesley.

Galbraith, J. R. and Nathanson, D. A. 1978: *Strategy implementation: The role of structure and process*. St. Paul, MN: West.

Ghoshal, S., and Bartlett, C. A. 1988: Creation, adoption, and diffusion of innovation by subsidiaries of multinational corporations. *Journal of International Business Studies*. 19, 365–388.

Ghoshal, S., and Nohria, N. 1989: Internal differentiation within multinational corporations. *Strategic Management Journal*, 10, 323–337.

Gupta, A. K. and Govindarajan, V. 1991: Knowledge flows and the structure of control within multinational corporations. *Academy of Management Review*, in press.

Harrigan, K. R. 1984: Innovation within overseas subsidiaries. *The Journal of Business Strategy*, 4(4): 47–55.

Hymer, S. H. 1976: *The international operations of national firms: A study of direct foreign investment*. Cambridge, MA: The MIT Press.

Miller, D., Kets de Vries, M. F. R., and Toulouse, J. M. 1982: Top executive locus of control and its relationship to strategy-making, structure, and environment. *Academy of Management Journal*, 25, 237–253.

Mintzberg, H. 1978: Patterns in strategy formation. *Management Science*, 24: 934–948.

Nadler, D. A. and Tushman, M. L. 1987: *Strategic organization design*. New York: Scott, Foresman.

Porter, M. E. 1986: Competition in global industries: A conceptual framework. In M. E. Porter (Ed.) *Competition in global industries* (pp. 15–60). Boston, MA: Harvard Business School Press.

Prahalad, C. K., and Doz, Y. L. 1981: An approach to strategic control in MNCs. *Sloan Management Review*, Summer: 5–13.

Rotter, J. B. 1966: Generalized expectations for internal versus external control of reinforcement. *Psychological Monographs*, 80, 1–27.

Salter, M. S. 1973: Tailor incentive compensation to strategy. *Harvard Business Review*, 49(2), 94–102.

Tannenbaum, A. S. 1968: Control in organizations: individual adjustments and organizational performance. *Administrative Science Quarterly*, 7: 236–257.

Teece, D. J. 1976: *The Multinational Corporation and the Resource Cost of Technology Transfer*. Cambridge, MA: Ballinger.

Thompson, J. D. 1967: *Organizations in action*. New York: McGraw-Hill.

Tushman, M. L. 1979: Impact of perceived environmental variability on patterns of communication. *Academy of Management Journal*, 22, 482–500.

Van de Ven, A. H., and Ferry, D. L. 1979: *Measuring and assessing organizations*. New York: John Wiley.

Van Maanen, J., and Schein, E. H. 1979: Toward a theory of organizational socialization. In B. M. Staw (Ed.), *Research in Organizational Behavior: Vol. 1* (pp. 209–264). Greenwich, CT: JAI Press.

Vancil, R. F. 1980: *Decentralization: Managerial ambiguity by design*. New York: Financial Exectives Research Foundation.

V

Self-Examination: Some New Approaches

Finally, the book presents three relatively new perspectives on the strategy process: evolution, autopoiesis, and chaos.

McKern studies the processes of strategic change through analogies from cultural evolutionary theory when examining how an international firm operating in similar and related market niches can continuously and incrementally develop strategic competencies through learning and imitation. Applications of evolutionary theory in management literature have often been used to depict global changes in organizational populations and the evolutionary model can be adopted to explain processes of strategy making within organizations. One such way is taking a Lamarckian approach to the inheritance of new traits, or competencies, within a generation of multinational firms, as opposed to a strict social Darwinian view which argues that traits can be inherited only through intergenerational processes. A Lamarckian view provides an active role for management in engineering the evolution of organizational competencies by influencing the odds of variation, selection, and retention processes of learning and imitation in desired directions. Thus, while selection forces outside the firm in the industry environment play an important role, corporate strategies of diversification and international expansion represent important levers to manipulate variety generation and selection mechanisms, which can increase a firm's adaptability and its ability to maintain a moving equilibrium over time.

Vicari and von Krogh study the theory of autopoiesis which views strategic learning from a more cognitive and cyclical perspective. In contrast to evolutionary theory, autopoiesis theory represents a much more self-referential and cognitive view of the process of learning. While an organization is open with respect to external stimuli or signals, it can only learn, or develop useful information, by giving new meaning to the signals. Learning is facilitated through errors and experiments which create a pool of various signals from which an organization can enact, recode, and construct new meanings, and thereby develop variety in its knowledge base. Thus, an autopoiesis approach to building organizational competence involves managing strategic experiments. It consists of three cyclical activities: (1) triggering and discovering experiments; (2) retaining knowledge about the experiments; and (3) applying knowledge from the experiments by raising new questions or identifying new opportunities not considered before by the organization.

Zimmerman studies a firm where it enters the zone where it is pushed out of its equilibrium orbit. In this chaotic zone, uncertainty and complexity are so high that order and learning can only be created through self-organization, in which the concept of fit is self-referential rather than adapted to the organization's environment. Traditional scientific models have assumed natural stability, equilibrium, linear processes and deterministic predictability; however, physical scientists, such as Prigogine, Lorenz, and Mandelbrot, have discovered a number of phenomena which refute all of these assumptions. Instead, it is necessary to admit that these chaotic phenomena are nonrecursive, dynamic, non-linear and may exist in states which are far from equilibrium. Although chaos theory is still in its infancy, it may shed light on many phenomena which have been inexplicable before.

15

An Evolutionary Approach to Strategic Management in the International Firm[1]

Bruce McKern

Introduction

The theme of this paper is that analogies drawn from evolutionary theory can provide an alternative perspective for understanding the international expansion of firms. According to this view, managers are motivated to expand internationally not only by profitability and cost considerations, but also by a drive to enhance the firm's resource base. In the early stages of a firm's expansion, profitability and cost minimization are likely to be uppermost as objectives. The basis of the firm's ability to surmount entry barriers in the international domain depends in the early stages largely on product-market advantages acquired through experience in the domestic product-market domain. These advantages are in the form of operational competences, and are influenced by characteristics of the firm's home country product-market environment.

As a firm gains experience of international business, a further motivation becomes important. This is a concern for enhancement of the firm's organizational competences through learning. The ability of an established international company to respond to changing relative pressures from the product-market and geographic domains, traditionally seen in the adoption of global, multidomestic or international strategies, will depend on its ability to adapt its operations, and this depends on learning acquired through internalizing operational competences.

Firms which successfully learn from international operations possess an additional source of competitive advantage in the form of strategic competences, which may explain differences in performance amongst established international companies. The strategic competences encourage variety and support new directions, sometimes at the expense of short-run profitability and growth, and are analogous to processes of mutation and selection. Strategic intent acts as a selection mechanism to support init-iatives which are consistent with the development of competences of long-term value to the firm.

The evolutionary perspective is a promising approach to the task of uniting two strands of theory in the study of strategy in the multinational enterprise: the theory of the international firm, on the one hand; and the theory of strategy choice in the international domain, on the other. While the empirical evidence is no more than suggestive, it is hoped that the paper will add to the emerging resource-based view of firm strategy and provide a stimulus for further research.

Evolutionary Theory and Firm Strategy

In recent years there has been an awakening of interest in applying concepts from evolutionary and ecological theory to the study of the behav-iour of social organizations. Alchian (1950) and Hirshleifer (1977) pion-eered the application of biological evolutionary ideas to economic problems, and Penrose (1952) was an early critic. Nelson and Winter (1982), in a seminal volume, applied evolutionary concepts to the theory of economic change, modifying a number of the assumptions of classical econ-omic theory. Sociologists have also developed a stream of theory in apply-ing biological ideas to organization change and development, including Hawley (1950), Campbell (1969) and Hannan and Freeman (1977; 1989), who pioneered the population ecology theory of organizations. A collection which presents recent papers and views on the direction of this work is pro-vided in Singh (1990). Lawrence and Lorsch (1967) stressed the conformity of the organization to environmental influences, and the concept of fit be-tween the strategy of the firm and its environment has been a continuing theme in strategy theory (Chandler, 1962; Christensen *et al.* 1978; Galbraith, 1983).

Yet applications of evolutionary concepts to strategy theory have been surprisingly few. The work of the population ecologists (Carroll, 1988; Hannan and Freeman, 1989) is the most comprehensive, built on careful empirical testing of an evolutionary theory of structural change in organizational populations, and poses a challenge to the view of strategy as a management-led adaptive process. A somewhat different evolutionary ap-proach is taken by Burgelman (1991), who focuses on strategic processes within the firm. He proposes two forms of strategy formulation, based on an intra-organizational selection process. This research is discussed later in this paper.

Firm, industry and environment

Since there is some variety of 'evolutionary' approaches, ranging from 'evolution' as synonymous with 'change' to the selection approach of population ecology, it is desirable to set out briefly the premises of the analogy used in this paper.

The evolutionary analogy is used here as an organizing framework rather than as a literal model. For this purpose, an industry is a population of firms, analogous to a species, of which the firms are individual members. By analogy with the biological equivalent (Gould 1982), the industry is adapted to a particular market environment through a process of selection, as the firms within it compete for the market under the drives of profitability and growth, the main objectives of managers described below. However, whereas the modern synthesis of Darwinian theory depends on micromutation processes and the random mixing of genes to produce variation amongst successive generations of individuals in a species, some of which turns out to be adaptive for the environment and thus selected, the theory outlined here posits an active role for management in adapting the competences of the firm, a process analogous to learning and its transmission between generations.

The firm's fitness, an outcome of its level of adaptation to the environment of its industry, depends therefore not only on its inheritance in the form of routines and operational competences (discussed below), but also on its ability to effect adaptive changes in its behaviour, or its strategic competences. The theory assigns an important role to selection forces outside the firm in the industry environment and to internal inertial forces, but argues that processes within the firm can effect adaptation within a time period relevant to the speed of environmental change.

Environment

I define the notion of *environment* for the industry in terms of two principal domains. First, the firms of a particular country develop initially in a national economic environment or climate which is broadly similar for all firms, independently of industry sector. For firms which become multinational, this domain is complicated by the varied environments of other nations. Second, the market for the products of each particular industry, or 'mission' in Ansoff's (1965) terms, defines environmental characteristics which are specific to each industry. The market domain also influences the configuration of the firm's functions.

The first characteristic is analogous to the general environment of a geographic area or climatic zone which is host to a number of species. The second, the market, is akin to the specific combination of terrain, plant and animal life that constitutes the ecological niche of a particular species. It is the interaction of these characteristics which influences the initial fitness of the firms of a nation for competition in the international environment.

National environment

Differences between national environments select for differences between countries in the general fitness of firms for international competition, by shaping the competences of national firms over time. The factor endowment theory of Hecksher-Ohlin-Samuelson (as described for example in Caves, 1960) ascribes differences in the comparative advantage of countries in international trade to differences in factor endowment. Leamer (1984) provided empirical support for Hecksher-Ohlin-Samuelson and explained shifts in comparative advantage over time as a function of changes in factor endowment. Porter (1990) expanded this framework to explain comparative advantage in international direct investment as well as in trade by adding three additional variables: related industries which support the value chain of the industry's firms; the specific characteristics of customer demand to which national firms respond; and the structural, competitive and strategic features of each industry. According to Porter, these three characteristics, plus traditional factor endowment, (collectively termed the 'diamond' of competitive advantage) determine the comparative advantage of nations in international competition.

The Porter framework builds on the factor endowment theory by adding additional *national* environmental forces in the form of externalities (related industries) which enhance the competences of the firm, and selection pressures from the *market* (domestic demand and competition). It is consistent with the evolutionary view of the firm's environment as outlined to this point, although it neglects two other factors. The national environment includes the nation's culture[2] and its government, and these two factors are also of importance in shaping the heritage of a country's firms and their behaviour. By adding these additional elements, a more complete description of the national and market forces influencing firm competitiveness can be developed, which is, however, beyond the scope of this paper. Firms' strategies are conditioned by the national environment in which they develop, and all of the six elements outlined above condition the nature of the resource base developed in a firm.

The Porter framework also ignores the presence in a firm's national environment of competitors from other countries, with advantages which stem from exposure to a different national 'diamond'. The most important implication of this presence is the impact foreign firms have on the host country's internal environment and the competitive position of its firms in world trade, matters which have traditionally been of great interest to scholars of international direct investment. Such implications at the level of the firm are taken up later.

Market environment

Market demand is critical to achieving profitability and thus ensuring short-term survival. It can also be viewed as one of the major 'stakeholders' to which managers have to respond (Donaldson and Lorsch, 1983). Satisfaction of domestic demand selects firms with abilities which may or may not prove adaptive in expansion into the international arena, depending on the speed of globalization of the product, the quality and cost standards of the domestic market relative to foreign markets, and the intensity of home competition.

Markets call into use the routines (discussed below) required by firms to serve them, but individual firms differ in their understanding of marketplace conditions, choice of segment, and ability to deploy routines effectively. This differential ability to deploy routines lies at the heart of competitive advantage, and is due to organizational competences, considered in more depth below. Firms within an industry are also in competition for inputs to their industry and frequently compete with firms in other industries for the same resources (Pfeffer and Salancik, 1978) However, resource inputs are not the analogue to the biological food supply; customer demand is the prime resource for which firms compete.

The competitive positions of national firms change as result of a shift in any of the national or market forces. The national environment is influenced by government fiscal, social and monetary policy; changes in infrastructure, education or immigration which change factor endowment; and inwards foreign investment and broader international forces such as the formation of free trade areas, which bring in new competitors and change industry structures. Changes in consumer taste affect the responses of firms, the routines they employ and their resource base. National culture changes only slowly, but has a profound effect on strategy and managerial culture in the firm. In the early stages of a firm's growth, these national economic and market forces are the most critical for its subsequent strength in international competition. As argued later, learning and strategic competences provide an additional souce of advantage as the firm gains experience of international operations.

One difference in perspective should be noted between the evolutionary analogues of industry and environment. Industry populations are sometimes small in number and often contain individuals of considerably different size, a variable not usually considered significant in population ecology studies. As Winter argues in a recent review of evolutionary theories of organization (Winter 1990), treatment of the size variable constitutes a crucial difference between the theoretical perspectives of evolutionary economics and organizational ecology. Winter argues that since firm growth is linked to profitability, initial success on the part of some firms in an industry, whether because of differences in initial competences or as a result of adaptation, results in differing growth rates and thus leads to differences in firm size. Larger firms are better able to withstand unprofitable periods, and are more likely to survive a variable environment. As an industry matures this process leads to fewer firms and an asymmetrical size distribution. Changes in the structure of an industry, as measured by the number of surviving firms, are attributed by population ecology theory to processes *external* to the firm: the entry of new firms as a result of legitimation, and the exit of firms as a result of selection forces. Winter argues that such changes are also consistent with an adaptation process *within* the firm. The position taken in this paper is that international industry structure changes, at least in part, as a result of the adaptation of individual firms, and that firms expanding abroad benefit from learning and increasing size. This view is consistent with the product cycle theory of international investment and trade (Vernon, 1966).

Managerial objectives: profitability, growth and the resource base

The general manager faces three major tasks: determining the businesses or environmental niches in which to operate, developing and deploying the skills necessary for success in those businesses, and managing strategic change.

In performing these tasks managers respond to the demands of several constituencies under the constraint of uncertainty. Donaldson and Lorsch (1983) make clear the multiplicity of objectives managers attempt to reconcile in responding to the pressures of numerous stakeholders, which can be grouped into three constituencies: the capital market (investors), the product market (customers), and the organization (employees). To these three should be added a 'social' constituency, comprised of government and interest groups concerned with such matters as corporate control, market concentration, equal opportunity and the environment (Olson, 1982). Each of these constituencies has different objectives to which managers attempt to respond.

In attempting to attain a degree of freedom of action from the variety of constraints imposed by these constituencies, managers seek to increase the 'wealth' of the enterprise – wealth expressed not solely in terms of stock value, but in terms of both the financial and long-term strategic strength of the corporation. Financial strength releases management from the immediate pressure of the capital market, while strategic strength mitigates some of the pressures of competitors, suppliers and customers, while simultaneously making possible partial satisfaction of organizational goals and social objectives. Financial and strategic strength are reflected in the resource base of the firm, which I describe below as including a portfolio of *routines* and *organizational competences*. The resource base of the firm is strengthened through emphasis on the goals of profitability and growth, which are themselves closely related through the sustainable growth equation.

Profitability and homeostasis

In evolutionary terms, the firm's drive for profitability is analogous to the basic tendency for certain systems in individual organisms to attain *homeostasis*, the condition underpinning critical physiological drives.[3] In the firm homeostasis is the maintenance of adequate profitability as a short-term objective, and this results from 'fit' between the firm's strategy and the current environmental conditions. The firm maintains its system in balance by performing the routines which implement its current strategy. These provide goods and services fitted to an environmental niche and thereby partially satisfy the stakeholder groups identified earlier. One result of the drive for profitability is the creation of structural inertia in the firm's strategic process, a tendency to maintain the perceived fit with the environment. Structural inertia is a key element of the population ecology theory of industry evolution, providing the rationale for lack of adaptation (Hannan and Freeman, 1977).

Growth and growth strategies

Profitability is the indicator of homeostasis in the firm;[4] it also provides the resource base for growth, the second major goal of the firm, which has a parallel in the evolutionary drive underlying reproduction (Dawkins, 1976). The genetic identity of the corporation, like a clan or lineage, outlives the current membership of the organization and is reproduced, not through the multiplication of family members (although spin-offs and the formation of subsidiaries can be seen in this light), but through the continued performance of its business by successive generations of managers who carry and transmit the collective memory of the firm, including its current concept of its strategy, its technologies, market knowledge, culture, organization structure and management policies.[5] Growth adds to the firm's resource base or repertoire of routines and competences, and enhances managers' degrees of freedom in balancing constituency demands.

The objectives of profitability and growth need not be inconsistent with maximizing shareholder stock value but, as Donaldson and Lorsch argue from their observations of managers, managers' objectives tend *not* to maximize shareholder equity value, for two reasons. The first is that the objective function motivating managers is a more complex one than share value; they may attempt quasi-resolution of other objectives (Cyert and March 1963), which can be given greater priority from time to time. The second reason is that managers tend not to maximize but to 'satisfice', by setting standards of *relative* performance (relative to competitors or to the stock market average, for example).

Growth is achieved through three strategies: stable expansion of sales at the same pace as the market; market penetration and vertical integration which increase share of a sector; and horizontal diversification. A number of studies have indicated that each of these growth strategies depends on a different strategic process (Bower, 1970; Quinn, 1980; Mintzberg, 1990).[6] There are evolutionary analogues to alternative growth strategies and to the appropriate strategic processes, which will be considered later in relation to international diversification.

To summarize, managers are motivated not only by the short-term profit objective of classical microeconomic theory, but also by the impetus to grow. Growth and profitability strengthen managers' degrees of freedom, by enhancing the resource base of the corporation. For many managers this is an addititonal objective. In terms of the strategic process in the international firm this implies that managers make decisions not solely on the basis of profitability; growth and contribution to the resource base are also important criteria. It is likely that profitability and growth considerations dominate in the early stages of international expansion, but as the firm gains experience of the international domain, the enhancement of competences assumes greater importance.

Routines and organizational competences

Routines

Routines are the capacity for repetitive performance of the firm's operations in a particular market, which are embodied in physical and human assets (Winter, 1990). They are both the configuration of the firm's physical assets and the knowledge about using these assets residing in individuals, who collectively comprise the organization's memory. While the above view of routines is not too different from that of Nelson and Winter (1982), it is narrower, excluding organizational competences, along the lines recently suggested by Winter (1990).

Evolutionary analogues of the notion of routines can be seen in the gene (Nelson and Winter, 1982). Although elements in the genetic constitution of each individual or phenotype in a species are shared with its conspecifics, the reproductive process, by varying their combinations, yields variation between members of a species. The constraints of the environment determine which resultant phenotypic characteristics are most fit, i.e. which individuals thrive. Just as genes persist through succeeding generations of phenotypes, routines can underlie generations of products or services.

Routines provide the basis for the firm's response to the industry-specific 'key success factors' necessary for adequate performance in an industry. To the extent that the firm's routines match these success factors, it can be a contender in an industry. The Porter (1980) competitive strategy framework helps to specify the deployment of routines in terms of alternative generic positions responding to the general key success factors needed in an industry. However, as Sousa and Hambrick (1989) showed in the industrial goods sector, general key success factors can be deduced from knowledge of an industry, so most firms should be able to discern over time the routines needed for participation in a business.

Therefore, routines themselves are not the basis for lasting differences in competitive strength among firms. Instead, distinctive *organizational competences* are the discriminators.

Organizational competences are of two kinds: operational and strategic.

Operational Competences

A firm's operational competences provide the ability to integrate routines and perform them in a consistent manner. They are the set of managerial policies and practices, conventions about how things are done, organization structure and culture, systems for managing innovation, motivating and rewarding employees, and relations with customers, employees and others (corporate culture), which ensure that standards of quality and efficiency are established and maintained. They are largely explicit, in part implicitly embodied in attitudes.

The firm's operational competences provide structure and focus to an assortment of routines in order to address a market niche, and can be seen as analogous to the genetic structure of a particular phenotype. Operational competences, including knowledge about routines, are transmitted as information from generation to generation of managers, and successful firms are skilled at replicating accurately the specific successful combination. Operational competences allow the firm to adapt to moderate change in the environment over time, much as the reassortment of genes produces a limited variety of phenotypes, some of which may be adapted to changed conditions. However, there are strong inertial pressures which limit the speed and extent of the firm's adaptation, and these have implications for the firm's strategic process.

Dawkins (1976) and other biologists view the organism as merely the carrier of the genes, which are themselves the key elements in the reproductive process. Those genes are selected which successfully assort themselves in combinations leading to the development of a biologically effective organism, i.e. an organism that is best adapted to the environment. In this view, selecting routines, managing the interconnections and ensuring complementarity and synergy between them is at least as important as the routines themselves. This explains why some firms are able to maintain an edge over competitors in industries where the general skills appear to be available to all. A competence for managing complex operations provides an integrated proprietary linkage between routines such as customer knowledge, technologies and production processes, and is the most difficult competence for a competitor to imitate.

Prahalad and Hamel (1990) see competences primarily in terms of technology and manufacturing skills underlying successive generations of products, such as Honda's engine and power train skills. However, this view is too narrow. Other skills, such as Coca-Cola's management of its trade name and marketing power, are also sources of distinctive competitive advantages. Their approach also fails to distinguish between routines and organizational competences. Toyota's routines, for example, include its assembly lines and technological skills, which foreign companies have imitated, whereas its operational competences include its management of the product development process and the Toyota Production System, which tightly integrates supplier relations, inventory control, assembly line operations and workforce skills. These organizational competences have proved more difficult to imitate.

In the international airline industry, the key routines appear to be well known and there are limited opportunities for a firm to gain an advantage in hardware, yet there is a wide dispersion in performance amongst firms. Singapore Airlines, for example, stands out in profitability and customer quality rankings (McKern, 1990). Its success is the result of a very clear set of objectives which provide consistent focus and direction,[7] coupled with delegation to staff close to the customer of the responsibility and power to take action, and operational competences which control each operation or routine and integrate them efficiently. These include strict cost control and operational discipline; continuous active monitoring of the marketplace and customer satisfaction; communication of customer complaints and satisfaction rapidly inside the organization; personnel policies which emphasize careful selection, regular training, and comprehensive performance appraisal; and incentives based on company performance which constitute a large part of employee remuneration. These operational competences, achieved through learning and experience carefully transmitted to succeeding generations of staff, are difficult for competitors to imitate.[8]

Strategic competences

The firm's strategic competences include its processes for detecting environmental change, deciding what adaptation, if any, is needed, and shifting resources so as to develop new routines and operational competences for implementing new strategies. A firm's strategic competences are expressed in its processes for scanning the environment, for initiating and approving new projects, and its culture towards innovation and change. This is the strategic context of the firm (Bower 1970): its strategic process and the firm's cultural conventions towards change and growth.

Strategic competence is partly explicit, often largely implicit. Because of inertia, a firm's strategic competence tends to match its prevailing concept of environmental change. If the environment has been highly stable, as for a single business firm in a protected national market, operational competences may have the predominant role. The firm's strategic competences will then be directed towards maintaining stability and may as a result respond poorly to environmental challenges.

Strategic competences which allow for reassortment of existing routines, as well as acquisition of new ones, are likely to be more adaptive in a dynamic environment or when the firm enters new fields. If change is the norm, for example in a rapidly internationalizing firm, the strategic competences may include a strategic competence derived from experience with dealing with change. This idea is expanded in the last section of the paper.

An Evolutionary View of Strategy and the Strategic Process in International Firms

In this final section, the evolutionary analogy is addressed to the international firm and its strategic process. As noted earlier, the international firm deals with environmental complexity in two broad domains. In the first, the product-market domain, it faces complexity similar to that of a purely domestic firm, corresponding to its degree of product diversification. The second domain, that of nationality and geography, adds considerably greater environmental heterogeneity, which places greater demands on the firm's operational competences, and also stimulates in some firms the development of a particular strategic competence.

Enhancing operational competences

A number of actions taken by multinational enterprises appear to be motivated by the drive to expand competences. These can be enhanced in a number of ways:

Exposure to different customer tastes in existing product-markets but in new national environments

The benefit is experience which improves product development and marketing skills and increases product variety, which can then be extended to other markets, including the home market.

Acquisition of new skills, particularly technology, through direct contact with researchers operating in a different national context

The benefit is access not only to individuals (who could otherwise be hired to work in the firm's home country research labs), but to the research network of a different country. In Porter's terms, the firm benefits from direct exposure to specific strengths in another country's 'diamond'.

Exposure to different government or industry standards, in order to develop a base of experience for penetration of foreign markets

Industry standards often constitute a barrier to foreign firms, and direct exposure may be the only way a firm can develop the competences needed to compete.

Experience of operating conditions in a foreign market, as a precursor to a major commitment

Gaining direct access to industry clusters which may not have a strong base in the firm's home country

This is an attempt to gain the benefits of a foreign country's national competitive advantages (Porter, 1990) by direct association with the cluster of suppliers of technology, equipment, materials and components, important for new product development and manufacturing. When the ties between firms in a national cluster are very close, operating in the country may be the only way a foreign firm can be exposed to these stimuli.

Direct exposure to foreign competitors in their markets

The rationale is not only to penetrate competitors' markets, but also to gain experience of their organizational competences and tactics, to force improvement of one's own competences and to predict competitors' behaviour in other markets. Clearly the benefits depend on the company's ability to learn, and this is related to its strategic competences.

Establishing countervailing power in a competitor's 'profit sanctuary'

While perhaps not very different from the preceding rationale, a firm may enter a foreign market where a competitor earns a large part of its global profit in order to distract the competitor from the firm's home market.

Following home country competitors

As described by Knickerbocker (1973), firms sometimes expand into foreign markets in 'oligopolistic reaction' to other home country firms, on the rationale that they cannot afford to be absent from a market which competitors find attractive. One might expect that it could be more profitable for a firm to seek out other markets than to be a follower. But if learning and enhancement of operational competences are important objectives, follower behaviour can be beneficial and there may also be a free rider benefit.

Becoming an insider in closely integrated markets

This is a combination of several rationales described above. Penetrating certain national markets, such as telecommunications equipment in Europe or Japan, is particularly difficult because of the close associations between suppliers, customers and government. Long-standing relationships between a country's national firms, which have facilitated the introduction of new generations of products or technology in the past, are difficult for a newcomer to displace, particularly when the customers face large switching costs and uncertainty regarding the newcomer's long-term commitment. An investment in a local presence, even one entailing losses over some time, may be essential to build the network of associations and the credibility with buyers to break into the business.

The implication of these examples is that the rationale for the international expansion of firms needs to be extended beyond the traditional view, to include the firm's drive to strengthen its resource base through the improvement of operational competences.[9] The firm's profitability and growth goals may be temporarily suspended by such actions, while organizational competences are enhanced.

The ability to compete in foreign markets: strategic competence as an additional source of advantage

International expansion is a special case of diversification, but the environmental challenges faced by the international firm are far more extreme than in the case of diversification in the market domain, since they include not only differences in customer tastes (the product market constituency) but also differences in the other three constituencies, which include supply and distribution systems, government taxation, regulation and monetary policies, employee relations, managerial culture and social norms.

In the considerable body of literature on the international firm, the basis of the firm's ability to overcome these difficulties has traditionally been seen to lie in intangible assets in the form of routines and operational advantages developed in the home country's market. Caves (1982) and Porter (1990) suggest sources of this advantage, some derived from the product-market, some country-specific. In the initial stages of a company's expansion abroad, these advantages are most likely to be the basis of entry.

However, the actions described in the previous section may be undertaken by well-established multinational enterprises despite the lack of competences developed in domestic product markets, and sometimes, in fact, in order to compensate for such a deficiency. Clearly, operations in foreign markets which run losses for several years need substantial financial resources, but if one of the firm's objectives in expanding abroad is the enhancement of its organizational competences, it must also have an ability to learn and adapt. This implies that there is an additional source of competitive advantage in established multinational enterprises, in the form of a strategic competence which promotes organizational learning and adaptation to new environments.

International Diversification and Strategic Competences

Diversification requires an internal strategic process in the firm somewhat akin to the biological processes of mutation and selection. This includes a means of generating a variety of strategic alternatives, an internal evaluation mechanism which selects useful opportunities according to some criterion and rejects the inappropriate ones, and a retention process which shifts resources into new routines and develops the operational competences which allow the new strategy to flourish.

Mokyr (1990), in his historical study of technology and economic growth, observes evolutionary parallels in the dynamics of technological change and, in particular, both mutative and variational processes in the emergence of new technology. He notes that while technological change sometimes occurs in the form of a major breakthrough (mutation), it also frequently occurs through the accretion of numerous minor developments (variation), some of which are necessary precursors of the breakthroughs. These processes are enhanced by the firm's strategic competence.

As the strategic emphasis changes through diversification, an appropriate strategic competence is needed to stimulate and guide the necessary shifts in operational competences. An example is the semiconductor industry, in which most US firms have shifted away from standard products to more complex, customer-tailored devices demanding more sophisticated organizational competences. The nature of the operational competences needed to gain an edge on competitors has changed as the market has evolved, and semiconductor companies have changed their strategic processes in order to develop new competences.

National Semiconductor has defined its business in terms of two major business groupings, one of which, Standard Products, is a mature business which generates cash and is managed strategically according to a process like the 'induced' process described by Burgelman (1991). The other, more recent, business grouping is defined as Silicon Systems Solutions, and focuses on sophisticated semiconductor chips designed to provide system applications unique to the demands of particular customers. Managing such a business depends on strategic competences which allow for variety to emerge so that new opportunities can be grasped. National Semiconductor fosters this variety by allowing great autonomy to the managers of the businesses in this group, regarding them much like start-up companies. Each of the three businesses is run by independent managers who have a call on the corporate competences outlined above, and in effect reassort the company's technical and marketing competences according to their interpretation of market need. The strategic process encourages innovation and diversity in this grouping of businesses, while confining the Standard Products business to more mature products.

Successful international diversifiers are more likely to have developed a strategic competence which is sensitive to new opportunities, allocates resources for experimentation and investigation of new markets, and facilitates consideration of challenging proposals. These processes encourage strategic variety. However, since resources are finite, the firm has to limit the scope of 'mutant' strategies by a selection mechanism, which screens out proposals unlikely to prosper. The selection mechanism in some firms approximates the 'struggle for existence' by forcing new proposals to fight for support and demonstrate demand in the marketplace. An example of these processes is Intel Corporation's 'Weird Ideas' fund, a small enterprise fund to provide resources on a competitive basis for exploration of novel ideas outside the mainstream business. Corporate values which ratify this process, allocate financial and human resources to projects which demonstrate their viability, and provide recognition and reward for successful performers, act as a retention mechanism which completes the process. Successful international firms are to be expected to employ similar processes, both in the product-market domain and in the geographic domain.

Strategic competences in the international firm

I have proposed that a firm's organizational competences can be viewed as being of two kinds: operational and strategic. Building on his studies of internal corporate venturing (Burgelman, 1985), Burgelman develops the concept of the strategic process further by distinguishing between the internal processes which deal with current strategy and those which elicit and support radical initiatives. He describes the mechanism used for coping with current strategic objectives as an *induced* strategic process, whereas major strategic shifts result from what he terms an *autonomous* strategic process. Burgelman proposes an ecological view of the autonomous strategic process, based on variation in new strategic proposals originating in the firm, an internal selection process which corresponds to external environmental forces, and a retention or organizational learning mechanism (Burgelman, 1991). The structural context of the organization determines, in his view, the induced strategic process, while the strategic context determines the autonomous process. Applying these ideas to the view of the enterprise described in this paper, the 'structural context' describes the firm's operational competences, which are concerned with implementation of the firm's current strategy. The 'strategic context' is the firm's strategic competences, and it is to be expected that in internationally diversified companies these will be characterized by the culture, resource allocation mechanisms and incentives mentioned in the previous paragraph.

The 'transnational' corporation envisaged by Bartlett and Ghoshal (1989) has attributes consistent with such strategic competences. Organizational learning is the centrepiece of the transnational, and this is critical to a strategic competence which responds flexibly to environmental change. The differentiated roles which Bartlett and Ghoshal describe for subsidiaries of the transnational help create strategic variety without loss of efficiency. ASEA-Brown Boveri, for example, has adopted a differentiated approach to its international subsidiaries by identifying 'centres of excellence', each of which has the leading role in developing the competences related to a specific group of businesses.

Examples of other processes in multinational firms which encourage innovation and learning are seen in Nestlé and Matsushita. Nestlé achieves integration between its sixteen internationally decentralized and sharply focused research companies ('recos') through processes which encourage easy informal contact, great use of project teams and working groups, and rotation of researchers between research centres. Nestlé has a formal research fund allocation process, directed from the centre by the general manager of research and development (R & D), who is a member of the corporation's general management group responsible for strategy.[10] This process provides consistency between the R & D effort and the company's strategic direction, and channels the variety generated in the research groups.

Matsushita allocates approximately half of its research budget to its product divisions, which sponsor research projects conducted by the research groups. The research groups bid for sponsorship from the product divisions by preparing proposals and holding 'exhibitions', with the result that their projects are obliged to be responsive to market needs. Matsushita's central laboratories also undertake novel and long-term corporate research projects which are decided jointly by the labs, the product divisions and corporate management.[11] These processes stimulate variety and promote the emergence of new products and, ultimately, new businesses.

The examples given above suggest that established firms which succed in global competition possess strategic competences which extend beyond the operational skills acquired through experience in the national product-market. The intangible assets seen as the traditional base of the firm's advantage, needed to surmount the obstacles in a new country environment

(Hymer, 1960; Vernon, 1971; Caves 1982), are in the nature of routines and operational competences, which may be sufficient for a firm expanding abroad in order to acquire resource inputs or to enter a market where competitors are not particularly strong. These operational competences are acquired as a result of product-market experience in the home country, where the 'diamond' of national forces (to which should be added culture and government, as suggested earlier) determines the nature of parent company operational competences. This is the base of competitive advantage for firms in the early stages of international expansion, as established in the traditional theory of the international firm (Buckley and Casson, 1976; Dunning, 1981; 1988). But the examples quoted above indicate that the successful multinational acquires an additional base of competitive advantage in the form of strategic competences, the source of which appears to be prior international experience, a restless search for improved operational competences, and an ability to learn. These strategic competences are consistent with the long-term development of the firm's resource base, which is a major objective. Experience in operating an international network is not a guarantee of developing this base, but it is probably a necessary condition.

Choice of market or hierarchy: internalization and strategic intent

Internalization

The choice of the organizational mode employed by the firm in serving foreign markets has traditionally been explained in terms of transaction cost theory and market failure, derived from Coase (1937) and Williamson (1975). The international firm attempts to minimize the global cost of its operations (Buckley and Casson 1976), which impels it to operate in foreign markets. Further, like a domestic firm, the international firm chooses to *control* the foreign activities by bringing them under its direct administration when the cost of internal control is lower than that of transacting at arm's length with independent contractors (Williamson, 1975; Caves, 1982).[12]

The theory did not purport to explain how a firm develops the competences or intangible assets which are at the heart of its competitive advantage in international markets, how these advantages can be sustained, or the managerial processes which promote successful adaptation to the new environment. These questions have been tackled by extension of the emerging theory of strategy and the strategic process to the study of the international firm, which has led to the integration-responsiveness paradigm (Stopford and Wells 1972; Doz, 1980, 1986; Porter, 1986; Prahalad and Doz, 1987). While this work was consistent with a cost minimization framework, there has recently emerged an interest in a resource-based view of international strategy (Hedlund, 1986; Bartlett and Ghoshal, 1989). This recent view is consistent with an evolutionary perspective.

Given managers' concerns for growth and development of the resource base, the decision to engage in direct ownership of foreign operations, such as R & D facilities and manufacturing, rather than to contract with other parties, may often be based on the expected contribution to corporate resources rather than global cost-minimization considerations. This is not to argue that estimates of the benefits and costs of alternative modes of operation, if they were made, might not generally favour administrative control, as internalization theory concludes. However, in the instances quoted above, even if a cost calculation favoured contracting, managers who regarded learning and operational competences as central objectives would opt for control of an expanded resource base within the hierarchy of the enterprise. In so doing, they enhance the opportunity to learn by doing, which is critical to strengthening the firm's resource base. The value of organizational learning is difficult to estimate, but contracting out activities of this kind would contribute little to organizational learning, and thus contractual modes are seen as having lower value. The motive for internalization is thus not uniquely cost minimization, but also resource development.

Strategic intent

Priorities have to be set in developing organizational competences. In National Semiconductor, Intel and other successful companies there is an understanding of which kinds of new ideas will be tolerated and which will not. How do managers decide what competences should be emphasized through internalization? In the preceding discussion I proposed that the development of new strategies over time depends on a strategic competence which includes both variety generation, a selection mechanism and a retention process. The selection mechanism often used by firms is a financial criterion (Bower, 1970), expressed as profitability or present value maximization. If, however, the objective is to expand competences, then a broader criterion for selection is needed. This can be provided by the idea of strategic intent (Hamel and Prahalad, 1989).

A firm's strategic intent is both a vision of the firm's long-term direction and at the same time a statement of the firm's current strategy, expressed in terms of human needs. Just as the future forms of new organisms cannot be foreseen, the firm's future products cannot be completely predicted. A clear strategic intent, however, helps to clarify the routines and organizational competences likely to be needed in the future to fill those needs over successive generations of products. Strategic intent can be used to impose a selection force on the strategic process.

In the international domain, the concept of strategic intent can help to define the critical routines and organizational competences which should be internalized, even when cost considerations might favour contractual arrangements. Singapore Airlines, for example, has diversified only into areas which are directly concerned with the airline business and which strengthen the company's operational competences, such as aircraft maintenance, catering, ground handling, and a reservation system.[13] It imposes a selection force on these operations by requiring them to sell services to other airline companies, and they are often structured as separate business entities or profit centres.

As has been argued earlier in the paper, it is organizational competences which distinguish successful firms from the unsuccessful ones, and my hypothesis is that the competences which support the firm's strategic intent should all be internalized. This is not to say that *routines* should all be internalized. A routine, such as production of an input, should be internalized if: it is immediately less costly for the firm to do so; or the learning associated with performing the routine contributes substantially to operational competences supportive of the strategic intent, despite higher cost in the short term.

Conclusion

The evolutionary framework places emphasis on the organizational basis of the firm's competitive advantage. The routines of any business, which are potentially accessible to competitors, cannot constitute the basis for competitive advantage, except transiently. Instead, operational competences are the basis for long-term advantage. Successful firms in dynamic markets employ a strategic competence characterized by processes which stimulate variety, a strategic intent which selects among alternative strategies, and mechanisms which foster appropriate operational skills.

International firms are motivated to expand not only by reasons of cost minimization, but also to extend their organizational competences, which are more likely to be enhanced by internalization of foreign activities. Internalization theory has provided an explanation motivated by global cost minimization for the ownership of activities by international firms. The evolutionary analogy developed here proposes an additional rationale for internalization: to strengthen the firm's resource base through learning, and this may explain differences in internalization choices among established multinationals. Internalization of competences through the internalization of activities may also be a significant distinguishing difference between successful multinational companies and unsuccessful ones over the long term. 'Hollow' corporations, which co-ordinate activities undertaken largely on contractual terms, appear to be based on a narrow organizational competence which is transient, and are unlikely to survive as viable organizational forms in the long term.

There appears to be a significant difference between US-based and Japan-based multinationals on this dimension. Japanese corporations seem to have placed greater emphasis on development of organizational competences in the post-war period than have US corporations (Abegglen and Stalk, 1985; McCraw, 1986; Imai, 1986). Japanese firms see their long-term competitive strength in terms of organizational competences, rather than narrowly in terms of routines.[14] Maintaining research, development, design and manufacturing activities within the hierarchy of the firm might not always make sense to a firm in terms of short-term cost minimization. The apparently irrational behaviour of Japanese firms in so doing is sometimes explained away as attributable to a lower cost of capital. But if enhancement of organizational competences is the key to long-term competitive ability, a firm with long-term ambitions acts quite rationally in keeping such activities within the corporation. The evolutionary perspective outlined in this paper contributes, it is proposed, to understanding the benefits of internalizing activities for organizational competences, and also to explaining differences in strategic competences amongst international firms with different home bases, which are important topics for international comparative research.

Notes

1   Based on a paper presented at the Strategy Processes Research Conference at the Handelshøyskolen BI (Norwegian School of Management), Oslo, June 19 – 21, 1991. The author thanks participants at the conference, and in particular Andrew Van de Ven, for helpful criticism and comment.

2   The relevance of culture to economic performance is shown in Franke, Hofstede and Bond, (1991). See also Kelley, Whatley, and Worthley (1987) and Kogut and Singh (1988).

3   Penrose (1952) noted that homeostasis in the biological case was an automatic response to disequilibrium, whereas only limited aspects of firm behaviour could be regarded as automatic.

4   Alchian did not regard profit *maximization* as a necessary goal, arguing that selection would lead firms with realized *positive* profits to dominate in an industry.

5   In this respect, the genetic analogy is not entirely consistent, as Winter (1990) points out; firms reproduce by continued performance and by expansion in size, whereas in the biological world the genotype is reproduced in successive phenotypes whose size is genetically limited.

6   Qualified support for the expectation of fit between strategy content and strategic process is provided by Segev (1987), although the research site was a business game rather than a sample of real firms.

7   Singapore Airlines, *Perspectives*, December 1988.
8   These policies are detailed in the case study, *Singapore Airlines in the 90s*, Graduate School of Business, Stanford University, No. S-IB-8.
9   This rationale is mentioned in Dunning (forthcoming 1992).
10 See the case study *Nestlé, S.A.*, INSEAD 1987.
11 Described in the case study *Matsushita Electric Industrial (MEI) in 1987*, Harvard Business School, No. 9-388-144.
12 Dunning's eclectic paradigm combines Heckscher-Ohlin-Samuelson factor endowment theory with the market failure-internalisation theory mentioned above, in explaining the international location of production activities [Dunning, 1981 and 1988].
13 J.Y Pillay, Singapore Airlines, *Perspectives*, December 1988.
14 Such an organisational competence is expressed in the concept of *Kaizen*, aimed at the continuous improvement of operational skills through the participation of employees throughout the company.

References

Abegglen, J. C. and Stalk, G. Jr. 1985: *Kaisha*. New York: Basic Books.
Alchian, A. A. 1950: Uncertainty, Evolution and Economic Theory. *Journal of Political Economy*, 58.
Aliber, R. Z. 1970: A Theory of Direct Foreign Investment, in C.P. Kindleberger (Ed.), *The International Corporation*. Cambridge, Mass: M.I.T. Press.
Ansoff, H. I. 1965: *Corporate Strategy: An Analytic Approach to Business Policy for Growth and Expansion*. New York: McGraw-Hill.
Armour, H. O. and Teece, D.J. 1978: Organizational Structure and Economic Performance: A Test of the Multidivisional Hypothesis. *Bell Journal of Economics*, 9, (Spring).
Bartlett, C. A. and Ghoshal, S. 1989: *Managing Across Borders: The Transnational Solution*, Boston, Mass: Harvard Business School Press.
Bower, J. P. 1970: *Managing the Resource Allocation Process*. Boston, Mass: Harvard Business School.
Buckley, P. J. and Casson, M. J. 1976: *The Future of the Multinational Enterprise*. London: Macmillan
Buckley, P. J. 1991: *Recent Research on the Multinational Enterprise*. London, Edward Arnold.
Burgelman, R. A. 1985: Managing Corporate Entrepreneurship: New Structures for Implementing Technological Innovation. *Technology in Society*, 7.
Burgelman, R. A. 1991: Intraorganizational Ecology of Strategy-Making and Organizational Adaptation: Theory and Field Research. *Organization Science*. 2, No. 3 (August).
Campbell, D. T. 1969: Variation and Selective Retention in Sociocultural Evolution, *General Systems*, 14.
Carroll, G. R. (Ed.) 1988: *Ecological Models of Organisations*. Cambridge, Mass: Ballinger.
Casson, M. 1987: *The Firm and the Market*. Cambridge, Mass.: MIT Press.

Caves, R. E. 1960: *Trade and Economic Structure*. Cambridge, Mass.: Harvard University Press.

Caves, R. E. 1982: *Multinational Enterprise and Economic Analysis*. Cambridge: Cambridge University Press.

Chakravarthy, B. S. 1982: Adaptation: A Promising Metaphor for Strategic Management. *Academy of Management Review*, 7, No. 1.

Chandler, A. D. 1962: *Strategy and Structure*. Cambridge, Mass.: MIT Press.

Christensen, C. R. *et al*. 1978: *Business Policy*. Homewood, Ill.: Richard D. Irwin. [most recent edition (1990) edited by Bower, Bartlett, Christensen, Pearson and Andrews].

Coase, R. 1937. The Nature of the Firm, *Econometrica*, 4

Cyert, R. M. and March, J. G. 1963: *A Behavioral Theory of the Firm*. Englewood Cliffs, N. J.: Prentice-Hall.

Daniels, J. D., Pitts, R. A. and Tretter, M. J. 1984: Strategy and Structure of U.S. Multinationals: An Exploratory Study. *Academy of Management Journal*, 27.

Dawkins, R. 1976: *The Selfish Gene*. New York: Oxford University Press.

Donaldson, G. and Lorsch, J. 1983: *Decision Making at the Top*. New York: Basic Books.

Doz, Y. 1980: Strategic Management in Multinational Companies. *Sloan Management Review*, (Winter).

Doz, Y. 1986: *Strategic Management in Multinational Companies*. Oxford: Pergamon Press.

Dunning, J. H. 1981: *International Production and the Multinational Enterprise*. London: Allen & Unwin.

Dunning, J. H. 1988: The Eclectic Paradigm of International Production: A Restatement and some Possible Extensions. *Journal of International Business*, 19, No. 1, (Spring).

Dunning, J. H. forthcoming, 1992: The Nature of Transnational Corporations and their Activities, in Dunning, J. H. (Ed.) *The Theory of the Transnational Corporation*. New York: United Nations Centre on Transnational Corporations.

Franke, R. H., Hofstede, G. and Bond, M. H. 1991: Cultural Roots of Economic Performance: A Research Note. *Strategic Management Journal*, 12.

Galbraith, J. R. 1983: Strategy and Organization Planning. *Human Resource Management*, 22, No. 1 / 2 (Spring-Summer).

Geringer, J. M., Beamish, P. W. and daCosta R. C. 1989: Diversification Strategy and Internationalisation: Implications for MNE Performance. *Strategic Management Journal*, 10.

Gould, Stephen J. 1982: Darwinism and the Expansion of Evolutionary Theory, *Science*, 216 No. 23, April.

Hamel, G. and Prahalad, C. K. 1989: Strategic Intent. *Harvard Business Review 3*, May–June.

Hannan, M. T. and Freeman, J. F. 1977: The Population Ecology of Organisations. *American Journal of Sociology*, 92.

Hannan, M. T. and Freeman J. F. 1989: *Organisational Ecology*. Cambridge, Mass.: Harvard University Press.

Hawley, A. 1950: *Human Ecology*. New York: Ronald Press.

Hedlund, G. 1986: The Hypermodern MNC-A Heterarchy? *Human Resource Management*, Spring.

Hirshleifer, J. 1977: Economics from a Biological Viewpoin:. *Journal of Law and Economics*, 20.

Horst, T. 1972: Firm and Industry Determinants of the Decision to Invest Abroad: an Empirical Study. *Rev. of Econ. Statistics*, 54 (August).

Hymer, S. H. 1960: *The International Operations of National Firms: A Study in Foreign Direct Investment*. Cambridge, Mass.: PhD Dissertation, MIT.

Imai, M. 1986: *Kaizen*. New York: McGraw-Hill.

Kelley, L., Whatley, A. and Worthley, R. 1987: Assessing the Effects of Culture on Managerial Attitudes: A Three Culture Test. *Journal of International Business Studies* 19, No.2.

Knickerbocker, F. T. 1973: *Oligopolistic Reaction and Multinational Enterprise*. Boston: Harvard Business School.

Kogut, B. and Singh, H. 1988: The Effect of National Culture on the Choice of Entry Mode. *Journal of International Business Studies*, 19, No. 3.

Lawrence, P. R. and Lorsch J. W. 1967: *Organisation and Environment*, Boston, Mass.: Harvard Business School.

Leamer, E. E. 1984: *Sources of International Comparative Advantage: Theory and Evidence*. Cambridge, Mass.: MIT Press.

Lecraw, D. J. and Morrison, A. J. forthcoming, 1992: Transnational Corporations and Business Strategy: the Foundations of an Emerging Field, in D. J. Lecraw and A. J. Morrison, Eds., *Transnational Corporations and Business Strategy*. New York: United Nations Centre on Transnational Corporations.

Lodge, G. C. and Vogel E. F. 1987: *Ideology and National Competitiveness*. Boston, Mass: Harvard Buiness School.

McCraw, T. K. Ed., 1986: *America versus Japan*. Boston, Mass.: Harvard Business School Press.

McKern, R. B. 1990: Evolving Strategies in the International Airline Industry. Technical Report No. 77, Graduate School of Business, Stanford University, (August).

Mintzberg, H. 1990: *The Design School: Reconsidering the Basic Premises of Strategic Management*. Strategic Management Journal, 11 no. 3, (March–April).

Mokyr, J. 1990: *The Lever of Riches*. New York & Oxford: Oxford University Press.

Morgan, J. C. and Morgan, J. J. 1991. *Cracking the Japanese Market*. New York: Free Press.

Nelson, R. R. and Winter, S. G. 1982: *An Evolutionary Theory of Economic Change*. Cambridge, Mass.: Harvard University Press.

Ohmae, K. 1990: *The Borderless World*. New York: Harper Collins.

Olson, M. 1982: *The Rise and Decline of Nations*, New Haven: Yale University Press.

Pfeffer, J. and Salancik, G. R. 1978: *The External Control of Organizations: A Resource Dependency Perspective*. New York: Harper and Row.

Penrose, E. T. 1952: Biological Analogies in the Theory of the Firm. *American Economic Review*, 42.

Penrose, E. T. 1956: Foreign Investment and the Growth of the Firm. *Economic Journal*, 60.

Porter, M. E. 1980: *Competitive Strategy*. New York: Free Press.

Porter, M. E. 1986: Ed.. *Competition in Global Industries*. Boston: Harvard Business School Press.

Porter, M. E. 1990: *The Competitive Advantage of Nations*. New York: Free Press.

Porter, M. E. and Salter, M. S. 1982: *Diversification as a Strategy*. Boston, Mass.: Harvard Business School.

Prahalad, C. K. and Doz, Y. 1987: *The Multinational Mission*. New York: The Free Press

Prahalad, C. K. and Hamel, G. 1990: The Core Competence of the Corporation. *Harvard Business Review*, 68 No.3 (May–June).

Quinn, J. B. 1980: *Strategies for Change: Logical Incrementalism*. Homewood, Ill: Richard D. Irwin.

Roth, K. and Morrison, A. J. 1990: An Empirical Analysis of the Integration-Responsiveness Framework in Global Industries. *Journal of International Business Studies*, 21 No. 4.

Segev, E. 1987: Strategy, Strategy-Making, and Performance in a Business Game, *Strategic Management Journal* 8, No. 6 (Nov–Dec)

Singh, J. V. 1990: *Organizational Evolution: New Directions*. Newbury Park, CA: Sage Publications.

Sousa de Vasconcellos E Sa, J. A. and Hambrick, D. C. 1989: Key Success Factors: Test of a General Theory in the Mature Industrial Product Sector. *Strategic Management Journal 10*.

Stopford, J. M. and Wells Jr., L. T. 1972: *Managing the Multinational Enterprise*. New York: Basic Books.

Vancil, R. F. and Lorange, P. 1975: Strategic Planning in Diversified Companies, *Harvard Business Review*, January–February.

Vernon, R. 1966: International Investment and International Trade in the Product Cycle, *Quarterly Journal of Economics*, May.

Vernon, R. 1971: *Sovereignty at Bay*. New York: Basic Books.

Vernon, R. 1977: *Storm over the Multinationals: The Real Issues*. Cambridge, Mass: Harvard University Press.

Williamson, O. G. 1975: *Markets and Hierarchies: Analysis and Antitrust Implications*. New York: Free Press.

Winter, S. G. 1990: Survival, Selection and Inheritance in Evolutionary Theories of Organization, in J. V. Singh, *Organizational Evolution: New Directions*. Newbury Park, CA: Sage Publications.

16

The Inherent Drive Towards Chaos

Brenda Zimmerman

Introduction

Equilibrium models have influenced our studies of organizations (Russett, 1966), entrepreneurs (Stevenson and Harmeling, 1990) and strategic processes (Zimmerman, 1990). This influence is evidenced by the presumption of an evolutionary drive towards equilibrium or stability (Perrow, 1967; 1984; Kagono, Nonaka, Sakakibara and Okumara, 1985). Strategic processes therefore are often designed to reduce uncertainty and decrease the complexity for organizations (Cyert and March, 1963; Thompson, 1967; Williamson, 1975; Andrews, 1980; Tichy, 1983). Models of adaptation have been used to study the information processing aspects of organizations to further the understanding of how different types of equilibrium fit with the environment (Chakravarthy, 1982). The purpose of this paper is to offer an alternative to the equilibrium perspective by using chaos theory as a lens to understand strategic processes. The evolutionary drive assumed in chaos theory is towards a far-from-equilibrium or chaotic state in which uncertainty and complexity are increased (Prigogine and Stengers, 1984; Janstch, 1980). Strategic processes are seen as a route to decrease the routine aspects of an organization, to add complexity and uncertainty. Order is created through self-organization (Prigogine and Stengers, 1984) in which the concept of 'fit' is self-referential rather than fit with the environment. The organization and the environment are seen as co-evolving (Janstch, 1980). The role of information in organizations is seen as information creation or the creation of meaning rather than information processing (Nonaka, 1988).

The intent of the paper is to show how viewing strategic processes through a chaos theory or self-organization lens provides different insights than those gained by interpreting strategic processes from an equilibrium or adaptation perspective. The paper begins with a description of the

Table 16.1   Adaptation versus self-organization

	Adaptation	*Self-organization*
Stream analogy	Steering in the stream	Being the stream
Organizational renewal	Renewal of fit with the environment	Renewal of 'self' or self-transcendence
Need for complexity	Increasing the requisite variety to allow renewal of fit as environment changes.	Search for novelty and meaning (self-transcendence) to enhance evolution of social processes.
Openness	Open to environment	Open to evolution
Domain	Organization within the environment	Social system within which the organization is embedded
Order and dynamics	Structure based stability Periodicity	Process based stability Aperiodic, nonrecursive patterns
Structure	Equilibrium	Far from equilibrium

differences between the equilibrium model of strategic management based on adaptation to the environment and contrasting it to a model based on self-organization or far-from-equilibrium conditions. This section highlights several dimensions of chaos theory which differ from equilibrium based theories. The second section of the paper will exemplify these distinguishing characteristics between equilibrium and chaos models by critiquing Perrow's well-known theory of organization design. Finally, the paper will examine a strategic organization design process from a chaos perspective based on an ethnographic case study of a Canadian metals distributor.

Equilibrium and Chaos Theory

Although any natural science model has limitations when applied to organizations, it is believed that chaos theory can shed light on many organizational phenomena which are seen to parallel physical science phenomena in their nature, structure and line of development. Traditional scientific models have assumed natural stability, equilibrium, linear processes and deterministic predictability. Scientists have discovered a number of physical phenomena which refute all of these assumptions (Prigogine and Stengers, 1984; May, 1973; Lorenz, 1963, among others). Instead it is necessary to admit that these chaotic phenomena are non-recursive, dynamic, non-linear and may exist in states which are far from equilibrium. Although chaos theory is still in its infancy, it promises to shed light on many unexplained phenomena which the law of large numbers excludes from analysis.

Table 16.1 highlights several dimensions on which equilibrium-based adaptation models differ from a self-organization model based on chaos theory. Each of these dimensions is explored in this section. Two perspectives emerge from this analysis with fundamentally different assumptions about the sources of order and change in systems.

Janstch describes the differences between the perspectives of equilibrium or adaptation and chaos or self-organization using a stream analogy.

> Standing on dry land on one bank and watching the stream go by corresponds to a *rational* attitude. If we try to steer our canoe *in* the stream, in direct interaction with its forces and keeping proper distance from both banks, we are taking a *mythological* attitude – we enter into a direct relationship with the life forces around us, we deal with them at their proper level, we become involved and try to influence the overall process. But if we imagine that we *are* the stream, just as a group of water molecules is the stream and at the same time only one of its aspects, we are experiencing an *evolutionary* attitude. (Janstch, 1980: 267).

In this paper, the *mythological attitude* is the adaptation model based on equilibrium and the *evolutionary attitude* is the self-organizing model of chaos theory.

Adaptation to the environment is a mainstay of strategic management literature. Chakravarthy (1982) epitomizes this approach by providing a comprehensive adaptation model for strategic management based on changes in the external environment and processes internal to the firm. He defines the role of adaptation as 'to fit the firm more particularly for existence under the conditions of its changing environment' (Chakravarthy, 1982: 35). Self-renewal of organizations in his model involves renewal of fit with the environment. In chaos theory, systems in a far-from-equilibrium or chaotic state are defined by dynamics which are self-organizing and the reference point for the system is 'self' rather than the environment. Organizational renewal is seen as self-renewal or self-transcendence (Janstch, 1980). The environment is viewed as an integral part of the organization rather than an external entity in which the organization must survive.

Adaptation with the environment through increasing the requisite variety (Ashby, 1960) or the proactive strategy of a neutral fit (Chakravarthy, 1982) fall within Janstch's mythological approach or steering in the stream. The fundamental logic to steer or navigate in the stream is survival of the organization and addresses the question of 'how to structure relations in a system so as to keep it viable' (Janstch 1980: 268). Requisite variety is necessary to ensure the organization has the capacity to react and adapt to environmental changes. This paper is an attempt at describing the evolutionary approach in which the guiding image of being the stream is seen as the management or catalysis of social processes to define the appropriate system dynamics (Janstch, 1980: 268). The search process becomes one of looking for meaning and novelty to enhance co-evolution.

The adaptation model (Chakravarthy, 1982) assumes organizations are open to the environment and describes three states of adaptive fit, all of which are defined as equilibrium conditions. The openness to the environment is a necessary condition for adaptation processes and a return to an equilibrium condition. In contrast, a self-organizing system can be viewed as open to evolution. The idea is to enhance evolution. The journey is the destination rather than a process to achieve a desired end.

Another way to understand the distinction of openness in the two models is in terms of domain. The domain of interest in an equilibrium model is the organization within the environment. In a physical system which is in equilibrium or near equilibrium, the boundary conditions between the system under study and its environment are the major or even the sole determinate in the end state of the system (Prigogine and Stengers, 1984, p. 139). In a far-from-equilibrium state or chaotic condition, the boundary conditions play a much less significant role in determining the end state. Consequently the term self-organization is used to explain the system dynamics of far-from-equilibrium conditions.

One of the key axioms of chaos theory is process-based stability. Chaos theory describes an order without periodicity. Stability arises from the processes which keep the parts connected, rather than from structural arrangements which impose shape. Nonequilibrium is seen as a source of order. However, before we can relate this notion to organizational strategy we need to understand what this means by citing some examples from physics. Prigogine argues that in equilibrium molecules act as independent entities. There is no 'inter-molecular' communication. He refers to the molecules in this state as 'sleepwalkers' because they ignore the molecules around them. However, in nonequilibrium states the molecules 'wake up' and begin to 'communicate' with the molecules around them. Patterns of order are established which allow molecules to be seen to act in synchronous ways. The stability of the system in this state is due to the communication or information transfer between the molecules which creates and sustains new patterns of behaviour. In essence, *equilibrium's stability relates to structural components* whereas in *nonequilibrium stability is a function of communication or process components*. This is the key – the stability of chaos is an order of different logical type than the stability of classical equilibrium theory.

Janstch describes three approaches to change using the stream analogy. Table 16.1 deals only with the equilibrium or adaptation perspective and the chaotic or self-organization perspective. One perspective or approach does not replace the other, both are necessary components of management. The adaptation model is critical for understanding the strategic processes which enhance the ability of an organization to survive. The purpose of this paper is to indicate that chaos theory may provide new ways to understand strategic processes by focusing on the far-from equilibrium aspects of the organization, the self-referential rather than environment-referential components.

Technology and the Drive to Absorb Uncertainty

Perrow's (1967) framework for comparing organizations was the precursor to much of the contingency literature of the past two decades. His basic argument is that organizations can be classified on the basis of their technology, which he defines as 'the work done on raw materials'. Perrow's basis of classification allows for fruitful contrasts by limiting comparisons to other organizations within a defined set of criteria. His framework is used here because of its direct and indirect impact on the field and also because of its implied evolutionary trend.

In Perrow's (1967) classification scheme, organizations, and by implication subunits and individuals, are assigned to a category depending on: (1) the number of exceptional cases encountered in the work; and (2) the search process that occurs when exceptions arise. The search may involve problems that are analysable and thus can be dealt with in a logical, analytical and reasonably detached manner. If the search process involves unanalysable problems, then the method of resolution is more intuitive than analytical. Both dimensions are seen as continua as shown in figure 16.1.

Perrow argues that the appropriate task and social structures are determined by the technology classification. Thus a firm in the nonroutine cell would fit a task structure akin to Burns and Stalker's (1961) definition of 'organic' structure, where the overall organization is flexible and polycentralized. Perrow cites an aerospace firm as an example of a nonroutine organization because there tend to be many exceptions to the work processes and many unanalysable problems. An aerospace firm needs a

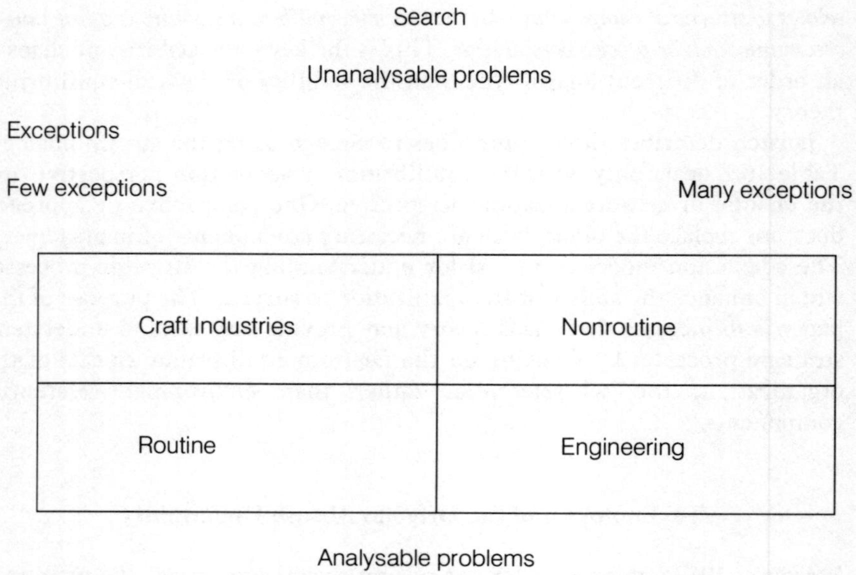

Search

Unanalysable problems

Exceptions

Few exceptions   Many exceptions

Craft Industries	Nonroutine
Routine	Engineering

Analysable problems

Figure 16.1   Industry types based on Perrow's (1967) typology

structure with loose task forces, which will allow the high-technology and research areas to be creative. This type of business should not have too much structure superimposed upon it.

A firm which fits in the routine cell is like Burns and Stalker's 'mechanistic' structure, and is ideally formal and centralized in response to the routine nature of the technology. The best way to manage this type of business (e.g. steel mills) is through bureaucratic methods based on rules, control systems and formal structures. The upper left quadrant is characterized by organizations which have few exceptions but where the problems are unanalysable, and calls for a decentralized structure. Perrow describes these as craft industries and cites speciality glass as an example. Finally, the lower right quadrant is characterized by organizations in which the search process for the many exceptions that arise is systematic, logical and analytical. Organizations in this cell are ideally suited to flexible, centralized structures. Perrow suggests these are engineering type organizations and provides an example of a heavy machinery manufacturer. Perrow argues that the non-task related or social interactions also differ from one cell to another.

One of the most important aspects of Perrow's analysis for this study is his contention that the technology of an organization determines the appropriate task and social structure, and that significant deviations from the

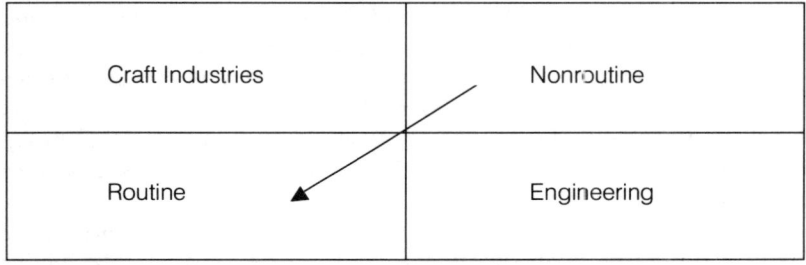

Figure 16.2   Perrow's (1967) assumed management direction

appropriate structures will result in a high cost in terms of output (Perrow, 1967: 204). But even more important to the argument here are his claims that the nonroutine cell is 'undesirable' because it is so difficult to manage and that the aim of most organizations is to move from nonroutine to routine (Perrow, 1967: 197). This implies that the job of management is to increase the analysability of problems and reduce the number of exceptions. The role of management is to absorb uncertainty.

Of particular interest here is the assumed evolutionary direction. Perrow argues that the natural trend is towards decreasing uncertainty and increasing predictability. Management's role is to move the organization as quickly as possible along the path of increased routinization, albeit within the constraints of the technology and the environment. In other words, the 'natural' drive is towards equilibrium as shown in figure 16.2. The research undertaken for this paper revealed some organizational activities congruent with a drive towards chaos.

Perrow (1967: 208) and Crozier (1964) argue that most people overestimate the variability in their jobs and very few classify their organizations as routine. Both Perrow and Crozier implicitly assume that people are therefore not objective in assessing their own work, especially on a comparative basis. However, perhaps there is something else at work here. Using the evolutionary paradigm underlying chaos theory, one could argue that the employees must find the nonroutine or must discover the far-from-equilibrium aspects of their job in order to evolve. Once they begin to see their jobs as repetitive, routine and boring, they may lose their resilience or their ability to absorb change within the job. They may lose their openness to evolution. Static equilibrium is a precursor to death because it is the enemy of change (Crozier, 1964: 172).

Research Methods

The organization studied was Federal Metals Inc. (Fedmet), a Canadian metals distributor and trader with major national and international holdings. Fedmet generated approximately $1 billion of revenue the year of the study. They are owned by Federal Industries, a conglomerate based in Winnipeg, Canada. Fedmet had four divisions at the time of the study, two of which became important comparison points for this paper: Russelsteel and Drummond McCall.

The research involved an ethnographic study for five months in 1989. The researcher was a full-time participant during those months having an office at the headquarters of the site. The bulk of the time at the site was spent on unstructured interviews. Archival research involved reading annual reports, planning documents and other relevant internal documents. During the orientation phase of the research, the documents introduced various members of the organization, provided information on the industry, and outlined a history of the organization. A journal article which described some of the history of Russelsteel was used as an early introduction to the organization (Hurst, 1984). The documents were later used as a source of questions for the interviews. During the five-month empirical study, the researcher was regularly updated with memoranda, planning developments, transcripts of speeches and other relevant documents. These shaped the research and provided evidence to construct the theoretical framework.

Many structured or semi-structured interviews were conducted over the five months. An emergent sampling design was used to determine who should be interviewed. The interviews averaged an hour in length but one lasted over six hours. Over two dozen members of the parent and the subsidiaries were interviewed, some several times. With few exceptions, most interviews were tape recorded. Having an office at the research site provided the opportunity to pick up on chance meetings as well as attending prearranged meetings and interviews (Whyte, 1984). All of the strategic planning meetings were attended. These meetings were usually half a day in length. There were eleven formal strategic planning meetings during the five-month period. Approximately one hundred hours of meetings and interviews were taped and transcribed. Social events, casual conversations or informal interviews, attending a three-day residence seminar and tours of plants also were part of the research activities. Sometimes these events or conversations were not a key source of data, but provided an opportunity to get closer to the participants. This seemed to allow greater access to information at later dates.

A variety of techniques were employed to establish the trustworthiness of the research including prolonged engagement (Glaser and Strauss, 1967), persistent observation (Jorgensen, 1989), triangulation of sources and methods (Jick, 1979), peer debriefing (Lincoln and Guba, 1985) and member checks (Lincoln and Guba, 1985; Jorgensen, 1979). Member checks played a key role in this research both in the form of informal conversations and a formal presentation to Fedmet's executive committee. These member checks brought systematic doubt into the inquiry by testing the concepts with the participants. The research methods are further described in the full case report and analysis (Zimmerman, 1991).

Empirical Findings

At the time of the study, Fedmet had four divisions. The two Canadian metals distributors, Russelsteel and Drummond McCall, were important comparison points for the research. Russelsteel and Drummond McCall are wholesalers of metals, primarily steel. They bought from the mills and resold in smaller lots to customers. The only physical value added to the product was to be found in the refinement process of cutting or slitting the metal. With a few exceptions, the equipment to cut the metal had not changed significantly for decades. As an example, a saw which was used thirty years ago, if well maintained, can still function today. There was very little new technology in the industry. There were some CADCAM operations in the industry, but they were simply for the purpose of two-dimensional drawings, and functioned mainly to save time. Fedmet used computers in order processing, but mainly for record-keeping purposes. Pat Eckersley, president of Drummond McCall, described the business as 'apologetically Canadian'. Fedmet's 1988 long-range plan described the industry as 'dirty and grubby'.

On the whole, the business was highly repetitive and 'boring'. The pejorative term 'boring' is used rather than 'routine' because a number of people interviewed, especially those in Drummond McCall, argued that they were concerned that the direction the company was headed in was going to make their business boring and increase the tedious repetition. There was an ongoing battle against becoming routine because they saw it as becoming 'boring'.

Fedmet could not rely on either the product or the production process to alleviate the boredom since they were the very source of it. They were the source of the stability which was so critical for survival in the shortrun. In other words, the product and the production process were a source of stability and strength for the organization, making it easier to 'steer in the stream', but because of the extent of the stability that goes along with them, they were also the source of boredom and thus a threat to survival in the long run because they could lose their ability to focus on 'being the stream'.

So how did they deal with the boredom which could eventually lead to equilibrium and death? The Fedmet group and the two main service centre divisions, Russelsteel and Drummond McCall, dealt with the problem in different ways.

Alleviating Boredom: Comparing Drummond and Russel

Drummond McCall and Russelsteel were direct competitors in many centres across Canada. They were both large steel distributors with some ability to do primary processing of materials, i.e. cutting of the metal in basic shapes or to certain lengths. None of the people interviewed in either company described themselves as fabricators. All described their business as steel or metals distribution. The companies both had long, and in some ways similar, Canadian histories. Jack Fraser, CEO of the corporate parent Federal Industries, described the acquisition of Drummond McCall as 'simply more of the same'. He said: 'We can buy steel service centres just like that,' as he snapped his fingers. *'It is repetition in business that is so important. Because every time you do something you get a little better at it. You do it over and over and over until all of a sudden you are doing it better than anyone else in the business.'* Fraser saw these companies in the same vein. He said there were differences in the product mix but 'the management techniques are identical,' because they both needed to have good asset management for inventory and receivables, good contacts with suppliers and with customers. it was a 'see spot run' business, said Fraser.

The focus of the Federal Industries team working with Fraser was to move towards quadrant four of Perrow's analysis. Their role was to increase the analysability of the industry, to increase the predictability, to decrease the number of exceptions, that is, to increase the routinization of the businesses they purchased. They did this by challenging industry assumptions of the operations management teams. Federal Industries continually challenged these assumptions and the thrust of the business strategy until there was agreement between the division and corporate office. When they reached that point Fraser said 'it self-corrects or it is automatic'. It seemed that once the problems had become analysable and the exceptions few, the repetition in the business allowed things to run smoothly and effectively. Fraser admitted that the process was never finished, but once you had the

basic plan everything else was quite straightforward. One of FIL's fundamental management principles was 'keep it simple'. This fits with the idea
of moving things towards quadrant four.

But the drive for chaos balances this movement with a need to 'keep it
complex'. In other words, there is a drive to keep the options open or create
the uncertainty and to create meaning in a broader social context. Complex
need not imply complicated. Complexity is necessary for the ability to
evolve (Janstch, 1980). A system must incorporate differences within itself
in order to have options.

Both Drummond and Russel therefore had a push from the environment,
from their technology and from their corporate parent to keep things
simple or routine. Using Perrow's classification scheme described earlier in
the paper, organizations are assigned to a category depending on: (1) the
number of exceptional cases encountered in the work; and (2) the search
process that occurs when exceptions arise. The search may involve
problems that are analysable and thus can be dealt with in a logical, analytical and reasonably detached manner. If the search process involves
unanalysable problems, then the method of resolution is more intuitive
than analytical.

Based on this classification, steel distribution falls into Perrow's routine
industry cell. Most of the work involves buying steel in large quantities and
reselling it in smaller quantities. There are few exceptional cases in the
work. When exceptions arise they are usually easily analysed. For example,
if a client asks for sheet metal to be cut in a particular shape for a
manufacturing process, the specifications for tolerance and width can often
be entered directly into the cutting equipment. Steel distribution appears to
fit into the routine business cell based on technology.

Perrow argues that the appropriate task and social structures are determined by the technology classification and that significant deviations from
the appropriate structures will result in a high cost in terms of output
(Perrow, 1967: 204). The task structure of a business in a routine industry
should be formal and centralized, similar to Burns and Stalker's mechanistic structure (Perrow, 1967: 199). The social interaction or the bases for
non-task related interactions should primarily be instrumental identity, in
other words job security, pay and protection from arbitrary power (Perrow,
1967: 200).

Yet examining the social interaction of the two divisions, it was found
that they fit much more comfortably into Perrow's cells for a craft industry
(Russelsteel) and an engineering type organization (Drummond McCall).
Russelsteel employees spoke frequently about the importance of identifying
with the firm and a sense of family. The social interaction for Perrow's craft
industry firms is social identity and a sense of community (Perrow, 1967:
200). Drummond McCall employees were more likely to emphasize the

technological gains of the company including up-to-date production equipment and CADCAM. Perrow argues technical satisfaction and work- or task-identification as the dominant social structure for engineering-type firms (Perrow, 1967: 200). At least in the realm of social structure, neither Russelsteel nor Drummond McCall have the appropriate attributes for a business in a routine industry.

The issue then becomes why, if their environment and technology dictate that the appropriate fit is in the routine cell, are they acting as if they were a craft industry and an engineering organization? It would appear that there is a poor fit between their technology and their social structures which should affect their ability to perform. However, in recent years Fedmet had been highly successful in achieving revenue growth and returns. One could argue that the environment had been so favourable that they had been successful in spite of the poor fit, and that with a less positive environment the flaws would evidence themselves in the performance. Nevertheless, a review of the statistics for 1989 and 1990, when the market took a very serious turn for the worse, shows that Russelsteel continued to be an upper quartile performer in the Canadian metals distribution industry in return on net assets and in gross profit and Drummond continued to be above the industry median in these areas. It is conceivable that this 'poor fit' actually plays a positive role. From the perspective of the conceptual framework of this study, it can be explained by the evolutionary drive towards complexity. The next two sections provide a few examples of this drive in Drummond McCall and Russelsteel.

The Search for Meaning in Drummond McCall

To a great extent, Drummond's method of creating the uncertainty (i.e. creating the nonequilibrium conditions), was to make the product or process less boring, and perhaps even exciting. It had a much wider product range than Russelsteel. For example, Drummond's product mix in 1988 included 36 per cent non-ferrous products (compared to only about 1 per cent at Russelsteel) and they had experimented with distributing plastics as a substitute for metal in certain industrial applications. Drummond had increased the number of exceptions in their work by extending their product range.

The distinction between ferrous and non-ferrous products is important. They are two different businesses with different customers and different demands from a metals distributor. Consequently, the selling skills and even the warehousing skills are different. Hugh Clancy, executive vice president of Drummond McCall, described the differences.

The companies who use a lot of non-ferrous products are different from the guys who buy a lot of steel.... People who use a lot of stainless steel, brass and copper, usually have very clean, neat, well organized shops. Steel is dirtier, the shops are dirtier, the welding smoke is dirtier. When you are using non-ferrous products, you are using a product that is worth $2 a pound versus one that is worth $0.25 a pound so there is more care taken. So when you go into these shops you see they are more careful whereas when you go into a steel shop the guy is in there hitting the metal with a hammer and he doesn't care. I believe it rubs off in our business, in that we have to project ourselves in a different manner.... They have more sophisticated buyers, higher skills in their plants. It is just a higher skilled business.

Drummond had a much higher proportion of university graduates in the management ranks and elsewhere than Russelsteel. Russelsteel had virtually no university graduates, other than those in support functions like accounting. Unlike Russelsteel, Drummond had a metallurgist on the staff. They also tended to spend more money on fixed assets in the plants than Russelsteel did. Drummond's fixed asset base was proportionately 13 per cent higher than Russelsteel's in 1988. The Drummond plants looked less 'grubby' than Russelsteel's and more high-tech, or at least more like a manufacturing operation. They had concrete floors, whereas most of the Russelsteel plants had dirt floors. Compared to Russelsteel, Drummond had much more CADCAM and more new, advanced flat-rolled equipment. Drummond's flat-rolled equipment was newer and more advanced than that of Russelsteel. Drummond's potential growth in non-ferrous, Clancy says, gave them certain advantages over other non-ferrous houses because they had some 'very good' production machines. He stated: 'We are setting ourselves up as a quality supplier of slit products .... We have the ability to get extremely tight tolerances, and we paid a lot of money for that.' Gino Motaferri, Quebec regional controller for Drummond, argued that their product was respected in the marketplace because the equipment they had could provide the tolerances demanded in the market.

In essence, Drummond had reduced the apparent 'boringness' of the product and the process. It was the product and the process which they had spent effort on in alleviating the boredom. They had created more exceptions by expanding the product base and increasing the emphasis on processing. They had pushed the organization toward the engineering cell in Perrow's chart, where technical expertise plays a high role and those who can plan the technical exceptions are granted high power and discretion. An excellent example of this was Drummond's contract to provide the cut steel plate for the Olympic tower in Montreal, Canada. All of the managers interviewed in Montreal mentioned the project and the prestige it brought the company. From the standpoint of social structure, Perrow predicts that employees of engineering type businesses identify with the work itself, and achieve technical satisfactions (Perrow, 1967: 200). Although one can argue that Drummond had aspects of all four of the cells in its social structure, it was clear that the technical satisfactions were dominant. They created meaning by stressing their expertise and the 'cutting edge' and saw themselves as pushing the technical aspects of the industry forward. This is in stark contrast to the management focus of Russelsteel as described in the next section.

Creating Meaning – Russelsteel

Recently, Russelsteel had met with more financial success than Drummond. How had they managed the boredom at Russelsteel? They did not do it through the product or physical process in the plant. This was not to say that they hadn't made the work flow as efficient as possible and purchased some equipment over the years. But they hadn't tried to put any glamour or excitement into the product or its movement through the plant. They were almost entirely a steel rather than a metals distributor. Many of the warehouses had dirt floors. Some of the branches kept inventory and the cranes to move it outside. Their equipment was generally ancient, and they had spent very little on CADCAM or other technological advancements. The people who had been hired had little formal education.

The people interviewed at Russelsteel from the president through to warehouse workers, said that the company was an exciting place in which to work. The principal way they created excitement, options and non-equilibrium conditions was through their 'people processes'. This included internal interactions between employees and external interactions with customers (e.g. tours of customer plants) and suppliers (e.g. meetings with steel mills). The company motto was 'People Making Difference'. This is not surprising, given the fact that Alec Shkut, president of Russelsteel, said that his job was personnel manager and always had been. 'Nothing that I do is more important than getting to know the employees and how they are feeling about the company and telling them what management is thinking about these days,' said Shkut.

He was not a great fan of planning. He complained bitterly about 'overplanning' and how it took him away from the job he should be doing. However, Shkut was a firm believer in feedback and communication. Consequently, he and the rest of the head office management team had calendars filled with meetings. Shkut said these meetings were some of the best and most important things they did, in spite of the fact that they were costly in money and time.

The rejection of planning and the acceptance of feedback at Russelsteel are very much in line with Perrow's notion of the appropriate way to structure task-related interactions for organizations in the craft industry quadrant. Coordination by feedback is the preferred supervisory approach (Perrow, 1967: 199). Perrow also argues that organizations that fit in this cell tend to have higher levels of discretion and power for supervisors than for technical people. Again one sees the parallel with Russelsteel because of their lower emphasis on technical expertise.

The people at Russelsteel frequently used the word 'family' when referring to everyone from the top executives to the data entry clerks. Almin Goode, manager of human resources, said that much of the management effort was directed to making people feel like part of the family. Russelsteel executives argued that it was the concept of family that allowed them to openly disagree with each other and still continue working together. Alec Shkut claimed that this was because of the trust factor. 'Something I'm very proud of at Russelsteel is the trust factor ... we can do an awful lot with our people on the basis of "trust me"', said Shkut. By creating this environment of trust and sense of family, the management team argued that they increased the options examined because people felt comfortable expressing their views. The 1988 Russelsteel long-range plan said that employees should 'dare to be different' because one has more to add to the organization as a result of one's differences than one's similarities. Complexity and the creation of unanalysable problems are enhanced by this focus on people processes.

Perrow's comments on the appropriate social structure of craft industry firms mirrors that of Russelsteel:

> The category social identity (in this cell) is meant to convey that the non-task-related interactions of personnel that are organizationally relevant revolve around communal or personal satisfactions born of long tenure and close working relationships. This is true especially at the supervisory level, which is a large management group in this kind of structure. (Perrow, 1967: 201)

Their management staff was almost 'totally home grown', which meant that managers generally had long tenure with the company. Long tenure requires patience, according to Jim MacDonald, operations manager for Russelsteel.

> Patience is a word that really captures what the company is all about.... The patience comes through in a lot of different ways. It comes through in that we don't tell people what to do.... You might

see something that could be done better but rather than shoving it down the throat of the operator, we make a very determined effort to let it evolve. No doubt we are shaping the process but we don't want it to be our push. We would rather see it as a pull situation. We want the operator to be pulled towards the division or corporate level in terms of learning.

Social identity does not necessarily lead to complexity, nor does it increase the nonequilibrium aspects of a company. The management team at Russelsteel was well aware of the threat of group think and made a conscious effort to combat it. Almin Goode commented that the Monday morning management meetings at head office were filled with arguments and genuine disagreements. 'We spend so much time in the discussion stage for everything we do, the arguing, the bickering ... before anything is committed to paper,' she said.

Another method of combating group think is the notion of champions. It is a word that was frequently used at Russelsteel and, as Goode saw it, was tied to the Fedmet vision of 'Every Person A Manager'.

In this company it is possible to believe in 'Every Person a Manager'. This is the first place that I've worked where if you see an area that is not receiving attention or something that should be done and no one has time to do it, you can take it over as your own project. There is no structure which says that this is not your job. If you are willing to devote your time to champion that particular cause, it is possible to do so.

Goode's comments were mirrored by several other managers and non-management personnel at Russelsteel.

The Russelsteel management team viewed almost all of its activities and programmes as an opportunity to communicate. Fedmet initiated a profit-sharing scheme for all employees in 1987. It was called a stakeholders plan and employees were rewarded depending on the performance of their branch and their tenure with the company. Russelsteel viewed this not simply as a monetary incentive scheme, but as a vehicle for communicating results on an ongoing basis. In addition, Russelsteel had used it as an opportunity to initiate an employee poster programme in which employees designed posters which talked about non-financial aspects of the stakeholders plan, like sharing and teamwork.

Discussion

Fedmet's divisions in some ways acted contrary to what the model of adaptation or environmental fit would predict. Viewing these processes, activities and participant mindsets through an equilibrium lens would suggest that these are inappropriate activities for the survival of the organization *vis-à-vis* the environment and its potential changes. However, when viewed through a chaos theory lens, these same activities, processes and mindsets may have positively enhanced the system's evolution. The search for novelty is not designed merely for amusement, but rather may serve the individuals' need to search for meaning beyond the tasks and adaptive steps required in their daily operations.

The equilibrium or adaptation concept assumes that strategic processes should be designed to absorb uncertainty and the senior executives act as leaders. Information processing models which are implict in much of the environmental adaptation literature assume that humans have bounded rationality and that goal congruence should be an aim for the organization. The dominant evolutionary drive is for organizational survival and hence fit with the environment.

In contrast, chaos theory assumes uncertainty should be created or expanded and that humans have limitless ability to create connections. The role of senior executives is to be catalysts in this evolutionary process. Counterforces within a system are seen to be positive in the evolutionary drive to requisite destabilization and self-presentation. The following table outlines some of the linkages between the chaos theory concepts and the empirical evidence of the research site. The rest of this section expands on these linkages.

In the previous section of the paper, a number of activities at Drummond and Russelsteel were described which seemed to be deliberately designed to create novelty. These activities to introduce novelty in the divisions increased the uncertainty for the organization. Drummond increased the complexity of its processing of metals and expanded its product offerings. Russelsteel increased the complexity of its people processes by including more people in the decision making processes and inviting open disagreement and dialogue. These increases in complexity were the defining features of their organization for the participants in the research. Members of Drummond invariably discussed their product line and processing capabilities and waxed enthusiastic about 'state-of-the-art' technology. Russelsteel employees and managers talked at great length about the role of individuals and teams at Russelsteel. There was often no mention of the product or equipment in the Russelsteel interviews.

One of Fedmet's guiding principles was 'Let it Happen'. This phrase depicted their idea that the role of senior management was to create the environment and learning experience for their employees but not to predetermine the exact outcomes of the processes. The deliberate aspects of management related to process elements. They argued that their role was to create the environment to let it evolve. The senior executives were catalysts in

Table 16.2 Mapping the empirical link between chaos/nonequilibrium and strategic processes

	Nonequilibrium/ chaos theory	Empirical evidence (Fedmet's approach)
Uncertainty	Creation / expansion	Drive for chaos (Drummond-increasing complexity of product and production process – Russelsteel increasing complexity of people processes)
Role of senior executive(s)	Catalyst(s) Enactment of strategies by members of org.	We make a determined effort to let it evolve
Human capacities	Limitless ability to create connections	Russelsteel posters asking members to create meanings out of organizational activities
Assumption of ideology	Counterforces	'Dare to be different' – open conflict / disagreement balanced with humour
Dominant evolutionary drive	Requisite destabilization & self-presentation in a search for meaning (self-transcendence)	Fight against conventional wisdom

the process and spent a great deal of their time creating conditions where multiple perspectives on issues could be presented to allow for the creation of new meanings.

One of the assumptions underlying information processing models is the processing limitations of human capabilities. At Fedmet and Russelsteel the assumption was often that humans had infinite capacity to create new connections and new meanings from organizational events. Seminars sponsored by Fedmet were held on a regular basis which included a vertical slice of the organization. During these seminars, truck drivers and receptionists as well as sales people and managers were asked to contribute their ideas and analyses of the organization. Russelsteel had a poster programme asking employees to create meanings out of organizational activities. At several Fedmet management meetings, individuals stated that their employees had incredibly creative insights and ideas for the organization but managers implicitly or explicitly prevent them from expressing those ideas.

Alec Shkut, president of Russelsteel, challenged his employees to 'dare to be different'. This idea was mirrored by many of his management team who said that disagreement is valued in the organization and indeed consensus created a sense of unease. Teams were designed throughout the Fedmet organization to ensure that multiple and conflicting interpretations would be brought to bear on the issues facing the organization. The meetings observed provided further evidence of the open conflict in the organization. This conflict was revered rather than disdained. Humour seemed to be one of their methods of handling conflict and disagreement.

Wayne Mang, CEO of Fedmet, said he was uncomfortable when things were too balanced, too smooth or too predictable. He said one of his roles is to 'fight against conventional wisdom'. He felt the need to continually destabilize the organization using processes which: (1) created or exposed differences or counterforces; (2) reinforced the differences; (3) built on the differences to create new ways of acting; and (4) encouraged retrospective reflection on the experiences. The reflection stage was critical because that was where they said much of the learning took place. Senior management were deliberately creating the processes or conditions but not deliberately structuring the outcomes.

Conclusion

A central feature of the idea of far-from-equilibrium fields is the notion of evolution. Systems cannot evolve, i.e., generate new patterns, in either an equilibrium or close to equilibrium state (Prigogine and Stengers, 1984). There is a need for this third field of far-from-equilibrium to break contexts and develop evolving patterns. Consequently, evolution seems to presuppose and require an inherent drive towards the far-from-equilibrium field, or an inherent drive towards chaos.

Chaos theory is proving to be useful in enriching our understanding of strategic management processes and innovation (Nonaka, 1988a; 1988b; 1990). This paper has focused on one particular axiom of chaos theory – the drive for chaos or the drive to create uncertainty. This drive is at odds with much of the strategic and organization literature and yet provides a complementary level of analysis for researchers and managers. Great strides have been made in understanding the need to enhance environmental fit, decrease uncertainty and in creating mechanisms, structures and processes to ensure these will happen in systems. This drive fundamentally stems from a theory of equilibrium. If indeed, theories of nonequilibrium, chaos and self-organization have merit in understanding social organizations then we must also recognize the evolutionary need to increase uncertainty. Pascale (1990) argues that organizations need to focus on resilience or change absorption rather than stability which suggests resistance to change. Chaos theory and the drive to increase uncertainty may provide some insights into the resiliency of organizations.

Evolution based on a vision of self-transcendence creates an optimistic broad perspective on order and change. The paper is a modest attempt at identifying some of the implicit assumptions of our models of strategic management which, in spite of their obvious value in the understanding of certain adaptive actions, may prevent us from understanding other dimensions strategic processes and change.

References

Andrews, K. R. 1980: *The Concept of Corporate Strategy*. New York: Dow Jones Irwin, 1971; reprint, Homewood, Ill.: Richard D. Irwin, Inc.

Ashby, W. R. 1960: *Design for a Brain*, second edition, Wiley, New York.

Burns, T. and Stalker, G. M. 1961: *The Management of Innovation*. London: Tavistock Publications.

Chakravarthy, B. S. 1982: Adaptation: A Promising Metaphor for Strategic Management. *Academy of Management Review* 7, no. 1, 35–44.

Crozier, M. 1964: *The Bureaucratic Phenomenon*. London: Tavistock Publications.

Cyert, R. M. and March, J. G. 1963: *A Behavioral Theory of the Firm*. Englewood Cliffs, N.J.: Prentice-Hall.

Glaser, B. G. and Strauss, A. L. 1967: *The Discovery of Grounded Theory: Strategies for Qualitative Research*. Chicago: Aldine Publishing Co.

Hurst, David K. 1984: Of Boxes, Bubbles and Effective Management. *Harvard Business Review* (May–June): 78–88.

Jantsch, E. 1980: *The Self-Organizing Universe*. Oxford: Pergamon, Inc.

Jick, Todd D. 1989: Mixing Qualitative and Quantitative Methods: Triangulation in Action. *Administrative Science Quarterly* 24 (December): 602–11.

Jorgensen, D. L. 1989: *Participant Observation: A Methodology for Human Studies*. Newbury Park, Calif.: Sage Publications.

Kagono, T., Nonaka, I., Sakakibara, K. and Okumara, A. 1985: *Strategic versus Evolutionary Management: A U.S.–Japan Comparison of Strategy and Organization*. Amsterdam: North-Holland.

Lincoln, Y. S. and Guba, E. G. 1985: *Naturalistic Inquiry*. Beverly Hills: Sage Publications.

Lorenz, Edward. 1963: Deterministic Nonperiodic Flow. *Journal of the Atmospheric Sciences* 20, no. 2 (March): 130–41.

May, Robert M. 1973: *Stability and Complexity in Model Ecosystems*. Princeton, New Jersey: Princeton University Press.

Nonaka, I. 1988a: Creating Organizational Order Out of Chaos: Self-Renewal in Japanese Firms. *California Management Review*. (Spring): 57–93.

Nonaka, I. 1988b: Toward Middle-Up-Down Management: Accelerating Information Creation. *Sloan Management Review* (Spring): 9–18.

Nonaka, I, 1990: Redundant, Overlapping Organization: A Japanese Approach to
Innovation. *California Management Review* 32, no. 3: 27–38.

Pascale, R. T. 1990: *Managing on the Edge*, Touchstone Books, Simon & Schuster
Inc., New York.

Perrow, C. 1967: A Framework for the Comparative Analysis of Organizations.
American Sociological Review 32, no. 2, 194–208.

Perrow, C. 1984: *Normal Accidents: Living with High-Risk Technologies*, Basic Books,
Inc., New York.

Prigogine, Ilya and Stengers, Isabelle 1984: *Order out of Chaos: Man's New Dialogue
with Nature*. Toronto: Bantam Books.

Russett, Cynthia Eagle. 1966: *The Concept of Equilibrium in American Social Thought*.
New Haven and London: Yale University Press.

Stevenson, Howard and Harmeling, Susan 1990: Entrepreneurial Management's
Need for a More Chaotic Theory. *Journal of Business Venturing*. No. 5, pp. 1–14.

Thompson, J. D. 1967: *Organizations in Action*. New York: McGraw-Hill.

Tichy, N. M. 1983: *Managing Strategic Change – Technical, Political, and Cultural Dynamics*, John Wiley and Sons, New York.

Whyte, W. F. 1984 *Learning from the Field: A Guide from Experience*. Beverly Hills:
Sage Publications.

Williamson, O. E. 1975: *Markets and Hierarchies: Analysis and Antitrust Implications*.
New York: The Free Press.

Zimmerman, Brenda J. 1991: *Strategy, Chaos and Equilibrium: A Case Study of Federal
Metals, Inc.* unpublished doctoral dissertation, York University, Canada, March.

Zimmerman, Brenda J. 1990: *Nonequilibrium: The Flipside of Strategic Processes*.
Presented at the Strategic Management Society Conference, Stockholm, Sweden,
October.

17

An Autopoiesis Approach to Experimental Strategic Learning

Georg von Krogh and Salvatore Vicari

Complexity is the best stimulus to knowledge and development. (Seres)

Introduction: Conceiving of the Firm as a Cognitive Entity

Recent years have seen an extensive growth in the cognitive sciences aimed at explaining how the brain works. This research has influenced the study of the firm in at least two different ways. First, it has provided new understanding of the cognition and behaviour of the single manager. The research pioneered by Sperry (Sperry, 1968) indicated that the brain consists of two separate hemispheres, each of which is different in character; while one part works in a rational and analytical manner, the other part works in an emotional and synthetical manner. This insight has been applied in the study of management behaviour, and can for instance be recognized in the works of Mintzberg (1976), Isenberg (1987), and Taggart and Robey (1981).

Second, and more important, the research on cognition has contributed to our understanding of the concept of organization. Researchers have started to ask the following question: assuming that the firm is a collection of brains, is it possible to construct a model of the firm as a brain? Morgan (1986: 356) describes the stage at which researchers find themselves attempting to answer this question:

> Compared with the complexity and mystery of modern brain research, use of the (knowledge) in organization theory is still in a humble stage of development. (Application of the knowledge of the) brain ... helps us to appreciate that the organization itself can be regarded as a cognitive system, embodying a structure of thought as well as a pattern of action.

Different approaches to the firm as a cognitive system have been suggested. Smircich (1983) for instance, argued that the firm resembles a cognitive system through its organizational culture. Following her argument, Gioia, Donellon and Sims (1989) proposed that organizational culture may be found in the shared cognitive 'scripts' of organizational members. It is further assumed that by developing a common language for expressing observation of events in the organization, organizational members may share cognition (Daft and Weick, 1984; Weick and Bougnon, 1986). Yet, following Gioia, Donellon and Sims the firm is to be undertstood as a collection of individual cognitive systems (Gioia and Sims, 1986). Here, the firm is understood not only as a collection of individual brains but also as a cognitive system. We assume that 'organizational thinking (can be seen) as something more global than the aggregate of individual cognitions' (Ginsberg, 1990: 520). Given this assumption, we are forced to consider advances in the cognitive sciences as well. One recent and important contribution of the cognitive sciences is the theory of autopoiesis (auto = self, poiesil = production), which has its roots in the field of neurobiology and is used to explain cognition in living systems (Maturana, 1958; 1960; Varela, 1979; Maturana and Varela, 1987). Although the theory has been introduced in the study of the firm, it has not yet been fully explored or applied in the social sciences.

The purpose of this paper is to demonstrate that the theory of autopoiesis provides a new understanding of strategic learning. In the first part of the paper, a brief description of the theory of autopoiesis and of autopoietic systems will be presented. The aim here is to highlight a select number of topics from the theory in order to show how these ideas may improve our understanding of the firm as a cognitive system.

It will then be argued that the firm may be understood as an autopoietic system and, therefore, that firms may learn by creating errors. The implications of the approach for strategic learning are then discussed and a new concept – the management of strategic experiments – is presented.

The Autopoiesis Theory

The notion of autopoiesis was developed to answer a question that had never found a convincing solution: what distinguishes living systems from other systems? It was possible to give a list of features of living systems, but the key question of what produces these features was without answer.

Maturana understood that the answer could be found in the concept of autonomy. The problem became how to define autonomy. The systems' theoretical concepts of finality and purpose were inadequate and Maturana concluded that the concept of autonomy needed a redefinition. This new concept was *self-referentiality*: each living system may be characterized only with reference to itself; the autonomy results precisely from this. All other systems by contrast, may be defined with reference to an external context.

Applying this concept to a particular case of living systems, in this case the cognitive systems, Maturana was able to develop these ideas further. For example, in the human brain it is not possible to distinguish between hallucination and perception: this can be explained only if the perception is determined by internal self-referential processes of the system and not by an external environment. Thus, the cognitive process must be circular.

The most radical proposition of the theory is that a thinking system cannot be externally steered by the input or output of information like any 'general' open system (see von Bertalanffy, 1968; Katz and Kahn, 1966). The cognitive system is closed, autonomous, and thus constructs its own reality. Reality construction is a process which involves the making of distinctions in observations (Spencer Brown, 1972; Luhmann, 1986). For example:

> When a woman observes a painting by Gauguin, it is her own mind that determines what she sees. She makes a distinction between persons and things, between ground or sky. If practicing the subtle language of art, she can tell others that the painting belongs to a particular stream of paintings. She can also distinguish the painting from other paintings based on her feelings. Due to her own personal experiences, distinction making is in essence different from those made by any other person.

It is postulated that the brain creates its own components (distinctions), and that it uses these components in the further recreation of components (Maturana, 1981), hence the term autopoiesis. This process of applying distinctions is a normative one (Varela, 1979). In effect, the same distinctions may be applied by a broader audience, but this does not necessarily mean that the distinctions are used in a uniform manner. The use of distinctions is dependent on norms which are different in each individual. For example, two people may apply similar distinctions (ugly/pretty) but use them differently (this painting is ugly/this painting is pretty). Thus we may choose to talk about a normatively closed system.

Yet, a brain must also have some degree of openness in order to register something like a painting. The brain is open with respect to stimuli; which we will refer to as signals, not information. Information means literally 'put in form', that is to give meaning. The subject does not *receive* information, it can only *create* information by assigning meaning to signals, that is, relating them to previous information. Thus, in autopoiesis theory, the adjectives 'open' (signals) and 'closed' (norms), are complementary system descriptions that accompany each other.

The Example of the Legal System

In spite of the fact that the theory was developed quite recently, it has been applied in several fields.

One of the most important applications of autopoiesis theory has been within sociology of law. Here, a somewhat taboo question has been how law and each singular judgement is based on reference to previous legal practice (Fletcher, 1985). Lawyers as well as judges refer to previous cases and judgements in each case, thereby behaving in a self-referential manner and creating normative autonomy for the legal system. The autopoiesis approach has made two major positive contributions to research in this field. First, autopoiesis theory has given a positive connotation to legal self-reference and autonomy, because as follows from the theory, when the legal system closes upon itself with respect to norms, it becomes increasingly aware of environmental change (open to stimuli) (Teubner, 1988). The discussion has focused on how legal practice may be increasingly efficient in self-reference, and how laywers simultaneously become increasingly aware of environmental changes. Second, autopoiesis theory has helped to identify and to raise debate about important problems that had been previously neglected: for example, the partial inability of law to affect other systems like society and economy. A possible answer rooted in autopoiesis theory is that the legal system, like the other two systems, is autonomous and assumes as well a causal relationship between legal decisions and societal or economical effects. Autopoiesis theory here suggests that the legal system should attempt to change itself, i.e. its own norms, and thereby affect the environment. The prescription is control through self-control (Kennealy, 1988).

It is our belief that autopoiesis theory may result in similar contributions in the administrative sciences if debated and analysed.

The Autopoietic Firm

In an attempt to apply the theory of autopoiesis to the field of sociology, Luhmann (1986; 1989) postulated that social systems in general are autopoietic and, in effect, construct their own reality. This construction of a social reality results from the interaction of individual realities. Building on Luhmann's work we propose the following:

P1: Firms are autopoietic systems (Vicari, 1991); firms are production networks which produce their own components (like distinctions) in a recurrent way through interaction.

As cognitive system, the firm acts as other cognitive systems or, more specifically, as a human cognitive system that has knowledge, observes, decides, and learns. The firm, for instance, applies distinctions like economical/not economical, right/wrong, professional/non-professional, technical/non-technical, product/process. Moreover, the firm reconstructs its reality by applying internally-generated norms and distinctions. In effect, we may label reality construction 'a self-referential process'. For example, when a firm distinguishes between a seasonal downturn in demand and a stable decline of sales, this very distinction refers to previous understanding related to the buying behaviour of clients. The previous experience allows the firm to make particular distinction and to apply its norms.

It should be noted that autopoiesis theory here suggests a 'total' self-reference; reference is made not only to past experiences, but also to *distinctions to be made*. Norms and distinctions limit the set of *future* possible norms and distinctions. For example, when implementing a diversification strategy, firms may find that the only available acquisition target does not meet an internal requirement of return on investments (ROI). In effect, the acquisition is not undertaken. The profitable/not profitable distinction and the internal ROI-norm have limited the development path; the firm will not gain new norms and distinctions through post-acquisition experience.

Another important implication from applying the autopoiesis theory is that for the firm there is input and output of signals, but not of information. According to the firm's established distinctions and norms, it finds meaningful events, signs, and stimuli in the environment. The environment consists of facts, and the firm seeks and collects data about these facts in a very selective manner. Furthermore, it creates information from this data through applying established norms and distinctions. In effect, 'information is not seen as something that the firm takes in from the environment. Pieces of information don't exist out there, waiting to be picked up. As (distinctions), they are produced by the firm itself in comparison with something else' (Luhmann, 1986: 175). Findings from researches under development illustrate the latter:

> Two companies were competitors in one market. One gave attention to data about consumer satisfaction, and the other to retailer margins. Confronting an increase in market share, the first company created the information: 'Customers are changing attitudes'. The second company created the information: 'It is necessary to continue with our new retailer policy'. In order to understand the diversity in their behaviour, it is necessary to see them as responding to internally generated information.

Another implication of autopoiesis is a concept of knowledge in the firm. Recently, the concept of knowledge and the processes of knowledge development in firms has received attention from a number authors (Itami, 1987; Winter, 1987; Morgan, 1988; Vicari, 1989; Pralahad and Hamel, 1990; Cohen and Levinthal, 1990). To date the concept of knowledge has not been clearly defined in studies of the firm, however. The perspective of autopoiesis allows for such a conceptualization. According to this approach knowledge of the firm results from processes of social interaction and may be understood as the ability of the firm to make distinctions in observations. Very broadly stated, individual skills, attitudes and behaviour, technological capabilities, marketing abilities, administrative procedures, financial resources, organizational structures and mechanisms, the relations with various stakeholders, and the relation between all of the mentioned components are part of the knowledge of the firm. There is knowledge in each individual, each subunit, in each procedure, and in each relation of the firm. Furthermore, the notion of organizational cognition as more than the sum of individual thinking allows us to recognize that in a process of knowledge development, individuals, machines and so forth may move (physically) out and in of the firm. Such a temporary contribution however does not necessarily mean that a contribution is lost for the future (Hedberg, 1981).

In conclusion we suggest that the firm is an autopoietic cognitive system and must be regarded as autonomous with respect to knowledge, creation of information and the application of distinctions and norms. This autonomy stems from the self-referential characteristics of the firm.

Autopoietic Learning in Firms

Learning is a major characteristic of cognitive systems, and is of major importance in the study of the firm. Several approaches to learning may be identified in the literature: Cyert and March (1963) suggested an experience-based adaptation of decision rules; March and Olsen (1988) attempted to link individual learning, organizational learning, and environmental change; Argyris and Schon (1978) analyse levels of learning and obstacles to organizational learning; Hedberg, Starbuck and Nystrom (1976) examine crisis-triggered learning, Barr and Huff (1990), Ansoff (1984) and Grinyer and McKiernan (1990) identify distinct processes of strategic learning. These approaches all assume that organizations are open systems. According to autopoiesis theory applied here, however, organizational and strategic learning assumes a very different form in which the learning subject is a closed system. Thus we propose that:

P2: In order to increase the ability to learn (make distinctions), it becomes necessary to create errors.

It was seen above how an organization constructs its reality through the making of distinctions, and past distinctions determine future distinction making within the firm. Distinction making, in fact, is the most crucial point of any study of cognitive systems because it is through this process that we may understand why the reality of the firm 'is in place' or 'is out of place'. The possible distinctions that firms may make rely on the auto-poietic process. In this picture, strategic learning would mean to stimulate the self-reproductive process, so as to increase the ability of the firm to make distinctions among observations of its environment. In a changing environment, if the firm continues to formulate the same distinctions without change, it is not learning, but only reproducing itself in a 'pathological' manner. Thus, the learning process is crucial for the survival of the firm.

Differences between autopoietic learning and traditional organizational learning.

Studies on organizational learning often distinguish between first order and second order learning (Argyris and Schon, 1978). First order learning occurs when organizational members adjust their behaviour in order to ac-complish the goals and strategies of the firm. Second order learning, by contrast, occurs when the internal understanding of the firm and its en-vironment, goals and strategies become subject to change. The learning processes may be labelled adaptive rational, a notion we borrow from March (1988). In this case the firm becomes better at avoiding error, that is, handling deviance from a fixed norm. Alternatively the firm becomes better at changing the norms. If the fixed norm is the best adaptation to environ-ment, we may also say that the firm seeks an equilibrium with its environ-ment through reduction of error (Le Moigne, 1985).

From the perspective of autopoiesis, the adaptive rational model may be criticized for putting too little emphasis on error creation. The perspective of autopoiesis in fact, underlines the need for errors as impetus for change and knowledge development. An example may help to highlight this point: according to the action learning theory of Argyris and Schon (1978) errors in the firm are negative because they indicate disequilibrium between firm and environment. A detection of an error is the trigger for organizational inquiry aimed at finding a possible solution that may restore this equilib-rium. A very different approach proposes that firms should to some extent engage themselves in producing crisis and errors in order to bring about changes (Nonaka, 1988). The proposition becomes evident if we follow autopoiesis theory. Self-reference in distinctions and norms firmly limits the variety in goals and strategies, and it is difficult, if not impossible, to transcend or break the autopoietic process. As a response to this difficulty, firms use errors in order to increase their ability to make distinctions. Without errors, for instance, it is impossible to make distinctions between a desired and an undesired state in the firm (the difference between states is the error).

According to autopoiesis theory, the only way a firm can stimulate the self-reproductive process is *to create new distinctions using the errors* provided by *experiments*, and by selecting new data from an environment. In the example of the acquisition decision given above, this would mean that the company would acquire as an experiment and thereby gather new data and increase the ability to make new distinctions.

'Experiments' resemble very much Popper's (1957) idea of a scientific experiment or Hedberg's (1981) suggestion to experiment with alternative environments. Both works, although very different from the origin of autopoiesis theory, call for a plan for the experiment, an intention behind the experiment, and hypotheses to be tested. Thus, the basis for the provoked experiment is a set of distinctions that allow for a sufficiently precise articulation of a plan, intention, or a hypothesis. However, as Runco (1990) observed in his research on creativity, the limitations in language may in themselves prevent possible directions of development. Thus, the provoked experiment can at its best only lead to incremental improvements in the firm's ability to make distinctions.

The self-referentiality in distinctions and norms may hinder the detection of errors. Moreover, autopoiesis theory emphasizes that ineffective learning results from self-referentiality in information. Adaptive rational learning is limited by the self-referential processes in the firm; firm members have trouble 'seeing a real error'. Rather they adapt to an environment they themselves have participated in constructing, and to which they have conditioned others. If they do see problems, basic understanding, goals and strategies are changed in a planned, adaptive and therefore very limited way.

The solution to this problem is the shift from a concept of adaptive rational learning to a concept of experimental learning. The latter addresses how the firm creates random events, errors, crazy ideas, etc. and develops knowledge around these. Unlike the case of scientific experiments, companies may be without a plan, intention and hypothesis behind the experiment. Firms may never even articulate certain experiments whose development may therefore be restricted by the limits imposed by the existing language of the firm (see Runco, 1990). Experiments may be planned (Hedberg, 1981), but more important, they may just occur and represent a pattern of knowledge development. Thus, the concept of experimental learning addresses the ways firms manage to obtain knowledge from the production of, and encounters with, error.

According to our view, experimental strategic learning would cover both *provoked* and *natural* experiments, although natural experiments are of most interest. Revolutionary leaps in strategic learning are associated with events that the firm has not planned, intended and hypothesized. These events, assuming that they are realized by the firm, enforce distinctions that were not previously present. Here strategic errors are of particular importance because they allow firms to distinguish among desirable and undesirable states. The error that results from the natural experiment allows firms to experience directly the appropriateness of distinctions.

A Knowledge-Based Framework for Company Performance

Both provoked and natural experiments provide variety in the firm, because each error creates a situation that differs from the existing one. At the end variety is found, for instance, in different attitudes, beliefs, practices, behaviours and conflicting interests among people, the emergence of diverse subcultures, the presence of not-fully-homogeneous procedures, organizational mechanisms, not-completely-compatible machines, products, technologies, customers, distribution channels and markets. Thus, we propose the following:

> *P3: All else being equal; in an environment increasing in complexity (from an external viewpoint), a firm that develops variety in its knowledge base will perform better than a firm that continues to develop redundancy in its knowledge base.*

Taking into consideration that firms are autopoietic systems (P1), that they learn though creating errors (P2), and that they build variety in order to face complexity in an environment, we propose that:

> *P4: All else being equal, a firm that learn through promoting and recognizing experiments will be more successful in developing variety in its knowledge base than a firm that learns through adaptation to a constructed environment.*

Having established an understanding of the socially constructed knowledge of a firm, we would now like to make a note of a possible relationship between the environment and the evolution of knowledge in a firm. In addition, we will examine how this relationship might influence the performance of the firm.

In theory on strategic management, the environment has been described by terms such as turbulence, degree and rate of change, volatility etc. However, when studying the environment as a medium for learning, it might be useful to describe it in terms of level of complexity (i.e. Hedberg, 1981). Complexity in the environment produces strategic issues. The firm or an external observer may, for instance, experience this complexity according to the following scheme:

1 An increasing number of strategic issues
2 Decreasing stability of the issue
3 An increasing degree of interconnectivity between strategic issues
4 An increasing diversity among strategic issues
5 Reduced time required for a strategic issue to develop from a weak signal
   (Ansoff, 1984)

It should be noted that, because the level of environmental complexity is dependent on the firm, it cannot be assessed in objective terms. Some preliminary research findings illustrate this:

> Firm A sold a large percentage of its total sales to a domestic buyer in the telecommunications industry. This buyer was acquired by a foreign group that has its own supplier of the products of firm A. As a result firm A suddenly was faced with a more complex environment. The environment for the domestic competitors of firm A, however remained unchanged and far less complex. This example demonstrates that complexity is defined by individual firms, and not by the environment. What may be classified as a 'simple' environment by external observers, may be seen as very complex from the view of one firm.

The firm copes with any environmental transition and the resulting complexity through exploiting its knowledge base. It can be suggested that in order for the firm to increase or maintain performance when the level of environmental complexity increases, the variety in the knowledge base of the firm must increase correspondingly. The latter argument is not very satisfying, however, as it does not take into account the process characteristics of autopoietic systems. It is necessary to add that since knowledge and reality are continuously created and recreated, knowledge cannot be modelled as stable even if the level of environmental complexity is unchanged. Rather, knowledge evolves from a process of social interaction in two ways; increases in depth or increases in breadth. To use notions of information theory, one may choose to speak about variety and redundancy in knowledge.

A firm that operates in a low-complexity environment encounters few, stable, slow developing, independent and uniform strategic issues. In effect, the firm develops a redundancy in knowledge through a recurring process of coping with similar strategic issues. The firm develops an increasingly fine set of distinctions which allow for an efficient detection of small variances in the environment. Strategic issues are easily detected and understood in the context of the firm, and there is knowledge present to cope with the issue. A redundancy in knowledge can, for instance, lead to incremental product and process innovations, an increasing effectiveness in selection of distributors, a dynamic price policy accounting for seasonal down-turns and an improved efficiency in administrative routines.

In the transition from a low to a high level of environmental complexity, the performance of the firm will be negatively affected unless the knowledge base of the firm increases in variety. An increasing level of environmental complexity implies that the firm encounters an increasing number of interconnected, fast-changing, and diverse strategic issues. An increasing variety in the knowledge base, however, allows the firm to distinguish several developments and trends in the environment, and it allows for effective response to the strategic issues. For instance, in the findings reported above, a firm which had 'enough' variety in its knowledge base (technological skills interesting for foreign customers), may have viewed the foreign acquisition as an opportunity to increase sales rather than as a potential loss of sales. As indicated previously, the way to increase the variety in the knowledge base is what we call 'experimental learning'.

Managerial Implications: from 'Strategic Issue Management' (SIM) to the 'Management of Strategic Experiments' (MSE)

Many interesting implications for management may be drawn from a complete exploration of the autopoiesis theory. As far as strategic learning and strategic management practices are concerned, some of the principal implications are:

1 Strategic management is primarily concerned with how to maintain the best fit between the firm and the environment, by adapting the environment through change in the knowledge of the organization. Focusing on the learning process is the way to change the environment.
2 The only way managers can hope to break the vicious circle of firms being able to perform better than that which the existing knowledge base allows is to create the conditions to change the knowledge base.
3 When the complexity of the environment (that is the complexity of the firm, in our perspective) increases, managers may improve company performance by creating the conditions for developing knowledge variety through the introduction of different cultures, technologies, skills, practices, interests, and so on.
4 It is possible to 'use' environmental complexity to improve variety through the learning process. Procedures promoting organizational learning must be implanted.
5 Strategic management may direct the development of knowledge, by providing the organization with new opportunities to learn, and thereby allowing the firm to develop new distinctions. The procedures and

practices that may be used to effect such learning may be grouped under the title the 'management of strategic experiments'.

The management of a firm in an increasingly complex environment faces two major problems: (1) How does the management detect increasing complexity? (2) How does the management cope with increasing complexity? The literature on strategic management offers a solution termed strategic issue management (Ansoff, 1980). Strategic issue management was originally developed as a technique to handle unforeseen events in strategic planning. Traditional strategic issue management (SIM) consists of the three activities; scanning, diagnosis and response development. Responsibility for SIM lies within the top management and staff or in some cases the middle level management.

Strategic issues play an important role as learning events. When faced with strategic issues firms undertake changes in strategy, structure, culture etc. in order to cope with the issue. If such a change is for some reason absent or inadequate, the firm experiences a decline in performance. Precisely for this reason, a firm's strategic management capability may be based in part on the way in which it manages strategic issues (Houlden, 1986).

Here a strategic issue is defined as a development or trend that a firm recognizes in its external environment. These developments or trends must be powerful enough to affect potentially the performance of the firm (Dutton and Ottensmeyer, 1987; Ansoff, 1980; 1984; King, 1982). Strategic issues are also understood as environmental facts (Ansoff, 1980), rather than symbols interpreted in the context of a firm (Dutton and Jackson, 1987). Strategic issues are characterized by having different degrees of impact and urgency for the firm (Dutton and Duncan, 1987). According to the autopoiesis perspective, firms classify strategic issues according to impact and urgency, collect data about strategic issues as well as produce information related to the issues. As a result, in the 'same' environment (from an external assessment), firms produce completely different strategic issues.

In the office furniture market in Italy some small companies have chosen to consider their environment (clients, sellers, retailers, competitors, etc.) as stable in spite of the fact that changes in the European Common Market require response (as seen from an external observer). According to their large competitors, they should worry about the internationalization of the market, and should in effect, change their behaviour quickly.

The knowledge base of firms plays an important role when executing SIM. By directing the scanning for environmental facts, it will apply distinctions and norms that will in turn affect both the outcome of the diagnosis and the design of an appropriate response. It is also important to recognize how the

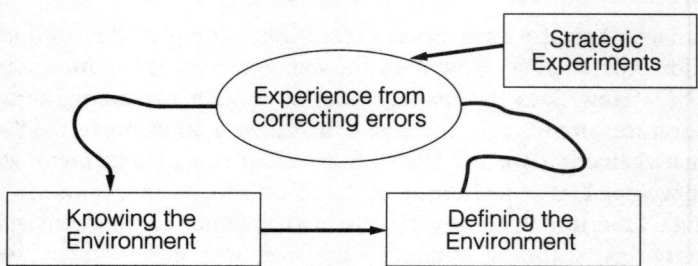

Figure 17.1   Blackboard sketch of the role of strategic experiments

knowledge base of the firm actually constrains the activities of strategic issue management. The knowledge base constrains the scanning activity (how can you scan for something unknown?) and the diagnosing activity by attempting to categorize everything in existing categories, and it constrains the responses possible by the firm.

It should also be noted that there is mutual causality between the evolution of a knowledge base and the ability to cope with strategic issues in an environment. The firm operates in a constructed environment defined by its knowledge base. The knowledge base in turn is developed through a process of 'adaptive rational learning'; that is by adapting to a constructed environment. In cases where the level of environmental complexity increases, this circle may become vicious if not broken; more knowledge leads to a more solid definition of the environment, which leads to more knowledge, which leads to .... The breaking of the circle requires the management of strategic experiments. The mutual causality and the function of the strategic experiment is indicated in figure 17.1.

The management of strategic experiments has a twofold purpose: (1) to produce knowledge about the knowledge in the organization; (2) to increase the variety in the knowledge of the firm. The purpose can best be illustrated by an example:

> In the Norwegian offshore petroleum industry requirements concerning product quality in engineering companies underwent a sharp change in the 1980s. Quality became a strategic issue: only those companies able to satisfy the standard of quality could continue to supply the operating oil companies. As a response, the suppliers had to develop knowledge on quality management through experimentation (with Japanese techniques). On the Gullfaks C platform, at that time the world's largest offshore project, an engineering firm responsible for structural design worked continuously on improving their quality management. At one point the concept of Quality Circle

(problem solving groups) was introduced. The instrument was abandoned later, however, due to what was explained as 'a difference between the working culture and the Japanese assumptions' behind the Quality Circle.

As the example very briefly illustrates, the firm experimented in order to gain knowledge both about the issue of quality itself and about the firm itself. Using the example we may also note that the management of strategic experiments consists of three activities:

Triggering and discovering the experiment

The strategic experiment may be triggered and discovered on several levels within the organization. However, top management's commitment to carry out strategic experiments, to promote and to recognize experiments that occur, are important. The experiment may take several forms corresponding to a general framework of strategic alternatives; product and market development projects, mergers and acquisitions, strategic alliances, corporate venturing etc. Top management may also attempt to assemble various experimental efforts to let them form a strategy for the firm (Quinn, 1980).

Retaining knowledge about the experiment

In order to retain knowledge from the experiment at least three precautions seem necessary. First, people implementing the experiment (making errors) should be kept rather than fired. They may serve in special roles of advisors to top management and play important parts in ongoing projects. Second, the lessons to be learned from the experiment should be shared rather than kept secret with a limited number of organizational subgroups. When the environmental complexity increases, in fact, the firm must be forced to deal with conflicting knowledge (see Prahalad and Bettis, 1986). Third, local or global restructuring may be necessary in order to retain knowledge gained from the experiment.

Applying knowledge from the strategic experiments

Post-experiment information is used to challenge assumptions that underlie existing strategic plans and perspectives in a dialectical process (Mason and Mitroff, 1981). The experiment may indicate answers to important questions such as: Do we have the knowledge to carry out existing strategic plans? Are strategic plans based on correct assumptions? Can the experiment be followed up by further investment in knowledge development? The experiment may raise new questions or indicate new opportunities not considered before.

Conclusions and some Implications for Future Research

This paper has demonstrated that the theory of autopoiesis applied to firms leads to a focus on experimental learning. The paper introduced autopoiesis theory and demonstrated how the firm could be understood as a cognitive system. Further, the paper proposed relationships between environmental complexity, the nature of a firm's knowledge base, experimental learning practices, and performance. Implications for managers were discussed and the concept of managing strategic experiments was introduced.

Other implications of the autopoiesis theory have to be explored in order to account for all of the applications of experimental learning in strategic management. Further analysis might examine how to distinguish the knowledge of the firm and its limits, how to analyse and evaluate the learning process and how to assess performance measures.

But future explorations of autopoiesis research should also raise new questions related to experimental practices of firms as a means to cope with increasing complexity. One should develop a set of hypotheses to test the complexity-learning-experimenting-performance framework.

Acknowledgements

We appreciate the comments of Andrew Van de Ven, Peter Lorange, Bala Chakravarthy, Ian MacMillan, Harbir Singh, Anil Gupta, Johan Roos and Pamela Adams.

References

Ansoff, H. I. 1984: *Implanting Strategic Management*, Prentice Hall: London.

Ansoff, H. I. 1980: Strategic Issue Management. *Strategic Management Journal*, 1, pp. 131–148.

Argyris, C. and Schon, D. 1978: *Organizational Learning*. Reading, Mass.

Barr, P. S. and Huff, A. 1990: Understanding Performance: The Process and Effects of Strategic Learning. Paper presented at the Tenth Annual Meeting of the Strategic Management Society, 24–27 September, Stockholm, Sweden.

von Bertalanffy, L. 1968: *General Systems Theory*. George Braziller: New York.

Cohen, W. M. and Levinthal D. A. 1990: Absorptive Capacity: A New Perspective on Learning and Innovation. *Administrative Science Quarterly*, 35, pp. 128–152.

Cyert, R. M. and March, J. G. 1963: *A Behavioural Theory of the Firm*. Prentice Hall: Englewood Cliffs.

Daft, R. and Weick, K. 1984: Towards a Model of Organizations as Interpretation Systems. *Academy of Management Review*, 9, pp. 284–295.

Deggau, H. G. 1988: The Communicative Autonomy of the Legal System in G. Teubner (ed.), *Autopoietic Law: A New Approach to Law and Society*, de Gruyter: Berlin.

Dutton, J. E. and Duncan, R. B. 1987: The Creation of Momentum for Change Through the Process of Strategic Issue Diagnosis. *Strategic Management Journal*, 8, pp. 279–295.

Dutton, J. E. and Ottensmeyer, E. 1987: Strategic Issue Management Systems: Forms, Functions and Contexts. *Academy of Management Review*, 12 pp. 355–365.

Dutton, J. E. and Jackson, S. E. 1987: Categorizing Strategic Issues. *Academy of Management Review*, 12. pp. 76–90.

Fletcher, G. P. 1985: Paradoxes in Legal Thought. Columbia Law Review.

Ginsberg, A. 1990: Connecting Diversification to Performance: A Socio-Cognitive Perspective. *Academy of Management Review*, 15, pp. 514–535.

Gioia, D., Donnellon, A. and Sims, H. P. 1989: Communication and Cognition in Appraisal: A Tale of Two Paradigms. *Organization Studies*, 10, pp. 503–530.

Gioia, D. and Sims, H. P. 1986: Introduction: Social Cognition in Organizations. in H. P. Sims and D. A. Gioia, *The Thinking Organization: Dynamics of Organizational Social Cognition*, Jossey-Bass, San Francisco.

Grinyer, P. and McKiernan, P. 1990: Generating Major Change in Stagnating Companies. *Strategic Management Journal*, 11, pp. 131–146.

Hedberg, B. 1981: How Organizations Learn and Unlearn. in W. Starbuck and P. C. Nystrom (eds.), *Handbook of Organizational Design, Vol. 1*. Oxford University Press: Oxford.

Hedberg, B., Starbuck, W. and Nystrom, P. C. 1976: Camping on the Seesaws: Prescriptions for Self-Designing Organizations. *Administrative Science Quarterly*, 21, pp. 41–65.

Houlden, B. T. 1986: Developing a Company's Strategic Management Capability. *Long Range Planning*, 19, pp. 89–93.

Isenberg, D. 1987: How Senior Managers Think. in D. Bell, H. Raiffa, and A. Tversky (eds.), *Decision Making*. Cambridge University Press: Cambridge, Mass.

Itami, H. 1987: *Mobilizing Invisible Assets*. Harvard University Press: Cambridge, Mass.

Katz, D. and Kahn, R. L. 1966: *The Social Psychology of Organization*. Wiley: New York.

Kennealy, P. 1988: Talking About Autopoiesis: Order from Noise? In G. Teubner (ed.), *Autopoietic Law: A new Approach to Law and Society*. de Gruyter: Berlin.

King, W. R., 1982: Using Strategic Issue Analysis. *Long Range Planning*, 15, pp. 45–49.

Le Moigne, J. L. 1985: The Intelligence of Complexity. In *The Science and Praxis of Complexity*, United Nations University: Tokyo.

Luhmann, N. 1989: *Ecological Communication*. Polity Press: Boston, Mass.

Luhmann, N. 1986: The Autopoiesis of Social Systems. In F. Geyer and J. Van Der Zouwen (eds.), *Sociocybernetic Paradoxes*. Sage: Beverly Hills.

March, J. G. 1988: *Decisions and Organizations*. Blackwell: London.

March, J. G. and Olsen J. P. 1988: Organizational Learning Under Ambiguity. in J. G. March (ed.), *Decisions and Organizations*. Blackwell; London.

Mason, R. and Mitroff, I. 1981: *Challenging Strategic Planning Assumptions*. Wiley: New York.

Maturana, H. and Varela, F. 1987: *The Tree of Knowledge*. Ask: Copenhagen, (in Danish).

Maturana, H. 1981: Autopoiesis In M. Zeleeny (ed.), *Autopoiesis*. North-Holland: New York.

Maturana, H. 1960: The Fine Anatomy of the Optic Nerve of Anurans – An Electron Microscope Study. *Journal of Biophysical and Biochemical Cytology*, 7, pp. 107–120.

Maturana, H. 1958: Efferent Fibres in the Optic Nerve of the Toad. *Journal of Anatomy*, 92, pp. 92–121.

Mintzberg, H. 1976: Planning on the Left Side, and Managing on the Right. *Harvard Business Review*, 54, pp. 49–58.

Morgan, G. 1988: *Riding the Waves of Change: Developing Managerial Competencies for a Turbulent World*. Jossey–Bass: San Francisco.

Morgan, G. 1986: *Images of Organization*. Sage: Beverly Hills.

Nonaka, I. 1988: Creating Organizational Order Out of Chaos. *California Management Review*, Spring, pp. 57–73.

Popper, K. 1957: *The Poverty of Historicism*. Routledge and Keegan Paul: London.

Prahalad, C. K. and Hamel, G. 1990: The Core-Competence of the Corporation. *Harvard Business Review*, May–June, pp. 79–91.

Prahalad, C. K. and Bettis, R. A. 1986: The Dominant Logic: A New Linkage Between Diversity and Performance. *Strategic Management Journal*, 7, pp. 485–501.

Quinn, J. B. 1980: *Strategies for Change: Logical Incrementalism*. Irwin: Homewood, Ill.

Runco, M. 1990: Implicit Theories and Ideational Creativity. In R. Runco and R.S. Albert (eds), *Theories of Creativity*. Sage: Newburry Park, Cal.

Smircich, L. 1983: Concepts of Culture and Organizational Analysis. *Administrative Science Quarterly*, 28, pp. 339–358.

Spencer Brown, G. 1969: *Laws of Form*. Allen and Unwin: London.

Sperry, R. W. 1968: Hemisphere Deconnection and Unity in Conscious Awareness. *American Psychologist*, 23, pp. 723–733.

Taggart, W. and Robey D. 1981: Minds and Managers: On the Dual Nature of Human Information Processing and Management. *Academy of Management Review*, 6, pp. 187–196.

Teubner, G. 1988: Evolution of Autopoietic Law. In G. Teubner (ed.) *Autopoietic Law: A New Approach to Law and Society*. de Gruyter: Berlin.

Varela, F. 1979: *The Principles of Biological Autonomy*, North-Holland: New York.

Vicari, S. 1991: *The Living Firm*. Etas Libri: Milano, (in Italian).

Vicari, S. 1989: *New Dimensions of Competition: Strategies in Markets Without Boundaries*. EGEA: Milano, (in Italian).

Weick, K. and Bougnon, M. G. 1986: Organizations as Cognitive Maps: Charting New Ways to Success and Failure. In H. P. Sims and D. A. Gioia, *The Thinking Organization: Dynamics of Organizational Social Cognition*. Jossey-Bass: San Fransisco.

Winter, 1987: Knowledge and competence as strategic assets. In Teece, D. J. (ed.). *The Competitive Challenge. Strategies for Industrial Innovation and Renewal*. Cambridge MA: Bollinger Publishers.

Index